HOSPITALITY DIGITAL MARKETING ESSENTIALS:
A Field Guide for Navigating Today's Digital Landscape

The study guide for the Certified Hospitality Digital Marketer (CHDM) certification

www.hsmai.org/chdm

6th Edition

By Dan Wacksman, CHDM, CRME, CHBA and Holly Zoba, CHDM

Published September 2021 By:

HOSPITALITY DIGITAL MARKETING ESSENTIALS:
A Field Guide for Navigating Today's Digital Landscape

Dear Colleagues,

This book is the study guide for the Certified Hospitality Digital Marketer (CHDM) certification (www.hsmai.org/chdm).

If you've gotten this far, you're interested in refining your skills and becoming a certified digital steward—congrats! Whether you have been in your role for years, are just entering the exciting space of hospitality marketing, or are considering expanding your experience into digital, the investment to become CHDM certified will pay off.

In our work to provide hospitality professionals with information on the most pertinent, relevant, and in-demand topics, we are proud to deliver an updated 2021 edition of this book.

As part of its mission, HSMAI's Marketing Advisory Board seeks to inspire success for HSMAI members and those they serve through the creation, curation, and promotion of relevant knowledge in the digital marketing space. We hope you agree that this book is a strong step toward that goal.

See the Acknowledgements for a full accounting of the individuals who contributed countless hours to make this edition possible, and the following roster of all advisory board members as of the printing of this edition.

> "HSMAI's Certified Hospitality Digital Marketer (CHDM) certification is absolutely the number one educational opportunity for all hotel marketers at all levels. Now is the time to learn more about marketing in a digital age to set yourself apart professionally."
>
> –Christopher Robinson, CHDM
> *Director, Customer Success – Engagement + Training*
> Marriott International

WHY BECOME CHDM CERTIFIED?

- This globally-recognized digital marketing certification administered by HSMAI will set you apart as having legit digital literacy + skills.
- It's one of the few digital marketing certifications specializing in hospitality.
- Leaders with CHDM certification have increased confidence. Being certified means that you know what you're talking about–inspiring more trust in you and your recommendations.
- The curriculum was carefully built by fellow hospitality marketing experts who know the space, the pitfalls, and all the in-demand digital marketing skills. Who could be better to help guide you through everything from the basics to the most advanced practices and skills?
- Invest in yourself and your career. You won't regret learning more about how digital has and will continue to impact the hotel industry.

REASONS YOUR ORGANIZATION SHOULD INVEST IN YOUR CHDM CERTIFICATION

- The curriculum provides an increased comprehension in the digital space which can lead to improved performance and overall revenue for your organization.
- The CHDM can be used as a continuing education piece proving that your organization is invested in your professional growth. Because the certification requires resubmission every two years, it's a given that you'll always be up to date on the latest trends and news. Every CHDM whose certification is current receives a digital copy of the new edition of the study guide whenever it is updated.
- You'll be a part of a community of thousands of HSMAI members worldwide which leads to peer interaction, advanced networking, and a larger company footprint within an esteemed cadre of professionals.

HSMAI AMERICAS MARKETING ADVISORY BOARD

- Stuart Butler, CHDM, Chief Marketing Officer, Myrtle Beach Convention & Visitors Bureau
- Tammie Carlisle, Head of Hospitality, Milestone Inc.
- Jessica Davidson, CHDM, SVP, Digital, Wyndham Hotels & Resorts
- Cristina DiStefano, CHDM, Director of Enterprise Marketing, Turning Stone Resort Casino
- Kirsten Frazell. Industry Manager, Travel, Facebook
- Isaac Gerstenzang, CHDM, CRME, Vice President Digital Marketing & CRM, Atlantis Paradise Bahamas
- Michael Goldrich, CHDM, Global Head of Digital Marketing, Club Quarters
- Steven Gottlieb. Senior Vice President Sales & Revenue, Graduate Hotels
- Michelle Green. Senior Account Executive, Google
- Benjamin Hoeb, CHDM, Corporate Director of Digital Marketing, PCH Hotels & Resorts
- Theodore Holloway, CHDM, VP of Digital Marketing, Remington Hotels
- Carolyn Hosna, CHDM, Vice President, Marketing, White Lodging Services
- Debbie Howarth, EDD, Interim Assistant Dean - College of Business, Johnson & Wales University
- Ryan Hudgins, Director, Performance Marketing, IHG
- John Jimenez, CHSP, VP of E-commerce, Noble Investment Group
- Katie Johnson, CHDM, Global Director of Brand Marketing, Hyatt Hotels Corporation
- Meghan Keough, CRME, CHDM, Senior Director, Business Development, Expedia Group Media Solutions
- Brian Klein, Senior Business Strategist, MMGY Global
- Thomas McDermott, VP, Marketing, Tambourine
- Jeremy Murray, CHDM, Director of eCommerce, Apple Hospitality REIT
- Christopher Robinson, CHDM, Director, Client Services, Marriott International
- Stephanie Smith, Founder & Digital Matriarch, Cogwheel Marketing
- Katarina Stanisic, Senior Director, Marketing, Best Western Hotels & Resorts
- Paolo Torchio, CHDM, Chief Operating Officer, Cendyn
- Nima Vaez-Zadeh, CRME, Market Manager, Hopper
- Theresa van Greunen, AVP, Corporate Communications, Aqua-Aston Hospitality
- Dan Wacksman, CHDM, CHBA, CRME, Principal, Sassato LLC
- Misty Wise, CRME, CHDM, Corporate Director, eCommerce, Atrium Hospitality
- Michael Wylie, SVP, Head of eCommerce, Aimbridge Hospitality

HSMAI EUROPE DIGITAL MARKETING ADVISORY BOARD

- Monna Nordhagen, Partner, Mars Brand Strategy
- Jean-Charles Denis, VP Commercial Europe, IHG
- Edward Lines, Industry Manager, Google
- Chris Mcguire, Managing Partner, 80 Days
- Eric Brun, Senior Vice President Commercial, Hyatt Hotels Corporation
- Fiona Gillen, VP Marketing, The Hotels Network
- Paul Mulcahy, Managing Director Europe, Middle East, Africa, RCI Vacation Exchange
- Philippe B. Roy, Director Global Client Group Europe – Head of the Hospitality Vertical, American Express
- Ksenia Ruffell, Marketing Manager Emea, IDeaS
- Roman Sucharzewski, Director Hotel Distribution & Marketing – Europe, Diamond Resorts International

CENDYN

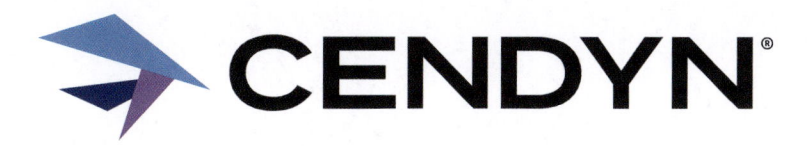

Dear Hospitality Colleagues,

Cendyn is proud to partner with HSMAI to sponsor this year's guide. Our mission has always been to provide hoteliers around the globe with the knowledge and tools that enable deeper, more profitable guest relationships by empowering hotel staff with the data they need at every touchpoint in the guest journey.

We proudly serve customers in 143 countries with software and solutions that remain at the forefront of innovation within our industry, driving sales, marketing, e-commerce, and revenue performance and alignment for tens of thousands of hotels across the globe. By providing best in class products that deliver measurable results and push the boundaries of what is possible in our industry, Cendyn enables hotels to make sense of their data and put guests at the heart of what they do.

On behalf of Cendyn and our hundreds of employees around the globe, we would like to thank HSMAI for the opportunity to connect with hospitality marketers and continue driving innovations for the entire industry. To learn more about our team and our hospitality solutions, please visit cendyn.com.

Tim Sullivan
CEO & President
Cendyn

TABLE OF CONTENTS

PART ONE: INTRODUCTION	**1**
Chapter 1: The Framework	2
Chapter 2: The History of Hospitality Digital Marketing	6
Chapter 3: Hotel Digital Marketing Strategy	16
PART TWO: OWNED MEDIA	**26**
Chapter 4: The Hotel Website	27
Chapter 5: Mobile	42
Chapter 6: Content & Merchandising	51
Chapter 7: Rich Media	65
Chapter 8: Search Engine Optimization (SEO) – The History of SEO and How It Works	70
Chapter 9: Search Engine Optimization (SEO) – Making SEO Work for Your Hotel	84
Chapter 10: Voice Search	94
Chapter 11: Email Marketing	98
Chapter 12: Customer Relationship Management (CRM)	106
Chapter 13: Loyalty & Recognition	110
Chapter 14: Digital for Pre-Stay, On Site, and Post-Stay	114
PART THREE: EARNED MEDIA	**117**
Chapter 15: Public Relations	120
Chapter 17: Social Media	136
Chapter 18: Influencers	151
PART FOUR: PAID MEDIA	**160**
Chapter 19: Paid Search	162
Chapter 20: Display Media	170
Chapter 21: Affiliate Marketing	176
Chapter 22: Metasearch	177
Chapter 23: Paid Social Media	181
Chapter 24: OTA Paid Media	189
PART FIVE: DIGITAL INTERMEDIARIES	**192**
Chapter 25: Online Travel Agencies (OTAs)	193
Chapter 26: Group Intermediaries	203
PART SIX: TRENDING TOPICS	**209**
Chapter 27: Virtual Reality & Augmented Reality	210
Chapter 28: Artificial Intelligence & Machine Learning	214
Chapter 29: Chatbots	225
PART SEVEN: MEASUREMENT AND MANAGING DIGITAL PERFORMANCE	**229**
Chapter 30: Website Analytics	230
Chapter 31: Marketing Analytics & Attribution Modeling	235
Chapter 32: Digital Marketing Organizational Structure	238
Chapter 33: Vendor Relationship Management	246
Chapter 34: Regulations Marketers Need to Know	254
GLOSSARY OF DIGITAL MARKETING TERMS	**258**
ABOUT THE AUTHORS	**267**
ACKNOWLEDGEMENTS	**268**
ENDNOTES	**269**

A NOTE FROM THE AUTHORS

Writing a book about the important elements of digital marketing for the hospitality industry is a bit of a daunting endeavor. What to include? How to frame it all to make the most sense? How to include enough to provide value without adding so much that it overwhelms? Should it be a how-to guide or a purely theoretical approach?

The good news is, we weren't starting from scratch. This study guide for the Certified Hospitality Digital Marketer (CHDM) certification, has been around and evolving since 2012, and the authors of this 6th edition have been a part of that evolution. We were part of all the discussions around how in-depth this guide needed to be, and what made the most sense to include or exclude.

Historically, this guide has been written by a committee of 10 or 12 people, each bringing their own area of expertise to the book—but then also writing in a different voice. There were sometimes duplications of content—framed a little differently. So, for this 6th iteration, two of us from HSMAI's Marketing Advisory Board were charged with making the updates and bringing it all together.

Of course, we didn't really write it on our own. We were able to consult with many of the greatest minds in hotel digital marketing today to ensure we kept in the expertise and current viewpoints on the subject.

The result, we hope, is something that anyone interested in a career—or even a hobby—in digital marketing will be able to pick up, peruse, and walk away with a comprehensive understanding of what makes up hotel digital marketing, how we got here, and where we are going. Our goal is to provide enough information to enable you to understand the big picture, know how the key components can contribute to your overall revenue strategy, and, in the end, help you make better informed decisions about all things digital marketing.

Important Note: This guide was published September 2021 and will be updated again within two years. At the time of publication all the information was accurate, but it is important, as digital marketers, that we all keep up to date on the changes in the discipline.

PART ONE: INTRODUCTION

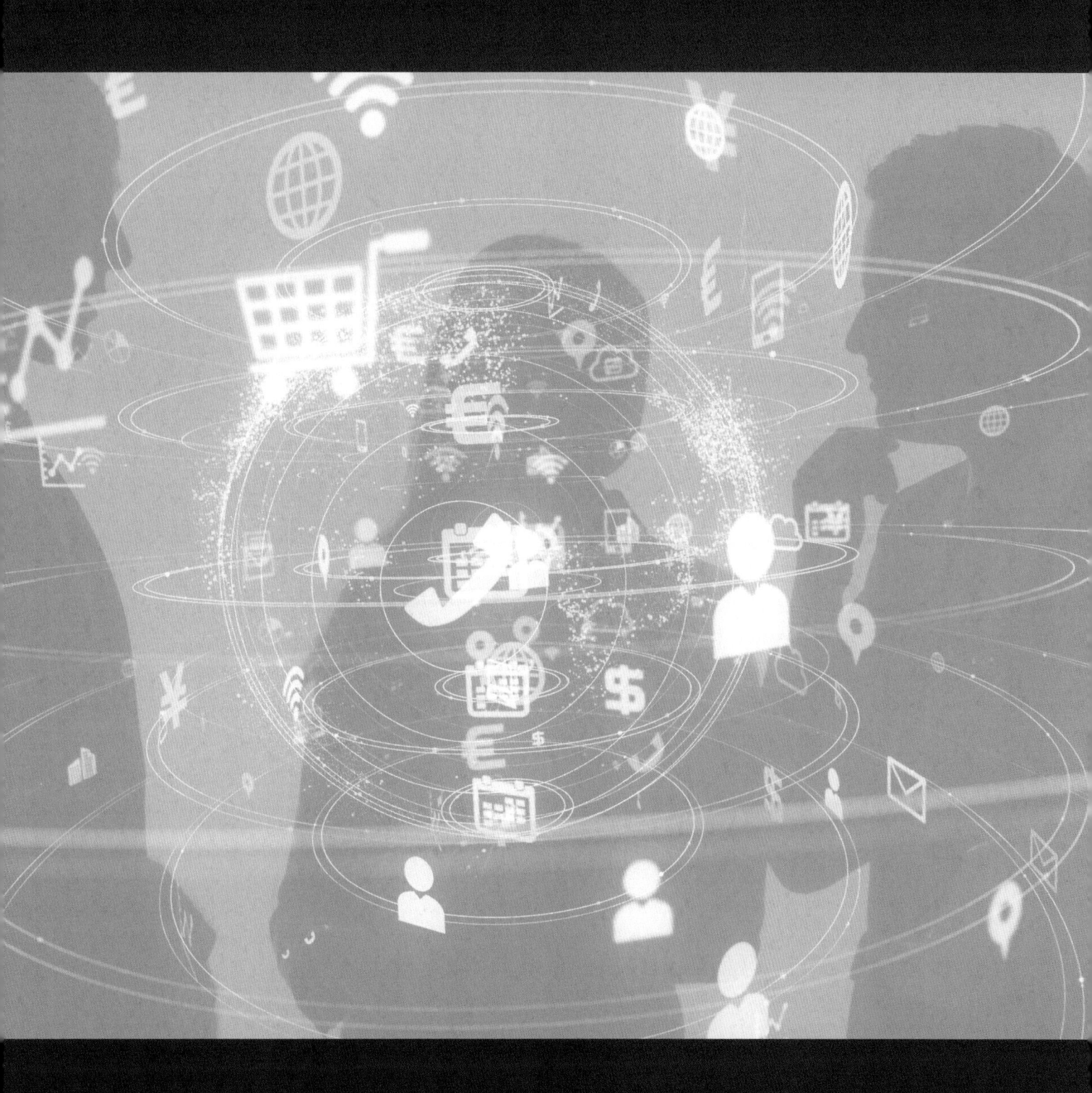

Chapter 1: The Framework

According to the American Marketing Association, "marketing is the practice of identifying and satisfying customer needs. This is a particularly important task in the business context, as successful marketing efforts can drive inbound leads and attract a large customer base. The traditional marketing cycle involves an analysis of market orientation, product mix and business environment."[1]

In short, marketing helps us find the right customers at the right time and offer those customers the right product at the right price.

Marketing began in antiquity, as soon as the need arose for products to be sold at a market instead of just between neighbors, replacing the barter system.

Throughout the centuries it evolved slowly, and it wasn't until the industrial era that it became formalized. Around the late 18th century, goods could be mass produced and the framework of marketing was very much "If you build it, they will come." Consumers never before had access to such a variety of products, so marketing was a matter of reach and distribution.

In the early 20th century marketing began to evolve because of competition. No longer could you just build it and they would buy it, because others were also building it. So, you had to brand and differentiate your product in order to assign it value.

Eventually, how you distributed your product became a competitive advantage, and increased the need for better marketing communication.

Then in the mid-1980s, digital marketing was born. The next chapter traces the evolution of digital marketing as it pertains to hotels. But in the larger context, digital marketing is "the use of the Internet, mobile devices, social media, search engines, and other channels to reach consumers."[2]

Throughout this marketing evolution, the fundamental goals remained the same—find the right customers at the right time and offer those customers the right product at the right price. The only difference is everything else:

- the methods we use to find customers
- the level of segmentation we can achieve, leading to greater personalization and better timing
- the rich media we can employ to present our product
- the interaction of the customer in real time to help us define and redirect our efforts to achieve our best results

And all of that is what we will try to unravel in the following chapters.

One important note here is the speed with which digital marketing has evolved. From print to radio to TV, the mediums and methods of marketing have changed dramatically over the years, but no medium has had such a huge impact so quickly as the internet and the evolving field of digital marketing.

What is the speed and reach of digital marketing? It took 75 years for the telephone to reach 50 million users and only 24 hours for Chewbacca Mum to reach 50 million views on Facebook live.[3]

How long to reach 50 million users?

- Telephone — 75 years
- Radio — 38 years
- Television — 13 years
- Internet — 4 years
- Facebook — 2 years
- Instagram — 19 months
- YouTube — 10 months
- Twitter — 9 months
- Angry Birds — 35 days
- Pokemon Go — 19 days
- Facebook Live 50 Million views — 24 hours
- Chewbacca Mum – 50 Million Views

[4]

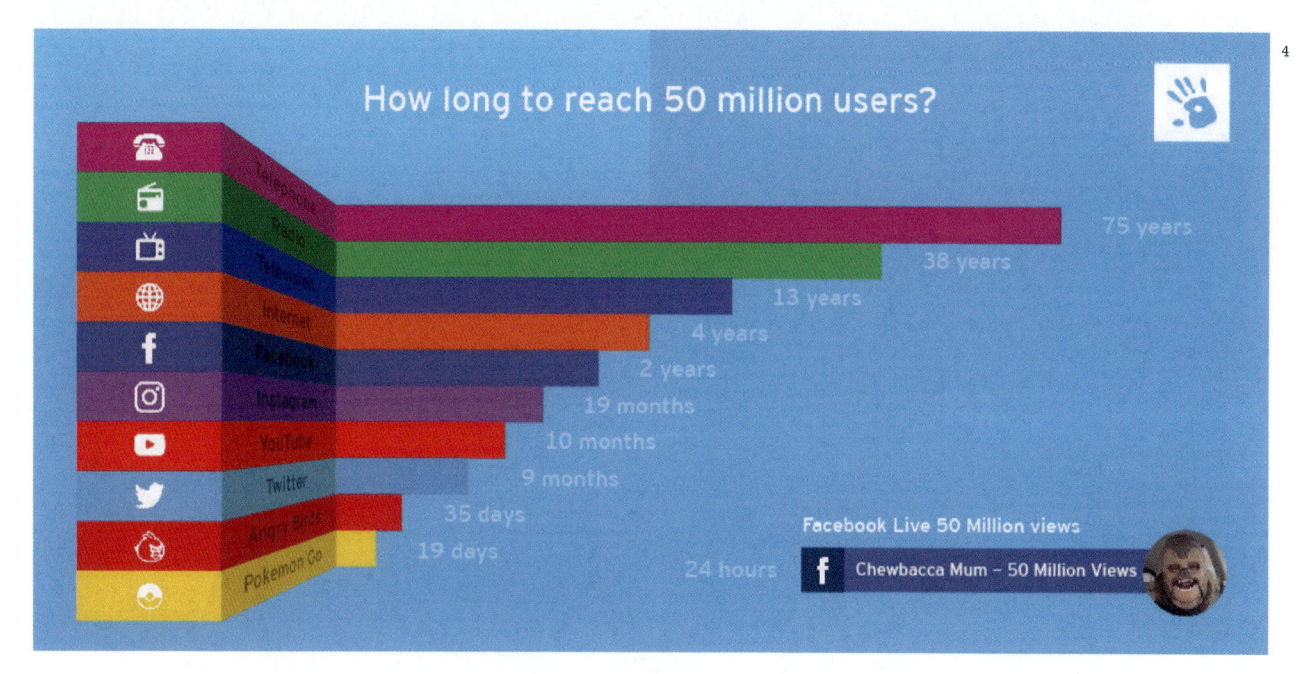

To help make sense of this complex discipline, we'll start with some context. How exactly did the current state of digital marketing evolve from a technology standpoint? What technology events triggered the evolution of digital marketing advances?

Once you understand how we got here, we will focus on the framework of digital marketing from beginning to end. From there we'll help you define your product and its value in order to segment your customers and create campaigns to target and reach them.

We will also address the buyer's journey. Digital has driven change not just for marketers but for our customers as well. We will look at their common buying patterns and introduce the modern marketing funnel.

We will then explore the available digital tools to get in front of those customers. These tools are categorized into three key components of digital marketing: Owned Media, Paid Media, and Earned Media.

Owned media includes any asset that you own and control. Primary to this component is your website. We can't talk about your website without also reviewing a key buyer behavior—search—and all that search encompasses, including voice search. Your owned media also includes your email marketing, your mobile website, and any other content that you create or curate.

Paid media is anything you pay a publisher for that gets you in front of your targeted audience. This includes paid search, display advertising, social media advertising (including boosting posts), subscription services, programmatic advertising, and paid metasearch.

Earned media includes media that you cannot buy—you must earn it. Traditionally it is public relations or word-of-mouth advertising. In the digital world it includes reviews, ratings, shares, and mentions. Even though it is the least controllable, it is often considered the most valuable media because consumers deem it unbiased.

Within each of these areas, and in Part 7, we will cover measurement—how to evaluate the results of your efforts.

How different marketing medias fit together

DIGITAL MARKETING TRIFECTA [5]
EARNED, OWNED & PAID MEDIA

- **SHARING**: MENTIONS, SHARES, REPOSTS, REVIEWS
- **EARNED MEDIA**
- Propel sharing & engagement with paid promotion
- **ADVERTISING**: PAY PER CLICK, DISPLAY ADS, RETARGETING, PAID INFLUENCERS, PAID CONTENT PROMOTION, SOCIAL MEDIA ADS
- **PAID MEDIA**
- SEO & brand content drive earned media (sharing) & traffic
- Leverage owned, earned, and paid media for a comprehensive marketing strategy
- **OWNED MEDIA**
- **WEB PROPERTIES**: WEBSITE, MOBILE SITE, BLOG SITE, SOCIAL MEDIA CHANNELS
- Gain more exposure to web properties with SEO and PPC

A Field Guide for Navigating Today's Digital Landscape

Why do these labels matter? Marketing lingo comes in and out of fashion and some might even question the use of these terms, but this is an easily understandable way to help explain avenues open to digital marketers, and it is useful to think in these terms (or terms like this). Everything the digital marketer does should be for a reason. Once a goal is set, these categories give you a good way to consider your options and determine how you will get your message out. For example:

Hotel A has a soft period in the next month and needs to do its best to fill those rooms. The general manager comes to the digital marketing team with a budget (or not) and asks, "What can we do?" The digital marketer should first ask themself:

- What should we do in paid media?
- What should we do in earned media?
- What should we do in owned media?

Each media source has pros and cons.

Media Type	Role	Benefits	Challenges
Owned	Build for longer term goals and relationships	· Control · Can be tailored for niche audiences · Cost efficiency	· No guarantees · Not always trusted · Takes time to scale
Paid	Attracts customers; feeds to owned media and creates earned	· Scalable · Control · Targeting · On demand	· Poor credibility · Declining response rates · Noise/clutter
Earned	Listen and respond; usually the result of well-coordinated paid and owned	· Most credible · Key role in most sales efforts · Transparent · Longer-term value	· Very little control · Can be negative · Hardest to measure

The ideal digital marketing strategy uses a holistic, or omnichannel approach, leveraging components from all three areas. As you can see from both the diagram and table, each can also overlap with the others and serve to bolster results if implemented strategically. We will explore each of these media in depth.

Finally, we will delve into what is coming next: the evolution of big data in descriptive, predictive, and prescriptive analytics in hotel digital marketing. This is where we will look at automation, machine learning, and artificial intelligence.

Of course we cannot ignore the impact that the Covid19 pandemic had on digital marketing for the travel industry. In some ways it accelerated our digital transformation further and faster, and in other ways it caused us to take a pause.

For an illustration of the dramatic shift the pandemic caused in the travel space, the Merkle analysis of daily Google search spend for retail versus travel through July of 2020 (on page 5).[6]

The post-pandemic recovery years will certainly provide a myriad of opportunities for the savvy digital marketer to use new strategies and tools to outpace their competitors.

Our goal for this book is to present a clear perspective on the strategies and tools that will drive better decision making for hotel digital marketing. This book also serves as the study guide for HSMAI's Certified Hospitality Digital Marketer (CHDM) certification, so we have included sample exam questions at the end of each section to help you periodically check your understanding of key points covered in each chapter.

Daily Google Search Spend Compared to January Average

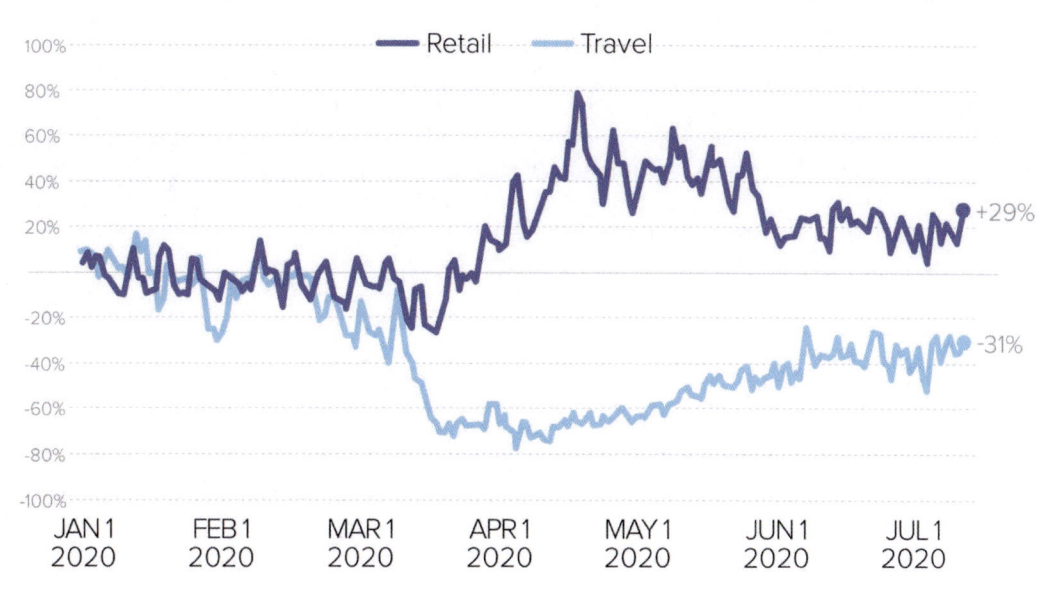

— Retail   — Travel

Retail: +29%
Travel: -31%

(Data from JAN 1 2020 through JUL 1 2020)

SAMPLE CHDM EXAM QUESTIONS

1. Which of the following media types is deemed "most credible" by consumers?
   a. Owned Media
   b. Paid Media
   c. Earned Media

2. Which media type would you use to realize the fastest short-terms gains?
   a. Owned Media
   b. Paid Media
   c. Earned Media

3. Websites, email, and blogs all fall under which category?
   a. Owned Media
   b. Paid Media
   c. Earned Media

Answers
1 = c
2 = b
3 = a

NOTES

_____
_____
_____
_____
_____
_____
_____
_____
_____
_____
_____
_____
_____
_____

A Field Guide for Navigating Today's Digital Landscape

Chapter 2: The History of Hospitality Digital Marketing

Today's technologically advanced travel marketplace sees travelers interacting with multiple digital devices, while expecting those encounters to address their personal needs and interests. This behavior is understandable, given the rise of always available apps and voice-based personal assistants. As a result, engaging travelers and satisfying their expectations is an increasingly complex endeavor.

Some context is required to fully appreciate the challenges facing today's hospitality marketer.

A HISTORICAL PERSPECTIVE

A century ago, Ellsworth Statler, the father of the modern hotel industry, proclaimed the keys to success using three maxims that remain relevant today:

1. "Location, Location, Location:" still the first rule of hotel Real Estate Investment Trusts (REITs)
2. "Life is Service:" a mantra of every successful luxury hotel operator
3. "The Guest is Always Right:" one that continues to be problematic for digital marketers

At that time, if a hotel offered a good product in a good location, and treated guests well, word-of-mouth referrals could sustain adequate traveler demand.

Fifty years ago, as automobile and commercial air travel increased, hotel brands incorporated new technologies including computerization and call centers to add consistency to the booking process—and simplify it—across growing property portfolios.

Brand messaging was tightly controlled through advertising and public relations. It highlighted product features and was broadcast to consumers largely based on the demographics of a particular distribution channel.

Two decades ago, hotel distribution was still mainly focused on traditional consumer media, travel agencies, corporate travel management companies, and group meeting planner channels. But the internet changed everything.

In the following pages, we outline the progression of events as they relate to both the internet and hotel digital marketing. The specific dates of occurrences matter less than the correlation between the cause and effects of different discoveries and advances, and the role they all played to shape our modern digital landscape.

Seven major step-changes required hoteliers to adapt since the birth of the internet:

1. The World Wide Web
2. Interface Standards
3. Social Media & User-Generated Content
4. Free Web Analytics
5. Smartphones
6. The Sharing Economy, Wearables, and Voice
7. Big Data, Artificial Intelligence, and Prescriptive Analytics

As in all things digital, we need to incorporate a bit of technology into our history lesson to accurately represent our today and help you to see our tomorrow. This review of the digital evolution includes some highly technical fundamentals. Understanding the basic building blocks of digital technology will only make it easier to understand the evolution of digital marketing strategy.

The World Wide Web is Born: 1989-2000

Tim Berners-Lee, a British scientist, invented the World Wide Web (WWW) in 1989 while working at CERN (the European Organization for Nuclear Research). The Web was originally created to help scientists in universities more easily share information around the world.[7]

Computers existed before the World Wide Web. All that Tim Berners-Lee, along with partner Robert Cailliau, really did was figure out a

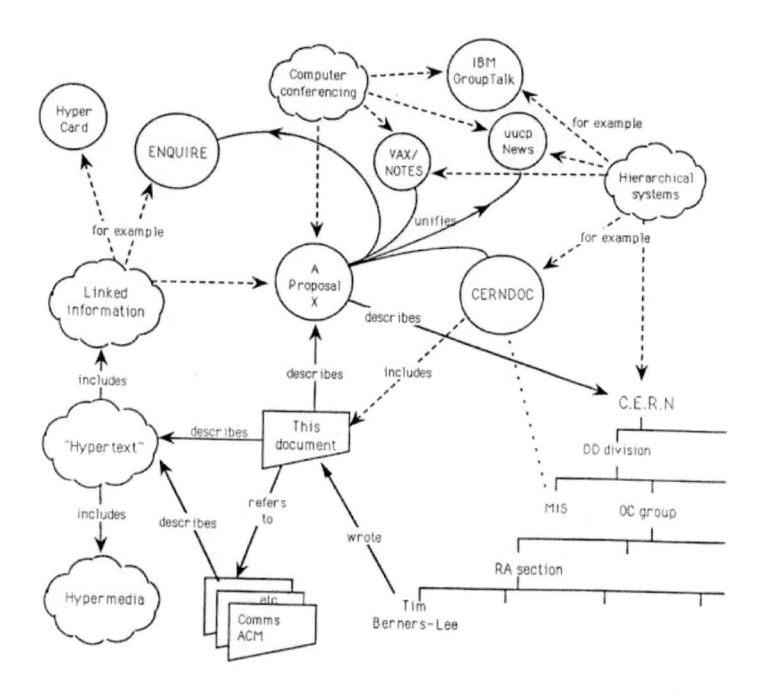

The first page of Tim Berners-Lee's proposal for the World Wide Web, written in March 1989[3]

protocol, or system, that enabled computers located in different places to share files centrally. They did this by using hyperlinks to direct signals to the correct address of a document and allowed that file to be displayed on your own computer through hypertext.

The address of the world's first website and web server was info.cern.ch, running on a NeXT computer at CERN. The first web page address was http://info.cern.ch/hypertext/WWW/TheProject.html. It worked by sending a series of header notes that told the computer a couple of important things. In the outbound message, when you typed in the URL (uniform resource locator), it told your computer key terms to find the correct computer housing the files.

In 1994, Berners-Lee launched Mosaic, which later became Netscape. Mosaic was the first browser that allowed the public to access files located on different computers outside of their own network. This free browser software could be downloaded by anyone with a computer and a telephone line. All that it really did, though, was make viewing websites much more appealing. Instead of code or data tables, you could see images and text. Suddenly, everyone decided this internet thing might actually mean something for commercial business, and websites started being built at a much faster pace.

By December 1994, there were more than 10,000 web servers around the world.

A Field Guide for Navigating Today's Digital Landscape

7

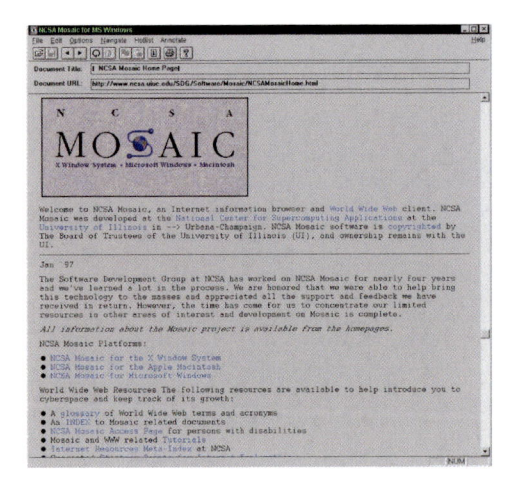

Mosaic 1.0 (an early browser) [9]

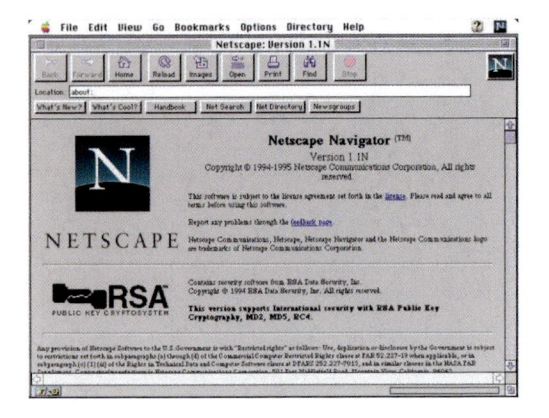

Netscape Version 1 [10]

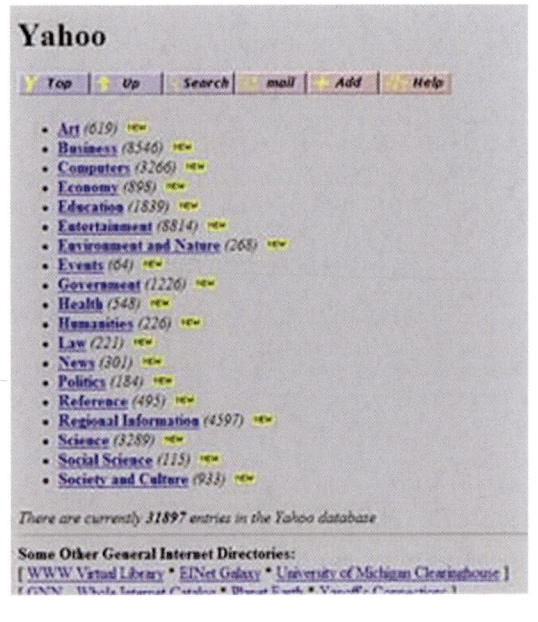

The original Yahoo directory from 1995 [11]

The only way you could access these websites was if you knew the address or URL; there was no real search capability yet.

Netscape was launched in 1995 and went public. This was the launch of the internet bubble, and it was an exciting time. Microsoft also released its browser, Internet Explorer 1.0.

The earliest search engines were really just listings of website addresses with hyperlinks organized by topics. The very first search engine was Yahoo—and was originally called "Jerry and David's Guide to the Worldwide Web." The founders, Stanford students Jerry Yang and David Filo, changed it to Yahoo which sarcastically stood for "Yet Another Hierarchy of Officious Oracle." A few other search engines were launched that took a similar approach, but soon the modern search engine was born.

As websites continued to proliferate, a better way to search started to emerge using computer robots—or bots.

Bots performed automated web tasks. One category of bots—web crawlers or spiders—"wandered" around the World Wide Web and collected information from the various websites to store in their databases. Early efforts focused on indexing by file names. So, if you typed in a keyword that matched a file name, that is the website result that would appear.

Next the bots indexed other content on the websites including page titles. During this time, a few other Stanford students launched a company called Backrub with a unique search concept. They believed that to give searchers the best results, they should see how many other websites linked back to a particular website.

So, the more sites that linked to a website, the more authority it must have, and the better the search results. Eventually, Backrub collected so much data, they overwhelmed Stanford's servers. These students, Larry Page and Sergey Brin, decided "Backrub" didn't evoke the huge quantity of data they were amassing and looked for a new name.

Sean Anderson, a fellow Stanford student, suggested googolplex. Googolplex is a large number—10 to the power of one followed by 10 to

The original Google search from 1998[02]

the power of 100 zeros. Larry Page liked the name googolplex but thought shorter would be better.

When Anderson searched to find out if the domain name googol.com was taken, he accidentally typed in google.com. Page liked the new name and Google was born. And their approach of tracking backlinks was Google's first search algorithm referred to as Page Rank (named after Larry Page).

While all this was happening, there was an explosion in email marketing, the first mobile payment was invented, and we saw insane valuation of almost every internet startup.

Hotels launched webpages, but in this early phase most hotel websites were little more than electronic versions of their printed brochures.

For a quick 5-minute video that reviews "How Search Works," see https://tinyurl.com/CHDMSearch.

Key Events–1989 - 2000
- Netscape goes public (1995)
- Microsoft Internet Explorer 1.0 launched (1995)
- Backrub (later to be called Google) formed (1995 – 98)
- Amazon.com begins selling books (1995)
- Expedia launched (1996)
- CTRIP (now Trip.com) launched (1999)
- Tripadvisor launched (2000)

Travel Interfaces Emerge: 2001 - 2003
For hotels, 2004 was a significant year because the Open Travel Alliance worked very hard to make it easier to exchange travel data between airline systems. What this meant for hotels is that travelers could finally book hotels online.

A few travel agent sites launched prior to 2000, and hotel websites existed. But to make a reservation, most sites suggested you call their 800 number, or fax a reservation request.

The new standards soon ushered in the ability for technology vendors and digital agencies to marry internet booking engines more easily with the content management systems (CMS) powering websites. Channel management systems were then created to more efficiently manage the growing number of systems capable of booking a hotel.

This new level of automation allowed for pushing information from a hotel to an online travel agency (OTA) and an OTA pulling data from a hotel, replacing reliance on cumbersome manual update processes. Websites became efficient for booking hotels, offering a greater variety of rates with more accurate pricing and availability, resulting in more customer adoption and improved booking conversion rates.

A lot of these advancements were due to the rapid expansion of bandwidth capabilities. Bandwidth is the amount of data that can travel between ports. Expanded bandwidth capabilities made data sharing faster and far more convenient.

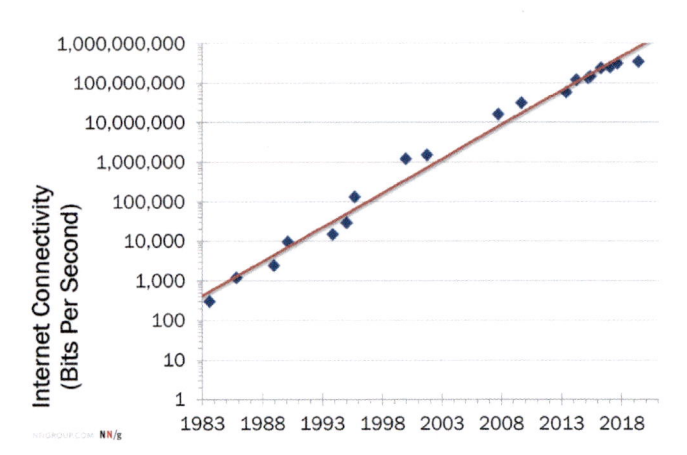

Nielsen's law of bandwidth growth from 1983 to 2019[3]

Bandwidth has doubled every year from 1983 onward, and this contributed to the speed of growth of all things internet related.

Key Events—2001 - 2003
- Email for Blackberry launched (2001)
- WordPress released (2003)
- LinkedIn launched (2003)
- Myspace founded (2003)
- First commercial mobile SMS (2003)

The Rise of User-Generated Content, Social Media, and Analytics: 2004 - 2006

Between 2004 and 2006, we saw the widespread adoption of social networks featuring user-generated content sharing. Notable advancements included Tripadvisor's pivot to consumer review forums, the launch of YouTube, and Facebook opening its network beyond students.

Prior to this phase, hotel marketers had a lot of control over the content that was shared with customers. But suddenly, the onset of user-generated content took that control away and led to a dramatic shift in the general public's trust in marketers in general.

The internet radically democratized the aggregation, communication, and consumption of information. For hoteliers, this was an unnerving development. Customer conversations might not involve management of the hotel, even though the property was a primary subject of discussion.

Brand positioning transitioned from controlled messaging that a hotel published to what consumers shared—descriptions, photos, and videos based on their experiences. This significant loss of control was countered with new reputation management tools that helped hoteliers proactively manage conversations, address customer service issues, and improve guest satisfaction.

As user-generated content grew, a new technological advancement came with the launch of Google Analytics allowing webmasters to better understand the sources and behaviors of site visitors. Basic analytics metrics that were once only available to large organizations (who were able to pay for analytics applications like Omniture SiteCatalyst, now part of Adobe's Marketing Cloud) were available for any website for free.

The ability to leverage tracking pixels and browser cookies to monitor and track user actions provided online advertising with an advantage over traditional offline broadcast media. It offered clearer evidence of return on investment (ROI). One challenge that arose, and continues today, was determining the attribution of booking intent from tracking data that extended across plural touchpoints, multiple websites, and various sessions.

Determining cause and effect remains a considerable task, even for those sporting the most comprehensive tracking technologies. In many cases, travel apps and websites use extensive A/B or multi-variate testing to compare results of experiments designed to improve usability, engagement, and conversion opportunities.

Key Events—2004 - 2006
- Facebook launched (2004)
- Web Analytics Association founded (2004)
- YouTube founded (2005)
- Urchin acquired by Google (April 2005)
- First rollout of Google Analytics (November 2005)
- Twitter launched (2006)
- Second rollout of Google Analytics (August 2006)

Smartphones Come of Age: 2007 - 2009

The introduction of the smartphone, most notably the launch of the Apple iPhone in 2007, produced a fifth phase of internet-induced change for hotels.

Beautiful websites designed for a guest's desktop computer did not translate well to the cramped real estate and width of a handheld mobile device. Notoriously impatient mobile users required a better user experience tailored to fingers and taps as opposed to the point and click of a mouse.

Native applications (apps) designed specifically for mobile devices evolved to take advantage of new mobile technologies including Global Positioning Systems (GPS), wireless networking (wifi/Bluetooth), messaging (SMS), cameras' fingerprint readers, contactless payments (NFC), and voice telephony.

Mobile-web friendly websites now offer many capabilities that were once exclusively the domain of native apps.

More than a decade later, hotels, OTAs, and metasearch websites continue to struggle with optimizing booking conversion on mobile devices, even though mobile website traffic in 2016 overtook desktop as the web browser of choice.

Many predicted the demise of the desktop, but instead we began to live in a multiscreen world. Instead of decreased time spent on a desktop, an increased amount of time was spent online overall.

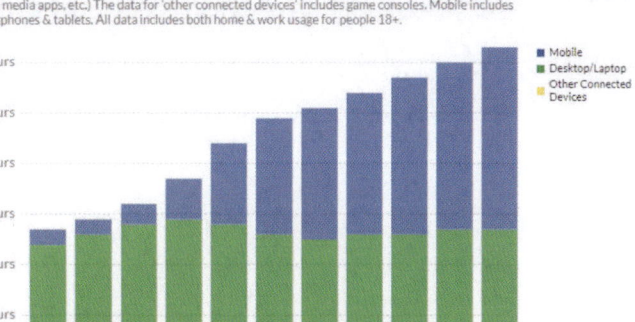

Our World in Data - Daily hours spent with digital media, United States, 2008 - 2018[15]

Key Events—2007 - 2009
- iPhone introduced (2007)
- Android smartphone launched (2008)
- Airbnb started (2008)
- Uber founded (2009)

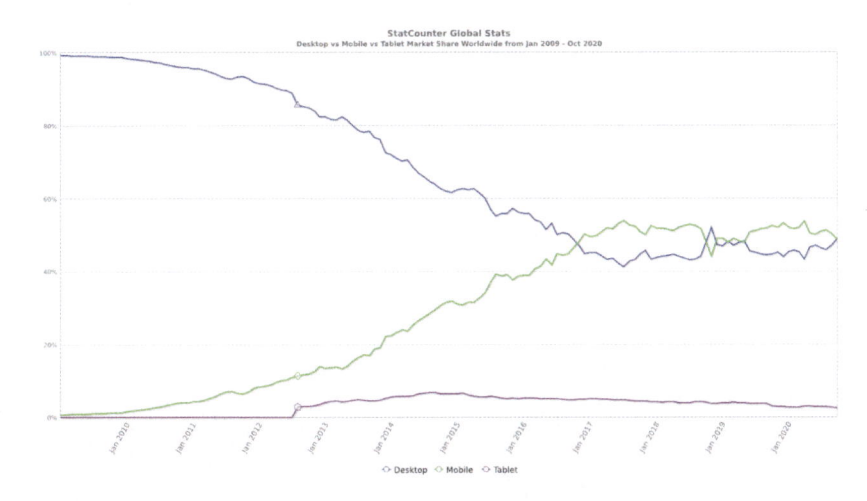

Statcounter Global Stats - Desktop vs Mobile vs Tablet Market Share Worldwide as of February 2021[16]

The Sharing Economy, Wearables, and Voice: 2010-2017

Mobile apps and websites, GPS, cookies, and mobile payment advancements led to new disruptors when the sharing economy emerged. Suddenly the taxi industry was threatened by Uber and Lyft, and hotels had a new segment vying for their customers with Airbnb. Mobile technology allowed for some visionaries to capitalize on new buyer needs for speed, ease, and personalization. No longer did we need to find the phone number of a cab company, call, and wait and hope they arrived. Uber and Lyft allowed us to use our smartphone to summon a ride, watch their approach, and even make a seamless payment.

Computing also expanded beyond our desktops and phones, and we were able to keep track of our steps and even text on our wristwatches. The Internet of Things began its takeover as "smart" went far beyond phones.

Instead of texting or typing, we began using our voice to issue instructions to virtual assistants like Siri and Alexa. There was a tremendous spike in smart speaker use between 2017 and 2018, but it has slowed considerably since.

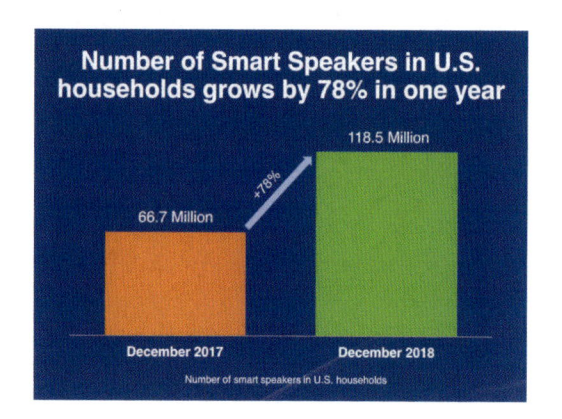

Marketing Land Survey: 118 million smart speakers in US, but expectation is low for future demand[16]

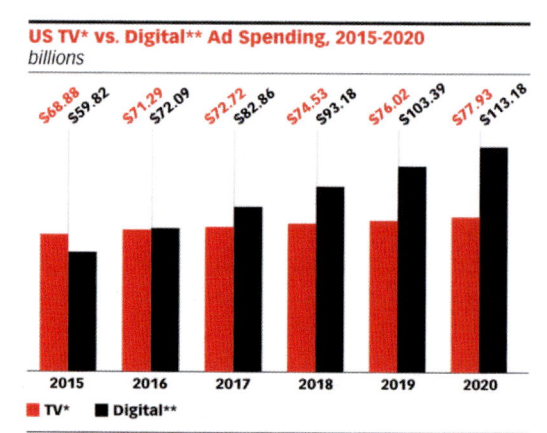

A peek at voice assistant and smart speaker use[17]

Speed, ease, and options dominated these years and hotels struggled to keep up. They had legacy systems that didn't adapt very well to one another. Airbnb was able to capture what the hotel industry believed should have been proprietary to hotels—the role of hosts—and handed that role over to an individual house or apartment owner. Airbnb made seamlessly communicating to their customers easier, while hotels competing with OTAs seemed to make options more overwhelming.

In the OTA world, it was a time of consolidation. Within just a few years, there remained only two primary OTAs—Booking.com and Expedia. Both companies had merged with or bought out most smaller OTAs.

Pokemon made augmented reality popular. Virtual reality made some progress in isolated sectors of hospitality, but fell short of the original hype they received initially.

Key Events—2010 - 2017
- Instagram launched (2010)
- Facebook Chat launched (2011)
- Google+ launched (2011)
- iPad introduced (2011)
- Device responsive website design became the new website standard (2012)
- Expedia purchased Travelocity and Orbitz (2015)
- GDPR (General Data Protection Regulation) was adopted in Europe (2016)
- Snapchat went public (2017)

Big Data, AI, and Predictive and Prescriptive Analytics

In 2017 the hotel industry entered another phase of internet technology impacts with the emergence of machine learning, big data, and voice interfaces.

Machine learning algorithms use big data technologies to capture massive quantities of information from a broad range of sources. They then identify patterns and signals to improve user experiences and optimize conversion rates, often using predictive models that would be too labor intensive and take too long for humans to calculate. This capability now informs everything from pricing and product sort orders to tactical promotions based on weather patterns or news events.

Advanced deep learning technologies, now utilizing neural networks, are being applied to the challenge of voice (natural language processing) and image recognition (computer vision), tackling not only identification of content but context. Artificial Intelligence (AI) is the natural extension of machine learning—point where systems are trained to make decisions and ultimately enhance their own applications without human assistance.

Web searches originally produced a list of links deemed best suited to offer relevant information. Now voice interfaces for mobile devices and home smart speakers leverage big data and artificial intelligence to offer what the user ultimately seeks: the BEST answer to their query. This requires hotel marketers to again adapt to a dramatic change in societal behavior and expectations prior to, during, and following a guest's stay.

Today, leading brand and property websites take advantage of all past advancements offered by internet-based technologies. Tracking user behaviors, they learned to present personalized content and alter website experiences based on customer profiles, navigation, and purchase behavior. They can now appeal to specific traveler personas for a particular property, destination, or customer segment. Behavioral retargeting presents context-relevant advertising across advertising exchanges for users who have previously visited a hotel website.

Major travel websites, whose business models are powered by data-driven strategies, adapt digital experiences based on a combination of historic and exhibited behaviors, even before they recognize the complex underlying motivations driving those user decisions. They employ a test-and-learn philosophy that knows no fixed objective—they seek continual improvement through a cycle of more data yielding better understanding to produce improved results.

Sophisticated digital marketers can dynamically create specialized promotional offers and alter cost-per-click (CPC) bidding strategies depending on the expected booking value, probability of conversion, and ultimately the lifetime value of a traveler.

Along with all these advancements came the threat of misuse of data and privacy. The European Union (EU) adopted the Global Data Privacy Regulations (GDPR) in 2016 to increase the security and transparency of what consumers were sharing across big data. The United States adopted the same measure in 2018, and the California Consumer Privacy Act took effect on January 1, 2020.

Privacy took center stage during the 2016 elections in the United States when consumers became aware of the concept of "You" as the product. If a service, like Facebook, is free to users, it is likely that the users are the actual products—or more specifically, their data and behaviors are. Cambridge Analytica was one company charged with scraping and using personal data collected from Facebook and other social sources to pinpoint political inclinations.

Cybersecurity saw a dramatic rise in importance as data breaches became widespread. Privacy issues will continue to impact digital marketing as more and more data is collected and used for personalization efforts.

Key Events—2018 - 2020
- GDPR was adopted in the U.S. (2018)
- TikTok launched (2019)
- Instagram removed the "following" tab (2019)
- Google launches new algorithm "BERT" (2019)
- California Consumer Privacy Act (CCPA) was enacted (2020)

TODAY AND THE FUTURE

The year 2020 will forever be associated with the Covid19 pandemic, and the long-term impact on hospitality is yet unknown.

Massive employee layoffs across all hospitality sectors stalled much digital marketing innovation and progress. Yet, due to work-from-home lockdowns and continued post-lockdown remote working, some digital transformations flourished.

Keyless check-in, virtual site inspections, and hybrid meetings took center stage, while social media marketing went dark for many hotels. Alignment of revenue management, ecommerce, and sales was forcibly elevated because staffing levels dictated more shared responsibilities.

How the industry emerges from the pandemic remains to be seen as of the time this book is published. Initial indicators suggest that recovery will be rapid once vaccines are widespread around the world. Pent-up demand for travel is evident, and sentiment to get back on the road is high. How the economy recovers in general will impact our industry.

Successful digital marketers must continue to adapt—using available technologies to research, segment, and target new customers. In other words, we will continue to present the right customer, at the right time, with the right product at the right price.

Digital Ad Spending in the U.S. 2019 - 2023
US, 2019-2023

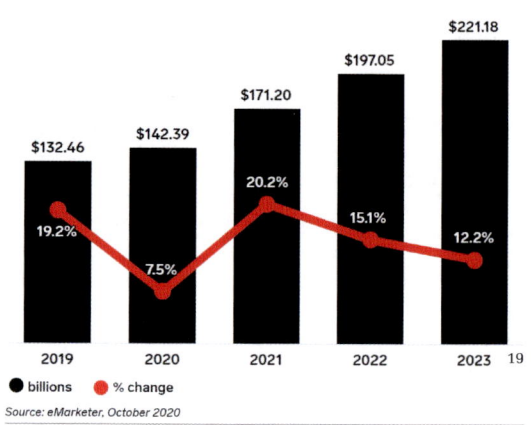

Year	Billions	% change
2019	$132.46	19.2%
2020	$142.39	7.5%
2021	$171.20	20.2%
2022	$197.05	15.1%
2023	$221.18	12.2%

Source: eMarketer, October 2020

eMarketer | InsiderIntelligence.com

Sample CHDM Exam Questions

1. The launch of browser software like Netscape and Internet Explorer is considered the start of the internet bubble because:
   a. It enabled commercial businesses to share files outside of their own networks
   b. It enabled consumers to search the world wide web for the first time
   c. It allowed both text and images to be displayed on consumers' computers from outside their network
   d. A & C
   e. All of the above

2. Responsive web design became significant in which phase of digital evolution?
   a. World Wide Web
   b. Interface Standards
   c. Social Networking
   d. Free Web Analytics
   e. Smartphones
   f. The Shared Economy, Wearables, and Voice
   g. Big Data, Artificial Intelligence, and Prescriptive Analytics

3. Attribution gained relevance after which phase of digital evolution?
   a. World Wide Web
   b. Interface Standards
   c. Social Networking
   d. Free Web Analytics
   e. Smartphones
   f. The Shared Economy, Wearables, and Voice
   g. Big Data, Artificial Intelligence, and Prescriptive Analytics

4. User-generated content (UGC) gained popularity in which phase of digital evolution?
   a. World Wide Web
   b. Interface Standards
   c. Social Networking
   d. Free Web Analytics
   e. Smartphones
   f. The Shared Economy, Wearables, and Voice
   g. Big Data, Artificial Intelligence, and Prescriptive Analytics

5. "Spiders" are:
   a. Travel Interfaces
   b. Automated computer tasks performed by robots
   c. A form of attribution modeling
   d. All of the above

Answers
1 = d
2 = e
3 = d
4 = c
5 = b

NOTES

_____
_____
_____
_____
_____
_____
_____
_____
_____
_____

Chapter 3: Hotel Digital Marketing Strategy

A strong marketing strategy should be the foundation upon which all media is applied.

THE FUNDAMENTALS OF A STRONG MARKETING STRATEGY

> Marketing = Business Model + Strategy + Segmentation + Tactics + Measurement

STEP ONE: KNOW YOUR BUSINESS MODEL

How do you create value?
A hotel must consider appropriate marketing strategies based on market conditions, competitive positioning, and product differentiation. Digital marketers must understand the underlying business model of the hotel or brand to create value by attracting and sustaining profitable business. However, the resources available to fund strategic initiatives depend on the business drivers of the enterprise.

As with all businesses, organizational strategy has three foundational pillars:

1. Business Model
2. Performance Measurement
3. Risk Tolerance

From a pragmatic perspective, strategies supporting well-defined, measurable goals more readily earn funding approval by helping decision makers understand risks.

Business models represent how a corporate strategy creates value. One of the major trends in the hotel industry has been the shift from capital-intensive to service-based business models. Major hotel groups that once owned and managed large property portfolios have gone "asset light," divesting the real estate assets on their balance sheets in favor of fee-based revenue streams.

The fragmentation of the hotel industry into hotel owners, third-party management companies, and hotel brands has created multiple parties that may have differing revenue streams, cost structures, and risk exposure emanating from a single property. It is critical for hotel marketers to understand how business strategies impact the profitability of these various constituencies.

The following table illustrates how different entities consider their value and risk formulas.

HOW DO YOU CREATE VALUE?

	Business Model	Performance Measurement	Risk Tolerance
BWH	Membership	Owner Retention	Low
Hilton	Fee based, capital efficient	team member opportunities, premium returns for owners/shareholders	Medium
TCOR	Acquistion of branded, premium select serivce in US, $10-20 million purchase, $3-7 in equity	Turnaround profit (5 year) targeting 18-20% levered IRR	Low
Agency	Labor based fee for services, independently owned	GOP, Client Retention	Medium

Source: Hotel Digital Marketing Essentials course materials. Learn more at https://americas.hsmai.org/career-development/hsmai-university/.

Hotel brands can extend a hotel's marketing reach substantially across a broader geographic region or additional market sectors, especially when able to successfully cross-sell to frequent guests of sister properties.

Property-level marketing and branding expenditures can represent risky propositions for hotel owners, particularly during times of economic uncertainty. Paying a franchise and/or marketing fee can reduce the financial exposure and cash flow impact of developing and executing marketing programs by basing expenditures on achieved sales and shifting some responsibility for driving revenue to a partner hotel group. This is why many hotel financing term sheets often require some form of brand relationship.

The growing market share of OTAs results from similar structural factors. OTAs spend billions of dollars on global marketing initiatives and technology platforms designed to convert travel demand into any hotel sale, not specifically for a particular brand or property. As hotel brands extend the marketing reach of a property, an OTA can extend the distribution of both a property and brand—again, with limited risk exposure.

Compensated only on arrived business, OTAs have successfully developed a business model that is best described as "Guests as a Service." While some hoteliers may complain about OTA fee levels (or brand fee levels, for that matter), in many cases those complaints overlook the pricing premium typically associated with any business model that creates value by eliminating risk.

All intermediary compensation levels are dictated by market conditions. If insufficient value is created, there is downward pressure on fee levels. Following nine years of economic recovery after the global financial crisis in 2009, the hotel industry was generally performing very well. That strength is reportedly translating into pressure on OTA margins.[20]

However, during the economic downturn brought on by the pandemic, hoteliers were motivated to seek incremental market share as core demand sources waned, and intermediaries gained an opportunity to grow margins as risks increased for hotel owners.

Mapping Out a Successful Strategy

Hospitality marketing has evolved into a discipline that encompasses every facet of the lodging business including:

- product design
- service delivery standards
- competitive positioning
- the more traditional marketing disciplines of pricing, promotion, and distribution

To efficiently execute successful marketing campaigns, hospitality marketers now need to get a lot of things right—far beyond the simpler approach of "the right customer at the right time at the right price." The four Ps of marketing—Product, Price, Placement, and Promotion—still exist, but digital has added to what marketers must address today:

- offering the right PRODUCT (beachfront hotel)
- in the right PLACE (Jamaica)
- including the right EXPERIENCE (all-inclusive package)
- to the right GUEST (family with young children)
- providing the right VALUE (ocean view upgrade)
- via the right MEDIA (retargeting ad)
- on the right PLATFORM (mobile)
- using the right CONTENT (family beach GIF)
- for the right PRICE ($299 per night)
- rewarding the right BEHAVIOR (clicking on an offer)
- at the right TIME (weekend evening)
- through the right CHANNEL (direct to hotel website)

STEP TWO: DIAGNOSE YOUR CURRENT STATE

Once you have defined your business model and understand how you create value, the next step is to diagnose your current state.

Product Diagnosis

Who is your product for? What is your current customer segmentation? What is your value perception? To answer these questions, look at your physical plant, the services you offer, your amenities, and your location. It is critical in this phase to define your competitors and diagnose your product relative to those competitors.

Market Diagnosis
What is your current positioning in the market? What is the overall strength of the market? Is there new supply coming in? Old supply being removed? What are the growth opportunities or concerns?

Channel Contribution Diagnosis
What is your current channel contribution and trend? This includes hotel direct, website bookings, GDS, OTAs, groups, and any other channels through which customers can find and book your property.

Opportunity Diagnosis
Based on your product, market, and channel diagnosis, this is where you should begin to hypothesize about your best customer segmentation and market mix. If you are not targeting your best audience now for your product, what should change?

We recommend a SWOT analysis as a critical step to evaluate your current situation. A SWOT analysis is a tool to evaluate a hotel's Strengths, Weaknesses, Opportunities, and Threats. Strengths and weaknesses are internal factors—the physical hotel structure, the location, its amenities, etc. Opportunities and threats are the external factors that may influence the hotel's business—the economy, health of key accounts, local construction, etc.

SWOT

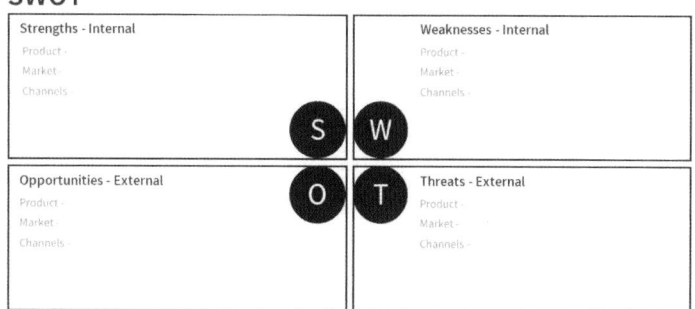

Strengths - Internal	Weaknesses - Internal
Product - Market - Channels -	Product - Market - Channels -
Opportunities - External	**Threats - External**
Product - Market - Channels -	Product - Market - Channels -

Source: Hotel Digital Marketing Essentials course materials

STEP THREE: DEFINE YOUR MARKETING STRATEGY VIA A MARKETING POSITIONING STATEMENT

With a thorough diagnosis of your current state, the next step is to define your marketing strategy by creating a positioning statement. A comprehensive positioning statement provides key direction for anyone who will aid in your marketing—employees or partners. It is the simplest way to convey a complex marketing strategy and align multiple departments to consistently deliver your best messaging.

While there are multiple approaches you can take to create your positioning statement, always start by answering five key questions:

1. What is your ideal market?
2. Who is your ideal customer?
3. What is your market category?
4. What is your product's key differentiator?
5. What are 2-3 of your key benefits?

Use this simple fill-in-the-blank template to get started.

Positioning Statement

For [target customer] who has [customer need], [hotel name] is a [market category] that [two or three key benefits]. Unlike [competition], the product [unique differentiator].

For inspiration, see the following sample positioning statement for Home2Suites by Hilton:

"Home2 Suites by Hilton understands the needs of value-conscious travelers, therefore our green-focused extended-stay hotels were designed with unique customizations, tech-savvy enhancements and plenty of space to call your own. From studio and one-bedroom suites to an Inspired Table™ breakfast, free Wi-Fi and other complimentary amenities, we're the kind of place you can kick back and be yourself."[2]

STEP FOUR: SEGMENT YOUR CUSTOMERS

All your research has led you here—to think through your ideal customer segmentation which will drive your campaign and tactical decisions.

What do we mean by customer segmentation? By defining segments, you can understand a hotel's different customer types including their purpose for travel, price sensitivity, booking lead times, and so on. This insight allows a hotel to price and apply inventory controls to maximize revenue from various sources of business, and tailor its sales and marketing efforts. Therefore, defining a hotel's segmentation mix is part of building a solid foundational strategy for a hotel. Once the mix is defined, strategies can be created to support it.[22]

As clearly and specifically as possible, identify your ideal customers. For marketers, far more detail than just "leisure" or "families" or "business travelers" is needed. Think about the many ways that customers can be segmented:

Identifiers	Potential
Demographics	· Age · Gender · Income · Education · Marital Status · Household or Business Size · Profession
Geography	· Country · Region · City · Urban · Rural · Climate
Life Stages	· 50+ Or Seniors · Families · Young Couples · Children · Young Adult · Newlyweds
Intent (linked to purchase choices)	· Lifestyle · Hobbies · Magazines Read · TV Watched
Psychographics	· Openness · Conscientiousness · Extraversion · Agreeableness · Neuroticism
Belief and Value System	· Religious · Political · Cultural

STEP FIVE: UNDERSTAND THE BUYER'S PATH TO PURCHASE

Before you can begin to identify what media you should use to drive more sales, there is one important factor you need to fully understand.

"Zero Moments of Truth" and micro-moments influence the customer experience in this digital age. Prior to the internet, this is the sales and marketing funnel that was introduced in 1898 by Elias St Elmo Lewis and was relevant for over 100 years.

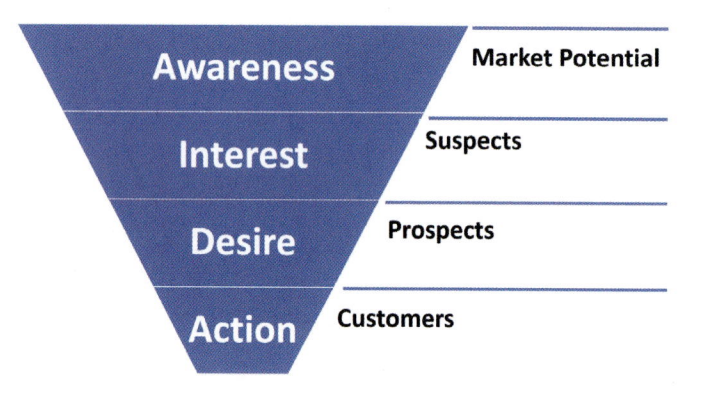

Source: Hotel Digital Marketing Essentials course based on the funnel developed by E. St Elmo Lewis in 1898

Source: Google

At the top of the funnel, marketing was charged with creating awareness for a customer or prospect and turning that awareness into interest. Once interest was assured, sales stepped in to create desire, and, ultimately, get the customer to make a purchase or act.

In the last 20 years, that marketing and sales funnel has undergone several evolutions as both buyers and marketers have changed.

With the onset of user-generated content, the funnel became more of a wheel as the path to purchase became less linear. Popular opinion was that travel marketers needed to appeal to buyers differently, depending on where they were in their buying lifecycle or journey. In the Dreaming phase, we created awareness by inspiring travel. We saw our customers doing their own research online—both on our websites and on sites like Tripadvisor where they got input from others like them.

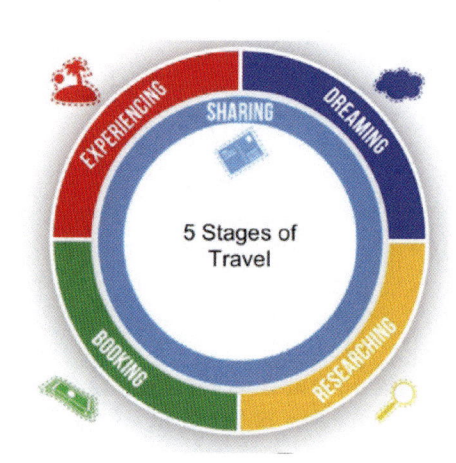

One of the biggest developments marketers saw was during the Booking phase: decisions were impacted by how easy or difficult the process was. With every click that a website forced, customers were lost, so the technology simply had to make it easier to purchase. So, there was much less of "call the hotel for a reservation," and much more of "click here for our booking engine."

We also realized that marketers could have an impact while customers were on property. By creating interesting backgrounds for photos, we could encourage in-house guests to help promote our properties through their social networks. During the Sharing phase—which could take place at any time during their journey—they could also share insights, reviews, or other word-of-mouth opinions about our properties.

Eventually realizing the vast opportunities for two-way engagement, the marketing and sales funnel morphed into an hourglass shape with more micro-steps throughout the pre-, during, and post-stay periods.

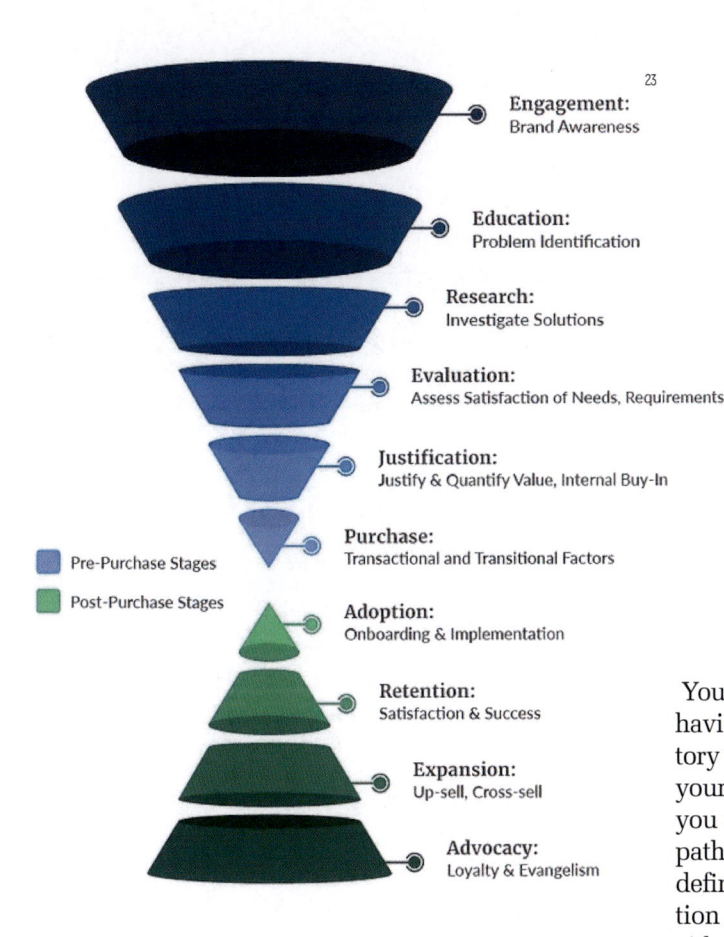

Engagement:
Brand Awareness

Education:
Problem Identification

Research:
Investigate Solutions

Evaluation:
Assess Satisfaction of Needs, Requirements

Justification:
Justify & Quantify Value, Internal Buy-In

Purchase:
Transactional and Transitional Factors

■ Pre-Purchase Stages
■ Post-Purchase Stages

Adoption:
Onboarding & Implementation

Retention:
Satisfaction & Success

Expansion:
Up-sell, Cross-sell

Advocacy:
Loyalty & Evangelism

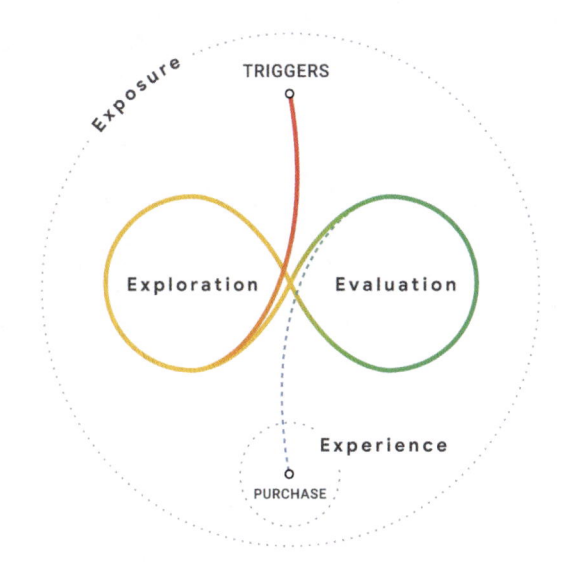

Think with Google[26]

Today, the most current thinking regarding the buyer's path to purchase is that it is a series of non-linear exploration and evaluation events with "the messy middle" in between the trigger and the purchase. "The 'messy middle' is a space of abundant information and unlimited choice that shoppers have learned to manage using a range of cognitive shortcuts."[24]

Your goal as a marketer is to influence your buyers' behaviors in the messy middle. So, the point of this history lesson on the customer journey is to say that once your market is defined and your customers segmented, you need to be acutely aware of where they are in their path to purchase, or customer journey, as that will most definitely impact your tactical campaigns. The question you must ask is, "How do my potential guests decide what they want to buy and from whom they want to buy it?"

For this book, we will use this simplified funnel model:

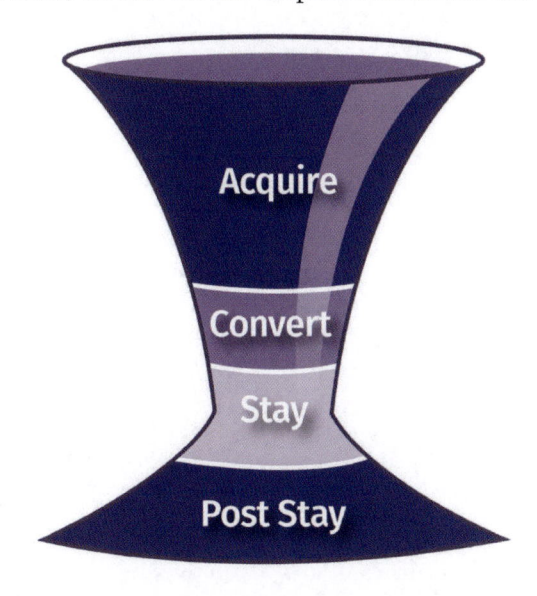

Amy had **419 digital moments** researching her trip over 2 months.

5 videos
34 searches
380 web page visits

87% of these digital moments happened on **mobile.**

Micro-moments as illustrated by Think with Google[25]

Acquire
Convert
Stay
Post Stay

Source: Hotel Digital Marketing Essentials course

A Field Guide for Navigating Today's Digital Landscape   21

At the top, customers are exploring, looking for ideas or inspiration, and the marketer's goal is to capture their attention and move them further in their decision.

In the conversion phase, the buyer is evaluating their research to determine if a certain property or brand is the best choice. Even after an initial purchase, it would be unwise to assume that they will move to the stay phase—as cancellations can occur, other brands can entice, or government regulations around something like a pandemic can change their decisions. In this phase we can continue to assure our buyers that we are still their best choice.

Assuming no cancellations or postponements, the buyer enters the stay phase where they experience our product and services. There are multiple opportunities in this phase to impact the buyer. Their delight or satisfaction will be a critical determining factor for their return, and for the photos they share and the reviews they post.

Upon departure in the post-stay phase, buyers can become advocates for the brand and help marketing efforts. Or, they can become detractors—never to return themselves and discouraging others from choosing your hotel. Even customers who enjoyed their stay will be tempted to stay elsewhere unless they are reminded of the value the property held for them. Loyalty should be reinforced at this stage.

CHINESE OUTBOUND TRAVELLERS

HSMAI has focused this publication on the best practices for hoteliers looking to apply digital marketing strategies to improve results. In most countries, there are several large players that dominate the search and travel landscape, so we have focused on processes and tactics which will work across local search engines and social channels regardless of which ones you use. The one large market that stands out is China; this is a market that needs to be addressed separately for two reasons: the sheer size of the market (China is already the world's largest outbound travel market), and because China has its own social and search engines.

FAST FACTS

- China is a country of 1.4 billion people and over 5,000 years of history. There are 33 provinces, municipalities, autonomous regions, and special administrative regions (SAR).
- The Chinese outbound hit an outstanding 155 million people[27] in 2019, and they seem to be recovering faster from the Covid-19 pandemic impacts than other countries.
- Chinese tourists are not homogenous; there are 8 archetypes with drastically different preferences and behaviors.[28]
- Chinese outbound travelers are getting younger, their spending behavior is becoming more rational, and more are seeking quality instead of being price sensitive.
- Fifty-six percent of travelers across all segments look for mid-range hotels. In pursuit of quality, 21 percent of aspirants seek luxury hotels, and base their choice on key opinion leaders and social media. The same proportion of individuals opt for a luxury hotel in search of a unique travel experience. Budget hotel operators should be thinking about the 31 percent of unplugged travelers who don't care as much about accommodation.
- Websites should be hosted on servers in China so they can get the .cn domain. Though as noted below, most companies just create WeChat pages due to expense and complications of creating websites in China.

WHAT CHANNELS DO CHINESE CONSUMERS USE?

Mobile is the predominant channel consumers use to access the internet in China. WeChat, Weibo, Baidu, and Trip.com are among some of the more predominant online tools Chinese consumers use.

- WeChat
  - Owned by Chinese tech giant Tencent, WeChat has more than a billion monthly users, just behind WhatsApp and Facebook Messenger. But it offers so much more than messaging, allowing its users to do everything from payments to booking flights and hotels. One of its key features is "mini-programs," which are apps within WeChat. More and more, hotels are using mini-programs instead of developing a Chinese language website.
  - If you're buying something online in China, there will be an option to purchase with WeChat Pay. You will need to put in a passcode or use

a biometric authentication tool to authorize the transaction. Instant money transfers to your WeChat contacts can also be made via the messaging function, which makes it easy to split bills or just move money around China. It is possible to be nearly cashless in China and go out for the day without a wallet.

- Weibo
  - Akin to Twitter in China, it is one of the largest platforms.
- Baidu
  - The predominant search engine in China, Baidu should be approached similarly to Google when it comes to advertising and SEO.
- Online Travel Agents for Chinese Consumers
  - Trip.com – the second largest OTA in the world with almost 40% of all online travel transactions in China leading back to it[29] – http://www.trip.com/
  - Meituan – a Chinese O2O (online-to-offline) local life service platform, currently focused on domestic travel, claims to have taken over Trip.com as the highest hotel bookings platform – https://www.meituan.com/
  - Qunar – a metasearch engine with 17.5% of China's 2020 online travel bookings focusing on domestic and discount travel[30] – https://www.qunar.com
  - Fliggy – online travel platform by Alibaba, that has gained in popularity – https://www.fliggy.com

HSMAI will continue to provide information and resources around this fast-growing source market. Follow developing information at https://hsmaiacademy.org/hotel-marketing-to-chinese-guests/.

STEP SIX: OUTLINE YOUR TACTICS & IDENTIFY YOUR CHANNELS

For each step of the customer journey, the marketer will likely use a different media type—or types—to target audiences.

For example, at the top of the funnel, when your buyer is in the explore phase, it is more likely that paid (see Part 4) or owned media (see Part 2) will reach them and help you acquire their interest. In the conversion phase, they are evaluating you so earned media (see Part 3) will likely be more relevant.

The pandemic highlighted an unprecedented and frequent stop along our customer journey: the cancellation or postponement of a trip. With waves of infections and business restrictions, marketers had to adjust their tactics based on this new and unprecedented disruptor. The following example is highly targeted and personalized owned media, sent to customers who cancelled their reservations during the pandemic.

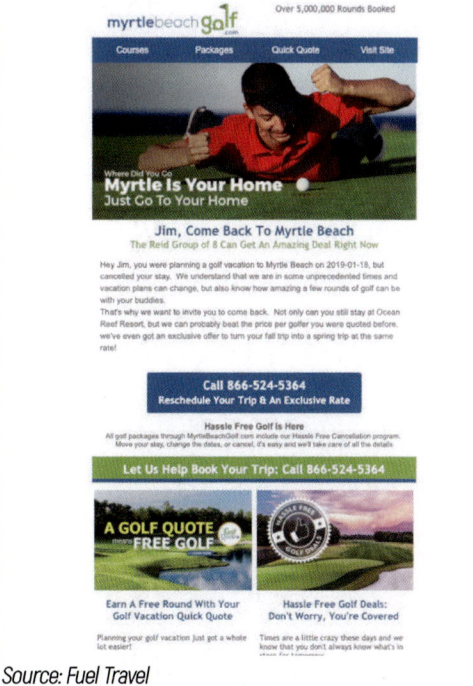

Source: Fuel Travel

A Field Guide for Navigating Today's Digital Landscape

As you outline your tactics, you are identifying your targeted customer's segment path to purchase AND the likely channels they will use to get there. All this falls under the tactics umbrella.

Channels in the Messy Middle

For channels, the approach can be messy. Gone are the days when buyers saw a billboard, called the 800 number listed, made their reservation, and showed up at the hotel.

Today, over the course of a couple days, a buyer may interact with your hotel through multiple channels—the hotel's website, an OTA, the brand, a wholesaler, and/or metasearch—and on several devices (desktop, phone, and/or tablet). That is the messy middle.

Our job as marketers is to create triggers, experiences, research points, and evaluation aids for potential guests to find us, book, stay with us, and share their own experiences. We design specific campaigns and marketing tactics and determine the relevant channels and customer journey approach—without spending all our revenues.

Throughout this book, we dive deep into those campaigns and tactics. For our marketing strategy, there remains only one more key step: measurement.

STEP SEVEN: SET GOALS AND PLAN TO MEASURE RESULTS

Every campaign should be mapped to a desired outcome, which may range from a principal business objective to a specific tactical result. Regardless of magnitude, goal setting must be directly tied to outcome measurement.

When success can be measured, success can be rewarded, and replicated. Even if a campaign is not successful, measurable results offer an opportunity for future refinement and improvement. It should also be noted that if success can't be measured, it becomes simpler for critics to describe it as failure.

The following table matches common success metrics with a particular buyer behavior:

Marketing Funnel Stage	Buyer Behavior	Marketing Objective	Media	Metric
Acquire	Trigger	Acquisition	Paid	Click Through Rate
Acquire	Exploration	Engagement	Owned, Paid	Visits, Time on Site, ROAS
Convert	Evaluation	Conversion	Owned, Earned	Video Views, Conversion Rate
Convert	Purchase	Validation	Owned	Arrived Conversion Rate
Stay	Experience	Satisfaction	Earned	Survey Responses, Net Promoter Score (NPS)
Post Stay	Exposure	Loyalty	Earned, Owned	Shares, Amplification, Membership Increase

There is no shortage of opportunities for measuring success. There is often a shortage of strategic planning for ideal outcomes. If you don't think through and map out your ideal outcomes and results, you won't be able to accurately assess your success, or make vital corrections along the way.

As we review each media type in the following chapters, keep in mind how each component fits into a larger strategic campaign. The most successful marketers understand how each individual tactic drives actions towards the ultimate success of the larger marketing strategy—which is a result of understanding how your business model drives value.

Sample CHDM Exam Questions

1. The customer journey is also referred to as:
   a. The marketing funnel
   b. Lifetime customer value
   c. The marketing tunnel
   d. Trip itinerary
   e. All of the above

2. Which of the following metrics best measures the success of a campaign designed to acquire guests?
   a. Shares
   b. Click Through Rate
   c. Net Promoter Score
   d. RevPAR
   e. None of the above

3. Which of the following questions should you answer in order to craft your marketing positioning statement?
   a. What is your ideal market?
   b. Who is your ideal customer?
   c. What is your market category?
   d. What is your product's key differentiator?
   e. What are 2-3 of your key benefits?
   f. All of the above

Answers
1 = a
2 = b
3 = f

NOTES

_____

_____

_____

_____

_____

_____

PART TWO: OWNED MEDIA

Chapter 4: The Hotel Website

KEY POINTS
- The hotel website represents the best opportunity for high-volume, low-cost bookings. It is your most valuable owned asset, and the website must be optimized for both prospective guests and search engines.
- Regularly updated content and professional imagery are essential for a successful website.
- Best practices for optimum revenue-generating websites include usability, search engine optimization, mobile optimization, and social interactivity.
- A website does not operate in a vacuum. Availability, rates, inventory (ARI)—and how they are presented in the booking engine—significantly impact performance.
- Usability is a key aspect of your website; your site must perform well on all form factors (desktop, mobile, tablet, other).

"When I started in the hotel business 52 years ago, the first impression customers had of our hotels was the lobby when they walked through the front doors. But in this digital age, often the first impression comes when they visit **Marriott.com**. It's our digital front door." - Bill Marriott

What began in the early 1990s as a digital brochure has evolved into a complex collection of marketing content, keywords, meta tags, visual images, widgets, and booking engines.

The hotel website represents the best opportunity for high-volume, low-cost bookings. It is your most valuable owned asset. Hotels must ensure that their websites are optimized for search engines, best represent their selling points, and are geared to an online customer.

When you boil it down to the basics, there are two key factors that will drive revenue on your site:

1. Site traffic
2. Conversion rate

Everything you do will revolve around these two areas in one way or another.

The hotel website has become the backbone of the hotel marketing mix and is the digital front door that most customers will see before they ever step foot on your property. In this age of omnichannel marketing, any type of hotel marketing initiative—from search engine marketing and display (banner) advertising to email and social media marketing—has the ultimate goal of driving the prospective guest to your website.

There are three major types of hotel websites.

1. Brand.com: If your property is part of a brand, it is likely your property is included in the brand website and booking engine. The property will have some level of control over the content and usually full control over rates and offers. But for the most part, the design, format, and functionality are controlled by the brand.
2. IndependentHotel.com: Hotels that are not part of a brand likely will build an independent website and utilize a third-party or homegrown booking engine.
3. VanitySite.com: Also called microsites, these sites are sometimes created by properties that have a presence on a brand site but for some reason need an additional property-specific site. Reasons may include uniqueness of the property that cannot be represented on brand.com, language needs that may not be represented on brand.com, or a specific market segment that is not targeted on brand.com. Vanity sites should be carefully considered as there are drawbacks to them. Please note that brands have different guidelines for vanity sites; some may allow them, while others strictly forbid them.

BRAND.COM

Typically, hotels that are part of a large brand (such as Marriott, Hilton, IHG, etc.) are provided representation on the brand.com site. These sites follow the brand templates (design, color schemes, and navigation). They have many of the critical features already built in, including booking widgets and other appropriate technology, textual content, imagery placements, and additional marketing components.

While the brand provides the framework, it is the responsibility of the property to ensure the website is well maintained from a content perspective, including:

- well-written and compelling textual content from both a marketing and SEO standpoint
- up-to-date, professional hotel and room imagery
- use of other components offered by the brand for promotions, additional hotel information, "product" highlights, and other "news and updates" for the hotel

Following are examples of two smaller brands' websites and two larger brands' websites.

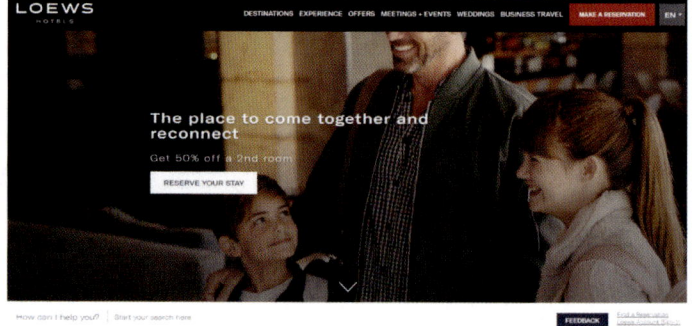

Brand.com website for Sonesta
Source: *https://www.sonesta.com/ as of February 17, 2021*

Brand.com website for Loews Hotels
Source: *https://www.loewshotels.com/ as of February 17, 2021*

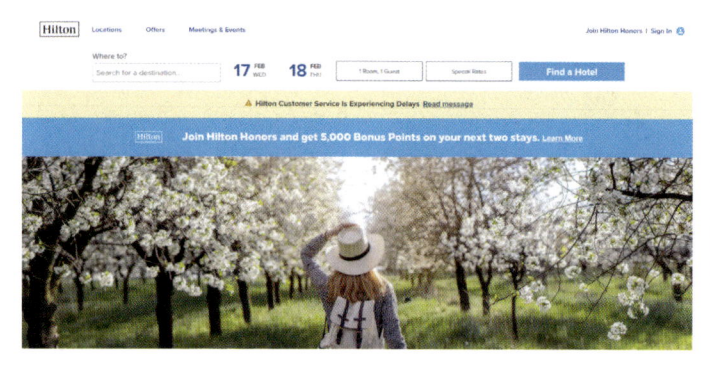

Brand.com website for Hilton
Source: *https://www.hilton.com/en/ as of February 17, 2021*

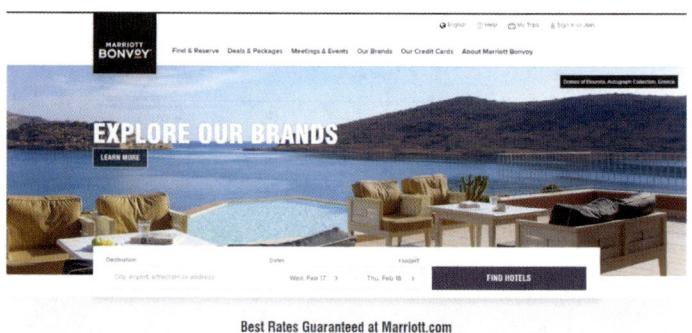

Brand.com website for Marriott International
Source: *https://www.marriott.com/ as of February 17, 2021*

INDEPENDENT-HOTEL.COM

The decision is simple for an independent hotel or resort—a website is an absolute necessity, and if you are not part of a brand, you need to build your own. In this case, the primary strategic decision is the level of investment appropriate for the site based on projected returns.

If it is a new hotel, you can build the site from scratch to meet all your requirements. If it is a hotel with an existing site, you need to consider if it is time to refresh or redo the site. Some key considerations include:

- Does the site creative represent your brand well?
- Does the website follow current best practices? For example, search engines algorithms place a high importance on sites that are mobile optimized and that load fast. If your site is not mobile optimized and/or does not load fast you will be penalized in your organic ranking (see Chapter 8).
- Are your year-over-year (YOY) website booking contributions growing, level, or slipping? How does that compare to industry benchmarks and other properties in your market?
- Are your website traffic and search rankings deteriorating? When was your website last optimized for SEO?
- Does your website have the most accurate descriptions of your hotel product and services from both a textual content and imagery perspective?
- Is your website integrated with the property's social media?
- Does your website support open graph tags—snippets of code that cause your selected picture and marketing text to appear when users share content from your site on Facebook, tweet links to your content, or post to Instagram?
- Is your website schema optimized?
- Does your website have a robust content management system (CMS) that allows you to manage visual and textual content, set up new specials and packages, post events and happenings, create new landing pages, and more?
- When was the site last refreshed or redesigned? If it has been more than a few years, it may be time to consider it. The last few years brought the deployment and adoption of schemas, open graph tags, and new algorithm updates including penalties for non-mobile optimized sites. Change is continuous and rapid, and hoteliers should consistently be considering site improvements, even if that means a full site redesign.
- Do you have staff capacity and capability to manage the site in-house, or will you need to outsource the site management?

Independent hotel website for Lotus Honolulu
Source: https://www.lotushonoluluhotel.com/ | As of February 17, 2021

VANITYSITE.COM

For branded properties, several factors must be considered prior to building a vanity site.

If the hotel is part of a brand, first determine the brand policies regarding property vanity websites. Many brands discourage or prohibit branded properties from creating stand-alone sites, preferring the resources be channeled through a central brand site or other online marketing activities. This enables product consistency, and in some cases is the wisest decision for a property. Some brands allow for vanity sites and may have preferred agencies to work with to build the sites. In either case, the best practice is to review your brand's policies and recommendations regarding vanity websites before investing time and resources.

Maintaining current information on a branded site is time consuming. Regardless of whether a stand-alone site is needed, maintenance should be a priority for any digital marketing strategy. Keeping photos, keywords, and information directed to key segments (and more!) up to date is primarily the responsibility of the property.

PROS — To Vanity Site or Not — CONS

Why You Might
- ✓ Unique property, not brand typical
- ✓ Marketing in feeder markets and translations
- ✓ Provide exposure to key segments that might not be addressed by brand
- ✓ Improve search engine results
- ✓ Create standalone site for an aspect of hotel (e.g., restaurant, spa, etc.)

Why You Might Not:
- ✓ Customer confusion (which is the "real" site)
- ✓ Brand inconsistency
- ✓ Cost and effort to maintain
- ✓ Inefficiencies in marketing spend
- ✓ Inability to effectively track results
- ✓ Prohibited by brand

Think about the following when considering a vanity site:

- Does the brand provide adequate marketing exposure for the property in your main feeder markets? More specifically, do you know where they are marketing your hotel? Most brands run extensive search marketing campaigns, but it is the property's responsibility to communicate your targeted feeder cities to the brand.
- How competitive is your location on the brand website? If you are in a primary, or even secondary, market with a strong brand presence—meaning multiple properties flying the same flag—a vanity site may be necessary to stand apart. Also, as noted previously, if your property has a non-standard brand component, a vanity site may be necessary to target your right customer mix.
- Are your booking contributions via the web competitive? Are you receiving your fair share of online bookings? If you are receiving more than your fair share on your branded site, is a vanity site necessary? If you see that your share is lagging, a great boost might be a new or upgraded vanity site.
- How easy is it for a customer to find your specific hotel on the brand site? In some cases, there are franchise naming issues—Hotel X Airport South, Hotel X Airport Southeast, etc.—that may be confusing to consumers, and a vanity site may more clearly differentiate your property.

> It cannot be emphasized enough that, before even spending time to consider a vanity site, you need to understand your brand's vanity site guidelines.

Following are examples of vanity sites for properties that also have presence on their brands' sites.

Vanity site for C Hotel, part of Carmen's Group

Source: https://carmenshotel.com/ | As of February 17, 2021

Vanity site for Grand Hotel Golf Resort & Spa Autograph Collection, part of Marriott

Source: https://www.grand1847.com/ | As of February 17, 2021

Vanity site for Intercontinental Sydney, part of IHG

Source: https://www.sydney.intercontinental.com/ | As of February 17, 2021

BEST PRACTICES: TEXTUAL CONTENT

Content should be written, first and foremost, with the customer in mind. The hotel should be positioned appropriately with the top-selling features and informative descriptions of the hotel and its services. What you write matters as much as any keywords you use.

You and your brand may have invested a lot of time, effort, and budget into driving traffic to your website. Now that you have a possible customer on your website, it's time to effectively market to them and convince them that your hotel is the best choice for their trip.

Search engine optimization (SEO) is extremely important for your hotel website and will have an impact on your textual content and meta data. Therefore, striking a strong balance between the use of content for marketing and SEO is very important. SEO and meta data is covered in Chapters 8 and 9.

When creating content, it is also important to understand WHY the customer is considering your hotel and, thus, how you should market to them. There are significant differences, for example, between a city center hotel, an airport hotel, and a resort hotel. Each has a different audience, a different reason for "being" (trip purpose), and various amenities and services. Your content should best relate to those differences and speak in the appropriate "voice," allowing visitors to quickly understand who and what you are…and what impression you wish to give of your hotel.

Make sure your website reflects the reasons why consumers travel to you or your area. One way to approach this is to think of your website in terms of how a director of sales (DOS) markets the hotel. Does your website reflect the demand generators that bring customers to your area? Are you appropriately featuring proximity to local attractions, amusement parks, stadiums, etc.? Are you a venue for weddings, family reunions, etc.?

Conduct an annual update of customer segmentation optimization to fully address all key segments, from meeting and group planners to corporate and leisure travelers, social event planners, and family travel planners.

Keep It Brief

As you write copy, keep in mind that web copy is very different than print copy. Web copy is "scanned" or glanced through…not "read" in the traditional sense. This is even more true on mobile platforms, which have become the leading source of online traffic and where visitors have much shorter attention spans. Most consumers will not read your website content word for word but look for appropriate keywords or phrases.

Ensure that all text relays important features and selling points quickly and upfront. Avoid long lists and overly-promotional content that visitors won't read. Content should be easily scannable, and paragraphs and sentences kept short and concise so visitors can find what they're looking for quickly.

Your most important points should always come first, whether written in paragraph format, bulleted lists, or icons (for branded hotels, the formatting is typically pre-determined at the brand-level template).

It is best to avoid needless repetition, jargon, and unnecessary words in your copy—keep it as simple as possible. Effective online copywriting is an art, so some properties will hire professional copywriters or vendors to handle this area for them. Check first with your brand to see if they have any internal services or vendor recommendations.

Keep It Fresh

The "freshness" of your content is extremely important, both from marketing and SEO perspectives. All content areas should be up-to-date and include the latest information on the hotel itself, new services and amenities, and the most recent local area content. Not only is this important from a consumer perspective, but it is also extremely important from an SEO perspective. Google and other search engines weigh the "freshness" of content in their ranking algorithms.

All promotional or event dates should be constantly updated (e.g., is your website still promoting a New Year's Eve event in February?). For SEO, it can be important to keep the addition of new content at a steady pace, keeping your site dynamic and continuously offering fresh content when and where possible. Consider updating key pages (those pages with the highest visitor view rates) at least once or twice a year. For sites that include customer reviews, the constant addition of reviews helps in this area as it is technically new content.

It is important to have proper room descriptions as these will help drive conversion and upselling efforts around premium room types.

In summary, is your website offering what your potential customers are looking for? Is it current? Can they find it quickly?

BEST PRACTICES: IMAGERY

Imagery sells…and can make all the difference. Strong photography is one of the most important aspects of your digital presence and your hotel website. A 2021 study from Expedia[31] indicated that accurate and abundant photos give travelers the confidence to book. Travelers reported that the most essential photos for them are of the guest room, bathroom, property exterior, and property amenities. Additionally:

- 57% said many detailed photos give them confidence to book an accommodation.
- 88% said it's important to see photos of amenities before booking a hotel.
- 9 is the average number of photos travelers view when considering a property.

Imagery should be shot by a professional photographer experienced in architectural photography. Handing a general manager a digital camera or using a wedding photographer is unlikely to result in professional hotel photography.

Your hotel website photo gallery and header images should represent all architectural features of the hotel, including the exterior, meeting space, lobby, fitness centers, pools, recreational areas, restaurants, bars, etc., and should provide the website visitor with enough visual knowledge to understand the offerings and services provided by the hotel. Pictures can tell a story, and a single image, if shot correctly, can convey information faster and more effectively than a paragraph of text.

Room photography is especially important. At the end of the day, the room is what the customer is purchasing. It is important for them to understand the features of the room, the size of the room, and the differences between various room types.

If you are selling a suite, focus on the size and layout of the room. If you are selling a "view" room, show the view. Too often, hotels simply repeat the same images (typically a bed shot) across various room types, in essence telling the customer that regardless of description and price, the rooms are all the same. We know that this is not the case, and you should show the rooms accordingly. This will assist in both conversion as well as upselling. If you can show a visitor how much bigger the Junior Suite is than a Standard room, or what that Ocean View looks like versus the Standard room through imagery, they will be much more likely to respond to higher cost room choices.

Effectively impact revenue generation through imagery:

- Tell the whole story with professional architectural photos. Be careful of over-staging, unnatural lighting, or props.
- Display a minimum of 2-4 images for each room type. The more high-quality images of the rooms and the hotel, the better. Trends have shown the number of images has an impact on customer engagement and bookings.
- Document the space with the best angles to give guests the visual information they look for when booking a room.
- Capture the benefits of the room to show layout, features, and amenities. Yes, bathroom shots are important as well!
- Document what is unique about a room type and visually represent the differences.
- Ensure that new photo shoots are scheduled as soon as possible during the opening process or after major renovations and enhancements.
- Avoid any stock hotel imagery. If customers realize you are showing them stock images and not actual images of the hotel, they will lose trust.
- If the website has the capability to show videos, 360s, and more immersive types of imagery, the property should take full advantage of this, as video (in particular) has been shown to have a big impact in the guest's purchase decision.

- Make sure that the imagery is "light" and does not slow the site down. Even if you have very compelling imagery, if it slows the site down it should not be used.
- While it is always important to put your best foot forward, never be misleading or dishonest. Do not "trick" customers by photo cropping or photoshopped enhancements. For example, do not use the one and only renovated room as the room you use for your website photos. Color correction, cropping for size, etc., is one thing, but providing false impressions of facilities to guests will result in lost trust and/or unhappy customers who are likely to communicate their dissatisfaction far and wide.

One area of hotel photography often debated is the use of models. While models can often convey the hotel "experience," there are downsides as well. Models are expensive, can date your photos quickly (clothing, hairstyles, etc.), and release rights are needed and must be kept up to date. Perhaps more importantly, models can provide unexpected perceptions of your hotel to possible guests.

Think of that image of the family with small children enjoying the pool. To some, that might mean loud and splashing children running amok, and not a great hotel for a quiet retreat or work trip. Or think about the image of the young couple at the bar. To some, that might mean it's not a great hotel for families with kids. While possible perceptions may not always align with the intent (or how different people may view the same images), they must be considered.

To look at hotel photography a different way, compare hotel shopping to how we act when shopping for other retail products online. If you searched Amazon for a product—an Espresso machine for example—would you consider purchasing any of the resulting choices if they had no images in their listing? Do you learn more about the product with highly professional and multiple images (the machine's size, materials, color, and build) or those with only a single image? Are there specific features you're looking for—perhaps stainless steel—that are conveyed through the imagery more effectively than in the text description?

In summary, imagery is one of the most effective tactics you have on your hotel website to increase conversion. Today's consumers are more visual than ever and will gain most of the knowledge they need to know in their decision-making process from the website imagery. Your imagery serves as your virtual hotel and will be viewed by far more people than will ever walk through your property. It should present the very best of the hotel in the most professional way possible.

BEST PRACTICES: ANCILLARY CONTENT

In addition to textual content and imagery, many brand.com sites offer additional opportunities for adding ancillary content on your hotel website. These may include the ability to add "product" pages to the website (think spa, golf, restaurants, meetings, etc.), additional promotional pages or elements beyond the typical "deals" listings, various timed marketing messages, renovations made and new hotel alerts, and posting of PDFs/informational items (menus, A/V service listings, directions, etc.). Be sure to check with your brand to ensure you are knowledgeable about all available enhanced products for your website.

BEST PRACTICES: USABILITY (UX)

Website user-friendliness refers to the quality of the user experience (UX) on the website. In human-computer interaction, usability usually refers to the elegance and clarity with which the interaction with a computer program or a website is designed. That is a fancy way of saying we need to make it EASY!

Website user-friendliness encompasses several key components that are crucial to the user experience, including:

- site architecture and page layout for both desktop and mobile
- tiered navigation structure (e.g., top/main navigation, sub-navigation, actionable navigation, footer navigation, etc.)
- logical flow of information
- content addressing your key customer segments
- rich media, videos, and quality imagery
- page load speed
- design aesthetics

- on-page/internal links
- call to action
- quick links

Every page should have a clear and easy way for visitors to make a reservation. Some sort of "Book now" or "Click here to make reservations" should have a prominent position on every single page. That may seem redundant, but the primary function of your hotel website is to generate bookings, and you want to make it easy for the visitor to make the reservation whenever they feel they have enough information. They may be ready once they visit your home page, or once they see the restaurants you offer onsite, or the directions from the airport—make it easy to book when they're ready. This point cannot be overstated: the process should be easy and friction points need to be eliminated or mitigated.

The same principle can be applied for those hotels that focus on group business. Prominently include clear navigation to information about event space and sales contacts so that meeting and event planners can find the information they need no matter how they have come into your site.

Redundant navigation is important. Show the main content areas across the top and duplicate them in text on the bottom of each page. Don't make the visitor scroll too far to find what they are looking for. The most relevant information should be top left, then top right. If you have a call to action (other than to make a reservation), give it a clear spot near the top. Don't bury it in the content.

Make sure your pages load quickly. If it's too slow, your visitor will abandon your site. This typically means you must carefully determine the number of images per page. And for every image, determine if it is inviting, and is it worth the load time?

Mobile users are even more impatient than desktop customers. With mobile, load time is even more important. Regardless of how amazing your fully loaded page is, if it does not load quickly, you will lose potential guests and be punished by Google in your page rank.

Text is important for search optimization factors, and it should always be relevant for your visitor. On your location page, are you telling your visitor what they need to know about your location? If you are an airport property, how clear is your proximity to the airport? Following the acronym EAT, your site should be seen as **Expert**, **Authoritative**, and **Trustworthy**. Not only will this put you in good stead with your customers, but it will also help you with your SEO.

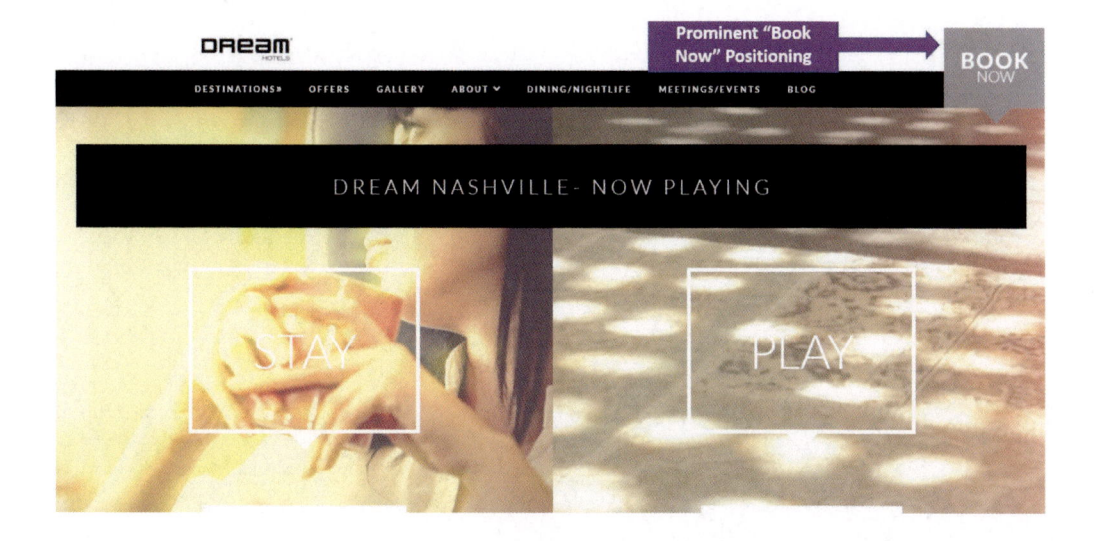

Notice the prominent "Book Now" positioning on Dream Hotels' home page

Source: https://www.dreamhotels.com/ | As of February 17, 2021

To test your site's usability, there are tools and services like usertesting.com that will allow you to test your site with visitors matching your customer demographics.

Ensure Compliance with ADA Regulations

Making your website accessible to users with disabilities is critical. Threats of lawsuits for noncompliance aside, Google also gives weight in ranking to sites that are trying to focus on universal accessibility factors, and of course it is important that your property and the website are ready to welcome all guests.

- Provide sufficient contrast between foreground and background.
- Don't use color alone to convey information.
- Ensure that interactive elements are easy to identify.
- Be sure there is clear and consistent navigation.
- Include visible links to transcripts of any audio you have.
- Include text along with image and media alternatives in your design.
- Add text along with icons and graphical buttons.
- Include captions and descriptions for tables or images.
- Remember ADA Rooms need to be bookable with same "ease" as other rooms.
- Know that, depending on the property, a certain number of rooms need to be ADA compliant.

To learn more, visit the Web Accessibility Initiative at https://www.w3.org/WAI/. And, to test the technical aspects of accessibility on your site, a tool is available at https://wave.webaim.org/.

BEST PRACTICES: EASY BOOKING PROCESS

The booker-friendliness of a hotel website is a direct result of how well it handles a whole range of complex issues that can influence purchasing behavior.

Build trust and credibility. Visitors are savvy; they will search among many sites during the booking process. How is your rate integrity? If you offer any sort of lowest rate guarantee, place it prominently on your website, in multiple places. A best-price guarantee is all you may need to build some trust.

Focus on the ease-of-use of your booking engine and the smoothness of the booking process. How easy/hard do you make it for someone to book your property? Is checking availability tedious? If it is, potential guests will move on and book elsewhere. Again, remember the goal is to make the process easy and remove or mitigate as many of the friction points as possible.

Put a reservation widget on your home page and include it as part of the global navigation of the site. Use a customized look-and-feel design that mimics the website design. When a customer clicks to book your property, are they worried they have gone to another site because the look and feel is different? That doesn't help with trust and credibility. Most usability studies and industry best practices suggest that the booking widget should be placed at the top left or center of the page. This is where you will find most widgets on brand websites and OTAs. If your reservation widget is a small icon, lower down on the page, or in a difficult-to-find location, you will pay a penalty in revenue and conversions.

There is a reason the big brands and OTAs have their booking widget front and center.

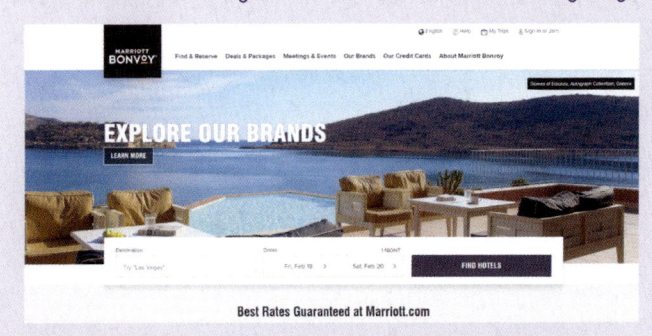

Source: https://www.marriott.com/default.mi | As of February 19, 2021

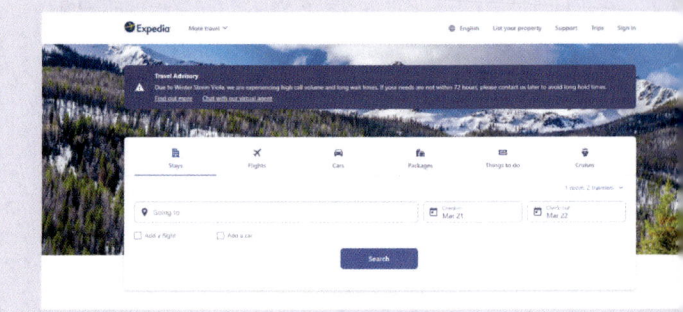

Source: https://www.expedia.com/ | As of February 19, 2021

Highlight the availability of bookable unique special offers, packages, and promotions with excellent perceived value propositions. You know your guests and your property better than anyone. Do your packages reflect what is unique about you, or are they what you can find anywhere? Keep your specials up to date. If they are expired, remove them. Otherwise, again, your credibility is in question.

Ensure good security and privacy policies, posting your privacy policy for visitors to see.

If one of your conversion goals is to receive RFPs from your site, make sure it is easy to submit them on your site. Even more importantly, ensure that whoever receives them responds within 24 hours.

BEST PRACTICES: ADDRESS SHOPPING CART ABANDONMENT

Taking a cue from retail, hotels have become more sophisticated about tracking and engaging with "lookers" who don't make it all the way through the booking process.

First, track what percent of your visitors go to your booking engine, and what percent of those visitors actually make a reservation. If you have a high abandonment rate, you should research to find out why. Is it a technical issue, a rate parity issue, or something else?

There will always be a percentage of prospects who will go to your booking engine and not book. One tactic is a trigger screen that will appear as they try to close out your website. A popup can offer a further special or invite the visitor to sign up for a newsletter.

If you have the customer's email and can recognize the customer through your CRM system, send a follow-up email later the same day or the next, potentially with a special incentive to return to complete the booking.

Finally, retargeting is an option, and is discussed in Part 4. In many instances you can retarget the shopper with ads as they surf around the internet.

The reality is that most people who visit your site will not make a booking; in fact, conversion rates are somewhere between under 1% to 5% on most hotel sites. However, even slight improvements to conversion can have a significant impact on revenue which is why it is important to understand why your visitors are leaving. If it is cumbersome to book online, they may pick up the phone to call or simply go to an OTA or other competitor's site. If your rate is not in line with what they have seen on the OTA or metasearch sites, they will likely leave to find the better deal.

BEST PRACTICES: SEARCH ENGINE OPTIMIZATION

Search engine optimization is extremely important as it determines if your site shows up when people are searching on Google and other search engines. Chapters 8 and 9 discuss this in detail but since it is such an important part of website design it is important to touch on some key points in this section.

- Make sure your web address, hotel name, physical address, and phone number are consistent on the site, and across all the websites, directories, and other locations that feature your hotel on the web. This information is referred to by the acronym UNAP (URL, name, address, phone number). Google refers to your UNAP as your business's digital fingerprint—it should be completely unique to you, and it should be consistent across the web as it is important to your site ranking.
- Ensure your navigation is clear and logical. Use an HTML sitemap to outline all searchable pages on your site.
- Use meta tags that are your most relevant keywords and have them vary based on the page being displayed.
- Be sure your content is relevant. Visitors who can't find what they want on your site will bounce away quickly. Make sure your content changes are up to date and relevant to your unique selling points.
- Ensure key listings are updated and pay extra attention to GMB (Google My Business).
- Have strong links to your site. If you are located next to a university, does that university link back to you? How about local corporate headquarters? Conduct search engine optimization (SEO) updates regularly (every few months is recommended) to take full advantage of the evolving search dynamics.

The Need for Speed

Site load time is important to consumers, and it is important to Google. Be aware that 47% of consumers expect a web page to load in 2 seconds or less, and 40% abandon a website that takes more than 3 seconds to load.[32] You can check your download speed at https://developers.google.com/speed/pagespeed/insights/.

Speed is even more important on mobile, and Google gives preferential treatment to mobile sites that take advantage of AMP—Accelerated Mobile Pages. AMP, backed by Google, was designed as an open standards project for any developer to access to help mobile pages load faster. Written in what is referred to as HTML lite, the concept is to encourage companies to deliver the product that consumers want—fast-loading mobile sites. In February 2016, Google officially began integrating AMP listings into its mobile search results.

If you believe ranking high on Google is important, this is a marketing investment with a strong ROI. While AMP is a great tool to help increase the speed of your site, it is no longer the only way to ensure Google gives you credit for a fast mobile site. If you have a mobile site that is fast, whether you do it through AMP or another method, Google will include that in the algorithm that ultimately determines your page rank.

BEST PRACTICES: SOCIAL INTEGRATION[33]

Hoteliers must align with the hyper-interactive behavior of today's travel consumer both on the hotel website and on the social web. The social interactivity of the hotel website is dependent on how well the website can intrigue users and enable them to provide comments, share content, and interact with various features and functionality. For a hotel to have a strong brand voice on the web, the relationship with customers must be a two-way street.

- Social interactivity features should be regularly implemented and updated to improve customer engagement on the site. For brand.com websites, much of this may be implemented by the brand, including Facebook sharing functions, links to social sites, etc.
- Include a blog on your website. Content can and should be changed frequently—it encourages comments, and it is also helpful for search optimization. One of the key benefits of having a blog is that the content can be re-purposed for other areas, like email campaigns, website content, social media, etc. Only do a blog if you have the time and resources to properly maintain it.
- Consider posting real reviews on your website. This is risky; if there is a negative review posted it will be front and center on your site, but from a credibility standpoint, mostly positive reviews on your website go a long way to inspire confidence. Many major brands, like Best Western, have already implemented reviews on their hotel websites. The property's responsibility is to ensure they are responding to those reviews through the brand's approved process or platforms.
- Share links to your social sites (Facebook, Instagram, YouTube, etc.) if you have them.
- Make it easy for your visitors to share information, to like it, and to post it to their Facebook pages, etc.
- Use open graph tags so that a photo and marketing text you determine is displayed when users post your content to their Facebook page, re-tweet links to your website, and post your content on Instagram. For more information on how to create open graph tags see https://ahrefs.com/blog/open-graph-meta-tags/. While the use of open graph tags doesn't directly impact your website SEO, it has a dramatic impact on how shareable your social content will be, which should ultimately lead to an increase in website traffic.

BEST PRACTICES: FEATURES AND FUNCTIONALITY

Ensure that your website is fully mobile optimized across the range of devices and associated browsers your customers use. The sites should automatically resize to fit the device they are displayed on, meaning you don't need to think in terms of a separate mobile site.

A hotel website should have a related content management system (CMS) that allows the property to, at a minimum:

- manage textual and visual content on the desktop site and the mobile site
- create new landing and content pages

- initiate real-time content push to social media
- update an interactive calendar of events
- manage imagery
- feature special promotions

Basic functionality that should be built into a hotel website includes:

- a reservation widget on the home page (and as many other pages as applicable)
- email capture functionality
- videos and rich media
- links from the site to Facebook, Instagram, and relevant social media
- A/B testing functionality
- the ability to accept RFPs (if applicable for your property)

BEST PRACTICES: CONNECTING WITH GLOBAL CUSTOMERS

In the ever-competitive world of travel, website localization is the key to success for a hotel to connect with new consumers, gain market share, and communicate a competitive differentiator. As more companies expand into new markets, competition grows. Hotels that don't localize will be left behind while competitors embrace translation as a means of growth.

In their report, "Can't Read, Won't Buy," CSA Research notes that 55% of global consumers only make online purchases on websites that offer content in their native language. And these consumers will spend more time browsing on sites in their own language, so a localized website is a must-have for engaging new customers around the world.[34]

With many detailed requirements, website localization can seem like a daunting task. But with careful planning and preparation, you can simplify the process and create a more impactful global website.

When tackling web localization/globalization, plan for these key tasks:

- Define your target markets and determine the most relevant languages for consumers in each locale. But be careful not to confuse a country for a locale. A locale refers to a region in which people speak a particular language—and it's not always defined by country borders.

- Decide whether you will have a standalone language site or present a "translation" of an existing site. Some people consider "localization" to be creating a very specific localized site while site globalization is taking an existing site and translating some or all the content to a specific language. While tools like Google Translate have improved, they are still lacking and it is obvious to any native speaker that it is a machine translation. This type of translation, while is arguably better than nothing, is not considered a truly viable option by most.

- Evaluate your website technology—particularly your content management system (CMS) and property booking engine. Ensure that it supports multilingual content.

- Check that your web content is written for translation—a method that prevents errors and re-work. This means using clear, short sentences without idioms; they're easier to translate and are better understood by global readers. Be cautious when using humor; it doesn't always translate linguistically or culturally.

- Perform a content audit to determine what web content should be translated—and if any should be locale- or region-specific. Content that is specific to a locale should be customized to meet local norms, regulations, and reader expectations. For example, local promotional content, visa requirements, weights, currencies, and payment processing should all be adapted by locale rather than language.

- Define a multilingual URL/domain structure so your site will be well indexed and SEO friendly. You have three options to choose from—each with pros and cons in terms of complexity, cost, and SEO performance:

  1. a country code Top Level Domain (ccTLD) structure, e.g., travelwebsite.mx
  2. a subdomain structure, e.g., mx.travel-website.com
  3. a folder structure, e.g., travelwesite.com/mx/

- Identify your global gateway strategy and decide how translated content will be delivered to the right consumer, in the right language in each locale. Assume that visitors won't be in their home country, will speak a number of languages, and will use a variety of devices. You'll need a user-friendly solution that guides visitors to locale- and language-specific content—no matter where they are or what language they speak.

- Select an in-region review team and develop a plan for including these team members in the translation process.

BEST PRACTICES: SELECTING A WEBSITE DESIGN/DEVELOPMENT VENDOR

Remember that your hotel website's primary objective is to generate as many direct bookings and group leads as possible. This objective requires not only building a website according to the industry's best practices, but also marketing the website according to the industry's best practices.

Some hotel marketers work with a full-service website design and internet marketing agency specializing in hospitality that build and then market their website, while others work with multiple agencies to leverage "best of breed" in each of the disciplines. Either way you go, vendor management is a very important aspect of building and maintaining your website. For further information, see Chapter 33.

Start by preparing an RFP outlining your vision of, and expectations for, the new website. Be sure to think about and address the weaknesses of your existing website, as well as any design elements, features, and functionality you like from your comp set or other websites.

From the proposals you receive, select the best three and require the vendors to make in-person or web-based presentations.

BEST PRACTICES: TRACKING PERFORMANCE WITH WEB ANALYTICS

Digital marketing is all about results. Unlike offline marketing, online we can track and analyze bookings, room nights, revenue, and ROI results from your website performance and online marketing campaigns quickly and accurately (mostly).

Best practices and common business sense require hotel digital marketers to constantly track and analyze website and campaign conversions as well as returns on investment (ROI), returns on ad spend (ROAS), content engagement, and behavioral metrics to shift marketing funds from less effective marketing campaigns to campaigns with higher ROIs.

- For a brand.com website, the brand will most likely have a suite of reporting tools and reports available to hotels. They may even have reports that can track traffic and web analytics from a stand-alone website to the brand's booking path.
- For a vanity site, choosing the right website analytics tool is important. For franchised/branded hotels, inquire with your brand about web analytics solutions that might be available or recommended for your vanity website.
- For independent properties, when budgeting for digital marketing, it is recommended that you include a separate line item for website and marketing analytics. A good place to start is with your online booking engine vendor or website developer. Ask if they support an advanced web analytics tool such as Google Analytics or Adobe Analytics and have your website developer implement it on your site.

There are two leaders in the web analytics space, Google Analytics (GA) and Adobe Analytics. GA is the market leader and offers both free and paid versions. Adobe is a paid service. In both cases the paid service is much more robust, but, especially for a small brand or independent hotel that might not have the budget, the free version of GA will often suffice.

SAMPLE CHDM EXAM QUESTIONS

1. For a franchised property, which of the following should NOT be a factor when considering investing in an independent/vanity website?
   a. Projected returns
   b. How well your brand site targets your primary visitor segments
   c. How easy it is for potential customer to locate your property on the brand site
   d. The cost of bookings generated through the brand site

2. The two core elements that will determine the success of your website are:
   a. Traffic and Conversion
   b. SEO and SEM
   c. Brand Site and Vanity Site
   d. Speed and Schema

3. For a hotel that is part of a large brand, what is the property responsible for on brand.com?
   a. Navigation
   b. Page templates
   c. Textual content and property imagery
   d. Booking widget
   e. All of the above

Answers
1 = d
2 = a
3 = c

Chapter 5: Mobile

KEY POINTS
- Mobile traffic exceeded desktop traffic in 2015 and continues to grow which means mobile optimization is extremely important.
- Your site must be optimized for mobile in terms of usability, content, and speed.
- Hotels have lagged in mobile conversion/revenue but that has started to change and ensuring the process is as frictionless as possible is paramount.

SUMMARY

In 2015, mobile surpassed desktop usage. For our purposes, we divide mobile into two categories: smartphones and tablets. While there are other mobile form factors, as of the writing of this book, these are the predominant ones. Consumer behavior varies broadly depending on the mobile platform they use, and to capture a fair share of the mobile market, we must not only understand why and how our customers use their devices, but how we can integrate our own digital assets into the buyer journey to create a seamless purchase experience and add value to their overall travel experience.

Today's consumers live in a multi-device world. They wake up in the morning and check their phones for texts, emails, news, and social media. At work they log onto laptops or desktops, all the while keeping their phones and tablets nearby. They return home at night, relax in front of whatever digital programming grabs their attention (probably streaming), and they keep a second or even third screen close at hand to tweet, Facebook, or TikTok about what they are watching or to Google information.

In 2015, Google coined the term "micro-moments."

"As mobile has become an indispensable part of our daily lives, we're witnessing a fundamental change in the way people consume media. What used to be our predictable, daily sessions online have been replaced by many fragmented interactions that now occur instantaneously. There are hundreds of these moments every day—checking the time, texting a spouse, chatting with friends on social media.

"But then there are the other moments—the I want-to-know moments, I want-to-do moments, I want-to-do moments, and I want-to-buy moments—that really matter. We call these 'micro-moments,' and they're game-changers for both consumers and brands."[35]

Since Google began talking about micro-moments in 2015, this phenomenon only accelerated. The way people use mobile means our sites need to not only work well on the form factor, but we need to understand how our prospective guests interact with our media and adjust our messaging and approach accordingly.

Source: https://gs.statcounter.com/

According to eMarketer, digital travel sales will reach $212 billion in 2024, and 38% will come from mobile devices.[36]

Transactional growth in mobile is only part of the shift in the travel marketplace. Increasingly, consumers see their mobile devices as an extension of their overall travel experience, whether preparing for their trip and creating activity agendas, looking around on site for activities or restaurants in the area, or finding ways to include their social network in everything they're doing while they're on their trip. And while the buyer journey continues to see a shift toward a seamless transition between desktop and mobile, more and more of the perceived value in digital assets is found in smartphone technology. See the following chart.

As a result, hotel marketers shouldn't view mobile and desktop in silos but rather as a consistent consumer experience across platforms from the dreaming stage of travel planning all the way through post-stay. By considering how users use mobile technology at each stage of the process, hoteliers can integrate their content seamlessly into the guest's experience, delivering personalized guest experiences that can lead to better trips/vacations, increased brand loyalty, and more bookings over the customer's lifetime.

This section provides insights into current mobile behavior to help hoteliers understand the mobile platform, and, most importantly, suggests how mobile behavior can be leveraged to a property's advantage. Mobile is now the dominant way people will access your site.

Smartphones have become a go-to resource for nearly every travel need

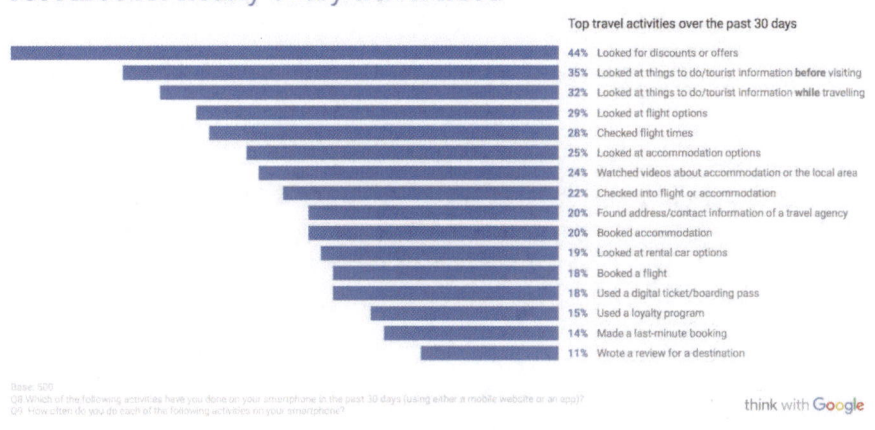

Top travel activities over the past 30 days

%	Activity
44%	Looked for discounts or offers
35%	Looked at things to do/tourist information **before** visiting
32%	Looked at things to do/tourist information **while** travelling
29%	Looked at flight options
28%	Checked flight times
25%	Looked at accommodation options
24%	Watched videos about accommodation or the local area
22%	Checked into flight or accommodation
20%	Found address/contact information of a travel agency
20%	Booked accommodation
19%	Looked at rental car options
18%	Booked a flight
18%	Used a digital ticket/boarding pass
15%	Used a loyalty program
14%	Made a last-minute booking
11%	Wrote a review for a destination

think with Google

Source: Think with Google

> During the Covid-19 pandemic, there was a shift to shorter stays in nearby destinations. It resulted in a significant increase in mobile traffic and bookings.

MOBILE DEFINED

Most web analytics tools track by three main categories: desktop, mobile, and tablet. In the past tablets were lumped together with mobile, but more sophisticated marketers are looking at these devices separately as user behavior tends to differ. It's important to recognize that people use smartphones differently than they use tablets due in large part to screen size, device size, and context.

HOW CONSUMERS USE MOBILE DEVICES...AND WHY IT MATTERS TO YOU

Increasingly, potential guests are visiting and transacting on hotel websites through mobile channels, not just on desktops. Today, more than half of all web traffic is mobile[37] For ecommerce in general, conversion on mobile—with tablets leading the way—is on the rise.[38]

2020 Global Smartphone Users [39]
Active Smartphone Users per Region | 2020

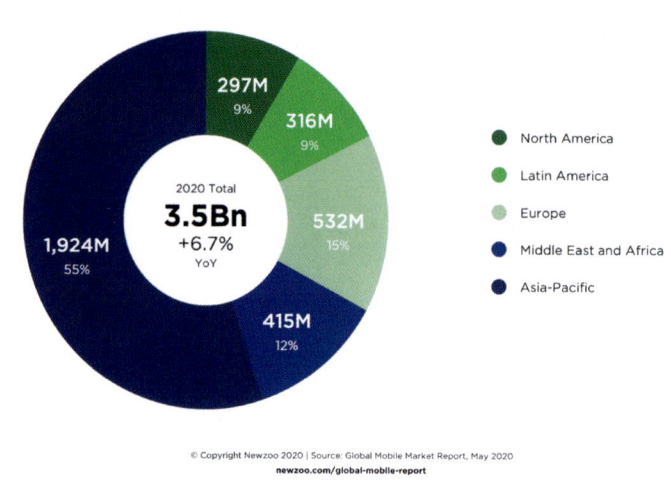

- North America: 297M (9%)
- Latin America: 316M (9%)
- Europe: 532M (15%)
- Middle East and Africa: 415M (12%)
- Asia-Pacific: 1,924M (55%)

2020 Total: 3.5Bn +6.7% YoY

© Copyright Newzoo 2020 | Source: Global Mobile Market Report, May 2020
newzoo.com/global-mobile-report

Clearly, mobile is extremely important in the consumer's digital journey. In a marketplace where brand loyalty is decreasing in favor of experience quality, any hotelier who has fallen behind in terms of creating a quality front-to-back mobile experience risks being passed over.

Failure to have a good mobile experience will lose you bookings. According to Google[40]:

- 50% of people admit they use websites less if the site is not mobile friendly
- Nearly half of all visitors will leave a mobile website if the pages don't load within 3 seconds
- 61% of users are likely to leave quickly if the site is not optimized well for mobile devices
- If your site isn't mobile-friendly, visitors are 5 times more likely to leave

CREATING THE OPTIMAL MOBILE EXPERIENCE

Mobile is the primary way guests will interact with your hotel website, and there needs to be a laser focus on mobile usability. This includes all aspects of the user journey; whether searching price and amenities, searching available dates, booking and receiving confirmation information, preparing for the trip, or getting the most out of the travel experience.

Website design requirements vary dramatically between desktop and mobile for multiple reasons. Desktop navigation is typically geared toward point-and-click functionality, while mobile requires tapping and swiping capability. A device-responsive approach (also known as device agnostic, responsive design, or liquid design) involves the development of the primary hotel website in such a way that the navigation and layout adjust based on the screen resolution of the device being used to view it. A point-and-click navigational schema intended for a consumer on a desktop would convert to a touchscreen interface for a consumer on the same website using a tablet.

All the major hotel brands and travel websites, including OTAs, metasearch sites, and review sites, have recognized the importance of being focused on the mobile experience. And while people at your hotel/brand may be spending time on the desktop site, most of your guests are on your mobile site. In fact, many websites today are built as "mobile first" sites, which means they are built first with mobile in mind and then desktop. This is a reverse from several years ago when everything was built desktop first.

NATIVE MOBILE APPS

It wasn't that long ago that everyone thought they needed a native mobile app, that is, an app specifically designed for your phone. A native mobile app must be downloaded from an app store. It requires that positive action be taken by the user, which is sometimes a gating factor, but it has many positives: it is quicker, can save personal information, and can be much more customized for a mobile experience. But as desktop sites moved to responsive design and other designs that make websites work well on mobile, many have moved away from having a native mobile app.

There are often good reasons to have an app. For example, if it is something that will be used frequently so the user would see the value of downloading the app, or if it has special functionality that makes it worth downloading (e.g., digital key, property information, etc.).

Apps tend to be adopted more by the bigger brands due to both frequency of use and functionality, but at times smaller brands or resort hotels find apps to be useful for their customers and for their profitability. As is always the case, the rationale for building an app should be strong, and the right resources need to be allocated to it or you risk doing more harm than good.

OPTIMIZATION

A website that is optimized for mobile will render properly on desktop and mobile alike. Text and images will display clearly, and users will easily be able to navigate the site with fingers and thumbs. It will take advantage of the device attributes and utilize features like pinch, zoom, portrait/landscape, and swiping. Contrast that with a website that is merely mobile compatible: the site will render on a smartphone, but without the proper device navigation features or appropriate use of the screen size it will make it virtually impossible to read and/or navigate.

CHOOSING THE APPROPRIATE WEBSITE BUILD

There are several approaches to creating a mobile experience based on marketing objectives and budget. Ultimately, the goal is a consistent experience, designed for usability, with features appropriate for each device.

Your best approach is to contact an experienced, qualified web developer which is up to date on current web best practices. Because the digital space evolves at an amazing speed, in-house teams may be behind the curve in terms of creating the most optimal experience for users who are flowing back and forth across multiple devices.

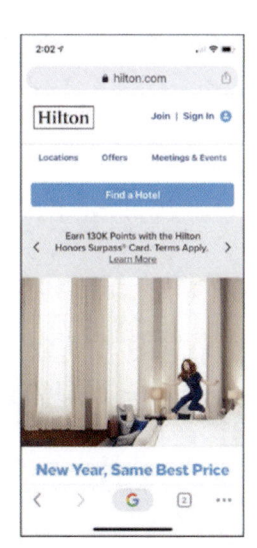

Make sure that you have clearly thought out what you want to accomplish with your marketing efforts so that you can create a clear, simple pathway for your customers. Always look for ways to test and tweak your site, looking for adjustments which may bring in an increased number of conversions or simply provide a better experience.

Before contacting a web developer, be familiar with the most common approaches to mobile websites:

- responsive website
- adaptive design
- progressive web app (PWA)
- mDot or mobile website

Responsive Website
A responsive website approach simply optimizes your one URL so that it functions well across multiple platforms. When a user visits the site, their screen size will determine the order and size at which each element will be displayed. In many cases, developers will take a "mobile first" approach, which ensures that the best web experience will take place on mobile, while the desktop or tablet performance might suffer some.

Responsive doesn't provide full flexibility in optimizing across each device, but it can still create excellent user experiences on both desktop and mobile. Google has typically recommended responsive design in the past, particularly because of its advantages in SEO. Because Google's "mobile first" index is set to begin rolling out in 2021, web developers are encouraged to migrate their mDot sites over to responsive as soon as possible to avoid any penalties.[41]

Adaptive Design
Adaptive design is a potentially faster and cleaner solution than responsive design, in that visitors do not have to download the entire site. Only the assets they need to view will appear in the version matching their device. However, this method requires significantly more server power and resources than responsive design.

Progressive Web App (PWA)
Progressive Mobile Web is a relatively new approach, emerging in the last few years as a more flexible, powerful alternative. Progressive integrates app-like functionality such as push notifications, full-screen mode, or offline mode into your site's mobile performance. Not only does it create better usability on mobile than mDot or responsive, it also typically delivers much faster speed,[42] since responsive design sites require the mobile user to download all the site assets, even the ones not used on the mobile version of the site.

Mobile Web Approach	Key Features
Responsive	• single URL for both desktop and mobile experience
	• screen size drives the order and size at which each element will be displayed
	• some take a "mobile first" approach
	• Google currently recommends this approach[43]
Adaptive	• like a mobile site but the software detects the device of origin and automatically redirects
	• visitors don't download entire site; only the assets they need to view the version that matches their device
	• requires more server power and resources than responsive
Progressive Web App (PWA)	• integrates app-like functions (push notifications, full-screen mode, offline mode)
	• faster download than responsive as it only calls assets needed for device of origin
	• no need to download an app; it loads in the browser
Mobile Website or mDot	• separate URL
	• designed for display on a mobile website
	• slower load time, confusing for sharing, two sites to maintain
	• has fallen out of favor, unless there is a specific use case

mDot or Mobile Website

One approach that was used widely but has fallen out of favor is mDot, or mobile website. This is a separate site with a separate URL, specifically designed for display on a mobile device. When visitors open your website on their smartphone, they have the option to a visit a different URL, which is set up specifically to deliver an experience for your mobile interface. Adaptive design is a similar strategy, except in this case, the site automatically detects device information and redirects traffic accordingly to either a desktop, tablet, or mobile version of your site.

Creating an mDot site requires maintaining and updating an additional website, and likely will add more load time to the user experience. In addition, the SEO benefits from visitors to the mobile site do not carry over to the desktop. Also, when someone shares your content on social media, they may be sharing the mobile version or the desktop version. Since social media visitors could be on either platform, they might end up with a poor experience if they click through the shared link.

BEST PRACTICES: THINK ABOUT INTERFACE AND SCREEN SIZE

Since smartphones and tablets are touchscreen devices, the user's fingertip will be the primary input device when navigating your site. Clearly marked, reasonably large buttons are generally far better than tiny hotspots, clickable images, or embedded text links. In addition, minimize the amount of typing and data entry required. Use location services to learn where the customer is and use cookies to recall previously entered data.

Make items fingertip-friendly—ensure links are easy to tap, allow swiping to move through tabs or photos, offer dropdown menus for selections, and include "Previous" and "Next" buttons to help guide users through the booking process.

Small and simple is necessary for smartphones. Although smartphones are generally trending upward in size, they are still pocket-sized devices. That small screen demands a different approach to user design, with a focus on clean, simple navigation. Display information in a single column (so users can avoid scrolling horizontally) and avoid cluttering pages with too much information.

Tablets offer a lot more room to play with than smartphones, so you can afford to take the experience up a notch. You can add tabs and more buttons to navigate deeper into your site. You can also include larger visuals to tell your story. However, keep in mind that these screens are still not as large as desktop screens. As such, it's important to clearly indicate what each tab or button does. Ensure links and calls-to-action are easy to tap, keeping in mind that "hover states" and mouse-over actions (that indicate where a link goes on a desktop) do not exist on a tablet. If buttons aren't appropriate, use clear contrasting colors or underlines in text links.

Keep your fonts large and crisp. Ensure a decent amount of padding around different elements—like buttons, links, text, and paragraphs—to avoid clutter. Increased white space can help give your site a clean, visually pleasing look.

BEST PRACTICES: ADD EYE-PLEASING VISUALS

Watching video is one of the most popular things people do on their mobile devices.

Options to consider include everything from promotional videos of your property to videos of events and things to do around town.

Don't stop at just video, though. Add virtual tours of your rooms and facilities. Provide tablet-optimized photographs showing off your property and the surrounding area. In other words, take advantage of the screen's size and clarity to show off your property!

BEST PRACTICES: DON'T SKIMP ON SPEED

While rich video and imagery will work just fine on mobile devices, you must properly optimize it, because the mobile experience requires speed. In a survey of U.S. smartphone users, 64% said they wanted a site to load within four seconds, with 16% of respondents saying they would abandon a site completely and never return if it didn't load promptly.[44] The probability of bounce increases by 90% after page load time increases from 3 seconds to 5 seconds.[45]

While you want to tell your story with great videos and beautiful photographs, you don't want those larger files bogging down the mobile experience to the point where visitors abandon your content. With this in mind, ensure that animation, video, and high-resolution photographs are properly sized and optimized.

There are many web tools available that can provide insight, such as Google Page Speed Insights or Google Lighthouse. These tools can highlight areas where your site may not be performing well across each device and offer suggestions to improve performance.

BEST PRACTICES: MAKE BOOKING EASY

Keep your "Book Now" button clearly visible on all pages of your optimized site, and make sure the check-out process is as simple and streamlined as possible. Always include a "Click to call" button, as there are always people who would prefer to ask questions or simply talk to a person when booking.

Your booking engine should be smartphone-optimized, because a visitor in a rush won't have time or patience to enter a great deal of text or mull over a lot of options. The booking path—picking dates, rooms, and options—should be straightforward, with drop-down menus and easy-to-tap buttons for selections. And of course, your booking process needs to be safe and secure, including confirmation screens to maintain the purchaser's confidence in the process.

BEST PRACTICES: TAKE ADVANTAGE OF THE PLATFORM

Smartphones and tablets are incredibly powerful multifunction devices, so it makes sense for your mobile-optimized site to take advantage of those functions as much as possible.

Leverage the smartphone's telephone capabilities—which are easy to forget in the rush to optimize the touchscreen experience. Sometimes, simply making a call is the best way to go, and some users will always prefer to transact by phone. Don't make your users copy and paste your phone number—they should be able to call directly from your website or app just by tapping your number. Or better yet, implement a "Call Now" button placed prominently on each screen.

Make use of maps and more. Mobile users shouldn't have to copy your address into their navigation app to find you or check out the surrounding area. Make sure you integrate mapping functionality on your "Location" page, letting visitors one-tap to open their default map app and immediately show your location in context. You can also take advantage of calendar, email, and camera app integration where applicable. Many phones also offer integration to social media apps.

BEST PRACTICES: MAKE YOUR MOBILE SITE SOCIAL-READY

Transform your visitors into brand ambassadors through social sharing features. Travelers like to share their vacation plans and activities with their followers: 55% of travelers "like" Facebook pages specific to their vacation, with 70% updating their Facebook status while on vacation.[46] Additionally, 80% of social media activity takes place on mobile devices.[47]

Make sure you're encouraging guests to share that they're staying with you when they check in, when they're by the pool, or when they're in the bar. And don't make them work hard to do it!

Regardless of device, word of mouth remains as important as ever in the travel sector, and social media is word of mouth on steroids. Adding Instagram, Facebook, Twitter, and "share-by-email" buttons to your mobile site is an easy way to encourage visitors to share their travel plans and build digital advocacy for your property.

BEST PRACTICES: DISPLAY REDEEMABLE SPECIAL OFFERS

Everyone loves a good deal—and mobile shoppers are no different. Most people across age brackets rated getting a coupon, deal, or discount as "extremely" or "very" influential, including 74.5% of millennials (ages 23 to 28) and 71.0% of Gen Xers (39 to 53). Promoting value-added special offers on smartphones and tablets not only grabs consumer interest and attention, but it also encourages them to book.[48]

To appeal to smartphone and tablet users during each period of their buying cycle—early research, booking, on-property time, and post-travel—ensure you have offers that will appeal to them at each distinct point in the journey. Not only can special offers entice booking, but they can create a more enjoyable stay, prompting more "wow" moments to share on social media.

Feature promotions that add value such as free parking, complimentary breakfast, bonus loyalty points, or happy hour specials at your restaurant, as well as special offers for tickets to local attractions and upcoming events.

- Ensure offers are easy to redeem by linking directly to your mobile booking engine with the appropriate offer code populated.
- Make offers easy to find and click on your home page or landing page.
- Enhance the way your offers are displayed by using large and relevant visuals.
- Leverage data you've collected on your visitors throughout the buying process to customize offers while they're on property. Learn their interests, travel preferences, and potential activities, and make sure you're offering relevant deals to make their stay more enjoyable.

MOBILE MARKETING TECHNIQUES

Since mobile is both a channel and a device,[49] what is true for traditional website marketing can and should be extended to mobile. At the heart of any great marketing strategy are clear objectives, a framework for measurement, and a detailed understanding of the user you wish to engage.

- Segment and target your strategy and messaging for mobile devices.
- Run mobile-specific campaigns that have ads, landing pages, and content targeted to the needs and behaviors of the mobile user.
- Use mobile banner advertising on mobile websites and within apps that are consistent with and a part of the overall hotel marketing strategy. Know that they do require some optimization in terms of the size of ads, the creative, and mobile landing pages.
- Mobile pay-per-click (PPC) is available via the major ad networks and can be run in conjunction with your regular PPC campaigns. The ad networks provide the ability to target (or not) mobile users. Think about focusing on keywords inherently used by a mobile consumer and apply your knowledge to ad copy and mobile landing pages. Additional targeting may be available by leveraging geolocation (the physical location of the user).
- Some "drive hotels" have seen good results from Waze, the driving app (and a Google company), and it may be worth testing if you in are a heavy drive market. Waze works on a CPM model, or cost per thousand views. Waze essentially has four advertising units within its mapping functionality: Pin, Search, Takeover and Arrow.
  - Like a store sign, Pins inform and remind customers that your business is on or near their route.
  - Search helps you be top of mind when customers browse for hotels in the area
  - The Takeover ad is a digital billboard. It is shown when vehicles are at a complete stop to prompt awareness and action at key moments.
  - Arrows help indicate your business is nearby, helping customers increase the association between a given location and your brand.
- QR (Quick Response) codes are another way to connect the physical and online worlds via mobile devices. The camera on a mobile phone is used to scan a QR code just like a bar code, which prompts the phone to open the designated website. QR codes have both advertising (e.g., QR code in a print ad scanned to see more info on the mobile phone) and on-property customer service applications (e.g., scan a QR code to see a menu). Use QR codes to connect your guests to Tripadvisor so they can easily write a review or access a "mobile only" special. While usage of QR codes in the U.S. lagged other countries, they were broadly used around the world for many "non-touch" activities (e.g., menus, information, etc.) during the Covid-19 pandemic and are much more widely accepted today.

LAST BUT NOT LEAST: MEASURE!

Before you put your mobile strategy into action, it's important to determine the business objectives you'd like to accomplish (e.g., branding, awareness, loyalty) so that you can determine

A Field Guide for Navigating Today's Digital Landscape

the right metrics to target (e.g., clickthroughs, average length of engagement, revenue). Remember, you can't manage what you can't measure.

In addition, make sure you can test toward those results. Perform A/B testing or multivariate testing on your site's booking functions and promotional pages and see what performs well. Never assume that a page that looks more visually appealing to you is going to convert more visitors. Take subjective decisions out of the equation whenever possible!

One of the leading indicators of whether a mobile strategy is working is the level of engagement that's being achieved with your target audience. If customers are increasing their interaction with your property via their mobile device, and with certain pieces of content, then they're seeing value in the mobile experience. Although sales are typically the ultimate measure of success, it's important for marketers to recognize that the impact of mobile marketing may not be realized immediately. Getting consumers to engage more often and more deeply with your hotel can lead to long-term success.

Ensure you enlist an analytics professional to set up your tracking, as this requires very specific knowledge to ensure credible results. Any click of a button can be tracked if you properly configure events and define goals to measure conversion success.

Some key performance metrics for consideration include:

- total traffic across all platforms (mobile + desktop)
- percentage of traffic on mobile (tablet + smartphone)
- bookings by platform and device type (desktop v. mobile)
- media (photos, videos, virtual tours) consumption by platform and mobile device type
- length of time on mobile site/page

To compete, hoteliers must provide content that's relevant, compelling, genuine, and fun. People treat mobile devices as extensions of themselves, enabling communication with friends, family, companies, and brands whenever and however they choose. Consumers are tied to their mobile devices and are innovative in finding new ways to use them. Hotels that approach this from a customer-centric position will gain competitive advantage and build stronger relationships with their guests.

SAMPLE CHDM EXAM QUESTIONS

1. Hotel marketers should view mobile and desktop in silos.
   a. True
   b. False

2. Desktop traffic exceeds mobile traffic.
   a. True
   b. False

3. Which of the following is NOT a method to mobile optimize your website?
   a. Responsive Design
   b. Progressive Web App
   c. Adaptive Design
   d. HTML Wrapper

Answers
1 = b
2 = b
3 = d

NOTES

Chapter 6: Content & Merchandising

KEY POINTS
- Your content—both text and visual—exists to answer guest questions and help them choose your property.
- All modern marketing depends on high-quality content; without content, your customers have nothing to find in search and nothing to share on social.
- Merchandising involves presenting your content—text and visuals—in an appealing and persuasive manner designed to encourage guests to consider and book your destination and property.
- Search engine optimization is a key consideration when creating content for your website.

SUMMARY

Content matters. It is one of your hotel's key "salespeople," available to guests whenever and wherever they are in their purchase path. Whether your guests are dreaming, planning, booking, experiencing, or sharing, content performs a vital role in the process. It inspires guests when they are dreaming. It answers questions when they are planning. It provides assurance when they are booking. It offers guidance while they are experiencing your destination. And it inspires, reminds, and delights them—and others as well—when they are sharing their experience with friends, family, and colleagues.s

THE IMPACT OF ONLINE SHOPPING BEHAVIOR

Like all online shoppers, those shopping for travel are looking for rich visual experiences that educate and help them better understand and feel comfortable about the purchase they are considering. Add to this the fact that much of the traffic to your site will be via mobile, so it is even more important that the story you tell is visual.

Travelers visit many different websites in a non-linear and very complex online shopping journey from inspiration to research, comparison, purchase, post purchase, and sharing stages. A typical guest will use many touch points to research a trip. This means that there are multiple opportunities to grab their attention and make a great impression. And brands and hotels need to differentiate their value propositions to stay top-of-mind.

Consumers are going to different sites for different reasons and at different stages of the travel shopping journey. According to Atmosphere Research Group, the top three websites that consumers cite as particularly helpful in the planning stage are travel supplier websites, online travel agencies (OTAs), and travel-focused ratings/review websites. Eighty-four percent of travelers will visit brand.com or several different brand.coms to get the hotel's direct perspective. Eighty-three percent will also visit an OTA, such as Expedia, to see what hotels are available in the market. Similarly, 83% will go to a traveler review site like Tripadvisor to read what others are saying, and 81% will check out a metasearch engine (like Kayak, Trivago, Tripadvisor, or Google Meta) to compare the prices.[50]

What consumers see about an individual hotel across these various sites must be consistent, relevant, and interesting; otherwise, a hotel risks not being in the traveler's consideration set.

Another trend that should not be ignored is the increasingly blurred lines between business and leisure travel. Both travel shopping segments want immersive, visually rich presentations. While there is a misconception that business travelers are not interested in researching their stay, 93% of business travelers watched travel related video online last year (versus 89% of leisure travelers). At the same time, 56% say that they plan to spend more time shopping around and researching before booking business travel to find good value for their money.[51]

WHAT IS CONTENT?

Fundamentally, your guests rely on four broad categories of content to help them decide where to stay.

A Field Guide for Navigating Today's Digital Landscape

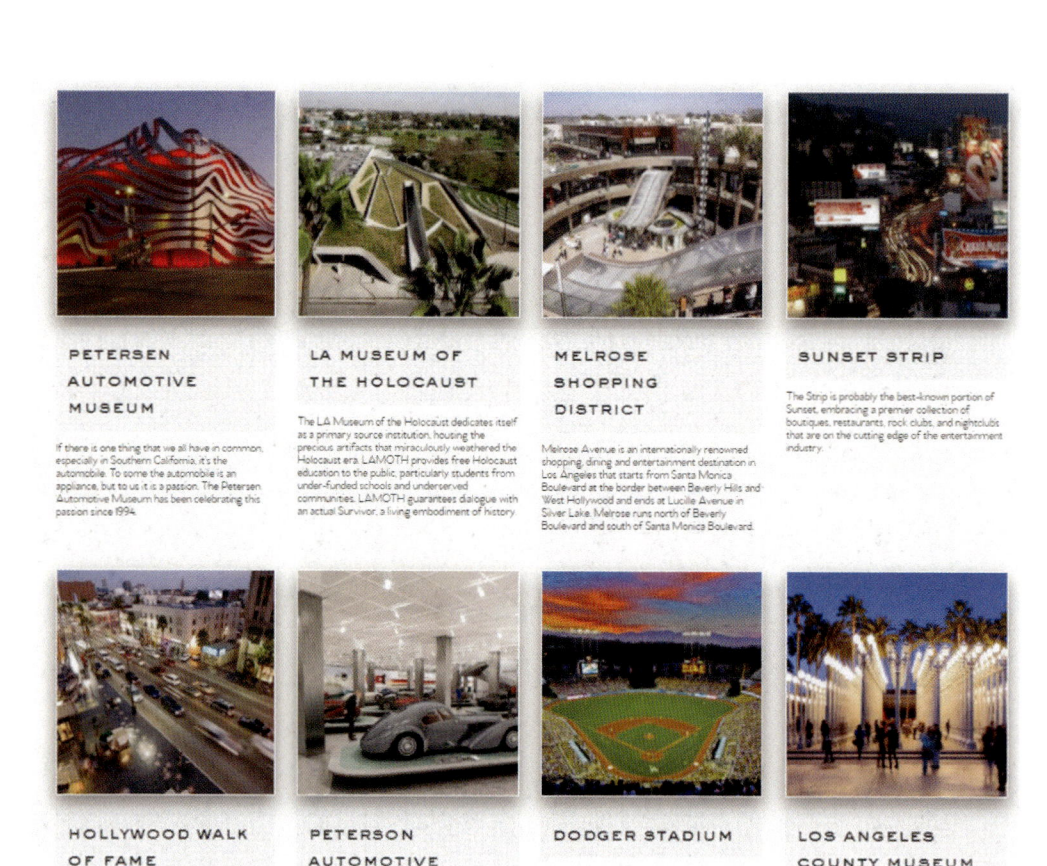

Example of destination content from The Farmer's Daughter Hotel

Destination Content

The first rule of selling travel to leisure consumers remains "sell the destination first." Travelers tend to start their travel planning by searching destination-related terms[52]. Whether you use blog posts highlighting area attractions, dedicated destination guides offered on your website, email marketing campaigns featuring local hot spots, or themed content targeting key audiences, guests must want to travel to your destination.

Property Content

Often referred to as "descriptive" content, or less commonly "static" content, this includes information about your property itself. Property content includes the number and type of guest rooms and meeting rooms, available amenities, its physical location and proximity to attractions, property name, brand affiliation, and other necessary attributes, that probably do not change very often.

Promotional Content

Promotional content includes the many offers, specials, and packages that your marketing and revenue management teams design to attract customers to book, enroll in loyalty programs or email lists, or respond to any other call to action (CTA) you can imagine.

Availability, Rates, and Inventory (ARI)

Availability, rates, and inventory present guests with information about what they'll actually book—descriptions and details of the room types, rate plans, and packages your property offers—as well as the dates when guests can book their stay. While ARI typically refers only to room types and suites, additional amenities, add-ons, and upsell items—including such varied items as bottles of wine, flowers, golf tee times, ski lift tickets, restaurant reservations, and the like—may also represent inventoried items within your property management system, central reservations system, or booking engine.

Content Type	Content Examples
Destination Content	• themed content targeting customer segments • blog posts about local hot spots and events • destination guides/itineraries of things to do • calendar of events nearby • information about nearby attractions/demand generators
Property Content	• descriptive, often static content • F&B and other amenities • # of rooms, meeting space, amenities • physical location and proximity to attractions
Promotional Content	• offers, specials, and packages designed to attract customers to book, enroll in loyalty programs or email lists, or respond to other calls-to-action
Availability, Rates, and Inventory	• descriptions and details of room types, rate plans, and packages • availability • rates • inventory

THE BOOKING ENGINE

While ARI is often considered the domain of revenue managers, the "machine" that enables the booking of the rates and offers loaded by a revenue manager is the booking engine.

One way to think about the website versus booking engine is that the website is everything that you do to drive people down the funnel and the booking engine is the conversion tool and the cash register. While most consumers don't see these as different things, most digital marketers view them separately. In many cases they are physically separate, often sitting on different technology and sometimes on different domains. This is starting to change as more hotels attempt to integrate the purchase path into the website, but many are not there yet.

Any time a customer searches for availability, rates, and inventory (ARI), they are in the booking engine. So, any time they click, tap, or swipe the "Search," "Book Now," or "Find Rates" buttons they are entering the booking engine. Having an effective booking engine experience is arguably the most important thing you can do to impact conversion.

Generally speaking, most smaller brands and independent hotels use third-party booking engines while the larger brands either have their own proprietary booking engines or highly customized versions of third-party engines.

Examples of third-party booking engines are Sabre, TravelClick, SHR, and Pegasus. Third-party booking engines usually make money by charging a fee per transaction or key, or by having a flat fee subscription.

While booking engines often have limited flexibility there are ways to optimize them. It is important that digital marketers ensure that the booking engine is optimized for conversion. Making the process simple and taking friction out of the process will have the biggest impact. Consider points where the customer may be confused:

- Are there too many rates, offers, or room types making it difficult to decide? Study after study has found that too much choice often leads to purchase abandonment.
- Are there points of confusion, like package inclusions or differences between room types?
- Is your navigation simple and straightforward?
- Is your room imagery compelling and does it contain enough detail so they do not need to abandon the booking to get more information?
- Are you instilling confidence that it is safe to book and that they are getting the best rate/offer by booking direct?

WHY DOES CONTENT MATTER?

Knowing what content is, however, is only half the battle. More important is how your hotel's content works as an "on-demand salesperson," telling an effective and entertaining story about your destination and property to guests whenever and wherever they may be. Most marketers understand the importance of search and social in selling their property. But without content, your property cannot appear in search. Without content, your guests have nothing to share across their social networks. Even technologies such as chatbots and voice-powered tools like Amazon's Echo depend on quality content to answer guest questions. High-quality content is what makes search and social media work.

As you use content to fuel your property's marketing, it's important to think about how each touchpoint assists guests in their purchase decision. Think about what questions your customers ask—and what answers they're looking to find. Google talks about "micro-moments" that explain what customers want as they move through each stage of the journey[53], and encourages marketers to "be there and be useful," offering answers to the questions your potential guests will ask as they make their decision. Your content must support guests before, during, and after their stay.

Beyond having informative and compelling content that appeals to your prospective guests and drives them down the purchase funnel, you also need to ensure that people will be able to find your website when they are searching on Google or other search engines. Website content in particular is essential for search engine optimization (SEO).

When creating website content, always keep in mind on-page SEO techniques (covered in detail in Chapter 9), especially:

- Know what your most important keywords are and strategically use them in your content.
- Make the content easily scannable (remember the majority of people visiting your site will be on mobile devices).
- Ensure meta tags, title, description and h1 tags are utilized effectively.

SEO is covered in detail in Chapters 8 and 9, while this chapter focuses on the "creative" aspects of content.

BEST PRACTICES: GUEST CONTENT NEEDS BEFORE RESERVATION AND STAY

Early in their shopping process, guests seek inspiration. While leisure travelers may understand that they're ready for a vacation or business travelers may wish to visit customers, these potential guests still have many questions. Research from Google shows that "37% of travelers in the U.S. think about vacation planning once a month,"[54] and that many have not yet selected their destination. This is your opportunity to capture their attention—and your content plays a crucial role in helping you do just that.

This inspirational content can be something as simple as a curated itinerary of things to do in your destination. Or it can be as complex and long-term as Accor's attempt to stoke the pent-up demand for travel during Covid-19 pandemic quarantines. See the "Fish Included" example.

Accor provided inspiration to travelers during the Covid-19 pandemic

All kinds of content can work to encourage guests to consider key destinations at this stage in their decision-making process and contribute to long-term brand engagement.

Most importantly, your "Dream" content must move customers along the funnel and help them take the next step in their travel decision.

Once guests have narrowed their options, they typically begin putting together the elements of their trip, a process Google refers to as a series of "time-to-make-a-plan" moments. The below illustration shows just how complex the search planning process can be for travelers, as well as what an integral part mobile is of this process.

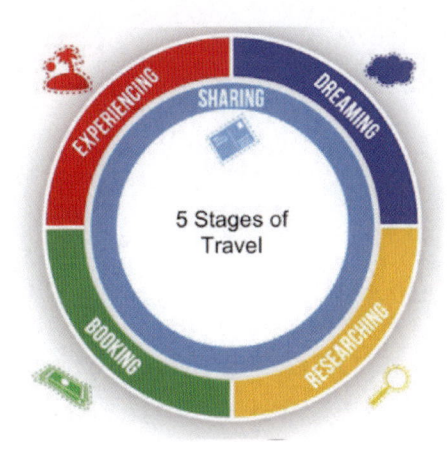

Source: Think with Google[55]

Regardless of the actual number of sites and sessions, you have your work cut out for you to connect with guests during each interaction to convince them your property represents the right choice for their stay. Following the mantra of "be there" and "be useful," your property content and promotional content must work together to answer the key questions your guests have about the features of your room product and the specific amenities you offer.

If your room types are sufficiently diverse and distinct, consider creating separate landing pages on your website for individual room types and suites to merchandise the specific benefits your guests will enjoy. But it is important not to "overload" the guest. Keep it simple and easy. When possible, allow them to easily compare differences to make their choice easier.

Don't forget to use images and photos to visually merchandise your product as well. Data from Trivago shows that "hotel profiles featuring high-quality images receive 63% more clicks than those with low-quality photos," and those hotels with a "high-quality main image" receive the lion's share of all clicks[56]. Or, in simpler terms, pretty pictures sell hotels.

This display from The Dunaway, a Hilton Hotel highlights key room features to answer guest questions in a simple but elegant format.

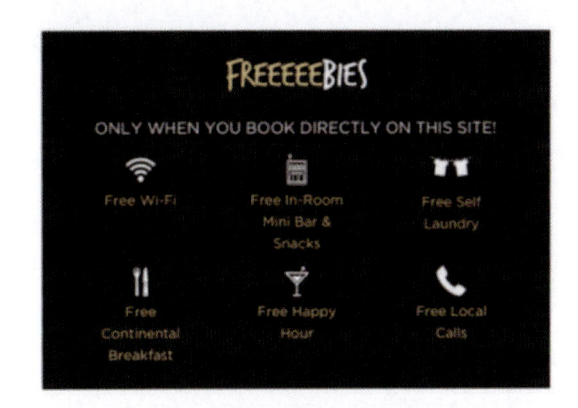

1888 Darling Harbour accompanies its room details with both photos and floor plans.

A Field Guide for Navigating Today's Digital Landscape

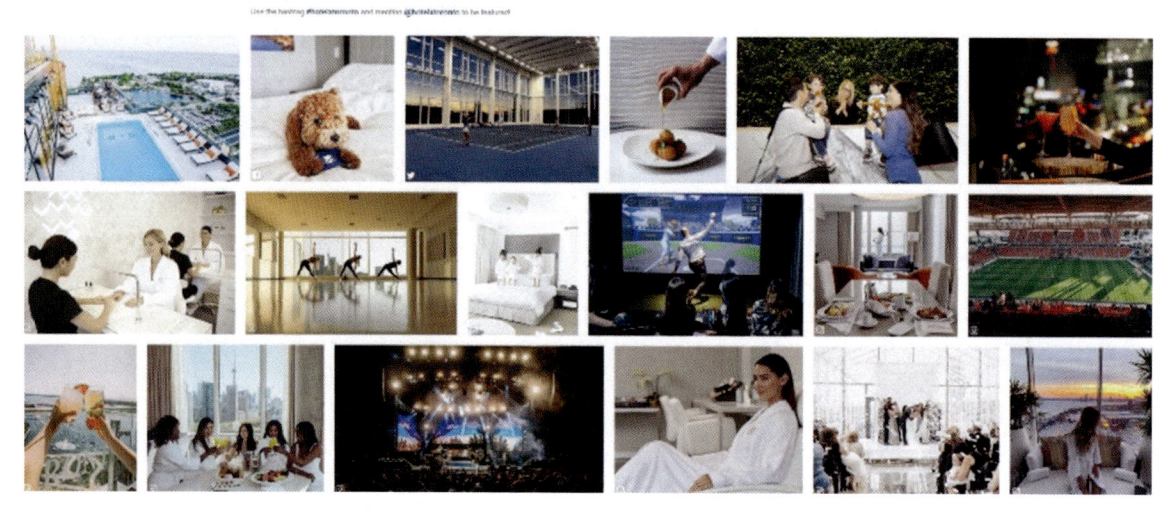

Hotel X uses professional and user-generated content (UGC)

BEST PRACTICES: CONTENT TO SUPPORT BOOKING DECISIONS

It will come as no surprise that the book stage of the guest journey represents a critical moment for your property—and for your content. While the number of visits and searches and sessions guests conduct prior to booking provide you multiple opportunities to catch their attention and interest, any missed chance during the booking process itself may send guests to seek a "better alternative." This is your shot at addressing their concerns and assuring them that your property will make their stay a pleasant one.

As you have likely seen, OTAs have invested heavily in this stage of the customer journey, focusing heavily on merchandising to close the sale.

Verbiage such as "In high demand," "Only 1 room left," "Great value today," "Last booked: 5 hours ago," "See our last available rooms," "x people booked this property in the last 48 hours," and other messages, as well as prominent ratings and reviews, signal to guests that they can feel comfortable that they're getting the right room at the right price and the right value for their trip.

Many hotels use tactics such as "best rate guarantees" and fenced rates to successfully convert guests. Work with your booking engine provider or brand to test additional message options designed to create desire, urgency, and confidence among guests that booking directly with your property will provide them a satisfactory stay.

The Library Hotel's confidence messaging

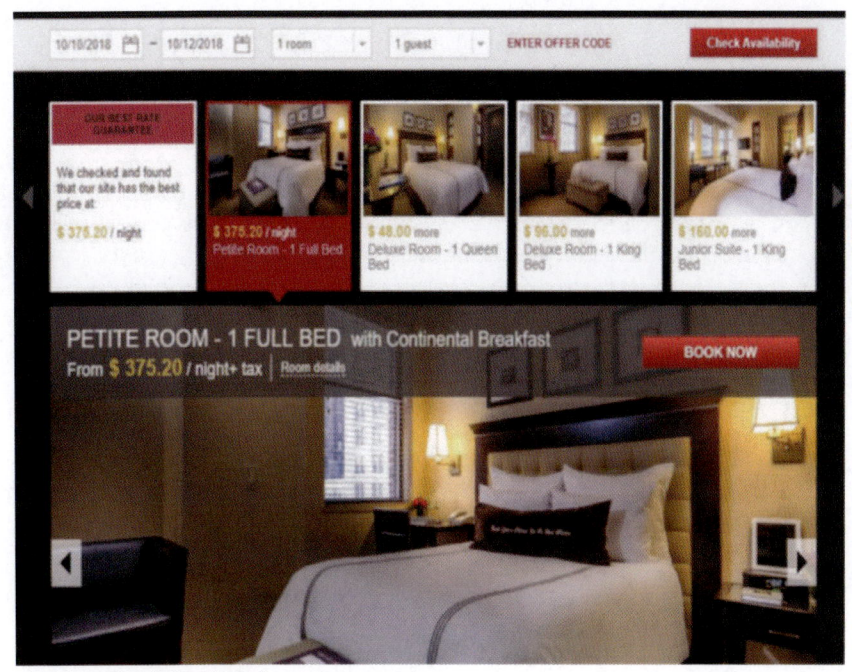

The Library Hotel's "Best Rate Guarantee" messaging

BEST PRACTICES: GUEST CONTENT NEEDS DURING THEIR STAY

Remarkably, research shows that most leisure travelers wait until after they arrive at their destination before deciding exactly how they'll spend their time while there. And almost 90% "…expect their travel provider to share relevant information while they are on their trip." Once again, this creates a great opportunity for you to provide useful content to guests that will improve both their stay and their view of the value they've received from you during their stay.

By far, the most common form hotel marketers use for providing content to guests on-property is the pre-arrival email, with some hotels also delivering post check-in emails highlighting directions to the hotel, and amenities and special offers in effect during their stay. Increasingly, major chains use their apps to connect with guests on-property to enhance the stay as well.

Content useful during the earlier research phase can also help guests enjoy their stay. Similarly, content from destination partners such as restaurants, museums, concert venues, and tour guides can provide useful and engaging information for guests while at your location. Look to work with those partners to remind guests why they've chosen your destination— and entice them to return in the future.

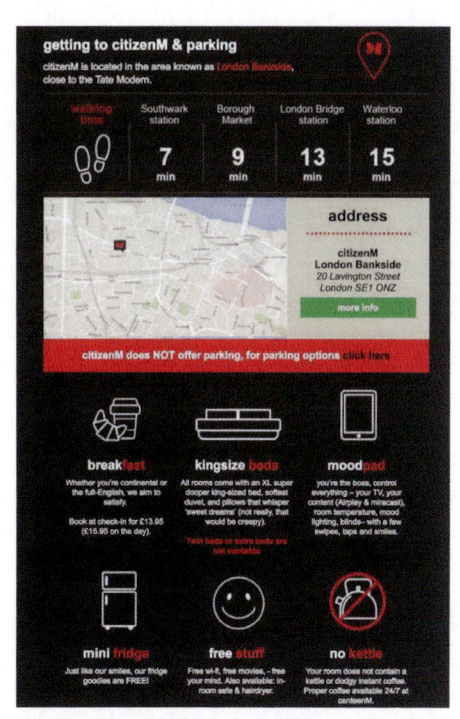

citizenM provides useful pre-arrival messaging.[57]

A Field Guide for Navigating Today's Digital Landscape

BEST PRACTICES: CONTENT FOR SHARING AND POST-STAY ACTIONS

You're not the only source of content for potential guests. Thanks to the rapid growth of mobile, your existing guests carry the internet in their pockets, and with it the equivalent of a printing press, professional camera, and HD television studio as well. They're using these tools to create immense amounts of "user-generated content" (or UGC) every day and during every stay. You can persuade guests to share their experiences with their friends, family, and colleagues via social media in the form of photos, videos, ratings, and reviews.

According to social media aggregation firm Stackla, 76% of consumers say "…online reviews from fellow travelers give them inside knowledge" about their destination while 40% of millennials say that they rely solely on user-generated content when making their purchase decision[58]. Additionally, your guests connect with an average of over 150 friends on Facebook[59]. Every one of your guests can promote content about your property and increase the number of potential customers you can reach—but only if you give them something positive to talk about.

By far the most common way to engage guests in the process of telling your property's story is through ratings and reviews on Tripadvisor, OTAs, and Google. Most hotel management teams actively ask for reviews from guests throughout their stay, but especially at checkout and in the post-stay email. Make certain your operations team has addressed any issues prior to asking for the review to avoid negative comments on ratings and review sites.

Some properties have expanded beyond traditional ratings and reviews and have developed "Instagrammable moments"[60]—cool visuals, distinctive artwork, and unique experiences on-property—designed to encourage guests to snap selfies and share them with their friends across social channels. Seek out opportunities to entice customers with visuals and experiences. Then build on these moments and ask guests to share them with their social networks to help you reach entirely new audiences. And consider whether social media engagement platform tools such as Flip.to, Sprout Social, Stackla, or others will work for your property to drive the discussion forward with guests.

CONTENT MARKETING PROCESS

Providing great content—content that is useful, informative, and entertaining—increasingly is "table stakes" for online marketing. But how can you do it well? Do you simply start writing blog posts, taking photos, or shooting video of your property? How do you know what to create and in which formats? And, once you have content, should you place it on your website, send it in an email, share it on Facebook, or post it on Pinterest? The following sections will guide you through that process.

Content marketing is a process. And it doesn't just involve creating content. Experts recommend that any content marketing process[61] includes four major components:

1. planning
2. production, management, and maintenance
3. distribution and merchandising
4. measurement and metrics

While the amount of detail needed in each component may vary depending on the size and scale of your organization, you will use these same basic steps whether you work for a 10-room inn, a 750-room resort, or a chain representing tens of thousands of rooms.

Planning

Failure to develop an effective strategy represents one of the biggest barriers to successful content marketing.[62] Planning helps you put together an effective content marketing strategy, drives each subsequent step in the process, and can easily make or break your overall success.

Consider the following questions when putting together your plan:

- What business objective(s) are you trying to address with your content initiative? This may represent the single most important question in any content marketing plan. Are you looking to drive leisure reservations, increase your wedding or meetings business, grow your loyalty program, or something else altogether? While content can help you do each of these things, it's unlikely that a single piece of content—or even a single campaign—can do all of them. Make sure you know what problem you are trying to solve before you begin.

- Who is the intended audience for your content? Once you know which objectives you are trying to address, think about the customer segment or segments for which your content is intended. Are you looking to reach new or repeat guests, business or leisure travelers, consumers, or the travel trade? Each audience will have different questions they need answered and preferred ways of finding answers to those questions. Define your audience up front to guide you to the optimal content, formats, and distribution channels for your content initiative.

- What will you need to produce the content? The answers to this question help drive your project plan. Think about where the content will come from, what resources you'll need, who will do the work, and who owns the result. Many organizations maintain an editorial calendar that outlines the key content they'll develop each season, month, or week, the audiences that content will target, and the roles and resources needed to manage their content initiatives. To improve efficiency and prevent waste during the process, think about who and what you'll need before starting to create content.

- How will you promote the content? A recent study[63] found that, across industries, "…20% of all content produced is never distributed." In other words, customers never even interact with content after it's created. Don't let that happen to you. Just because you build it, it doesn't mean customers will come. Ensure your plan accounts for distribution and promotion opportunities to ensure your content reaches its maximum potential audience—and delivers on your objectives.

- How will you measure the success of the program? Think about how you'll know your content worked before you begin. As the adage states, "you can't manage what you can't measure." Make sure you've defined what you'll measure and that you have any necessary tracking in place prior to launching your content to avoid the risk that you won't know what worked.

A proper plan can help you overcome one of the significant barriers to content marketing success. It helps you understand the outcomes you're looking to achieve as well as the necessary path to reach them. As the old saying goes, "by failing to plan, you are planning to fail." Make sure you're planning for success with your content efforts.

Production, Management, and Maintenance

Once you have your plan in place, the next major step is to produce your content. However, "producing" content is not the same as "creating" content. Creating new content from scratch can be expensive and time-consuming. Additionally, your team may lack the skills or time—or both—that is necessary to create great content. Instead, ask yourself, "what is the best way to get the content we need?" The "4C Framework"[64] provides a simple way to think about where your content might come from:

- COLLECT: Reuse and repurpose existing content, such as organizing photos into an interactive video, to lower the cost and time needed to produce content that answers guest questions.

- CURATE: Organize and share destination and property content from partners or local experts. Leverage others' expertise to produce quality content quickly and inexpensively.

- CROWDSOURCE: Let your guests tell your hotel's story. For example, gather ratings, reviews, and feedback from comment cards, or guest photos and videos, and share that information with potential audiences on Facebook, Instagram, or Pinterest. Or record an interview on video with your property's chef, concierge, general manager, or other staff about common questions they receive from guests or their favorite experiences at your destination, then transcribe that interview into a blog post or "curated experience" on your property website. Even better, the video can be reused on YouTube, Facebook, and Instagram to increase your reach and attract interest from new audiences.

- CONTRACT: Cases will exist where the content you need neither exists nor can it easily be gathered from other sources. In those situations, look to contract with local travel writers, bloggers, PR firms, or agencies for your new content. These resources can often provide a cost-effective means to augment your team on an as-needed basis.

How to acquire content

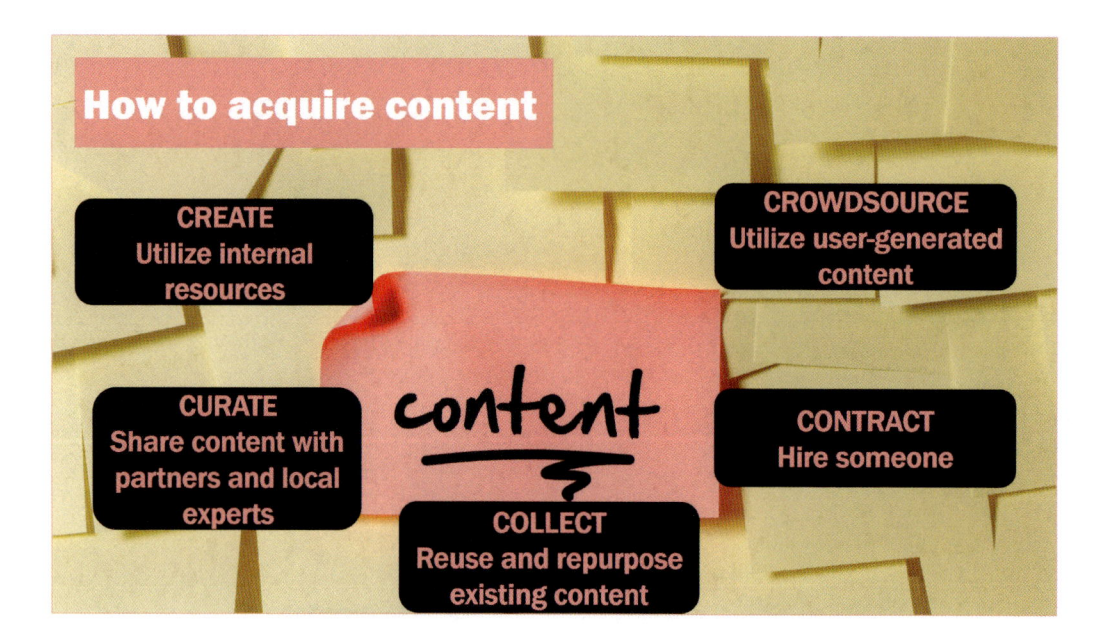

- **CREATE** — Utilize internal resources
- **CROWDSOURCE** — Utilize user-generated content
- **CURATE** — Share content with partners and local experts
- **CONTRACT** — Hire someone
- **COLLECT** — Reuse and repurpose existing content

During your content development process, think about the full content lifecycle as well. While some content pieces can last for years, others age quickly. A guide to beaches and national parks near your property may rarely change, while a list of the "best restaurants in town" might need updating every year. Your website's content management system (CMS) often provides tools to allow you to schedule when pages will be retired from your site.

Kings Courtyard Inn uses guest comments for social promotion.

Use website analytics, social media management tools, or your content calendar to periodically revisit older content on your site and social channels for relevance to your customers and alignment with updated business objectives. Once you've reviewed your existing content, update, replace, or retire it as appropriate.

Regardless of the method you use to produce and maintain your content, ensure it remains focused on the audience you defined during the planning stage. Speak to the needs of that audience using the language they use. Unless you're producing content for the travel trade, avoid jargon and industry terms. And even then, keep it clear and simple so less experienced travel agents and meeting planners can easily understand your message.

Finally, ensure that your content aligns with your brand and quality standards. As a "digital salesperson" for your property, make sure that your content presents an accurate view of the experience guests will have with your brand overall.

Distribution and Merchandising

One significant limitation for developing successful hotel and destination content is the sheer volume of it that exists online. Your content may be great, but it can't help your business if no one sees it. Author Mark Schaefer refers to "content shock," stating, "there is just too much content and too precious little time for people to consume it." However, Schaefer argues compellingly that "the real power only comes to those who can create content that connects, engages, and moves through the network through social sharing," search, and other distribution channels.[65]

It's not enough to build it and expect "they will come." Your plan must consider ways to put content in front of your intended audience. This is the core of your content distribution strategy.

While this chapter is in the Owned Media section of this book, it is important to note that content distribution can occur across paid and earned media as well. The specific channel you'll use may vary based on your audience and objectives. However, one common and highly effective approach follows a "hub and spoke" model—it leverages the reach of paid and earned media to drive traffic to your owned website.

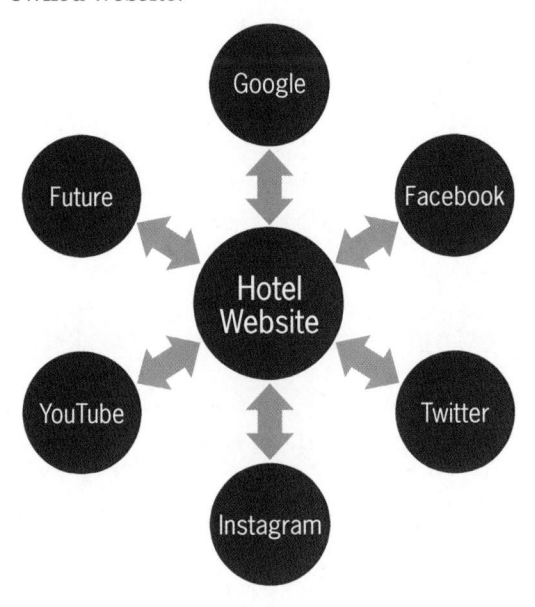

"Hub and Spoke" content distribution model

Providing a permanent home for your content on your website—a hub—increases the value of your site in search engines, demonstrates value to your guests, and establishes you as a trusted information source. At the same time, "spokes" enable you to get your message in front of the widest possible audience. It also makes it easier for guests to share your content with their friends, family, and colleagues, extending that reach and trust even further.

Measurement and Metrics

The process of making content work for your property is relatively straightforward. But to understand what "making content work" means, you must ensure you have the right measurements and metrics in place. As the Content Marketing Institute points out[66], "Content marketing is often no faster, cheaper, or more effective at moving customers down the funnel than other marketing techniques. However, its greater power lies in its ability to produce a better customer, a more loyal customer, or a customer more willing to share his or her story with others—which compounds the value he or she provides to the business."

Similarly, your measures should focus on understanding how content is helping you connect with better, more loyal, and more engaged customers for your property.

To that end, your metrics should seek to answer at least one of these questions:

1. **Did your customer see the message or the content in question?** Many marketers speak in terms of "engagement." In other words, did the customer view your content or spend time with it (in the form of time on site or additional pages viewed). While these are useful first steps, try to move your metrics deeper into the funnel to determine whether customers share your content or move towards a conversion. It's not enough to "go viral." Work to understand how visibility leads to business results.

2. **Did the customer take action?** Action demonstrates the real value of content marketing success. These actions don't have to be bookings but might include clicking through to your website; opting-in to your email marketing or loyalty program; sharing your content or property information with friends, family, and work colleagues; downloading meeting room specifications or wedding planning information; or other valuable steps towards doing business with your property. Ensure you've set objectives for action—and that your analytics are in place to measure those actions.

3. **Did the customer convert?** Conversions equal the holy grail of any marketing effort for many hotels. These conversions may include bookings or sales leads for weddings and group business. Tracking a customer's entire journey from their first view of your content through to a reservation isn't easy. But it is worthwhile to

begin testing which actions—whether shares, downloads, or opt-ins—correlate with increased conversion rate. Follow a "crawl, walk, run" process and continue building on your success to gain a clearer picture of the customer journey.

4. **Is your hotel seeing increased business?** This may take the form of additional reservations, greater repeat business, longer length of stay, increased on-property spend, and so on. As you build out your content marketing initiatives, note whether you're seeing increased business benefit along with your engagement and action metrics. Give your efforts some time to gain traction with customers, then adjust as necessary to drive value for your hotel.

Measuring the success of your content efforts takes time. But you must begin by working backwards from your objectives and putting in place the necessary analytics to assess its value for your hotel. Your content's job is to answer questions for potential guests 24 hours a day, 365 days a year. Ensure you're measuring its effectiveness at helping guests answer their questions to achieve your goals, too.

See Part 7 for additional information on measurement and managing digital performance.

BEST PRACTICES: CONTENT FORMATS

Content can take many forms. Hotels have successfully used tactics as diverse as blog posts, infographics, slideshows, destination guides, interactive trip planners, and incorporating text, images, and video to drive engagement, loyalty, and reservations from guests. No single rule exists that says you must use a specific format to achieve your objectives. Marketers have used the same formats to deliver both effective and ineffective content alike.

A few basic guidelines exist to help guide you to the right format for your messaging:

- **Align format with the correct stage in the customer journey.** While no one format consistently works better than others, some tend to support guests based on where they are in their journey. Presenting a detailed list of property amenities in a downloadable document probably won't help guests who've yet to decide whether they'd rather lie on a beach or hit the slopes. By contrast, a harried business executive may not want to sit through a video—no matter how beautifully crafted—just to learn how close your property is to the airport. Think about your guest's questions at each stage and consider the formats that best help them answer their questions.

- **Make each moment earn the next.** A common statement about online content states "shorter is better." While it makes a handy rule of thumb, it's also not entirely true. What is true is that customers don't have lots of time on their hands. Your content must provide support quickly and easily. Though, longer-form content can work. What all content must do is continue to provide value at each increment of time or risk losing the guest's attention and interest. When done well, you may find that longer content can prove effective for your guests. Yes, when in doubt, shorter is better. But understand why that's so and challenge yourself to make sure each extra moment you ask your customers to read, watch, or listen to your content is worth their time.

- **Think visually.** As we've already discussed, visuals help sell hotels. Where the channel and message allow, incorporate images or a brief video alongside your other content to let guests experience your property with their own eyes while making their decision.

- **Test and learn.** Test what works with your guests and learn from those tests. Build on your successes to find the content and formats that help answer guests' questions and improve your results. There's no one guaranteed path to success—and the pace of change suggests that even if there were, it would likely evolve in short order. Instead, learn to measure your efforts and apply the lessons learned to continue to grow.

An extremely important point to be considered when developing content is site speed. Studies indicate that if it takes more than 3 seconds for your site to fully load, you will lose a large percentage of your visitors. Even if you have the most amazing videos/content that anyone has ever seen, if it does not load fast, it will do more harm than good. Not only will users abandon your site, but Google will also punish you in its rankings as site speed (and mobile optimization) are important parts of the search algorithm that determines page rank.

WHAT DO WE MEAN BY MERCHANDISING?

Merchandising represents the practice of making your content attractive and persuasive to potential customers. While it's debatable whether "the medium is the message," the medium undoubtedly plays a role in what people think about your message. And, no matter which channel you use, your merchandising must support what you want guests to think, feel, and do when seeing your message.

Techniques for improving merchandising continue to evolve with changing customer behaviors, but several key approaches consistently produce results.

- **Define a clear call to action.** For any individual piece of content your team produces, make sure you've made it clear what you expect guests to do next. Whether it's "learn more," "enroll," "book now," or something else, help guide your guests to the next step on their journey. Additionally, ensure your call to action aligns with where your guests are in that journey. "Book now" may be appropriate in some cases, but not others. Test to see which calls-to-action support guests based on their current step in the buyer's journey.
- **Test urgency.** Which of these calls-to-action do you think generates more bookings?
  - "Only 1 room still available at this rate. Book now to save!"
  - "Plenty of rooms available. Book whenever!"

  Most people would correctly guess that the first tends to drive more reservations. Asking guests to act works; asking guests to act now works even better. Urgency drives results. Incorporate a sense of urgency into your content at appropriate points in the guest journey to increase action.
- **Use social proofs.** Human beings are inherently social. We all like to share experiences with our friends and family. At the same time, we want to feel like we belong. This entirely human need to connect often leads us to be influenced by the actions of other people. Social proofs use others' views of our property to influence our potential guests. We've already looked at examples of OTAs showing the number of people who've viewed or booked a given hotel. That's a social proof at work, frequently causing potential guests to say, "If everyone else likes this hotel, it must be a good one." Ratings and reviews work the same way. Look for opportunities to include social proofs in your messages to drive engagement and action.
- **Work towards personalization.** The best messages speak to each potential guest on an individual basis. Would you rather be addressed by your name or as a generic customer? If you're like most people, a personal touch works more effectively and produces stronger results. Work with your agency and technology vendors to begin the process of personalizing your content at each touchpoint to improve interactions with your guests and grow your bottom line.

CONCLUSION

Content and merchandising work together. For each piece of content your property creates—whether text, images, or video—consider its intended audience and how that content can help inspire, attract, or convert its viewer into a great customer for your hotel. Evaluate the appropriate next step in the guest journey and ensure you've presented effective calls-to-action to continue the dialogue with your customer and move them from simply dreaming to booking and from experiencing to sharing. Help your guests make the right choice for their stay and you'll both receive the benefits.

Content represents the cornerstone of all your digital marketing activities. And it's the key to unlocking your hotel's success at every stage of the guest's journey.

SAMPLE CHDM EXAM QUESTIONS

1. Collecting, curating, crowdsourcing, and contracting are four ways to acquire:
   a. Followers
   b. Content
   c. Social Influencers
   d. Search Rankings
   e. Reviews

2. Effective merchandising should always contain:
   a. A price point
   b. Images with people
   c. A call to action
   d. Testimonials

3. Which of the following is NOT true about booking engine best practices?
   a. Include as many rates and offers as possible to appeal to different personas
   b. Be simple and easy to understand
   c. Have enough information to make decision, but not to be overwhelming
   d. Have strategies developed by a team of marketing and revenue professionals working together

Answers
1 = b
2 = c
3 = a

Chapter 7: Rich Media

> **KEY POINTS**
> - Rich media has significant value in a digital marketing toolbox.
> - The targeted use of rich media can increase bookings.
> - Storytelling by visual methods impacts online shopping behaviors.
> - Understand the best practices for using rich media across multiple channels of your digital marketing strategy.

SUMMARY

Storytelling comes to life with rich media, and the better the story, the stronger the connection made between hotel and consumer. Travelers rely on rich media to inform themselves, help plan itineraries, and give them confidence to make their lodging purchases.

The power of visual merchandising should not be undervalued. It can be used to inform, inspire, and differentiate your hotel to drive awareness, sales, and guest loyalty. More than 90% of internet users watch video online and over 70% of video watched on YouTube was viewed on mobile.[67] In 2020, 92% of marketers say that video is an important part of their marketing strategy, up from 78% in 2015.[68] One study showed 4.8% as the average conversion rate for websites using video compared to 2.9% for those that don't.[69]

Today's rich media options are extensive, addressing the needs of all types of properties and budgets. A typical portfolio of rich media production includes full motion video, 360° virtual tours, interactive floor plans, 3D schematics, digital photo slideshows, and virtual reality. The type of media chosen depends on your hotel's marketing objective and budget.

FULL MOTION VIDEO

Videos tell stories and bring your hotel to life by creating emotional connections with guests. Video:

- helps a property stand out in a crowded online environment
- inspires and creates desire, and as consumers are drawn into a property or brand story, they become emotionally engaged and inspired to book
- encourages consumers' confidence in their selection because they have a better understanding of what to expect from the hotel and/or surrounding areas
- more effectively communicates key selling points than text or photos alone
- increases look-to-book conversion rates

Hotels can take advantage of the sight, sound, and motion of the medium to tell their story in new and creative ways. Whether a guided tour of the hotel narrated by the general manager, a "day in the life" story, or a series of videos showcasing different areas or behind-the-scenes takes of your hotel, video is your way to be creative, set your hotel apart, and inspire lookers to become bookers.

360° VIRTUAL TOURS

Virtual tours are popular for their versatility and low cost of production. Virtual tours:

- give consumers more complete and engaging visual information compared to static photos
- transform the photographic image from a flat two-dimensional world to a 360° virtual reality experience, allowing the consumer to explore a property as if they were physically there
- provide confidence and help set expectations among guests
- improve look-to-book ratios compared to just photos alone

Virtual tours showcase rooms and amenities from every angle and provide a realistic idea of what the hotel is like—what equipment is in the fitness center, how much storage space is available in the guestrooms, or even what types of amenities are available in the room or on property. Providing this information is important because travelers come from different generations, demographics, and behavioral groups. Some travel alone, others with spouses or families. Some are leisure travelers; some are business travelers. Today's guests have different needs and expectations; virtual tours can help guests easily evaluate whether your hotel may be a good fit for their needs.

DIGITAL PHOTO SLIDESHOWS

A digital photo slideshow, sometimes referred to as "photo video" or "photomontage," is built to balance function with budget for any type of hotel that has good quality digital photos. Digital slide shows:

- scale efforts that are economical and effective
- combine photography and traveler engagement with movement, music, and voice-overs
- combat commoditization by differentiating what a hotel has to offer above standard price comparisons
- increase consumer confidence
- inspire booking

CONSUMERS ARE VISUAL

Instagram, among other websites and apps, led the breakout trend of visual marketing in 2012 - 2013. When we look back (not that long ago) blogs were one of our earliest forms of social networking with people writing 1000-word posts, according to Dr. William Ward, social media professor at Syracuse University. When we moved to status updates on Facebook, our posts became shorter. Then "microblogs" like Twitter came along and chopped our updates down to 140 characters. Today, we're leaving out words altogether and moving towards more visual communication with sites like Instagram, SnapChat, and TikTok leading the way.

THE IMPORTANCE OF STORYTELLING

Always begin the process of producing media for your hotel by answering one central question: what is your story? Explain what makes your hotel or brand uniquely compelling to the travelers you wish to attract. Rich media is simply the medium through which you will show and tell this story—whether it is video, a virtual tour, or virtual reality.

Hotel marketing teams can develop a story that will attract more online travel shoppers—and more guests in general—by answering a few questions[70]:

- Who are your guests?
- What are guests saying about your hotel?
- What makes your hotel unique?
- What are your competitors' value propositions?
- What would excite and inspire you if you were a travel shopper?

Much of this information can found by reading online reviews about your hotel. Reviews are a good place to start because guests will tell you what makes your hotel unique and compelling and what doesn't.

Through this process, you'll know what sets your property apart, and you'll become much more skilled at conveying this message.

BEST PRACTICES: MAKE IT AUTHENTIC

When everything is available at the click of a mouse, having a clean and comfortable hotel product is not always enough to drive action. Creating authentic videos that capture the human element of your brand allows travel shoppers to connect on a personal level. This connection builds trust and drives action. Do not be afraid to go on camera and welcome your guests in the same way you would welcome them when they arrive at your hotel.

BEST PRACTICES: MAKE IT RELEVANT

With customers in control, irrelevant video is at best ignored and at worst will create a negative impression when viewers feel their time is wasted. Video that works shares compelling stories that resonate with the audience. Respect viewers' time and provide them with actionable content.

If you cater to young families on leisure travel, show them how their stay at your hotel will enhance their vacation. If you cater to business travelers, show them how their stay at your hotel will add to the success of their business trip. A good gut check could be: if you were the customer, would you find your video interesting and compelling enough to prompt action?

BEST PRACTICES: MAKE IT ENGAGING

With thousands of sites providing similar services and information, your online video must stand out from the competition. Entertainment goes hand-in-hand with engagement. Video must deliver content in a format that interests and excites users. This is why a story is so important and why just walking around the hotel with a video camera is not enough.

BEST PRACTICES: MAKE IT SHORT

Online shoppers have short attention spans. As such, considerable effort and thought must be put into developing the story that you want to tell and how you will do it. Short videos (best practices suggest 1 minute or less) force you to think creatively and distill your value proposition down to its very essence. Is it engaging from the start?

BEST PRACTICES: MAKE IT AVAILABLE

Your ability to distribute and show your video through search engines, destination sites, online travel agencies, and thousands of other specialty sites will enable you to welcome the travel shopper through your digital front door in a way that differentiates your brand.

BEST PRACTICES: MAKE IT SHAREABLE

YouTube taught everyone that video is portable and starts conversations between friends. Videos that fail to meet this expectation limit their own effectiveness. Sharing is an easy action that viewers can take to promote your business. By enabling conversations to spread, you're giving yourself an easy opportunity to gain viewership. To promote sharing, make sure your video can be embedded, emailed, and posted to the different social media sites.

BEST PRACTICES: MAKE IT ON YOUR BUDGET

Questions about production costs always come up quickly when the issue is video. The good news is that you can produce persuasive video in a way that matches your objectives and your budget. Hotels can produce enticing photo slideshows very economically. For those with very limited budgets, another option is to leverage user-generated content. A quick search on YouTube can yield some valuable content, and if repurposed appropriately with the owners' permission, user-generated content may even seem more authentic to future customers.

BEST PRACTICES: SOCIALIZE IT

There are some very good reasons why social media is critical to your success. Thirty-two percent of surveyed travelers chose a different hotel based on the impact social media had on them[71]; and according to research by Atmosphere Research Group, 62% of leisure travelers find travel brands' Facebook pages helpful.

BEST PRACTICES: OPTIMIZE IT FOR MOBILE

See Chapter 5 for a complete overview of the mobile topic. Ensuring that the consumer receives the information they are looking for on the platform, device, and operating system they are using is going to have a direct reflection on the success of your mobile marketing strategy.

INCORPORATING RICH MEDIA ACROSS MARKETING INITIATIVES[72]

In addition to ensuring that your hotel's story is being maximized across all the relevant websites and screens, there are additional opportunities to increase the size of the audience that your media is reaching by simply incorporating your visually rich story into marketing initiatives you're likely already doing.

Email Signatures

Add a button that says, "Take a Tour" to your email signature and link it to the gallery section of your website. This way everyone you email can easily explore your hotel and become immersed in a rich visual experience. Get all the employees at your hotel to do the same to further its reach.

Sales Proposals

If you have a great multimedia presentation that you can easily share, it can act as a sales proposal in itself. Send prospects a link that includes photos, floor plans, written descriptions, videos, and tours that are relevant to them. For example, a meeting planner wants to see your event facilities and learn about their features and capacities. Why send a long, written proposal when you can send them visuals with accompanying descriptions? This is far more effective than any written sales proposal, and hotels can vouch for that. Further, meeting and event planners who book their events at your hotel can share your multimedia tour with their registrants and attendees so they know what to expect when they arrive.

Online Advertising
Add relevant visual media to the landing pages from your online banner ads and PPC (pay per click) programs, or any of your other digital advertising campaigns. Studies show that online shoppers who watch video spend an additional two minutes on the site and are 144% more likely to purchase.[73] Present your best and most influential marketing assets—your hotel's story—using rich visual media along with compelling matching descriptions that will turn lookers into bookers.

Email Newsletters and Promotions
When sending newsletters and promotions by email, add a "Take a Tour" button that directs readers to your hotel's rich media. After reading your newsletter and hearing about what your hotel has to offer, prospective guests who have never stayed before will be able to see visuals of your hotel and envision what the experience would be like, while past guests will be reminded of how great their experience was. Rich visuals give travel shoppers confidence to book, so in both scenarios the visuals make them more likely to book or book again.

ATTRIBUTION & MEASUREMENT

As with all marketing initiatives, it is critical to remember that there is not a single silver bullet answer regarding how much to invest in each marketing medium or channel. A common best practice, however, is to not limit your perspective in only valuing the "last thing" that a consumer does before completing a booking. Rather, consider all your marketing programs when evaluating your ROI and ROAS for rich media and know that oftentimes a booking can be influenced by multiple sources, interactions, and touch points. Measuring the effectiveness of your rich media can be as specific as an ROI on your email campaign.

Similarities abound concerning the types of metrics specifically related to media measurement.

Audio
- subscriptions
- listening audience size
- duration of attention
- forwards
- evoked action solicited by the content

Video
- subscriptions
- views
- duration of attention
- forwards
- evoked action solicited by the content

Rich Media
- action count
- views
- frequency of use
- forwards
- evoked action solicited by the content

A partial list of other metrics to consider includes:
- increase in bookings
- increase in ADR before/after
- views of media
- site traffic
- time spent on website
- number of likes
- number of pins

Highway Property
- Average 200 views per month
- 1% conversion rate
- 200 x .01 = 2 bookings per month
- Sample ADR $80
- LOS = 1.2
- Incremental Revenue = $192
- Cost per month: $100
- 2 x ROI

Resort Property
- Average 1000 views per month
- 1% conversion rate
- 1000 x .01 = 10 bookings per month
- Sample ADR $115
- LOS = 2.4
- Incremental Revenue = $2760
- Cost per month: $200
- 14 x ROI

Downtown Property
- Average 2000 views per month
- 1% conversion rate
- 2000 x .01 = 20 bookings per month
- Sample ADR $210
- LOS = 1.9
- Incremental Revenue = $7980
- Cost per month: $300
- 27 x ROI

Above are simple formulas you can use to evaluate the ROI potential of your online visual marketing efforts.[74]

CONCLUSION

Start by figuring out what your story is. Think about location, style of property, staff, guests, experience, and positioning. Once your story is developed, ensure you're using all of the visual merchandising tools available to you. SHOW it, don't just tell it, in a way that compels people to take action. Optimize the experience for the consumer to ensure that they don't disregard your offering because of a bad visual experience. Use visual content on your hotel website, social media sites, and on all the channels where the property is represented to increase engagement, inspire sharing, and boost sales.

NOTES

SAMPLE CHDM EXAM QUESTIONS

1. Full motion video, 360° virtual tours, and digital photo slideshows are all examples of:
   a. Mobile Media
   b. Earned Media
   c. Rich Media
   d. Paid Media
   e. Social Media

2. Which metric is utilized with video?
   a. Views
   b. Duration
   c. Forwards
   d. All of the above

3. Mobile has made imagery and rich media less important.
   a. True
   b. False

Answers
1 = c
2 = d
3 = b

Chapter 8: Search Engine Optimization (SEO) – The History of SEO and How It Works

KEY POINTS
- The value of Search Engine Optimization (SEO)
- How search engines work
- The evolution of SEO
- The relevance of zero click

SUMMARY

The goal of search engines has always been to return the best possible results to searchers. That is still true today, but the complexity of the uses of data on the web has led to complex algorithms vetting out the most authentic, credible, and effective information to return to searchers—which today does not always mean serving up a website link.

This chapter covers the evolution of search and how search engines work, closely tracking closely with how buyers' behaviors have evolved. The following chapter recommends a series of both on-page and off-page best practices to ensure that your website—or at least the information about your brand—will be returned to your most relevant searchers. By the end of Chapter 9, you will understand that to be successful with SEO, it takes a village—meaning sales, marketing, revenue management, and operations team members must work together—and the results can help to solidify long-term revenue stability.

WHAT IS SEO AND WHY DOES IT MATTER?

SEO is the process of improving website visibility in unpaid web search engine results, which are also called "natural" or "organic" search results. The higher a website appears in search results, the more visitors it receives.

Accomplishing this goal is highly competitive in the hospitality/travel industry due to individual hotel sites, brand sites, destination sites, review sites, and OTAs competing for the top lines.

The differences between SEO and paid advertising (covered in depth in Part 4) must be evaluated in your overall digital marketing strategy. SEO takes more effort than running an AdWords campaign, and the results typically take longer to achieve. If you optimize your website today, you may not see results for two, six, or even nine months, whereas with paid advertising you will appear in the top spots as long as you are willing to pay. However, once you achieve a top spot organically, you won't likely lose it as quickly as the end of a campaign will eliminate your paid results. The ideal situation is to have both a well-optimized website and smart, targeted search marketing campaigns.

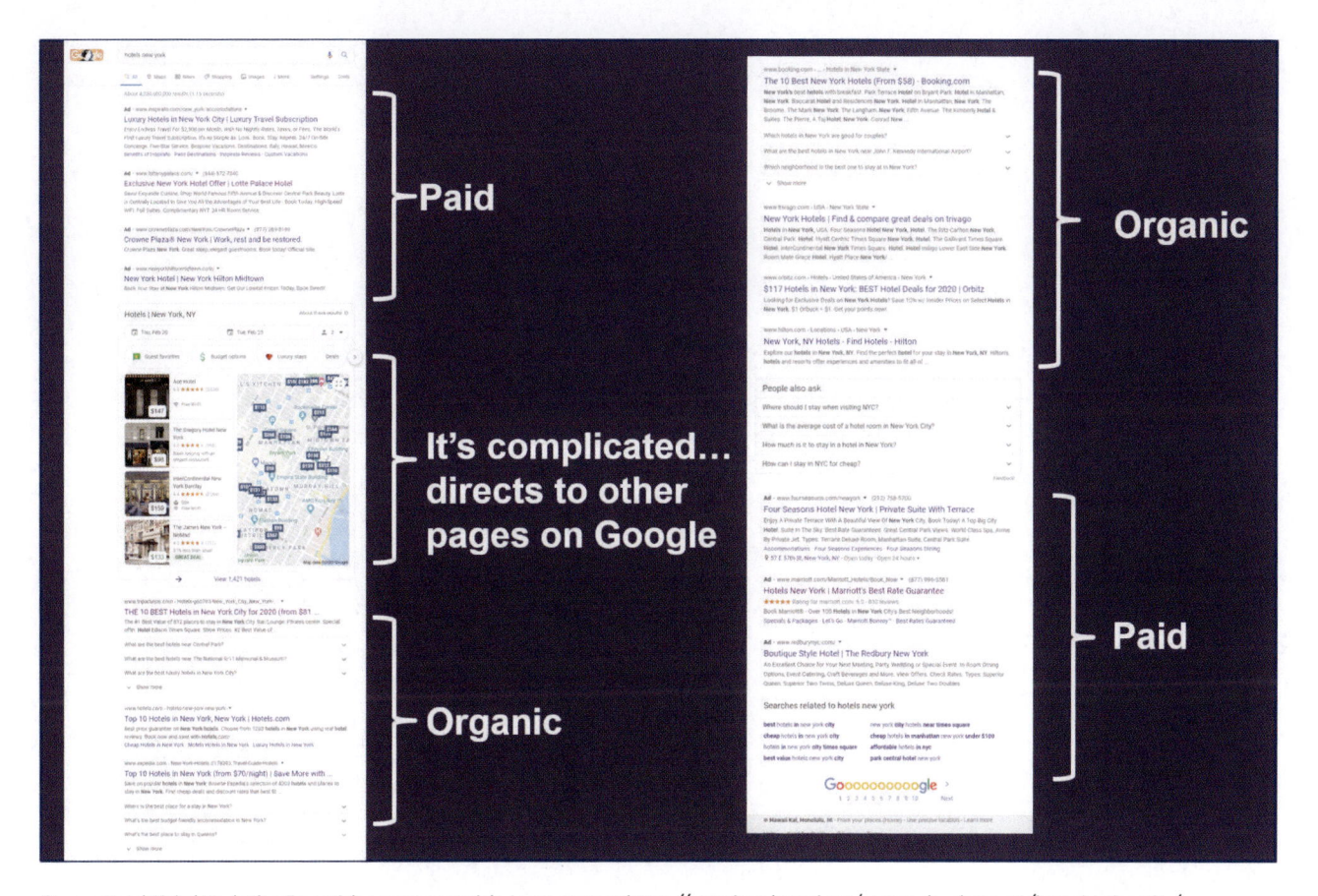

Source: Hotel Digital Marketing Essentials course materials. Learn more at https://americas.hsmai.org/career-development/hsmai-university/.

SEO is one of the most important components for driving revenue to your website's booking engine. The most beautiful website is rendered virtually useless if it has not been properly optimized.

Proper optimization techniques can help you rank high in search engine results for terms that target your ideal guest, whereas poorly performed optimization can harm your hotel's online presence, and even remove it from popular search engines altogether. Gaining a firm grasp of all the complexities of SEO practices and learning to use trusted tools are the first steps to a successful SEO campaign in a competitive online marketplace.

While Google owns the lion's share of search, search components exist on most websites—like Tripadvisor, the online travel agencies (OTAs), and YouTube. Understanding and strategizing around the elements that are included in each of these search engine algorithms will help you increase your share of searchers, and most significantly, conversions—or increased revenue. Today there aren't just website searches; now there are image searches, video searches, social searches, ratings searches, and voice searches.

Keep in mind a little jargon as we get started:

- On-page SEO includes things you can control on your site, like keywords and meta tags.
- Off-page SEO includes components like social media, articles, and references on other sites that give you "authority" according to Google.
- EAT is an acronym often used when people talk about SEO. It stands for Expertise, Authority, and Trust. The Google algorithm that determines page rank looks at these important areas.

WHAT SEO DOES NOT DO

SEO does not create demand. It is important to understand this upfront. Your content, CRM, and promotions all may inspire people

A Field Guide for Navigating Today's Digital Landscape

and create demand, but SEO simply helps drive searchers to your website. If there are no searches for a set of keywords, it doesn't matter how beautifully optimized your page is for those terms.

SEO does not directly close sales. A great SEO strategy will drive the right customers to your website, but once they arrive, pricing, website navigation, and other web page factors result in conversion. Ironically, better conversion factors on your website can help your SEO, but all that SEO can do is bring you the right customers. Driving the right customers to your website is a big deal of course, and certainly can have a significant impact on your closed sales, but SEO on its own doesn't close sales.

HOW SEARCH ENGINES WORK

Search engines like Google, Bing, and DuckDuckGo all have three key parts:

1. the database of information they collect from websites
2. the algorithms they use to return and rank the results of any given search
3. the format in which search results are displayed on the page

A search engine starts by using a scheduler to decide when and how often it will crawl—and recrawl a website. The URL is listed in the engine's scheduler and then a crawler is sent out to collect certain data within a website. That data is then parsed where the vital information from the site is extracted and indexed.

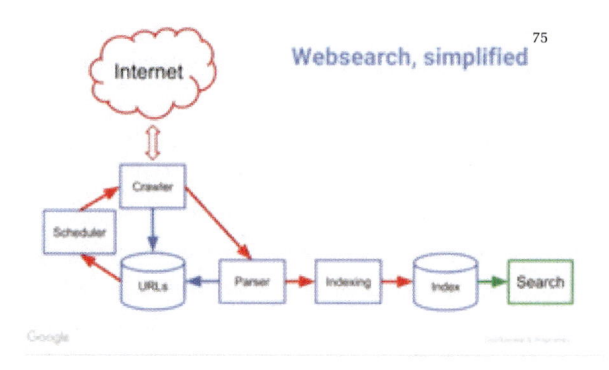

Which website results appear, and in what order, is determined by the search engine's algorithms—this is the unique "secret sauce" of each search engine that determines the most relevant matches to return the best results for its searchers.

Originally, search results were displayed as a list of blue links with a short description next to each. But today, results are displayed in a wide variety of ways—from blue links and snippets with images to knowledge graphs, answer boxes, and more. As the way we search for information has evolved, so has the way it is displayed.

This chapter mostly refers to Google as it dominates the search landscape—at least in the Western world.

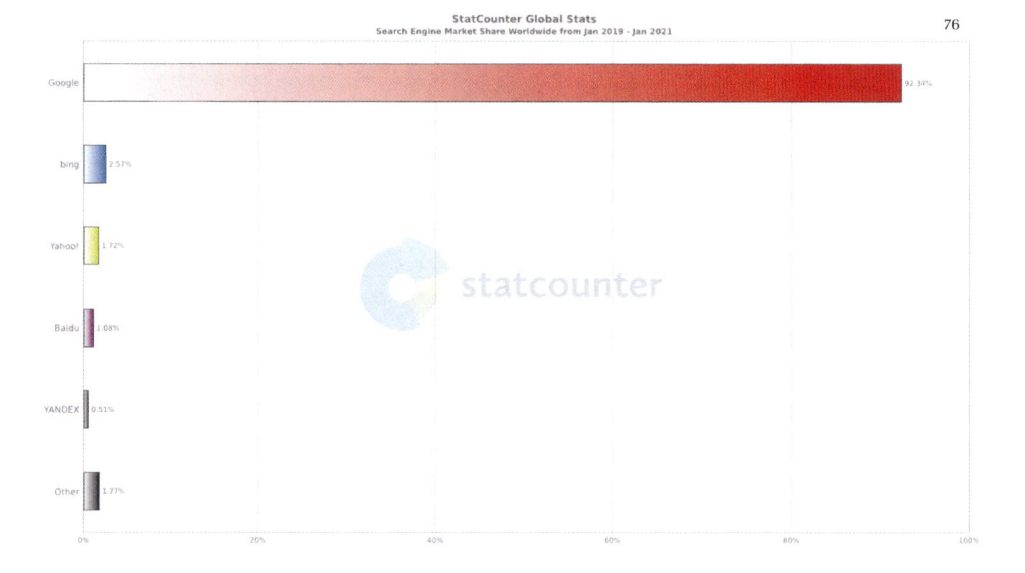

Why does Google dominate?

Since Google's early days, its founders have been consumed with returning the best results to their searchers. While everyone else was indexing title tags, Google was trying to find out how many other sites were linking to each website as they realized those websites were more satisfying to their searchers.

Today, Google has three distinct advantages due to its drive to return the best results.

1. It crawls and re-crawls websites more than any other site enabling it to maintain the largest and most up-to-date database in the world.
2. It has invested heavily in NLP—natural language processing—so that it can better understand the searcher's intent.
3. Its algorithms return the most satisfying and relevant results.

If we look back at the evolution of search (primarily Google), you can see that a search engine's success is driven by how tuned in it is to its customers.

THE EVOLUTION OF GOOGLE SEARCH[77]

The 1990s

The earliest search algorithms depended on meta data—information about a webpage that exists behind the scenes and describes what is on the page. Webmasters provided this information in the form of meta title tags, keyword tags, and meta description tags, and web crawlers used this information to index data for search engine results. File names were also indexed.

Because meta data could contain information that inaccurately represented the site's actual content, using meta data to index pages was found to be unreliable. Inaccurate meta data caused pages to show up in irrelevant searches.

Meta data is still used today by search engines. Not as much for determining which result gets displayed, but the description of what gets returned is often the meta description term used behind the scenes in the HTML of a website.

By 2004

Because the success of a search engine depends on the quality and relevance of its results, search engines developed more complex algorithms that took a variety of undisclosed factors into account to prevent system manipulation. For instance, Google said it used more than 200 different factors to determine relevance.

Items like H tags were added to indexes. H tags are HTML code that tells your browser how to display text. An H1 tag will typically display text the largest, so search engines assumed that was an important keyword for your site. Alt tags were indexed too because an alt tag was typically used to describe an image file—if a browser was unable to display an image file, an alt tag would take its place to let the user know what would have been there. Again, search engines assumed these alt tags would have some keyword relevance as the images you use should support your website content. Site maps also became important—because they helped the web crawlers or spiders find more areas of a website to index.

As you can imagine, in a battle to get the best search engine results on a page (SERPs), keyword stuffing became a problem. Some web designers would, for example, create a white background, and in white text add H1 tags with fake keywords. Or their alt tags for an image would have nothing to do with the actual image. This was an example of black hat SEO (techniques designed to trick search engine algorithms by manipulating content so that what the spiders see is different from what users can see). Search engines eventually caught on to this and websites that employed these tactics were punished by losing ranking.

A legitimate and effective alt tag for the following image is <img src="pancakes.png" alt="Stack of blueberry pancakes with powdered sugar">.[78]

A deceptive website might use a manipulated alt tag to try to "cheat," for example: <img src="pancakes.png" alt="pancake pancakes pan cake hotcakes hotcake breakfast food best breakfast top breakfasts breakfast recipes pancake recipe">. Search engines eventually caught onto this practice and discouraged it.

2007
In addition to the way Google was finding search results, how Google was displaying results was evolving. What began as blue hyperlinks to the web pages that Google found to be most relevant evolved over the years to so much more. The year 2007 was a pivotal moment as Universal Search was launched, which returned search results for images, maps, news, videos, shopping, and books.

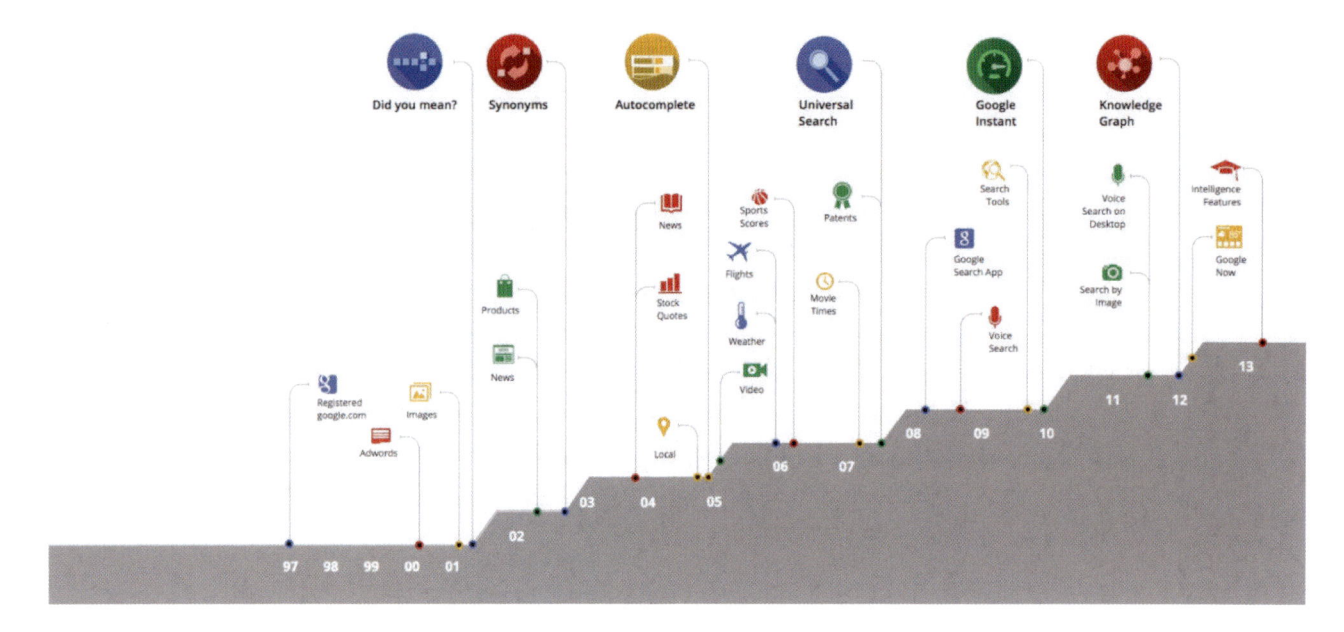

2009
Google added users' web search history as a factor in search results and introduced Google Instant which allowed new content to rank quickly. Historically, it could take months or years for sites to increase in search rankings, but the growth of social media and blogs created demand for more timely results.

This was an important step in the history of search, but it caused hotel owners and marketers quite a lot of confusion. Because the returned results were based on individual search histories, each search using the same keywords would get dramatically different results!

2011
Google released the Panda algorithm in 2011 intending to reward high quality websites and penalize low quality sites. One key factor considered was duplicate content.

Before 2011, copying content from one site to another helped sites rank faster. You would be able to have more relevant content quickly. However, duplicate content caused SERP problems—which duplicate content was the most relevant to return to searchers? In 2011, Google began penalizing websites for containing content duplicated from other websites.

However, sometimes duplicate content is important—even inevitable—on a site, such as for aggregators of content (like for metasearch sites that scrape other sites to display valuable information for searchers in one place). Also, having information on a site that is printable—without ad copy, for example—might be duplicate but necessary and user-friendly content. And most common, your own site URL might be accessible to web crawlers via https:, http:, https://www, or without a www. To humans, we know these are all the same destinations, but to web crawlers each is unique.

The concept of communicating to search engines about what content was the most relevant became "canonicalized." A canonical tag (a.k.a. rel canonical) is a way of telling search engines that a specific URL represents the master copy of a page.[80]

```
name="description" content="Looking to level-up your content game? The free Beginner's Guide to Content Marketing from Moz has you covered." />

<link rel="canonical" href="https://moz.com/beginners-guide-to-content-marketing" />
```

[81]

The rel=canonical tag in action. Here, it indicates that the page on which this tag appears should be treated as a duplicate of the specified URL.

Two other key developments happened around 2011: the creation of schema.org, and Google's rich snippet use of schema.

Berner-Lee, creator of the first browser, wrote a paper in 2001 suggesting the creation of a semantic web—a web that had an organized infrastructure that every webmaster would follow. It was a great idea but wasn't widely adopted.

That changed in 2011 when Bing, Google, and Yahoo (later joined by Yandax) created Schema.org. Schema.org was created to help lessen the confusion about the different markups used by webmasters for different verticals. For example, one set of markup language was used as a standard for calendar information exchanges, and a different set for business contact info. Markup was becoming very task specific. More on schema follows in this chapter.

2012

In 2012, social media sites played an increasingly important role in search engine results and rankings, and their evolution continues. If you search for a company name or organization, often, in addition to website pages, their social presence will also be displayed in your results. In the following image you'll see that, for a search for "HSMAI," first page results include both Twitter and LinkedIn results.

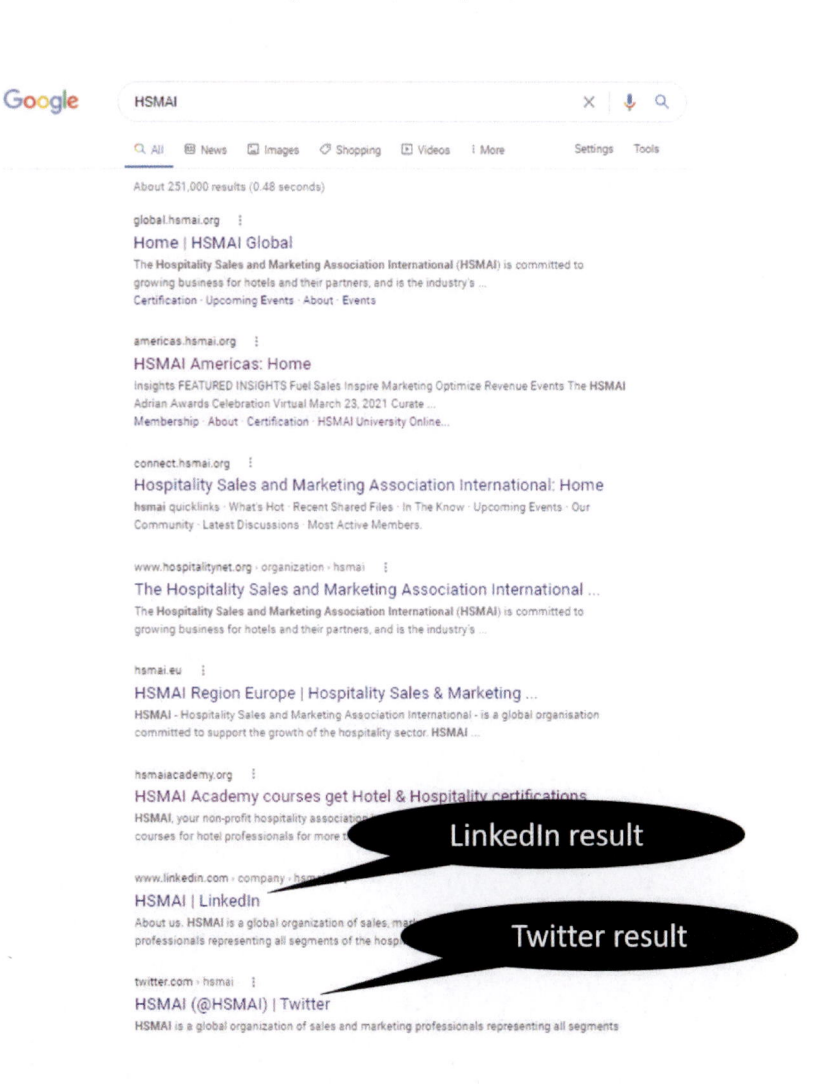

Note that each social site has its own search functionality. Social profiles are key today, just as meta tags were years ago.

The year 2012 also brought the birth of Google's Knowledge Graph. In its earliest days, the knowledge graph answered a search question or query on the SERP—saving the user time and energy by not having to click into a results page. Google took the information that previous searchers found useful and displayed it on the results page. This was the beginning of "things not strings," meaning the words used in search queries were more than a series of letters; they had intent behind them, and Google began understanding that intent is better than just the words.

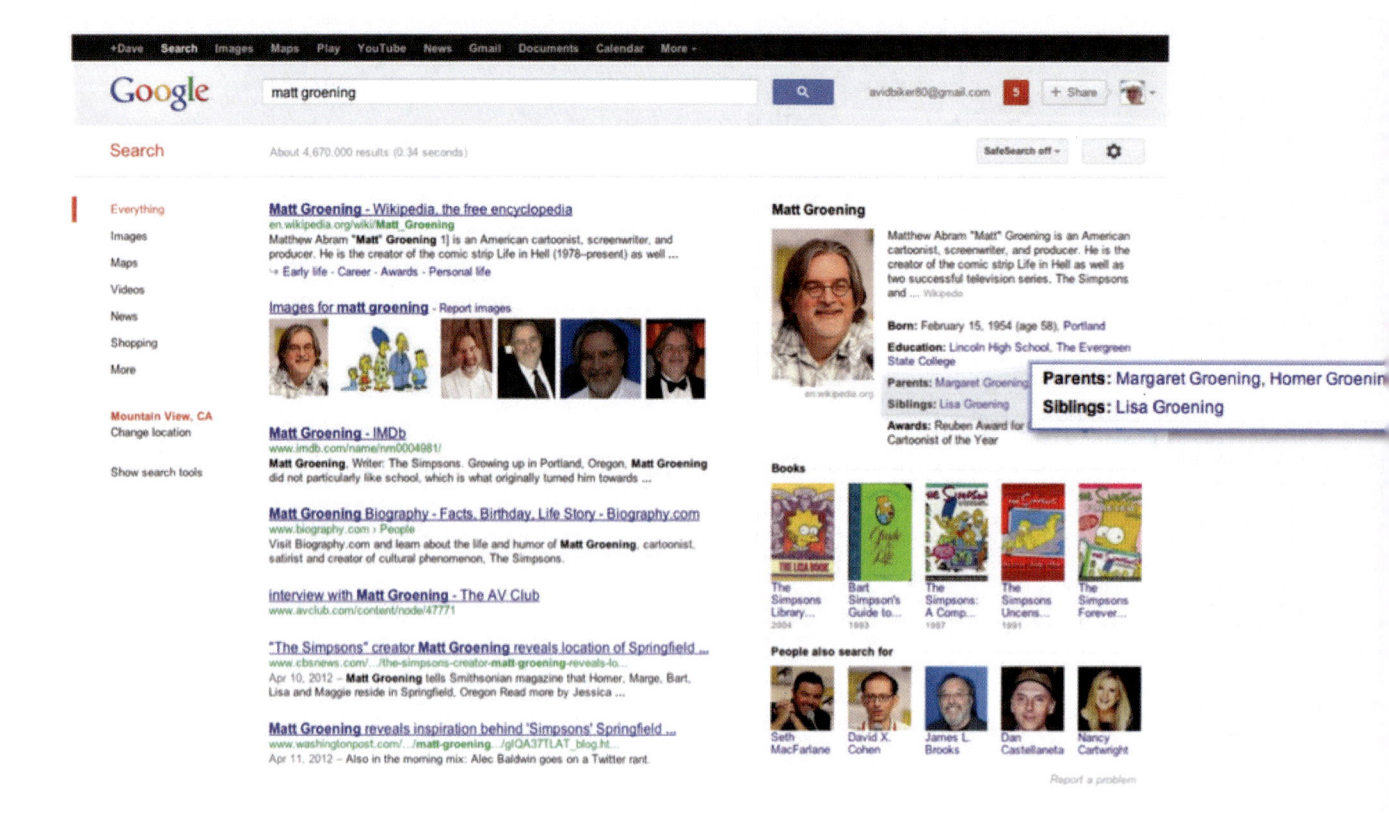

This snapshot of the knowledge graph for a search for "Matt Groening" delivered much more detail on the results page.[82]

2013

In 2013, Google released the Hummingbird and Pigeon algorithms, both entirely revamped versions of Google's search practices, not just a patch or update. Matt Cutts, the former head of the web spam team at Google, said that Hummingbird would affect 90% of all searches, albeit in a subtle way. Considering that at the time Google handled more than 3.5 billion searches every day, Google Hummingbird affected more than 3.15 billion searches a day.[83]

Hummingbird promised to change SEO dramatically from being keyword-driven to dynamic content-driven. Keeping fresh and interesting content was what Google was looking for, and those sites that delivered this relevant content would simply rank higher because Google understood the importance of the best user experience.

This was the beginning of semantic results—results based on the words, the context, and the user intent. It also laid the groundwork for voice search. You speak differently than you type and the Hummingbird algorithm began to address these differences in "conversational searches."

The Pigeon algorithm had an equal impact—but on local search. The goal of Pigeon was to tie local search algorithms closer to their web algorithms to take advantage of the hundreds of ranking signals that go into them.

For example, take the weather. Ask a human what the weather is, and they most likely will assume you want to know what the weather is where you are today. Prior to Hummingbird and Pigeon, Google would have returned results that included a definition of weather.

Today Google understands that you want the weather in your current location.

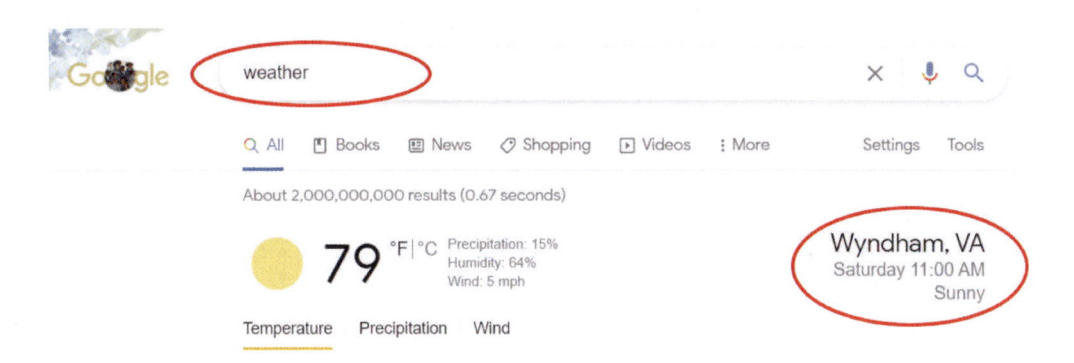

The introduction of intent and context allowed Google to return a variety of results that would more closely match what you were really asking for. The knowledge graph continued to evolve and tried to answer intent questions by providing a wrap of data it had indexed from various web sources.

Pigeon also introduced the 7-pack, which was later converted to a carousel, then cards, and reduced from seven to five and then three—although that differed based on the industry.

2014
This year saw multiple updates and tweaks made to Panda, Penguin, and Pigeon, all with the intent to reduce spammy, low authority websites in both web and local search.

2015
The Google Mobile Friendly Update (a.k.a. Mobilegeddon): Google announced this update in advance, and it centered around improving results for mobile-friendly websites. While the digital world braced for extreme changes in results, the reality was a much slower and more subtle change. Additionally, in 2015 there was a "phantom" change that many dubbed a "quality update," which Google later acknowledged as impacting its core algorithms.

Semantic search and NLP—natural language processing—continued to evolve, allowing Google to return results based on how people naturally speak (e.g., "beach hotels, Avalon, NJ" versus "where can I find a great beach hotel in Avalon, NJ?")

In 2015, Google also started using a machine-learning artificial intelligence system called RankBrain to help sort through search results. Post-RankBrain, it is believed that the query now goes through an interpretation model that can apply possible factors like the location of the searcher, personalization, and the words of the query to determine the searcher's true intent. By discerning true intent, Google can deliver more relevant results.[84] In 2015, about 15% of Google queries were processed through RankBrain. By 2016, 100% of queries were being processed.

For further reading, Searchmetrics released a whitepaper in 2015 which compared changes in SEO based on results. That detailed account of their findings is available at http://www.searchmetrics.com/wp-content/uploads/Ranking-Factors-2015-Whitepaper-US.pdf.

Also in 2015, Google released the Search Quality Evaluator Guidelines[85] which gave a clearer picture of what Google meant by a high- or low-quality site. The acronym EAT was first introduced. It stands for Expertise, Authority, and Trustworthiness.

2017
Google deployed AMP—Accelerated Mobile Pages—with the goal of finding the most relevant site with the best user experience. Mobile sites built with AMP significantly improved your mobile website's load time which in turn resulted in better ranking and lower bounce rates.

Site speed had been a ranking factor for desktops since 2010, but in 2017-2018, site speed became a noticeable ranking factor for mobile too. AMP is known as a framework—a light version of HTML. When initially launched by Google, AMP websites were given a preferred ranking presence, though that has since changed. AMP is not without controversy—many web developers suggest that simply focusing on increasing the load time and speed of your mobile site is preferable to using the AMP framework.

2018
In 2018, as misinformation online became widespread, Google made an important addition to EAT (Expertise, Authority, Trustworthiness). Not only did Google want to know the EAT of a website, it wanted to know the EAT of the website's main page author—especially if it was a YMYL (Your Money or Your Life).

This is particularly relevant for websites that impact happiness, health, or wealth. If content was about mental health, physical health, finances, or anything else that might impact YMYL, the EAT, or quality score, became more important. Google's goal was to push misinformation to the bottom of the search results and, as a result, credentials became more important than ever and continue to grow in value.

2019
In 2019, Google launched the BERT algorithm which was much more than a new set of search criteria. BERT is an open-source resource project and stands for Bidirectional Encoder Representations from Transformers. In simple terms, BERT is a natural language processing (NLP) framework that Google produced and then made available to the world as open source.

BERT gave Google the ability to understand the context of a word within a sentence regardless of the order in which it was presented. For example, if you said, "I like the way that looks, just like the other one." The word "like" is a verb when it follows a pronoun (he likes, she likes) but later in the same sentence it is a preposition and means something else completely. This is easy for humans to understand but challenging for computers—until BERT.

For search, BERT made it easier for Google to understand voice search—as we often speak search queries differently than we write them. It continued making progress in understanding intent based on where words fall in a sentence. It also helped with the nuances of the written word because people had begun searching with longer, questioning queries.

Can you optimize for BERT? Not really! But because of BERT, searchers may find your site as Google will do a better job of understanding what they were really looking for.

2021
As this book is being updated, Google has indicated that it will make a significant update in 2021. The focus will be "page experience," and the update has been referred to as the "Core Web Vitals" update.

According to Google: "The page experience signal measures aspects of how users perceive the experience of interacting with a web page. Optimizing for these factors makes the web more delightful for users across all web browsers and surfaces, and helps sites evolve towards user expectations on mobile. We believe this will contribute to business success on the web as users grow more engaged and can transact with less friction."[86]

The bottom line is that Google is looking to improve search results based on user experience, which will include site speed, design, usability, and more.

What exactly are Core Web Vitals? Over time, the meaning will likely expand, but currently, three factors are included—all around the user experience:

1. load time
2. interactivity
3. visual stability

There are three corresponding measurement tools that gauge how a website measures up around the Core Wb Vitals:

1. LCP (Largest Contentful Paint): with a loading time goal of 2.5 seconds
2. FID (First Input Delay): a measure of interactivity which should be at less than 100 milliseconds
3. CLS (Cumulative Layout Shift): with visual stability that should be less than 0.1

A tool is available in Google's Search Console to measure Core Web Vitals: https://support.google.com/webmasters/answer/9205520.

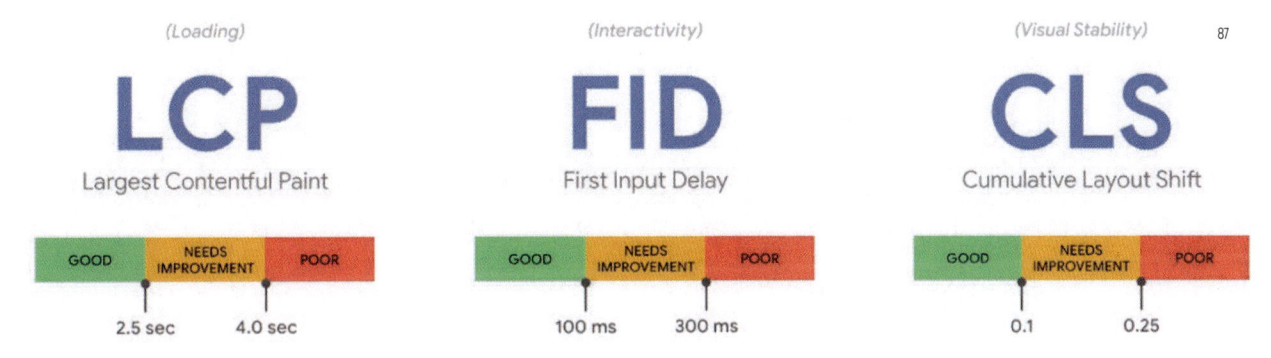

(Loading)
LCP
Largest Contentful Paint
GOOD | NEEDS IMPROVEMENT | POOR
2.5 sec — 4.0 sec

(Interactivity)
FID
First Input Delay
GOOD | NEEDS IMPROVEMENT | POOR
100 ms — 300 ms

(Visual Stability) [87]
CLS
Cumulative Layout Shift
GOOD | NEEDS IMPROVEMENT | POOR
0.1 — 0.25

THE RELEVANCE OF ZERO CLICK

It is important to note that the varying search result display options have shifted the way everyone uses, and optimizes for, the internet. Continuing evolution and behavior shifts will always impact hotel marketers' strategies around organic search.

The concept of Zero Click has become especially relevant—first on mobile but also on desktop. When you look at the CTR (click through rate) on a Google results page, what percent of searchers are clicking through to your website versus finding what they need on the SERP (search engine results page)? June 2019 saw a milestone: for the first time, a majority of all browser-based searches on Google.com resulted in zero-clicks.

According to a study by Rand Fishkin,"from January to December, 2020, 64.82% of searches on Google (desktop and mobile combined) ended in the search results without clicking to another web property."[88] When you breakout desktop and mobile, the gap is wide: almost 47% of searches on desktop did not generate a click and more than 77% of searches on mobile did not generate a click.

Google Search Desktop CTR, 2020
(worldwide data, via SimilarWeb's 100M+ user clickstream panel)
- Zero-Click Searches 46.48%
- Organic CTR 50.75%
- Paid CTR 2.78%

Data courtesy of SimilarWeb. Assembled & published by SparkToro

Google Search Mobile CTR, 2020
(worldwide data, via SimilarWeb's 100M+ user clickstream panel)
- Organic CTR 21.99%
- Zero-Click Searches 77.22%
- Paid CTR

Data courtesy of SimilarWeb. Assembled & published by Spar

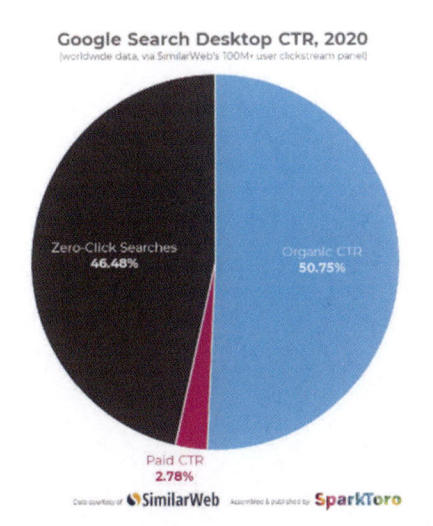

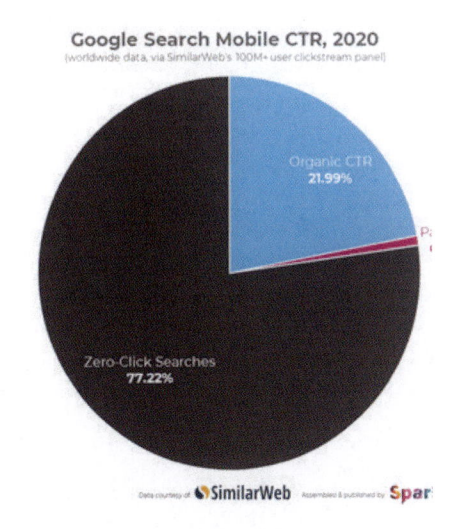

These changes have slowly skewed toward zero click for the last few years as more and more SERP features are offered. Some are concerned that Google is trying to have a monopoly on search results, and the counter argument is that Google is doing what it has always done—making it easier for searchers to find the information they want fastest.

SEARCH RESULT TYPES

Following are the different kinds of results Google currently returns on search terms[89] including information about where many web developers believe Google pulls the data.

Blue Link Results
The simple original search results—the webpage title in blue text that links to a page's URL—still in use today.

Rich Answer/Answer Boxes
Type or speak a question like "what is the temperature?" and Google knows to show your area's weather without having you click through to another website.

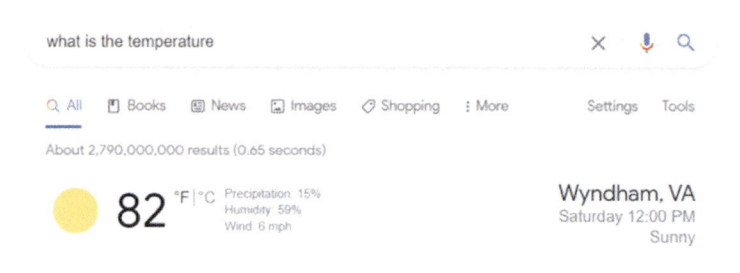

People Also Ask
Google anticipates what else you might want to know. Open the accordion arrow to see an answer, and the website that provided the answer.

Rich Results (Rich Snippet)
This is a normal SERP listing that includes additional information—usually ratings, prices, and additional links. You can add structured data markup or schema to optimize your content to display rich results. Rich Cards are the mobile-friendly version of Rich Results.

Knowledge Card
Specific data, for example the address of Hotel X in Toronto.

Knowledge Graph
Knowledge graphs are often in the right-hand sidebar and include images, facts, maps, and related search topics. This SERP feature is often shown for queries about certain topics, places, or people.

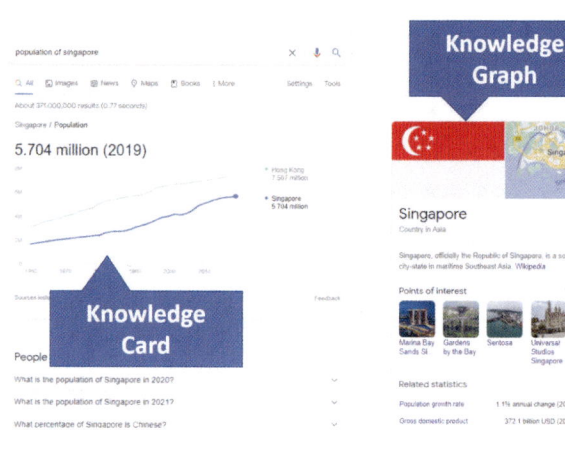

Knowledge Panel
Data is pulled from Google Maps or My Business listings. For hotels, a knowledge panel will likely include some paid information in addition to organic.

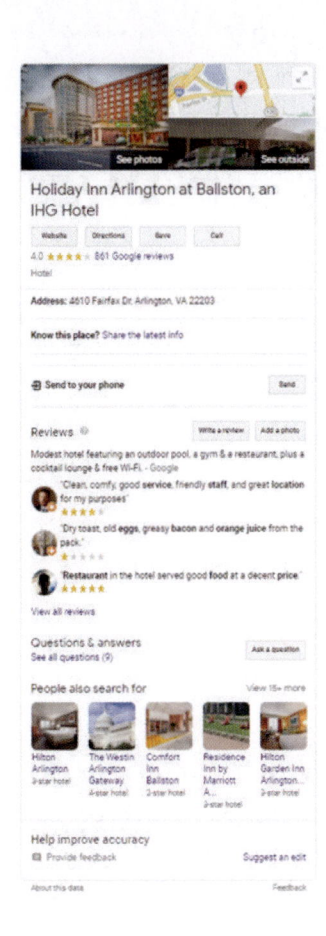

Local 3-Pack
The local 3-pack includes a map plus a list of three local businesses with rich results.

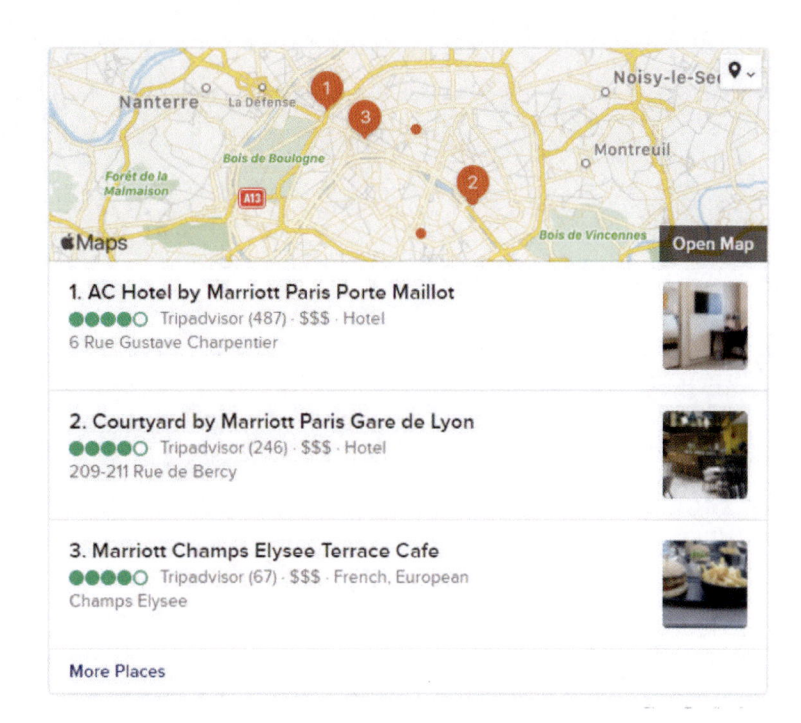

Image Packs
This feature is an array of images.

Videos
This feature is a carousel of three YouTube videos.

Sitelinks

Sitelinks are results with expanded links (with descriptions) to other pages on the same site.

Vertical Search

This is usually at the top of the page and frequently used when multiple sources of data—from images, video, news, etc.—are required to answer the query.

Top Stories

This is usually breaking news or trending news stories around the search topic.

Featured Snippets

This is a coveted return result, often referred to as "position 0." For hotel marketers, these are the best way to get in front of potential customers organically. However, it is challenging—99.58% of Featured Snippets are from sites that already are ranked in the top ten SERPS organically.[90]

There are six key types of Featured Snippets:

1. Paragraph
2. Numbered List
3. Bulleted List
4. Table
5. Video (YouTube and most popular for "how to" searches)
6. Twitter

Featured Snippet Example: Paragraph

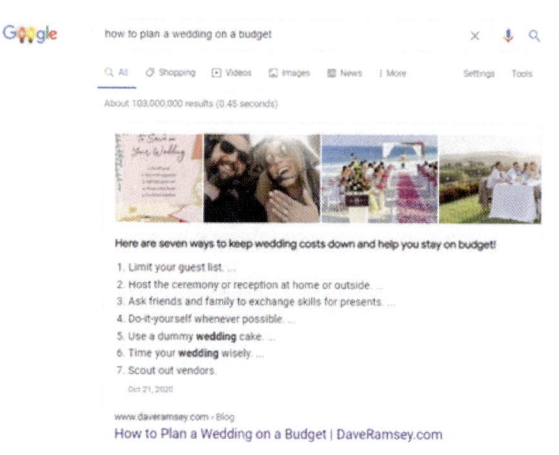

Featured Snippet Example: Numbered List

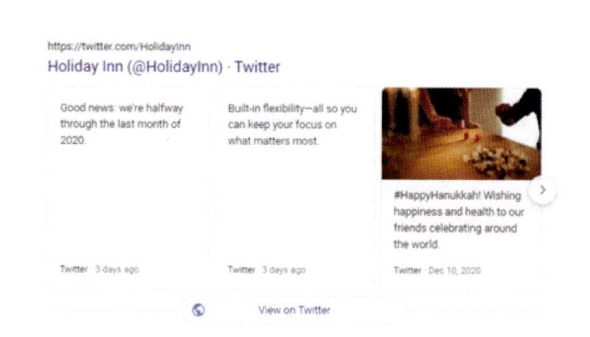

Featured Snippet Example: Twitter

Searches Related

At the bottom of the page

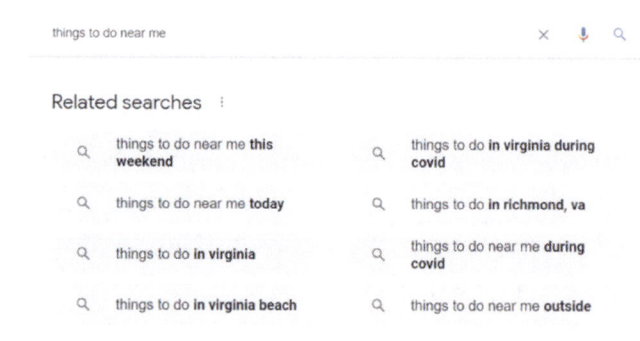

SAMPLE CHDM EXAM QUESTIONS

1. Which of the following does SEO NOT do?
   a. Create demand
   b. Drive searchers to your website
   c. Reward credibility by recognizing back links to your site
   d. Improve your site's visibility
   e. All of the above

2. There are 3 key parts to the search engine's process. Which of the following is NOT part of that process?
   a. An indexing process is created—determining when and how often sites will be crawled
   b. Algorithms are created to determine the most relevant matches for the sites they return
   c. How results are displayed is determined—like the blue link, or knowledge graph for example
   d. Advertising auction or bid rates are established to determine order of display

3. Today Google has distinct advantages that keep its search engine on top. What are they?
   a. Google crawls and re-crawls more sites than any other site
   b. Google invests heavily in NLP
   c. Google's algorithms return the most relevant results
   d. Google has the largest advertising base
   e. Google is the search engine of choice for all the digital voice assistants
   f. A & B
   g. A, B, & C
   h. B, C, & D
   i. All of the above

Answers
1 = a
2 = d
3 = g

NOTES

Chapter 9: Search Engine Optimization (SEO) – Making SEO Work for Your Hotel

> **KEY POINTS**
> - What SEO can and cannot do for your hotel
> - On-page and off-page best practices
> - The significance of schema to your website rankings
> - How to maximize local search

SUMMARY

The last chapter focused on the evolution of search and the current applicable ways in which your results are displayed on Google. This chapter continues with SEO with a focus on how to make the Google algorithms work for your hotel—starting by defining your goals, then leveraging keywords. Both on-page and off-page SEO best practices are important, and schema can significantly impact your results.

DEFINE YOUR SEO GOALS

As with any marketing initiative, start by defining your SEO goals.

Some of the limitations of SEO are addressed in Chapter 8 (e.g., SEO won't create demand or close sales), so make sure your SEO goals are tied to key marketing strategies because they will drive activities and investment. Consider the following example.

Business	Grow wedding sales by X
Marketing Goals	· Build brand awareness around the hotel's unique space · Grow top of funnel traffic · Attract newly engaged brides to the website
Potential SEO Goals	· Rank for low demand, high conversion keywords · Rank for high demand, low competition keywords · Rank for high demand, high competition keywords · Create content that will attract more links and influencer engagement to expand organic reach and in the future rank for more competitive keywords

Be realistic and consider your resources when setting goals. In the case of the example, ranking for high demand keywords would be fantastic, but there is a lot of competition for keywords like "weddings near me." So, to be successful, you will need a serious investment of resources. However, ranking for "weddings in City name with spectacular views of X" might be achievable without nearly as much of a time and resource investment.

It is critical to remember that SEO strategy doesn't impact much in the short term. If you need a quick fix for a low-demand weekend this month, paid ads are your answer. SEO is a longer-term investment. With SEO, you can see results that will have better staying power, but not in 24 hours…more likely in 6-9 months. If you stay consistent and follow other best practices including those outlined in this chapter, you may see even better results in 12-18 months.

CONDUCTING KEYWORD RESEARCH

Once your SEO goals are defined, conduct keyword research to find the words and phrases that are the highest value for your property. You don't have to guess what people are searching for. There are tools that provide valuable insights into exactly what potential customers want to know, and specifically how they are phrasing it. AnswerThePublic (https://answerthepublic.com/) is such a tool.[91]

There are five key steps for keyword research:

1. Understand the keyword research landscape. What are people searching for?
2. Create a list of terms and phrases for which you want to rank.
3. Prioritize those terms. What will get you the best return?
4. Determine the kind of results you want to optimize for. See page 80 in Chapter 8 for the complete list of options currently offered by Google (Answer Boxes, People Also Ask, etc.).

5. Match the keywords you've identified with your website. Do you have content and web pages that match the terms you want to target? If not, plan to add them (see Chapter 6 on Content & Merchandising, and the following pages for how to do that).

There are several tools available to help you discover which terms are searched more frequently than others, including:

- Google Trends (free)
- Moz's Keyword Explorer
- AHEFS Keywords Explorer
- SEMrush Keyword Magic Tool

Most of these tools will show the number of times a keyword or phrase shows up in a search. They also show the number of websites optimized for that keyword—meaning they are using that keyword in any of their anchor texts. This gives you an idea of how competitive the keyword is. In an ideal world you would find a keyword or phrase that has a high amount of use, but very little competition.

Consider what sets your property apart from your competitors. Are you pet-friendly or family-friendly? Do you have suites, a variety of business amenities, or a large meeting space? Are weddings—traditional or same sex—your target?

Compile a potential list of your target markets during your research phase and list what you offer that will be specifically appealing to that market. Look at your competitors' websites to see which words and phrases they use. You can view source code to see the meta tags and descriptions they are using—though keep in mind they can also look at yours! Simply Googling potential phrases can help as well, to see if keywords are worth targeting, to look for competition for the term, and to see what iterations of the term appear in search results.

RECOMMENDED PRIORITIES FOR KEYWORD RESEARCH

Brand, Location, and Local Demand Generators

Your own site, not third-party sites, should come up first in a search for your brand terms. Visitors and bookings to your direct website are ideal because you avoid paying third-party fees for bookings. After brand, the next most important set of terms to optimize relates to your location. Focus on the location by using words like hotels, lodging, suites, cabins, or resorts, and pairing them with the location, such as:

- Resorts in Orlando
- Suites in Miami
- Boston lodging
- Hotels in downtown Chicago

Keyword	Volume	Trend	KD %	CP...	Com.	SERP...	Results
hotels in phoenix az	18,100		89.05	1.41	0.28	+3	67.8M
cheap hotels in phoenix az	1,900		85.99	1.60	0.47	+2	3.4M
hotels in downtown phoenix az	480		87.53	1.55	0.28	+5	95
extended stay hotels in phoenix az	320		86.15	1.17	0.42	+2	83
pet friendly hotels in phoenix	320		85.21	1.90	0.32	+4	93

From Semrush's Keyword Magic Tool, you can see the volume of searches in the first column, then a trend graph. The next column tells you the keyword difficulty (KD%)—how competitive that keyword is. The tool is available at www.semrush.com/analytics/keywordmagic/.

To the location terms, add more targeted niche terms, such as "Miami beach hotels with conference rooms" or "Miami beach resorts for weddings." These terms are very specific, relevant terms to your property and are quite valuable.

Though the volume of searches will be lower for the more specific terms, the visitors you will attract will likely convert more often because they are looking for your product.

In addition to brand, location, and niche terms, consider local demand generators—local business and leisure attractions—that bring guests to your area, such as:

- corporate offices
- hospitals
- theme parks
- beaches
- museums
- historic districts
- convention centers
- shopping, dining, and entertainment districts
- popular annual events

Pair these with lodging and niche terms, for example:

- family-friendly resorts near Disney World
- beachfront suites in Miami
- Boston Marathon lodging
- pet-friendly hotels near Magnificent Mile

LONG & SHORT TAIL KEYWORDS

Long tail keywords are most likely to produce results for you. These are phrases that contain four or more words that are very targeted to your property. They receive fewer searches, but are very targeted, and result in a higher conversion rate because searching for more specific terms generally means the intent to purchase is further along. Examples of long tail keywords include: "pet-friendly hotels near Magnificent Mile" and "Sydney hotels with indoor pool." A searcher's intent is clearer when they search for more detail, so your conversion rate is likely to be higher.

Short tail keywords are broad phrases that receive a lot of searches but result in a lower conversion rate because they are so broad. The searcher is likely in the earlier stages of the buying process. Examples of short tail keywords include: "Barcelona hotels" and "Orlando lodging."

Rules of Thumb for Long and Short Tail Value
- Location: Many low-value searches
- Location + Hotel: More value, slightly fewer searches
- Property Name: Even more value, even fewer searches
- Specific Amenities or Niche Terms: very few searches but very high value

ON-PAGE SEO

Your goals are established, and your research is complete. The next step is to focus on your on-page SEO. On-page optimization is where you include information on your website to tell search engines and users what your site is about and make your site highly relevant to your target market. If you review the history of search, you see that on-page SEO used to be limited to checking meta tags and putting some keywords in the title tags.

Today, on-page SEO falls into three different areas of focus:

1. User experience
2. Technical keyword targeting
3. Content structure relevance

> This book goes into great detail on Google because it commands so much of the market. But do pay some attention to other search engines (each of which has its own specific set of algorithms) if they are relevant to your target market.
>
> For example, DuckDuckGo does not capture or use your private information. There is a growing segment of searchers who value this approach, and if they are a part of your target audience, you will want to review DuckDuckGo optimization tactics. A detailed comparison of DuckDuckGo and Google results are at https://www.searchenginejournal.com/google-vs-duckduckgo/301997/#close".

USER EXPERIENCE

One of the biggest mistakes you can make is to write the content on your website to keep the Google algorithms happy. Always keep the user experience in mind first and foremost because Google knows when people click through to your site and, like a pogo stick, bounce right off because it wasn't what they wanted. This could be an entire chapter unto itself, and we cover elements of it in Part 2 on owned media, but there are a few key tactics that are especially relevant to on-page SEO.

- **Provide an easy-to-use, fast-loading site that is a pleasant experience overall.** This is where web vitals come into play—make sure your site loads quickly, that the site navigation is clear, and that you present the content in a clear and completing manner. If your site is not responsive to mobile devices, or is slow to load, you will not only get penalized by Google SERPs but your users will quickly click away and move on.

- **Answer the searcher's primary questions comprehensively and with authority.** This is where you put your keyword research to work. Make sure that you know what questions are being asked and make sure to use your goal keywords to answer those questions thoroughly. Remember EAT (Expertise, Authority, Trust). If you want to rank for the most pet-friendly hotel in your city, you should have content that reassures searchers that you are extremely pet friendly. Include reviews supporting that information, specifics steps you take to ensure animals feel welcome, and images of happy pets. Use headlines and content written in a Q&A format to make it easy for Google to use in a knowledge panel.

- **Solve the searchers' next tasks and questions.** If you claim to be family friendly, and you have shared content focused on family activities, what other questions will searchers have that you can answer, stopping them from clicking away? Can you add an itinerary, or a link to your blog that features the top ten kid-friendly activities outside of your hotel? How about an interactive map with all those spots highlighted? Can you share reviews on that page about what other guests have said about your family friendliness? All these elements are considered buyer-enablement tools and are designed to give you a long-term competitive advantage.

This is a great example of how to make it easy for Google to include information in a knowledge panel while ensuring an engaging user experience (from Hotel Nikko San Francisco).

A Field Guide for Navigating Today's Digital Landscape

TECHNICAL KEYWORD TARGETING

After ensuring a positive overall user experience, you can incorporate some technical components into your page.

- Create a descriptive, compelling, keyword-rich title element for each page. Be specific—but don't keyword stuff (using a word or words so much that the content loses its meaning). Ideal length is 50-60 characters.
- Include a meta description designed to draw the click of the searcher. While meta descriptions are not used for ranking, they are displayed in basic results, so this is your best chance to entice the searcher. Ideally it should be around 160 characters.
- Include meta descriptions for Twitter and meta properties for open graph images and titles.
- Use easy-to-read, short URLs versus long, meaningless URLs with numbers and symbols.
- Optimize your first paragraph for appearing in featured snippets (include image and description).
- Use the keywords smartly in headlines, the first paragraph, page content, and internal link anchors.
- Leverage appropriate rich snippet options like star ratings and schema.org markup.
- Images and videos on the page should all have descriptive, keyword-rich filenames, descriptive alt attributes, and caption text. Ideally store them all in same domain.

CONTENT STRUCTURE RELEVANCE

Content Structure means the way you organize your HTML headings to break up your content into logical sections and help search engines interpret your intent.

- Ensure that each page is unique and valuable. Make sure to use canonical tags, or block bots if you need to have alternative pages that are similar or duplicates. For example, if you need to have a page specifically to print out, like a recipe or walking directions that is a duplicate of something you already have listed on another area, make sure to use canonical tags to indicate the primary reference area.
- Make pages accessible to crawlers that can be parsed for even text-only browsers. This means to make sure that even if a browser or spider can't read jQuery (a popular programming library), your HTML website story still makes sense.
- Remove thin or duplicate content. Thin content is any content that doesn't add value to your searchers. If you need to have a page with a lot of duplicate information in a summary form for a user, use a robot.txt indicator in your html to tell the search engine to ignore it.
- Aim for a wide, but not very deep, site. That means for all pages that contain valuable content, you must go no more than 3 clicks deep. It should be reflected in your URL—https://yoursite.com/services/pet-friendly-hotel instead of https://yoursite.com/services/roomtypes/amenities/pet-friendly-hotel.
- Include breadcrumbs and site maps for both a better user experience and spider crawlability.
- Ensure each page is responsive for every device and screen size.
- In your content structure design, use 301 for permanent redirects, 404 for dead pages, 503 for temporarily unavailable pages, and 200 for all ok—and nothing else if possible.
- Use https: instead of http: as it signals that this is a secured site, meaning the site has an SSL certificate. Google is now rewarding this delineation.
- One domain is better than several domains unless canonical tags are used.
- Subfolders are better than subdomains.

THE RELEVANCE OF SCHEMA.ORG AND STRUCTURED DATA

Schema helps Google understand the context of words on a website. Humans understand context more quickly and easily than search engines. If you talk about cars and bring up Jaguar, humans right away understand your context—the Jaguar car. But historically search engines would return results for the animal. Adding structured data markup to your website allows search engines (Google, Bing, Yahoo, and Yandax) to understand more deeply what your content means.

Schema matters because Google uses schema markup to generate rich snippets and knowledge graphs. As of early 2021, only about 1/3 of all websites use schema in any form, which presents opportunities to stand apart from your competitors. The easier you make it for Google to trust and share your content, the more likely you are to be featured.

How does it work? Schema markup can be added to your website in one of three ways currently: Microdata markup, RDFa (Resource Descriptive Framework in Attributes), and JSON-LD (Javascript Object Notation for Linked Objects).

To add schema markup through microdata, mark up your site's HTML using a few key techniques:

- itemscope: creates the item and indicates that the rest of the element contains info about it
- itemtype: describes the item and properties with a URL of vocabulary (like https://schema.org)
- itemprop: indicates that the containing tag has the value of specific item property (itemprop="name")
- itemid: indicates a unique identifier
- itemref: references properties of an element that aren't contained in the itemscope—they may appear anywhere in the doc

HTML Example Without Schema	HTML Example with Mircrodata Markup
<div>	<div itemscope itemtype="http://schema.org/Book">
<h3>Harry Potter and the Chamber of Secrets</h3>	<h3 itemprop="name">Harry Potter and the Chamber of Secrets</h3>
<table summary="Bibliographic Details">	<table summary="Bibliographic Details">
<tr>	<tr>
<th>Main Author: </th>	<th>Main Author: </th>
<td>Rowling, JK</td>	<td itemprop="author">Rowling, JK</td>
</tr>	</tr>
</table>	</table>
</div>	</div>
<table summary="Holdings details">	<table summary="Holdings details">

If you look at the hotel category on schema.org (at https://schema.org/Hotel) you will see the various identifiers that have been specified to help Google understand and present details for a property. A few examples include:

Property	Expected Type	Description
amenityFeature	LocationFeatureSpecification	An amenity feature (e.g., a characteristic or service) of the accommodation. This generic property does not make a statement about whether the feature is included in an offer for the main accommodation or available at extra costs.
audience	Audience	An intended audience, i.e., a group for whom something was created. Supersedes serviceAudience.
availableLanguage	Language or Text	A language someone may use with or at the item, service, or place. Please use one of the language codes from the IETF BCP 47 standard. See also inLanguage
checkinTime	DateTime or Time	The earliest someone may check into a lodging establishment.

Source: https://schema.org/Hotel

SCHEMA RESOURCES

The best resource is schema.org for all the hierarchy of available data types. However, there are several other tools that can help you add schema markup to your site:

- Hall Analysis JSON-LD Schema Generator For SEO: https://hallanalysis.com/json-ld-generator/
- Google's Structured Data Markup Helper: https://www.google.com/webmasters/markup-helper/u/0/
- Microdata Generator: http://microdatagenerator.com/generator.html
- Merkle Schema Markup Generator - https://technicalseo.com/seo-tools/schema-markup-generator/

Test your site to ensure you have working markup with Google's free testing tool: https://search.google.com/structured-data/testing-tool/u/0/

WHITE HAT V. BLACK HAT OPTIMIZATION

White hat optimization is any optimization technique that is recommended and approved by search engines, and that does not involve any form of deception. A basic guideline for producing an optimized site that search engines will approve of is that the content a search engine uses to index and rank your site should be the same content users can see.

Black hat optimization is any optimization technique of which search engines do not approve. Black hat optimization is designed to trick search engine algorithms by manipulating content so that what the spiders see is different from what users can see. Examples of black hat optimization include:

- using text that is hidden, either by making the text a similar color to the background, hiding text behind an image, or positioning text off screen
- offering a different page to the search engine than to a user (a technique called "cloaking")
- keyword stuffing—using a word in the content so much that the content loses its meaning

White hat optimization naturally produces long-term positive results, but black hat optimization only works as long as a site can get away with it. When a search engine discovers deceptive optimization techniques, it either temporarily or permanently bans the site from its search engine.

OFF-PAGE SEO

Off-page optimization is where you make your site more relevant in search engines by methods that don't involve making changes to your site. The most important aspect of off-page optimization is link building—increasing the number of quality inbound links, or back links, to your site. Each time another website links to your site for a particular phrase, it is a vote for your site for that phrase. If your site has a history of people visiting for that phrase, search engines will consider your content more relevant for that phrase, and your site will move up in search results.

Remember the EAT—Expertise, Authority, and Trustworthiness—relevance from Google? Off-page SEO has the greatest impact on these factors because Google believes what people say about you is more credible than what you say about yourself.

The quality of the sites linking back to you are also relevant for your off-page optimization. For example, if you talk about being located near an attraction, ideally that attraction would feature your property in an HTML readable link without any no-follow instructions (it could look like <a href= https://yoursite.com> Great hotel next door to X attraction</a>).

There is a hierarchy in the value of off-page links. Links from .gov, .edu, and .org sites seem to help a hotel's SEO more so than .com sites. However, keep in mind that you only want links back to your site that help you prove some relevancy. If you are nowhere near the White House, getting a link from the White House will not help you. However, if you have a page that promotes your Halloween specials and you have haunted rooms, an article in the New York Times linking to your hotel as a top haunted destination will be a strong asset for your authority.

In this age of influencers, links from relevant people who have credibility and trustworthiness in an area that you are trying to optimize for can be beneficial. For example, if a wedding planner includes photos from your venue on their blog or social pages, and includes a link back to your weddings page, that will add to your authority.

Having a number of irrelevant links or links from low quality sites can harm your SEO. Paying $100 to a "link farm" that simply creates sites with nothing but links will not help you appear more relevant to the search engines.

Be sure to link back to your site from any social sites you have. If you have a Facebook page, post periodically with a link back to a specific area on your website. A blog is a great way to help SEO because it enables you to frequently change and update content as well as encourage others to link to you if they are interested in what you have to say.

WHAT ARE THE BEST WAYS TO GET LINKS?

The best ways to generate links to your site are 1) content and 2) outreach. Share your content with influencers, client sites, attractions, and local demand generators, and ask for a link back. Provide the correct link to the page you have optimized for that partner's specific content.

Link reclamation can be another easy way to get links. If you used to have links from other sites to yours but they expired, or you changed URLs, be sure to update and reclaim them.

Look for opportunities with directories, groups, events, and resources pages. Try to be included with a relevant link for anything taking place at or near your property.

Finally, see who is linking to your competitors and be there too. The Link Intercept tool from Moz is very helpful for this.

OPTIMIZING FOR LOCAL SEARCH

It is important to ensure you have claimed and updated all the major directory listings including Google My Business, Yelp, Bing Places, Yahoo, and others. If you can only take care of one, ensure your Google My Business is claimed and up to date.

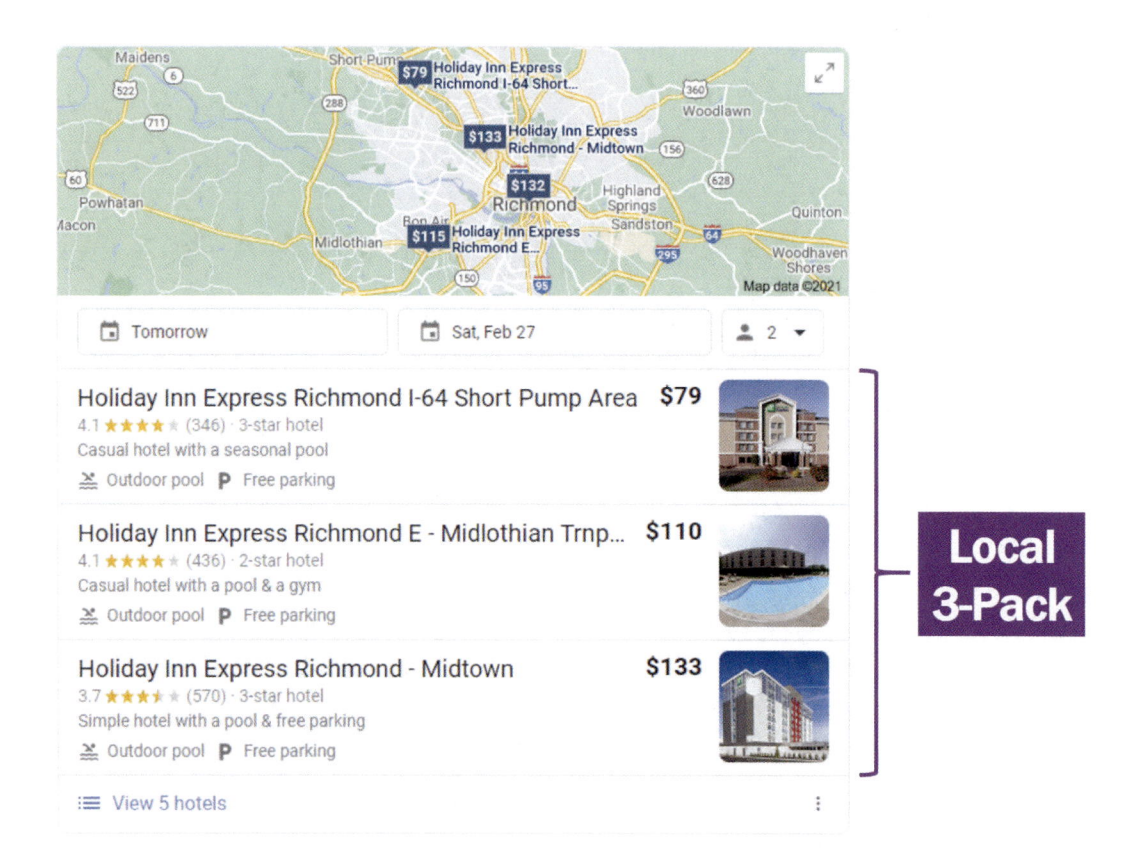

In Google, local search shows a "three pack" that appears below maps.

For most local search engines and directories, there are three primary criteria that determine your inclusion in search results:

1. Proximity: Are you near the search term?
   - Your location, determined by zip code and geo-coordinates, is important. Ensure UNAP (URL, business name, address, and phone) is correct and consistent.
2. Prominence: How important does Google think you are based on the search item?
   - What matters here is mostly off-page SEO links to you, site traffic, the number of reviews you have, and other items that position your site as the trusted authority on the property.
3. Relevance: Schema.org takes on an elevated priority in this area including:
   - Keyword-rich content
   - On-page SEO
   - Citations
   - Categories (make sure to keep Google My Business updated)
   - Business name
   - Review content (in your reviews, are people talking about what you are optimized for?)

SAMPLE CHDM EXAM QUESTIONS

1. Local demand generators are a good source for part of your keyword strategy.
    a. rue
    b. False

2. Which of the following is an example of a long tail keyword?
    a. Ocean City hotels
    b. Pet-friendly hotels
    c. Pet-friendly hotels in Ocean City Maryland
    d. Studio suites in Alabama
    e. All of the above

3. For most local search engines and directories, which criteria does NOT determine your inclusion in local search results?
    a. Proximity
    b. Schema
    c. Prominence
    d. Relevance

Answers
1= a
2 = c
3 = d

NOTES

Chapter 10: Voice Search

KEY POINTS
- Consumers are increasingly employing multiple devices and search channels–including voice search–throughout all stages of travel.
- Showing up as an answer for voice search is an evolving marketing opportunity.
- Driven by advances in artificial intelligence (AI), web and social optimization for voice search in hotel marketing is expected to increase significantly.

SUMMARY

Voice search is one of the fastest-growing types of search:

- 55% of voice search users ask questions on a smartphone.[92]
- 39.4% of U.S. internet users operate a voice assistant at least once a month.[93]

US Voice Assistant Users and Penetration, 2018-2022
millions, % change, and % of population

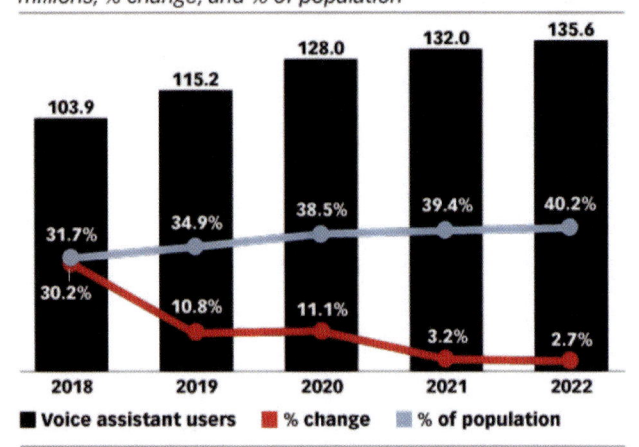

Year	Voice assistant users	% change	% of population
2018	103.9	30.2%	31.7%
2019	115.2	10.8%	34.9%
2020	128.0	11.1%	38.5%
2021	132.0	3.2%	39.4%
2022	135.6	2.7%	40.2%

Note: individuals of any age who use voice assistants at least once a month on any device
Source: eMarketer, July 2020[94]

Focusing your website (or parts of it) towards influencing featured snippets is an SEO technique that's been around for some time now, but the emergence of hands-free voice search devices brings a new importance to this strategy. If you are successful, you'll not only increase the influence of your content, but you'll also limit the influence of your competition and third-party sites by claiming the top spot—or in the case of hands-free devices, the only spot. Invest in local search and SEO, with an eye on voice search, to deliver schema-rich answers to customers' questions.

A MULTI-DEVICE WORLD IS DRIVING VOICE SEARCH

According to ComScore, the average consumer owns almost 4 connected devices. In such a fragmented, multi-device world, marketers must understand where and how their target consumers are using different devices and search channels.

Mobile devices started the revolution in search—all the way back to the original iPhone—but a new generation of "headless" devices, devices powered by AI engines like Alexa, Google Home, and Siri, are poised to further change how people search and find information. The increasing reliance on voice search has already changed the landscape of search engines—48% of consumers use voice assistants for general web search.[95]

DIGITAL PERSONAL ASSISTANTS AND HOW THEY WORK

In this world of voice-powered smartphones, speakers, home assistants, and bluetooth enabled automobiles, consumers are increasingly relying more on search to provide answers, not lists of results.

While a user might type "hotels San Francisco downtown," that same user is more likely to ask, "What five-star hotels with a spa are near downtown San Francisco?" Users are far more comfortable asking longer, more complex, more specific questions using voice than when typing. The improvements in voice-based assistants are driving this even further.

Alexa, Cortana, and Siri currently using Bing results to provide answers. Google Home uses a tool called "Google Assistant." Additionally, each system has its own unique features, which evolve regularly.

For instance, Google Assistant, benefiting from Google's enormous database of searches, does particularly well in understanding the context of what has been said. And, it now answers conversational queries—questions that are related to earlier answers—relying heavily on featured snippets (see Chapter 8) for the answers. For example, our same user might follow up the "five-star hotels" question with something like "which ones have a pool?" Obviously, with this conversational approach to search, the technology necessary to stay ahead is changing.

Due to the screen-less nature of these types of devices, the inherent difference between asking one of them a question or running the same search query on your phone is that the device will provide you with a simple answer to your question. There will be no opportunity to explore a results page, as you would on your screened device.

The Role of Structured Data in Voice Search

As covered in Chapter 9 (Making SEO Work for Your Hotel), structured data is "a standardized format for providing information about a page and classifying the page content."[96] A group effort by Google, Microsoft, Yahoo, and Yandex created Schema.org which provides a shared vocabulary that allows website content providers to more easily communicate the specific content contained on the site to search engines. By providing industry-specific content labels, content is more easily categorized for the most relevant returns. There is now even specific voice schema.

To understand the critical importance of structured data and schemas, we must look at how search engines use them. Take the question "How many five-star hotels near downtown San Francisco have a pool?" From a search engine's perspective, that question has 4 key elements:

1. Business category: hotel
2. Rating: 5 stars
3. Address: located near geolocation 37.773972, -122.431297
4. Hotel amenities: pool

Google uses your website's structured data to understand the content on the page, and to enable special search result features and enhancements like graphical search and voice search. Because the structured data labels each individual element describing the hotel, consumers can search for your hotel by rating, location, amenities, and more.[97] A current listing of data labels for hotels is at http://schema.org/docs/hotels.html.

The point? To be successful when it comes to voice search, you need to present as much of your content as possible as structured data.

OPTIMIZING FOR VOICE SEARCH

Just like the evolution of typed search, voice search has already seen its own progression. As humans tend to speak differently than they type, there are a few differences in how you should optimize for one over the other.

Context is important for voice, just as it is for any search component. Google recognizes a few different contexts currently such as location. For example, if you ask how far the airport is from the conference center, Google will take your current location into consideration and assume you mean the closest airport and convention center. Just like Google may take your previous searches into consideration, what you previously talked about may be considered.

For example, if you asked how many mountains are in Massachusetts and then asked where Mount Tom was located, you would likely get the location of Mount Tom in Massachusetts instead of the one in California.

Structured markup is very important for your site/information to show up in voice search results; in fact, there are voice schema specific markups. In addition to leveraging schema markup, employ additional best practices to optimize for voice searches:

- For voice, long tail keywords are better than short tail. Focus on optimizing for conversational long-term keywords. The easiest approach for hotels is to add a FAQ section to the website. Ask and answer questions conversationally and with detail. Or create your landing pages with the headlines as commonly asked questions by your audiences with the answers detailed in the body.

- Make sure you understand your target customer. This will help you write content more clearly targeted to that audience—using the words and phrases most often used by that demographic. Once you know your demographics, create very specific persona-based content that appeals to each key audience.
- The biggest opportunity, and threat, for hotels is that Google and Apple will take the answers to queries from any website that provides relevant answers. All major OTAs are making a significant push to dominate the organic rankings in voice search and featured snippets. It is imperative for hoteliers to ensure that the answers in featured snippets come from your website and not a third-party site. To turn content from your hotel website into a featured snippet and claim the coveted top spot, there are some general steps you can follow.

1. Identify what question(s) your content is trying to answer. It should be something relevant to your market area. It is important that the question literally appears (as it would in a search query) on your page within a header tag (e.g., h2, h3, etc.). Beneath that header, provide the content as you want it to appear in the featured snippet box. This content should be within a <p> paragraph tag.
2. Add valuable supporting information or content beyond the direct answer.
3. Make it as easy as possible for Google to find your content by adding structured data, which allows Google to better understand what type of content you have on your site.

FAQS THROUGHOUT YOUR SITE PROVIDE ANSWERS

Schemas can help you with voice-based searches that are non-branded. But how does a hotel respond to voice searches that are highly specific, and branded? For example, how do you ensure that your website answers the question: "Does the Hotel Nikko have a pool?"

Once again, part of the answer lies in schemas in your meta data, but another critical piece to the puzzle is having dynamic and properly formatted content on your site that supports what your schema is presenting. One approach that appears to be successful is the concept of Frequently Asked Questions, or FAQs. Your site can and should have a dedicated page for FAQs and the format should incorporate questions as they may be asked while speaking versus typing.

Additionally, you can provide content on multiple pages of your website to answer specific questions relevant to the page topic. For example, when you hover over the questions relevant to the hotel amenities, a pop-up answer box can be used as a voice answer. See an example of this in action at https://www.hotelnikkosf.com/amenities (available as of June 2021).

Home > Frequently Asked Questions

Frequently Asked Questions

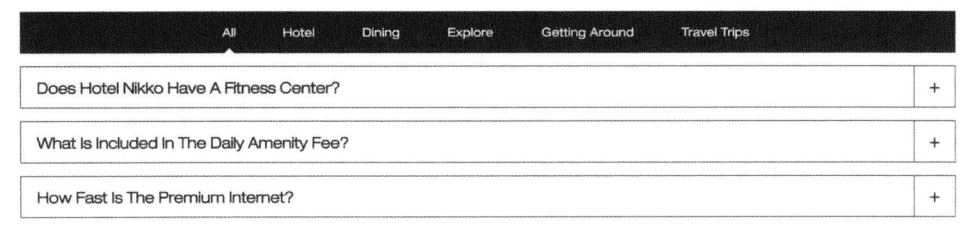

| All | Hotel | Dining | Explore | Getting Around | Travel Trips |

Does Hotel Nikko Have A Fitness Center?	+
What Is Included In The Daily Amenity Fee?	+
How Fast Is The Premium Internet?	+

The Hotel Nikko has a comprehensive FAQ page on its website.

SAMPLE CHDM EXAM QUESTIONS

1. What is a best practice for optimizing for voice? (select all that apply)
   a. Use long tail keywords
   b. Add structured data to your website to support your content
   c. Add optimized imagery
   d. Add an FAQ section to your webpage
   e. All of the above

2. There is a specific voice schema available.
   a. True
   b. False

Answers
1 = a, b, d
2 = a

NOTES

Chapter 11: Email Marketing

KEY POINTS
- Three primary categories of email: Transactional, Promotional, and Relational
- Six steps of the customer journey as it applies to email marketing
- Using email marketing to entice new customers through lead nurturing
- Email marketing analytics

SUMMARY

People have been ringing the death knell of email for years, but it is still the single best performing marketing asset in terms of return on investment. It is up to 40 times more effective than social media, and the buying process happens 3 times faster than on social media.[98] Statistically, there are indicators that show that there is still growing potential for email marketing.

Email marketing is the workhorse of digital tools available to marketers. But like any tool, it needs to be used for the appropriate job—as the guest moves along the digital journey from awareness through booking to after the stay.

EMAIL AND THE CUSTOMER JOURNEY

Email marketing is an integral part of the hotel's direct online channel strategy and marketing mix, and is crucial to digital customer relationship management. Hoteliers must always be searching for new guests, communicating with current guests, and maintaining contact with past customers as they are the most likely to book the hotel again since they are already familiar with the product. Email marketing serves a lot of different functions, and it is critical to identify the right time to send the right messaging to your guests. This means the creation and segmenting of customer lists, crafting compelling messaging, and making offers based on what is appealing to that customer at that time.

There are three primary categories of email—transactional, relational, and promotional.

Where your customer can be found along the journey to purchase and beyond will drive the type of email that should be utilized. In the world of email marketing, these are the steps of your customer's journey.

1. Awareness
Your customer is in the dream phase or in the very early planning stages of the hotel visit. They may be thinking of planning a wedding or a business meeting on the group side. For transients, this might mean they are planning a vacation, taking the kids on a tour of colleges, or moving across country. This is the very beginning of the journey and more likely than not, asking for a hotel booking at this juncture would be premature.

2. Engage
Once you have been able to make a prospective guest aware of your property or brand, the next step on the email journey is to engage them. Entice them by sharing what is unique about your destination, brand, or property.

3. Subscribe
In email terms this is the point in the guest's journey where they are willing to share some information with you because they are both aware of your property and engaged enough to want to know more. A typical email at this phase might include an invitation to join a brand loyalty club or subscribe to your blog or newsletter service.

4. Convert
At this point your prospect may have visited your website, or even done a site inspection of your property with your group sales managers. Your goal in this step is to move them to purchase.

5. Excite
Post-purchase, pre-stay is the stage where your future guest is most likely to read and respond to any email they receive. It will be critical to use this time to further educate and create enthusiasm on the part of your guest about your property or brand.

6. Stay
The guest is onsite, and the role of any email during this phase will be to further educate and engage your guest.

7. Advocate
The guest has left your property and your goal in this phase is to invite the guest to share their experiences (assuming they were positive!).

8. Promote
Invite your guest to return to your property or brand, or to invite their friends or business associates to try your property or brand.

It is critical at each step of the journey to apply the type of email that is appropriate. For example, in the awareness and engage phases, you will likely use promotional emails because you don't have an existing relationship with the guest, so both transactional and relational are not as likely to result in moving that guest to the next step.

The subscribe, convert, excite, and stay phases are best addressed through a mix of relational and transactional emails. The advocate and promote stages are typically covered by relational and promotional emails. The following lists break down each email category into the roles it often plays.

Transactional Email Examples
- reservation confirmation
- confirming loyalty membership
- sending receipts post stay
- loyalty account creation
- newsletter subscription confirmation
- support tickets
- password reminders
- unsubscribe confirmations

Relational Email Examples
- welcome series to new subscribers or loyalty club members
- newsletter/blog
- survey/review
- updates and information
- contest announcements

Promotional Email Examples
- promotional content
- flash sale announcement
- new product announcements—renovations, new services, etc.
- event announcements
- trial offer
- upgrade offer

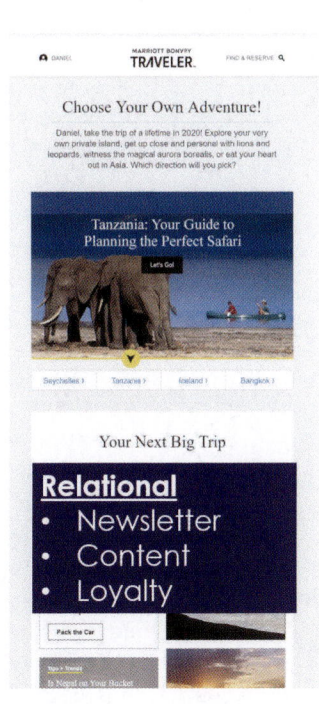

Source: Hotel Digital Marketing Essentials course materials

BEST PRACTICES: LEAD NURTURING

The focus of lead nurturing is on the ongoing relationship you have with a past or future guest, cultivating it not only through their experience at your property but also through their interaction with your hotel digitally.

Lead nurturing should have a large role in your digital marketing strategy. It begins with what is vital to your email marketing efforts: focusing on the collection of new email addresses as needed to grow your email marketing database. This collection can then be expanded and built on to foster a prosperous relationship with these new leads. It is important to remember that what you do once you have those addresses is just as important to the potential revenue-generating relationship as it is to gather them initially and amass a larger audience.

Bought or purchased lists do not constitute valid leads, as those recipients are not necessarily interested in your property, product, or offer and will likely either opt-out or their email addresses will be invalid. It is better to invest your time and resources in growing your database organically with leads that can be nurtured into a prosperous relationship.

BEST PRACTICES: GROWING YOUR EMAIL LIST

Consider the following best practices for gathering new email addresses and maintaining your relationships with your fresh, new leads:

- **Opt-in via a collection form on your website:** Make sure you provide leads with a place to indicate what they are interested in receiving (e.g., golf specials, dining offers, etc.) so that you can cater to those interests with your marketing materials later.
- **Upon making a reservation:** Whether a new reservation comes in through a phone call or a reservation request online, make sure those guests' email addresses are being collected. You can make it a required field on your booking engines or reservation pages.
- **Upon check in:** If a guest is part of a group or booked through an OTA, you may not have had a chance to collect their email prior to their stay and can certainly do so when they check in at the front desk.
- **Upon check out:** If the guest's email address still hasn't been secured by the time a guest checks out, make sure that you request a valid email address so that they can be sent a follow-up email after their stay.
- **At various outlets on property (restaurants, spas, etc.):** Email addresses captured to reserve dining or appointment times can also be used when sending interest-based marketing pieces.
- **With the sales team:** Email addresses collected by your sales teams at conferences and conventions are also great leads to nurture with digital marketing.
- **Through contests:** While buying lists is usually not effective, contests (e.g., win a weekend at the hotel) that get people excited about the potential of staying at your property, and at the same time collect email addresses, can significantly grow your list of prospective guests.

BEST PRACTICES: NURTURING NEW EMAIL ADDRESSES THROUGH DIGITAL MARKETING EFFORTS

Obtaining email addresses at any point in the reservation process allows you to not only secure those leads for future marketing purposes, but it allows you to start nurturing those guests and providing them with a higher level of service before they even step on property.

Prior to their stay send them reservation confirmations and pre-arrival pieces with options to upgrade or sign-up for specific requests. This allows you to paint a vivid picture of the high level of service they can expect from you while on property.

While on property, present them, via email, with an opportunity to take advantage of a special offer at an on-property outlet, or just inquire about their stay. You'll enhance your presence and start to build a dialogue with your guests.

After their stay, send a follow-up survey allowing them to provide feedback concerning their time spent at your property, continuing the dialogue after their stay, and helping to increase the quality of future stays. To increase repeat business, you can then send automatically triggered offers throughout the year, based on learned stay and booking behavior.

An email service provider (ESP) that directly interfaces into your property management system or customer marketing database will be able to provide you with customized, triggered emails, as well as the ability to send targeted marketing messages based on things like geography, preferences, etc. If you are not using an ESP that directly interfaces with your property management system, it may be time to incorporate that into your marketing budget. The hospitality industry has a huge advantage over other industries in that there is so much information about our past and loyal customers (guests) at our fingertips waiting to be extracted from the property management system or customer database. Combined with our opted-in leads, you can target them with specific messages in the future.

Digital marketing to any lead, whether it came from an opt-in system or a reservations system, should focus on and adhere to the best practices of email marketing.

BEST PRACTICES: EMAIL MARKETING

Several factors need to be considered prior to launching any email campaign.

- TARGETING: To whom will you mail? Past customers tend to be most responsive (assuming a generally positive past experience). It is better to have a smaller, well targeted list. Determining where you will obtain your list should be your first step. Does your list comply with opt-in compliance?
- COPYWRITING: What will your subject line say to entice your targeted list? What will you be selling? What will your offer be?
- DESIGN: Visually, how will you support your message? Is there a photograph that showcases the element of your property that would be particularly appealing to your targeted audience?
- DELIVERY AND DEPLOYMENT: How will you send the email? Will you use a software company like Constant Contact or ExactTarget? What links will you have back to your website? What action will you ask your audience to take? Are the links working and landing pages operational?
- MEASUREMENT: Start with a goal—opens, clicks, revenue producers—and then measure your results to that goal. If you fell short, at what point along the way did you miss the target? Was it the wrong list? Was it the wrong offer?
- TESTING: Each element of your email can have a dramatic impact on your success, so always test and verify results. Try new subject lines, change your offers, or change the visuals. Repeat successes and learn from failures.

Additional best practices include the following:

- Plan your email marketing campaigns the same way you plan any other quarterly or yearly marketing schedule. Start with a purpose, and make sure your emails are purpose-driven and will support your other marketing efforts to attain specific goals.
- Every email should be planned so that timing is taken into consideration on a large scale, with each email having a goal or specific purpose behind it. Do not send emails just to send emails. It will end up decreasing your response rates for future campaigns when you have something of value to offer or mention.
- Segment your email lists by market and customer type (meeting planner, leisure traveler, business traveler, geography, etc.) and tailor your marketing messages to target consumers strategically.
- Consolidate past guest email addresses from your property management system, booking engine, and past customer relationship management databases.
- Segment the data you have from your property management system not only to target customers by market or customer type but also by their past purchasing behavior (booking date, stay dates, amount spent, rooms stayed in, etc.) to even better tailor your messages.
- Each message should present a concrete offer, available only for a limited time to create urgency. Include a direct and easy-to-follow booking link or instructions.
- Ensure the landing page you are driving your customers to is consistent with the creative, the message, and the call to action that is in your email to provide the best customer experience.
- Design your pieces so that they are responsive to whichever device, email software, or browser they are viewed in, automat-

ically optimizing the piece to be viewed and responded to from any device.
- Strong and short subject lines are key.
- Create clean, enticing designs, in line with other branding and marketing efforts, so that the guests can associate the offer with your property.
- Be concise. In email marketing, less is more, driving deliverability rates upward as well as increasing the likelihood of response and action on your offer/message.
- Comply with GDPR, the CAN-SPAM Act, and other regulations while respecting customers' privacy and the frequency with which they desire to receive marketing messages.
- After a campaign has been sent, analyze the reporting statistics to see the response to different aspects of the email: day of week it was sent, time it was sent, how many links/materials were included, and bookings generated. Adjust aspects of your future emails based on the information learned from previous campaigns. It is all part of the process to determine what works best for your specific audiences and property.
- On property, request guests' business cards or contact information upon check-in or via in-room questionnaires to build your email databases.
- On the hotel's website, an email sign-up widget should be present on the home page so that email addresses can be collected from people who have an interest in receiving your email. Also, have a dedicated "Stay Connected" page.
- Your Facebook page should also have a "Stay Connected" widget that allows people to submit their email addresses directly to your database.

BEST PRACTICES: FUNCTIONALITY REQUIREMENTS FOR EMAIL MARKETING SYSTEMS

Your email marketing system should be able to:
- perform A/B testing
- resend bounces
- support multiple IP addresses
- allow for bounce/media domains

BEST PRACTICES: EMAIL TEMPLATE DESIGN

Because photos sell a destination and hotel, hotel email template designs should support multiple images. Templates should also allow for multiple sections of copy to appeal to various customer segments. Include social media icons (Facebook, Twitter, YouTube, Tripadvisor, etc.).

Though each email you send will have a slightly different purpose, all should include a call to action that links to the hotel's website. You might direct them to a custom landing page for the campaign, to specific content, or even straight into an offer in the booking widget. The key is to take them to a place that relates directly to the link on which they clicked.

BEST PRACTICES: EMAIL ANALYTICS

Email is one of your most effective owned media marketing tools. It is also one of the best marketing vehicles to track and optimize since you have full control over everything from messaging to tracking and testing.

You are likely using an ESP (Email Service Provider) or a CRM system to send your emails. This system, along with your analytics program, will give you key data points that will enable you to optimize campaigns, determine success, and gather key learnings for future campaigns.

Key Metrics: Health of Email List
- DELIVERABILITY RATE: Your email may never make it to the intended recipient for many reasons, like throttling, bounces, spam issues, bulking, incorrect address, and flagged content to name a few. When these issues arise, they need to be addressed. A good deliverability rate is 95% or higher. To calculate, divide Number of Delivered Emails by Emails Sent.
- BOUNCE RATE: Your bounce rate should not be higher than 3%. To calculate is, divide Bounces by Emails Sent.
  - HARD BOUNCES: the number of emails returned because the recipient address was invalid
  - SOFT BOUNCES: the number of emails returned because the recipient's mailbox is full, the server is temporarily unavailable, or the recipient no longer has an email account at that address

- EMAIL LIST GROWTH RATE: A healthy email list will continue to grow over time. Efforts should be made to grow this list, including front desk opt-in, wifi opt-in, website opt-in, contact center opt-in, contests that encourage opt-in, and so on. If your property or brand has a loyalty program, email capture is often done through them. Calculate by dividing New Subscribers minus Unsubscribes by the Total List Size.

Key Metrics: Email Effectiveness

- OPEN RATE: How many receivers opened the email, which tells you the effectiveness of the subject line. Calculated by dividing Opens by Delivered (Emails Sent minus Bounced Emails). If 1000 are delivered and 200 are opened, 200/1000 = 20%.
- CLICK THROUGH RATE (CTR): Provides insight into the overall effectiveness of the email. Calculate it by dividing the Number of Emails in Which Content was Clicked by emails Delivered (Emails Sent minus Bounced Emails). If 1000 are delivered and 20 clicked through to the website, 20/1000 = 2%.
- CLICK-TO-OPEN RATE (CTOR): This number of emails that are opened and then clicked gives you insights into the effectiveness of the content in the email. If 200 are opened and 20 clicked through, 20/200 = 10%
- EMAIL UNSUBSCRIBE RATE: This can be a sign that your email content is not effective, or that there is an issue with the health of your email list. Calculate it by dividing Unsubscribes by Emails Delivered.
- LANDING PAGE BOUNCE RATE: While this is more of a website metric, it is important to understand what happens to the clicks when they land on the site. A high bounce rate tells you the landing page is not as effective as it should be.

Key Metrics: Campaign Success

- CONVERSION RATE: How many of the people who received the email completed the email's desired action (book, enter contest, join loyalty program, etc.)? Calculate by dividing Those Who Completed the Desired Action by Emails Delivered.
- REVENUE: There are many ways to calculate the revenue generated for the overall campaign, like revenue per email, average order value, and so on. More often than not, you see this calculated at the campaign level.
- ROI: Determining your return on investment in email is sometimes difficult as often many of the costs are internal. Regardless, is still important to benchmark it. You will need to determine what is included in the "investment." For example, will you only include external costs (e.g., payment to agencies), or will you also include estimated internal costs of sending the campaign? Regardless of what you do, be consistent. To calculate, divide Revenue minus Investment by Investment.

Most of these metrics can be tracked in your ESP, but once the customer hits the website, you will need to use your website analytics tool (Google Analytics, Adobe Analytics, etc.) to track the performance. This requires the campaigns be tagged and set up on these platforms to track them properly. You can track email campaigns, using Google Analytics for example, by adding parameters to URLs in each email marketing message. These will denote which visitors arrive as a result of each email marketing campaign. The values contained in each link will report back:

- CAMPAIGN SOURCE: who is sending the message (an e-mail provider, for example)
- CAMPAIGN MEDIUM: which instrument is being used to send the message
- CAMPAIGN NAME: each campaign should be named, so one can differentiate the results and effectiveness of each one. Usually for an email campaign, it is the subject line.

Key Email Metrics

- **Delivery Rate**
  - ✓ If 1200 sent & 1000 delivered, delivery rate is 1000/12000=83%
- **Open Rate**
  - ✓ If 1000 delivered & 200 opened, open rate is 200/1000=20%
- **Click Through Rate (CTR)**
  - ✓ If 1000 delivered & 20 clicked to website, CTR is 20/1000=2%
- **Click To Open Rate (CTOR)**
  - ✓ If 200 opened & 20 clicked a link, CTOR is 20/200=10%

BEST PRACTICES: AUDIT, OPTIMIZE, AND TEST EMAIL MARKETING CAMPAIGNS

By using A/B testing, remarketing, and strategic variations of emails each month, hotel marketers can audit past campaigns and optimize future ones for the best results. Headlines can be tested, as can specific offers and specific calls to action (e.g., book now, request more information, have someone contact me, etc.).

Some email systems enable real time A/B testing. You can test two emails against each other for a subset of your database, and have the system select the "winner" to send to the rest of the database.

BEST PRACTICES: CONNECTING WITH GLOBAL CUSTOMERS THROUGH EMAIL CAMPAIGNS

Global email campaigns can reach and connect with customers effectively. But with billions of emails sent daily and a human tendency to have a short attention span, crafting emails that stand out is a challenge.

So how do you compete in today's noisy international markets? Include some language and locale-specific adaptation so your emails resonate with customers. You'll drive a stronger campaign return on investment and stand out from competitors.

Some useful suggestions for effective global email campaigns are:

- Above all, be aware and respectful of local opt-in laws and privacy regulations. They constantly evolve, and they differ from country to country.
- Segment your audience by language and locale preferences. This helps you target the right audience with the right content.
- Localize your emails so they are both in the reader's language and relevant to their culture. For instance, be aware of current local events (e.g., Singles Day in China, religious holidays, etc.).
- Use culturally appropriate imagery and colors that resonate with your audience.
- Be sure to craft your email greetings correctly. Email best practices recommend you use personalized greetings because they have a 6x higher transaction rate and 41% higher click rates. But remember that in many languages, the gender of the addressee changes the structure of the greeting.
- Optimize your emails so they 'respond' well to a smartphone email application and browser. They're likely to be viewed on mobile devices.

Key Email Components

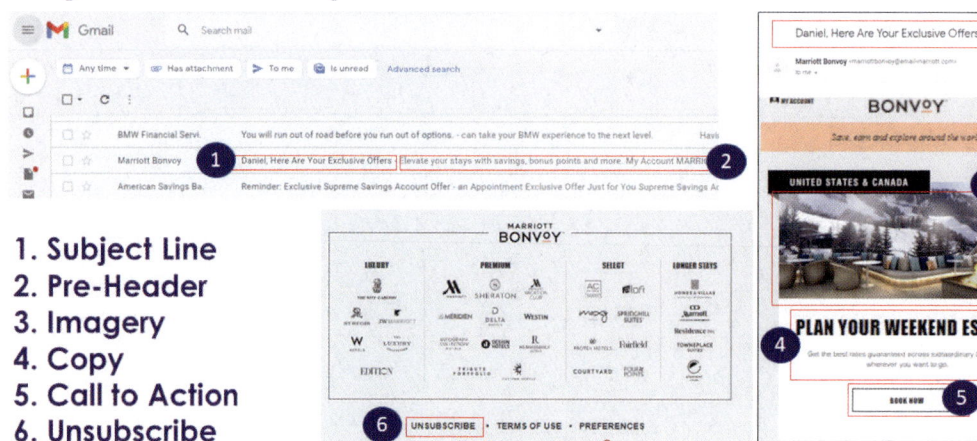

1. Subject Line
2. Pre-Header
3. Imagery
4. Copy
5. Call to Action
6. Unsubscribe

SAMPLE CHDM EXAM QUESTIONS

1. Which of the following metrics should be used in email marketing campaigns? (select all that apply)
   a. Bounce Rate
   b. Delivery Rate
   c. Click Through Rate
   d. Open Rate
   e. All of the above

2. Which of the following is not a primary category of email?
   a. Transactional
   b. Functional
   c. Relational
   d. Promotional

3. Which of the following metrics is used to measure email campaigns?
   a. Click to Open Rate
   b. Open Rate
   c. Click Through Rate
   d. Delivery Rate
   e. All of the above

Answers
1 = e
2 = b
3 = e

NOTES

Chapter 12: Customer Relationship Management (CRM)

> **KEY POINTS**
> - Hotels have so much data about their guests. Use that data to improve the guest experience before, during, and post-stay.
> - A strong CRM strategy helps hotels close the loop on the travel planning and booking journey, and helps hotels acquire, engage, and retain their best guests.
> - CRM data can help fuel new guest acquisition. By using the data hotels have about their own guests, they can build look-alike and act-alike audiences to reach future guests. Using this strategy, marketing dollars go farther and deliver higher ROIs.

SUMMARY

Today's customer journey is increasingly complex in the multi-device, multi-channel, and multi-touch point digital landscape. Considering this complexity, hotel marketers can no longer afford to have a fragmented customer engagement and acquisition approach. CRM can halt this fragmentation and help hoteliers develop a single view of their guest, which they can use to deliver more targeted and personalized messaging throughout the guest journey—ultimately providing a better experience on- and off-property and driving higher loyalty and guest conversion through direct booking channels.

WHAT IS CRM?

CRM (Customer Relationship Management) means using data to develop a 360° view of each guest, and ensuring they receive the most targeted, dynamic, and relevant communication no matter where they are in the customer journey. CRM also allows hotels to know who their best guests are in terms of how often they stay at the property or with the brand, their preferences, and how much revenue the guest spends. Once you know that, you can recognize and tailor the on-property experience to guests' preferences and determine the potential lifetime value (LTV) of your guests.

A good CRM technology platform must integrate into a hotel's existing tech stack and connect with systems like PMS, CRS, RMS, and other data sources.

FUNDAMENTALS OF A CRM STRATEGY

One Central View of the Guest

A guest data management platform (DMP) should be cloud based, able to store data profiles, and provide one clean view of the hotel guest. This DMP should serve as the "smart" data layer incorporating past guest data extracted from the PMS, CRS, and other guest data sources. It should continuously update, cleanse, and enrich customer profiles to serve as the main "guest knowledge depository" for ongoing guest engagement and retention, as well as new guest acquisition efforts. This platform should be able to dedupe and combine several guest profiles if they belong to one guest (i.e., one guest may have different profiles because they have provided different email addresses in the past). This allows the hotel to recognize their loyal guests on property, as well as on the hotel website and throughout digital marketing initiatives.

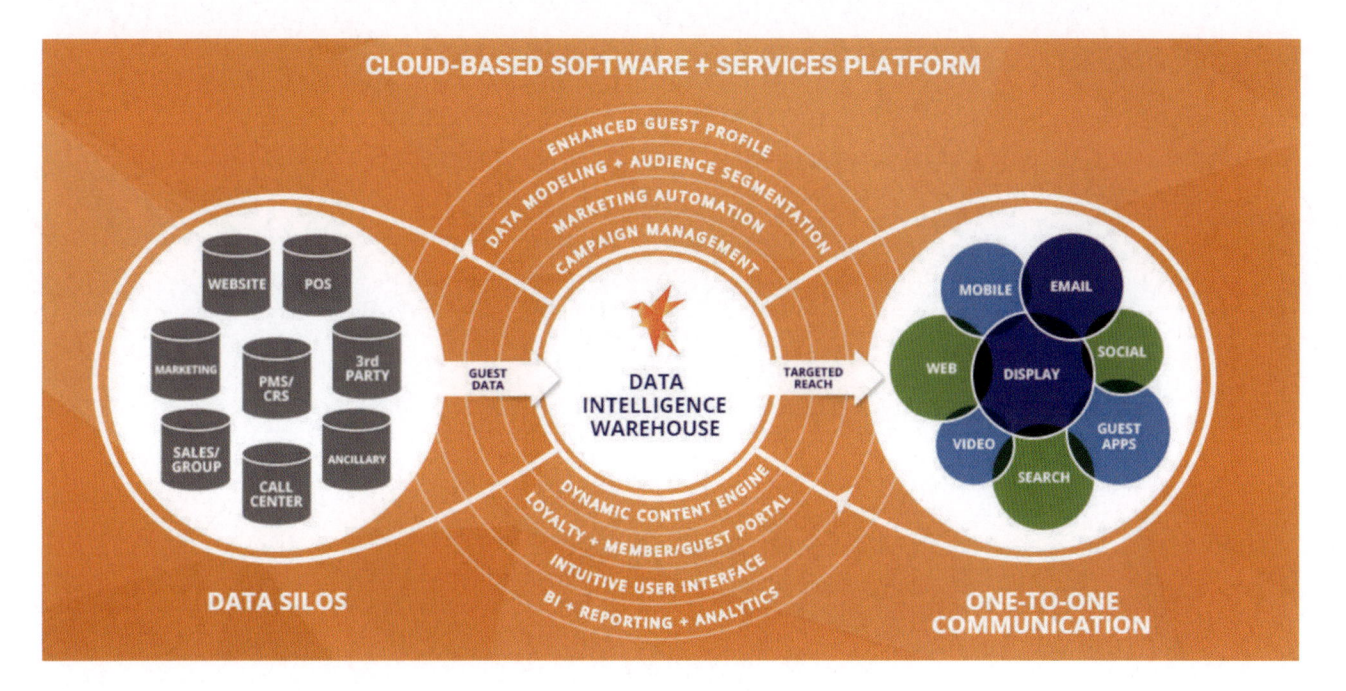

The potential complexity of a CRM system[99]

Guest Communications
Automated transactional emails engage customers with personalized guest communications, such as pre-stay, in-stay, and post-stay emails, cancellation emails, guest surveys, and more.

Guest Marketing Automation
Marketing automation tied to CRM data allows a hotel property to initiate or schedule targeted and highly personalized email marketing campaigns.

Loyalty/Guest Recognition
Mid-size and smaller hotel chain, luxury, or boutique hotel brands or even independent hotels and resorts must be able to recognize and reward repeat guests through either a comprehensive reward/loyalty program (points or perks) or through a guest recognition and appreciation program.

TODAY'S FRAGMENTED APPROACH TO HOTEL DATA

In years past, hotel data resided in silos and information was not readily shared by systems, either due to technology issues or vendors' reluctance to integrate with potential competitors. These systems were often referred to as "walled gardens" where everything was contained within the walls.

In recent years there has been greater understanding of the need to connect systems through APIs (Application Programming Interfaces) and allow disparate systems to share data. Through this, along with the adoption and accessibility of cloud computing, the hotel industry has seen an explosion of companies that can add functionality to a hotel's current tech stack, and fortunately many CRM systems are now able to "plug-in" to the hotel's various data sources. This allows hotels access to a real 360° view of the customer, enabling more effective marketing and better customer experience—leading us closer to the goal of personalization.

By tying a CRM strategy into a hotel's website, technology, and marketing strategies, the marketer can do a better job of engaging, retaining, and acquiring guests throughout the customer journey. Not only is this more efficient and effective for driving direct bookings, but it is incomparable when it comes to growing the hotel's bond with customers and their lifetime value.

HOW CAN CRM GO A STEP FURTHER?

Using CRM data, hotels can acquire new guests by capitalizing on the knowledge of past guests. Everything should function in one seamless ecosystem to "close the loop" in a hotel's past and future guest engagement, retention, and acquisition. This includes:

- PERSONALIZATION: Fully integrated with the guest DMP, hotel websites should be able to deliver dynamically personalized content and promotions on the hotel website based on users' past booking history, preferences, loyalty program affiliation, demographics, geolocation, website behavior, or market segment affiliation.
- SMART DATA MARKETING: Smart data marketing takes full advantage of "owned data" (past guest data, demographics, website data, etc.) and then layers on real-time travel planning insights and intent data points to target in-market potential guests during the travel planning process to a property's destination. Smart data marketing should utilize programmatic advertising and dynamic rate marketing.
- ACQUISITION MARKETING: This type of marketing should utilize knowledge from past guests to target and acquire new guests through direct response and evergreen digital marketing initiatives such as SEO, paid media, programmatic display, and dynamic rate marketing. Acquisition marketing also includes seasonal and targeted multichannel campaigns with one cohesive message across channels to answer occupancy needs, target current and new segments, capitalize on events and holidays, and more.

CONCLUSION

When a hotel CRM strategy is incorporated into the overall strategy of acquiring guests, a hotel can truly engage a travel consumer at every touchpoint in their travel planning journey. Here is a snapshot of what this journey looks like, and how hoteliers can be there every step of the way.

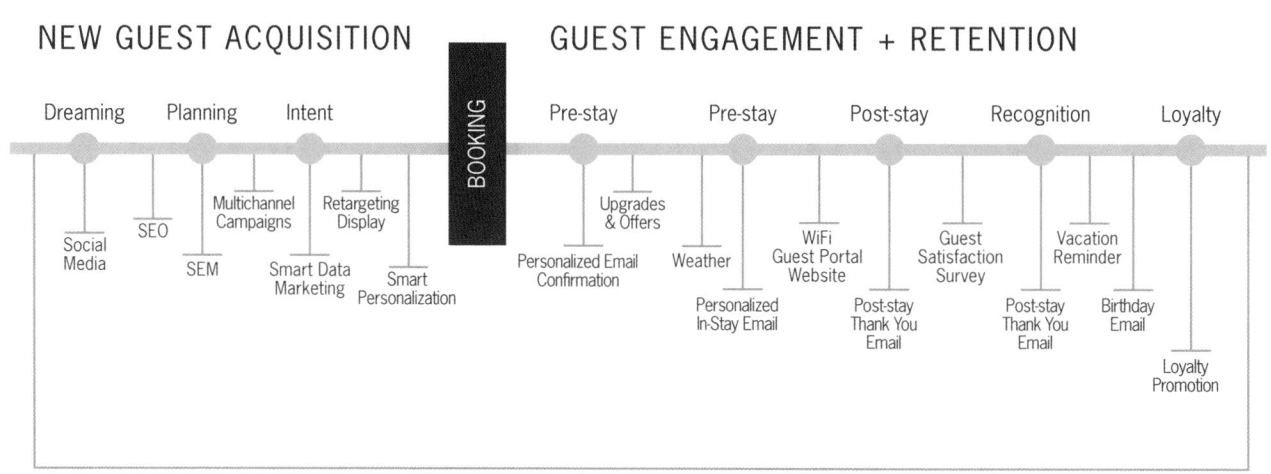

NEW GUEST ACQUISITION

- **Dreaming**: Social Media
- **Planning**: SEO, SEM, Multichannel Campaigns
- **Intent**: Smart Data Marketing, Retargeting Display, Smart Personalization

BOOKING

GUEST ENGAGEMENT + RETENTION

- **Pre-stay**: Personalized Email Confirmation, Upgrades & Offers
- **Pre-stay**: Weather, Personalized In-Stay Email
- **Post-stay**: WiFi Guest Portal Website, Post-stay Thank You Email, Guest Satisfaction Survey
- **Recognition**: Post-stay Thank You Email, Vacation Reminder, Birthday Email
- **Loyalty**: Loyalty Promotion

THE CUSTOMER JOURNEY COMES FULL CIRCLE

SAMPLE CHDM EXAM QUESTIONS

1. CRM is used to:
   a. Create financial forecasts
   b. Automate revenue management
   c. Enable customer feedback loop
   d. Give a 360° view of the customer

2. Effective hotel CRM systems can:
   a. Pull from multiple data sources
   b. Create customer profiles
   c. Integrate with marketing platforms
   d. All of the above

3. Which technology development has enabled CRM to become a reality in the hotel space?
   a. ARI
   b. RMS
   c. API
   d. XYZ

Answers
1 = a
2 = d
3 = c

NOTES

Chapter 13: Loyalty & Recognition

> **KEY POINTS**
> - Loyalty programs reward and recognize customers when they continue to engage in desired behaviors and build stronger brand ties.
> - Loyalty programs are not limited to points but can include leveraging deep knowledge of personal preferences to customize service, and surprise, delight, and enrich the traveler's journey with content. Recent studies have shown that recognition is often even more important than the rewards.
> - A new category of loyalty engagement is emerging fueled by mobile technology: guest experience management.
> - Loyalty marketing is emerging as a potential differentiator by brands to direct their bookings to the brand.com sites.

SUMMARY

In the previous chapter we discussed CRM, which allows you to get a better view of your customers. The logical extension of that is rewarding and recognizing your best customers through loyalty programs.

Loyalty programs have become a core offering for larger hotel chains, many online travel agencies, and increasingly, independent hotels. Large, branded point-based programs provide participants with several benefits including room upgrades, check-in amenities, preferred room availability, and the most sought-after reward—free nights.

Increasingly, however, independent hotels and small groups are leveraging the same program fundamentals and technologies to develop subtle, "behind the scenes" loyalty programs with guest recognition and preference management at their cores. The objective of these programs is to differentiate by providing customized service, and to "surprise and delight." These programs may not rely on a formal system, but they utilize CRM data to recognize best guests and reward them. In its simplest form it might be an arrivals list that is given to the front desk to welcome return guests in some manner.

These programs can be complex to manage and costly to offer, but many brands see them as necessary components of their marketing mix. Loyalty programs offer the digital marketer a treasure trove of data, as well as the holy grail of web analytics—multichannel customer tracking.

THE EVOLUTION OF LOYALTY

Although it was not the first loyalty program, American Airlines launched the first frequent flier program in 1981. Two important environmental changes set the stage: deregulation, and computerization of reservation systems. Prior to deregulation, airlines' advertising and marketing efforts were largely image based, and were used to differentiate commodity products from one another. Loyalty programs as we know them today would not be possible without data storage and data-mining systems.

Holiday Inn and Marriott were the first hotel brands to enter the loyalty program arena, with both launching programs in 1983. At first, these programs simply fed into the airline programs as additional ways to earn points or miles toward free flights. It didn't take long, however, for hotels to get into the business of redeeming loyalty currency for free room nights and other perks.

Today, a whole new category of loyalty has emerged around guest experience management with technology at its core, mobile devices as the point of engagement between the hotel and the guest, loyalty technology as the facilitator, and the fundamentals of a loyalty programs as the outcome. The digital marketer now has additional opportunities to leverage loyalty and build a relationship with the guest throughout the lifecycle: research (website, travel agent), booking (website, call center, travel agent, OTA), pre-arrival (e-concierge, mobile app, mobile check in, and using mobile as the room key), on property (PMS, mobile concierge app), check out (PMS, online, mobile app), and post-stay (loyalty program app).

GOALS OF LOYALTY MARKETING

Hotel loyalty programs are no longer just about accruing and redeeming points—they provide an enhanced, personalized experience for every member. Loyalty programs allow companies to gather data and insights on customers that they can use to provide a personalized experience. Digital technology allows companies to further personalize the experience and give customers more choice and control over their travel.

Loyalty marketing can have several goals, depending on your hotel's overall strategy, for example:

- retain the best and most profitable customers
- make good customers better
- acquire customers with potential to be best customers
- reconnect with customers who left the brand
- build strong brand ties by engaging with customers through the guest lifecycle with personalized content
- prevent customers from switching to competitors
- provide insights into customer behavior and preferences
- make each customer feel valued and appreciated

Loyalty programs, when well executed, recognize and reward the best customers who continue to engage in desired behaviors. These programs are promoted in ongoing conversations with a customer. They can entice customers to stretch beyond their normal behavior with aspirational elite tiers. In the airline world, for example, so called "mileage runs" are common among travelers looking to get to the next elite status. Similarly, hotel guests may book additional stays to qualify for elite perks in the next year.

By partnering with credit card companies, loyalty programs can also target customers who will potentially be among their best. These partnerships typically include extensive direct marketing and customer segmentation opportunities so the message can be customized and made appealing to various target markets.

Loyalty marketing offers a way for brands to reconnect with customers who may have left the brand. As with customer relationship management, loyalty programs offer several metrics and vehicles to identify customers who are likely to, or have already, left the brand. The digital marketer, can then create and deliver a rich offer to re-engage the customer. Retaining a customer is much cheaper than acquiring a new one.

TAKING BACK CUSTOMERS

Brands began seeing their loyalty members as a way to attract customers to book direct on their websites versus the OTAs to decrease distribution costs and create a stronger bond with their loyalty members. Some offer discounts for loyalty members to book direct on the brand.com site while others are beginning to offer upgraded services or perks. Continuing to enhance the loyalty experience once on site and post stay will likely be the winners in the battle for the customer.

There are five common characteristics of loyalty programs: accrual, redemption, elite tiers, partners, and acting on personal preferences.

Accrual

All loyalty programs are based on repeat activity. Loyalty programs develop their own currency, which members can earn by engaging in specified activities, such as staying a night in a hotel. For marketers, loyalty programs offer the ability to streamline the booking path and reduce friction by pre-populating form fields with customer name and address information, all provided by the customer upon registering for the program.

Accrual can also be non-point based, or what are known as soft benefits. Much the same way as room nights or stays can be counted and converted into points, soft benefits like upgrades can be accrued based on a repeated activity and redeemed from an accrual account. Most loyalty program management technology can accommodate this type of program.

Redemption

The "what's-in-it-for-me" element of loyalty programs, redemption involves exchanging the loyalty program's currency for something of value. Gamification has expanded the definition of "something of value" to include digital badges, access to exclusive online content (extra game levels), and "power-ups," items that have no value in the real world but enhance the digital experience for the customer.

Elite Tiers

Many programs offer members additional benefits when they reach certain thresholds of activity in a given period. These additional benefits are often combined into tiers, or status levels. Benefits vary widely by brand, but may include accrual bonuses, late check-out, special reservations line, free wifi, room upgrades, etc. These higher levels within the program serve as aspirational targets designed to drive more activity.

Partners

Nearly all loyalty programs offer some cross-promotional opportunities by incorporating partners. From the beginning, American Airlines partnered with Hertz and Hyatt to offer AAdvantage members access to additional travel benefits, or to allow members to accrue miles for activity with these partners.

Acting on Personal Preferences

By tracking and building comprehensive profiles of customers, personalized service can be structured, building loyalty. Also, deep insights into guest preferences and actions can be gleaned pre-stay, on property, or post-stay, and content customization can be leveraged to build loyalty and brand ties.

One of the fundamentals of all loyalty programs is a robust profile management system that can provide a single guest identifier and "single source of truth." Sometimes referred to as a "gold guest profile," it is the profile system of record that ties or updates all other systems involved in the guest experience.

Marketers have in loyalty programs the holy grail of analytics: a unique identifier. When joining loyalty programs, members are assigned a number, login, member name, or some other unique identifier that is attached to all activity. By encouraging loyalty program members to log in to the brand's website early in the visit, marketers can track the member across the site. This ID also solves the issue of how to track an individual across devices. In today's multi-screen world, customers may research on a laptop, transact on a tablet, and further engage on a smartphone. Cookies are widely cross-device, but a unique ID that a customer voluntarily offers allows marketers to connect the dots across devices.

LOYALTY & RECOGNITION AND THE INDEPENDENT HOTEL/BRAND

While loyalty programs have mostly been the domain of the big brands, smaller brands and independent hotels have developed approaches to try to get the benefits associated with these programs and to help better compete with the big brands. Approaches include building their own unique programs, like Kimpton Karma (prior to the IHG acquisition of Kimpton), joining a coalition like Global Hotel Alliance, being part of a soft brand like Preferred Hotels, choosing an "off the shelf" program like Stash Rewards, or looking at relatively new entrants in the space like TheGuestbook. Independent brands and hotels need to carefully weigh the costs and benefits of these approaches.

INCORPORATING LOYALTY PROGRAMS INTO A DIGITAL MARKETING STRATEGY

Best Practices: Call to Action

Always include a "join now" prompt in any digital communication; this serves for lead generation, as well as providing a secondary way for consumers not yet ready to purchase to interact with the business.

Best Practices: Customize, Customize, Customize

Through loyalty programs, marketers learn a lot about individuals. Use that information to customize the experience for that guest. Loyalty member data can also be used to customize content for non-members by establishing a "looks like" approach.

Best Practices: Connect the Dots

A unique identifier, such as a member number, can connect the dots across various programs and platforms, not only for the marketer but for the consumer as well. Providing a common experience in new media, such as logging into a loyalty program, extends the connection the consumer already has with the brand and makes the new engagement more comfortable for the consumer.

Best Practices: Incorporate Experience

Personalize content and promote soft benefits (non-point related rewards like upgrades). Leveraging all you know about a guest can be a great way to deliver personalized content during all phases of the guest experience. Leverage all the touch points in the guest experience to message the guest with relevant content and messaging.

SAMPLE CHDM EXAM QUESTIONS

1. What does LTV stand for?
   a. Long-Term Viability
   b. Last-to-View
   c. Long-Term Vacationers
   d. Lifetime Value

2. Loyalty programs are only viable for large brands.
   a. True
   b. False

3. Which is NOT a goal of hotel loyalty programs?
   a. To retain the best and most profitable customers
   b. To engage with customers through the guest lifecycle with personalized content
   c. To extract data to sell to third party marketers
   d. To provide insights into customer behavior and preferences

Answers
1 = d
2 = b
3 = c

NOTES

Chapter 14: Digital for Pre-Stay, On Site, and Post-Stay

> **KEY POINTS**
> - Digital provides the opportunity to establish a stronger relationship directly with guests through pre-stay, on-site, and post-stay communication.
> - Communicating the right message at the right time is key to creating more loyal guests.
> - Creating customer marketing advocates is more likely through digital.

SUMMARY

It is often said that the greatest wasted opportunity in the hotel booking cycle is the time between booking and stay. There is so much that can be done in this space to engage your guest, excite them about their stay, avoid cancellations, and create opportunity to generate ancillary revenue like upgrades, on-property restaurant reservations, etc.

Historically, the only communication our guests would receive before check-in might be a reservation confirmation. Communication on site was limited to a welcome letter in the guest room and then various front desk interactions. Once the guest checked out, they may receive a survey or an email asking how their stay was, but that was often the extent of planned guest communications.

Today, hotels recognize a multitude of reasons and opportunities to increase the amount and diversity of communication they have with guests—and the delivery systems used are equally varied. Eventually there will likely be widespread use of a single platform that follows guests from their first interaction searching online all the way to sharing information about your property with their friends and family via their own social networks after they have checked out. Currently, most properties and brands are taking a little bit more of a piecemeal approach.

WHY HAVE MORE FREQUENT COMMUNICATION?

The first thing we should look at is why we are communicating more with our guests—what are the benefits to them and to us? For the purposes of this section, we are going to look at the steps from booking all the way through the post-stay experience.

Of course, the primary reason is to develop a stronger relationship with the guest. The more you know about them, and the more they know about you, the more loyal the relationship. But in growing that relationship, there are several reasons for interacting along the way.

1. Upselling

The first reason for reaching out to a guest in advance of their arrival is to let them know how they might be able to enhance their stay. This period—between booking and arrival—is when guests are most likely to open and read your correspondence, so hotels should use this opportunity wisely. The guest will benefit from knowing what opportunities there are to have a better stay—Is there a suite they can have instead of a room? Do you have a spa that you want them to visit, or a golf course, or restaurant?

2. Education and Excitement Generation

Apart from upselling, informing future guests of all that the property and the surrounding area offer is of value to the guests—helping them plan their itinerary, or even helping them understand what kind of clothes to pack based on weather forecasts or activities that are available either on site or nearby. Enhancing the experience for the guest beyond the hotel room may prevent last-minute rate shopping that today's guest is often encouraged to do. If they have formed a stronger relationship with the hotel through information sharing, they are less likely to cancel and book elsewhere to save a little money.

3. Preventative

Are there restaurants or attractions in your area that fill up so quickly that reservations are required? This would be good information to pass along to your future guests to build a relationship. Is the parking facility your guests normally use closed so other recommendations might be suggested? Is your pool closed for renovation? All these items can be communicated in advance to your guests to ensure their check-in is seamless. Something as simple as communicating the weather forecast for their stay might be an opportunity to make a unique connection with your guest in advance of their arrival.

4. Data Gathering

By communicating about the likes or interests of your future guests, you can continually add to the data you collect about them. How responsive are they to offers? What types of offers do they find most appealing? What information are they clicking on to read more about? What special requests might they have for their stay? This is all valuable data you can collect that will help you maximize their spend on site and make future targeted offers of genuine interest to them, solidifying their attachment to your brand or property.

5. Social Network Sharing

Is there an opportunity for you to help your future guests share the excitement about their upcoming trip with their social networks? Providing enticing "out of office" visuals of your property or resort is an opportunity for your guests to let others know how they will be spending their upcoming vacation or trip.

6. Customer Service

Onsite communication, especially through SMS is becoming more and more prevalent to deal with onsite issues and requests (e.g., request more towels, report broken TV, etc.). Companies like HotSos, Zingle, and many others offer these types of services.

PRE-STAY COMMUNICATIONS[100]

Travelers value pre-check in information. A 2021 study by Expedia Group found that globally travelers find the following types of information helpful:

- general information—93%
- hours for onsite amenities like pools restaurants and spas—53%
- driving and parking instructions—48%
- insider knowledge about the area—46%
- restaurant recommendations—44%
- accessibility features—35%
- information about partnerships with local businesses—20%

ONSITE COMMUNICATION OPTIONS HAVE CHANGED

Once the guest arrives on site, the reasons, opportunities, and delivery systems continue for ongoing guest communication.

Some hotels have begun to utilize what is often referred to as a virtual concierge. Several companies have developed software or apps that allow guests to communicate with hotel staff in every area of the hotel—from inquiring about spa reservations to ordering room service or requesting an extra towel. Most companies in this space offer platforms so guests can connect with the hotel before, during, and after their stay.

Another trend is for hotels to provide in-room virtual assistants like Amazon Alexa and Google Home. As the population becomes more dependent on the voice activated assistants in their home, their expectation will be to also find it in their hotel room. Several hotel brands are experimenting with these in-room assistants, and this practice is likely to grow. Initial tests have seen happy guests who love having the devices they are accustomed to in their room and other guests who unplug them when they arrive because they are concerned about privacy, but testing and refinement continues.

POST-STAY COMMUNICATIONS

Probably the greatest opportunity in guest marketing is the opportunity to create customer advocates. Historically we might have sent a post-stay survey and then included the guest, segmented by stay type, for future emails inviting them back. But, outside of loyalty membership, that was probably the extent of our post-stay conversation with our guests. Today, that focus has shifted a bit. We still send surveys and include the guest in future emails based on their interests and history with us, but we are also trying to work our way into their social networks.

Many hotels have found that running things like photo contests is a great way to engage guests post-stay. The guest is invited to share a photo taken during their visit and enter it into a contest to win a future free stay. Once the photo is entered, they are encouraged to invite their friends to vote for their photo. The goal is to encourage the guest to share information about the property with all their social network connections. An added benefit is often many focused, positive, experience-based stories on the property website. During the Covid-19 pandemic some hotels used this strategy to keep past guests engaged and excited about returning when they could travel.

Another concept in this space is gamifying the guest experience. Once a guest is involved, they are offered points for different activities—like sharing a photo of the hotel, or writing a review, or sharing a blog post that the hotel has written with their friends and family. Points can be redeemed for future stays or other items.

Critical to most of these pre-, during-, and post-travel activities is a strong customer relationship management (CRM) component as discussed in the previous chapter.

CONCLUSION

Digital continues to evolve around increased opportunities to communicate with guests before, during, and after their hotel stay. The benefits of engaging more with guests are the antidote to the commoditization of hotel rooms. The more unique the experience of your guest, the more they feel loyal to your brand or property, the more likely they are to spend more on site, return to your property, and share their experience of your property with their own networks.

SAMPLE CHDM EXAM QUESTIONS

1. The time between booking and stay can be utilized to:
   a. Engage the guest
   b. Excite the guest about their stay
   c. Upgrade or sell ancillary products or services to the guest
   d. All of the above

2. Communication after the stay should be avoided.
   a. True
   b. False

3. One of the greatest opportunities in guest marketing is the opportunity to create customer brand/property _____.
   a. Advocates
   b. Concierges
   c. Passives
   d. Appreciatives

Answers
1 = d
2 = b
3 = a

NOTES

PART THREE: EARNED MEDIA

PART THREE: EARNED MEDIA

THE EVOLUTION OF EARNED MEDIA

Earned media is the most unique of all media to the digital age. Marketers have always had some form of both owned and paid media. Owned media used to include printed brochures and menus, and paid media included billboards and newspaper ads. The closest form of marketing we had to earned media was public relations. We would pitch an idea or an event and hope that someone would pick it up and write about it in their newspaper or magazine. Even so, public relations was still one way—from us as marketers, to them as consumers.

Earned media evolved due to two primary drivers: 1) the launch of social media communities like Facebook and Twitter, and 2) consumers' growing mistrust of marketers. At the same time, consumers were more able to share their own experiences and options—as user-generated content—on sites like Tripadvisor and YouTube. Consumers no longer relied solely on marketers to learn about products—they could talk to their peers and get first-hand insights. In the early days of social and review sites, users only wanted to talk to one another, and marketers were often excluded entirely from the conversations.

Fast forward a few years, and marketers were able to be a more active part of the conversation. Review sites and ratings were important, but management responses became valued as well. Social media channels like Twitter became a customer service point of contact—happy or unhappy customers could speak up, and savvy marketers would respond directly via the same channel.

Today, earned media is a two-way means of communication with past, present, and future guests. And thanks to the evolution of video and mobile, earned media has evolved into brand storytelling, inclusive of our audience's input.

The good news is that due to the perception of earned media as unbiased, it can garner the most trust and credibility. The bad news is that marketers have the least amount of control over earned media.

EARNED MEDIA TODAY

Today earned media is any media that contributes to the telling of a brand's story but isn't owned or paid for. When a post on social media gets shared over and over, that is earned media. When an influencer tells our story to an audi-

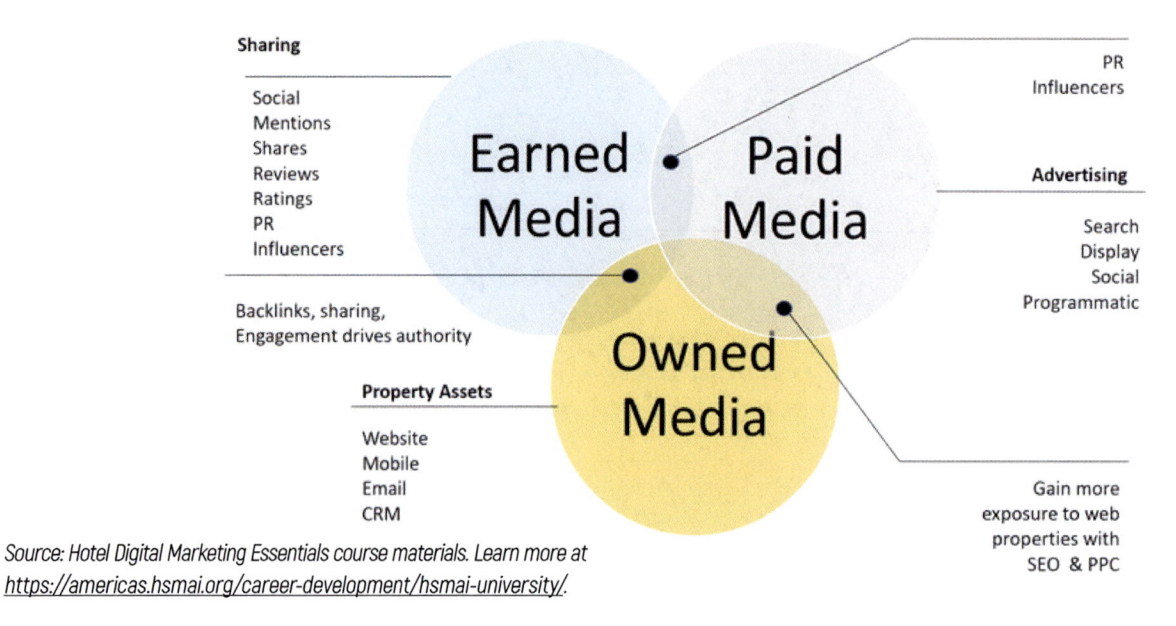

Sharing
- Social
- Mentions
- Shares
- Reviews
- Ratings
- PR
- Influencers

Backlinks, sharing, Engagement drives authority

Property Assets
- Website
- Mobile
- Email
- CRM

PR
- Influencers

Advertising
- Search
- Display
- Social
- Programmatic

Gain more exposure to web properties with SEO & PPC

Source: Hotel Digital Marketing Essentials course materials. Learn more at https://americas.hsmai.org/career-development/hsmai-university/.

ence, that is earned media. When a review site publishes ratings and reviews of our property that we don't control, that is earned media.

Earned media is valuable at multiple points in the buyer's path to purchase. At the top of the funnel, it is a tremendous asset for creating brand awareness. If a travel writer publishes a popular story about the top ten romantic hotels and includes your property, your brand awareness will likely skyrocket, as will visitors to your website. Reviews can make the conversion step of the buyer's journey easier—if other people like you, a consumer will be more willing to give you a chance. Finally, once a guest has stayed with you, they are in a great position be an advocate for you by sharing photos of their trip with their social networks. All of these touchpoints are highly trustworthy and most are far beyond your direct control. You can write the press releases, host travel writers, deliver stellar experiences and picturesque backgrounds, but what gets shared and consumed is up to your target audience. It is earned.

This part of the book covers the primary drivers behind earned media starting with the modern approach to public relations and influencers. We also cover the top social channels for travel reviews and ratings, and best practices around them. In each chapter we address the measurement of this media type.

Chapter 15: Public Relations

Historically, public relations (PR) was a way to tell the public your brand story by reaching out to print or other media publishers, pitching your story, and convincing them to cover it. Marketers used PR to create awareness of a new product, or to rebrand an older product. It was used to highlight an event or celebrate a milestone. Public relations was a way to spin otherwise bad news into a story of redemption or hope. PR was not charged with reflecting reality—anything was possible depending on the storyteller.

Today, while the press is still a significant player, public relations can bypass them and appeal directly to consumers via social media and other channels. The key to effective public relations, in crafting a narrative or simply having a conversation, is relationship building. Relationship building with the press or members of the media is as important as relationship building with current or potential guests with whom you can directly communicate via tools like Instagram, Facebook, or TikTok.

Public relations encompasses a broad scope of responsibilities for today's marketer, including:

- corporate communications
- crisis communications
- executive communications
- internal communications
- investor relations communications
- marketing communications
- integrated marketing/integrated marketing communications
- media relations
- content creation
- events promotion
- social media
- multimedia coordination
- reputation management
- speechwriting
- brand journalism

Influence and credibility were once easily assessed based on cornerstone periodicals, like major newspapers, magazines, and TV shows. Now the credibility of these media powerhouses has shifted, and media distribution includes countless blogs and social channels pushed by influencers. Your hotel or brand can build credibility by aligning with influencers to push your story line only if the influencer is authentic and can be trusted as a media source.

Media sources today include the traditional formats of print and broadcast in additional to internet media. Internet media is produced by writers on personal blogs or social media accounts. The lines get blurry where editors from traditional media sources use the internet as their distribution platform. There are countless examples of magazine editors resigning from their desk jobs to be full time influencers, usually using Instagram as their core platform, along with writing a blog for longform content.

PUBLIC RELATIONS CAMPAIGN DESIGN

A well-executed PR plan can have a much longer lifespan and wider reach than any individual promotion. The steps for designing a PR campaign are like other marketing campaigns:

1. Define your goals and specific outcomes.
2. Identify your target audience.
3. Determine distribution channels.
4. Create your story.
5. Amplify and engage.
6. Measure and analyze results.

DEFINE YOUR GOALS AND SPECIFIC OUTCOMES

To establish goals for your PR initiatives, start by identifying where in the funnel you want to have an impact.

Example Goal	Example Outcome
Increase brand awareness for a new product or program	Increased site traffic, increased email list, increased engagement on social channels
Increase awareness within a specific target market	Attract engagement of influencers for the specific market
Alter perception of property due to poor past management	Increased positive reviews and ratings around new service offerings

IDENTIFY YOUR TARGET AUDIENCE

Based on your desired outcomes or goals, specifically define your target audience. In some cases, your PR efforts will be designed to impact consumers directly; in other cases, your target audience may be a segment of the media, or niche influencers. You may target multiple audiences within the same campaign, but each should be clearly defined and sourced.

Audiences may include:

- media sources like Travel and Leisure, or The New York Times
- journalists—narrow your outreach based on their niche topics and audiences (e.g., general travel, meetings and events, LGBTQ, tech, weddings, etc.)
- influencers—macro or micro
- partners—destinations, attractions, associations, etc.
- consumers—Facebook groups, LinkedIn groups, etc.

DETERMINE DISTRIBUTION CHANNELS

Technology is essential for the aggregation and distribution of content. Properties large and small can easily increase online visibility and generate publicity through digital press release distribution via wire services. Wire services charge variable fees depending on the size of the distribution and formatting options. This distribution method provides more online exposure and links (hyperlinks embedded in your press release copy) pointing to your website, Facebook, Twitter, and other social channels. Valid links give your website and social platforms credibility, thus fostering search engine optimization (SEO).

There are multiple press release distribution services for traditional media PR approaches. The most popular are Cision, Business Wire, Issuewire, and PRWeb. You craft a press release to tell your story and sign up through these services to have your release distributed.

Email distribution to your list of press contacts is still a viable route—though competition is far greater for attention.

Targeting niche influencers for your desired audience can be a cost-effective way to broaden your reach. Connect via direct messages to micro influencers, or through a source for macro influencers. Tools for identifying ideal influencers include BuzzSumo, HYPR, and Followerwonk.

Look locally for unique partnerships with a destination or attraction management group. For example, if there is a large event in your city, partner with them to include your hotel's information in their PR plans. This can also work for larger brand initiatives as there is strength in joining forces—even with your competitors—to promote a specific city or destination.

Social media is an effective avenue to cultivate relationships with the media. There are several LinkedIn groups for travel writers that you can join:

- Travel Editors & Freelance Journalists (12,548 members)
- Travel Notes - Travel and Tourism Connections (2,888 members)
- Travel Media Pros (8,019 members)
- TravMedia, a forum for travel writers and travel communicators (1,450 members)

You can also join the Society of American Travel Writers.

More travel writers are on Twitter, so if you follow them and comment on their posts, you will get to know them and they may be more open to an invitation from you in the future.

Today there is no separation between traditional and interactive PR. Whether your in-house PR professional, or PR agency, is developing and pitching well-crafted stories to media, or telling a story to public followers on social media accounts, relationships must be built AND be authentic to garner success.

CREATE YOUR STORY

Your story should be crafted and based on your hotel's unique selling points. Start by identifying those unique selling points and then creating programs, special offers, and events to showcase distinctive features.

Think about what you would like writers to say about you. Create that experience. Do a semantic analysis of your reviews and see what your customers say is important to them. Think about your target audience and identify your most enthusiastic fans. What are they reading? Where is the best place to reach that market with a unique message?

The key to great PR is identifying what is newsworthy and aligning your hotel with events or programming that are already happening to gain brand awareness. Sometimes you don't have to create a new program to garner press—instead align yourself with a program or event that you know will trend. You don't need to reinvent the wheel to have media talk about your hotel.

A traditional approach is for marketers to align with an event (like a sporting event or film festival) via paid sponsorship (i.e., buying ad space for promotion). In the evolving world of earned media, marketers will create something to complement or contribute to the event theme. An added benefit of event-based PR is that it has a longer life span because you can build pre-event, actual event, and post-event buzz.

Your story is more likely to be picked up if the content is popular or trending. Conduct keyword research and think about trending words you find popping up again and again, and with which you can create or align your story? Trending words might include design, local, organic, yoga, spa, sustainable, rooftop, artisanal, authentic experiences, customized experiences, pet-friendly, eco-friendly, gay-friendly, human-friendly, tech-friendly, bleisure, or glamping. Glamour, love, and romance are always current but finding a fresh way to express them can be powerful. Use popular keywords, backed up by hashtags, in your press release, video, and other collateral.

The following questions will help you start generating story ideas.

Business Meetings
- Did your property host a large, successful conference? What about that conference exemplifies an up-and-coming trend? Did the event tie in any kind of fundraising or community outreach?
- Did a high-profile company and/or guest stay at your hotel? Did they enjoy something at your hotel that speaks to a current trend?

Unique Use of Event Space
- Have you noticed any business or cultural trends in weddings? Does your hotel specialize in a particular type of wedding or event?
- Did you have a famous speaker in a conference room?
- Have you provided space as an in-kind donation to a local charity or community organization?

Property
- Have you renovated and updated your property to provide a more modern experience for your guests?
- Do you meet any "green" certifications or standards of excellence?
- Have you recently added a major amenity such as a new restaurant, spa, or business center?
- Can you give a writer an idea for a story that highlights you—like the most unique privacy door signs, most extravagant turndown service, hotels with great libraries, best guest room views, or most extraordinary pools.

Promotions & Packages
- What special rates or promotions are you offering for an upcoming holiday, noteworthy concert/sporting event, or a local festival?
- Do you offer a military discount?

- Has your property been featured by any credible sources—travel magazines (print or digital), Tripadvisor Certificate of Excellence, any "Best of …" lists, etc.? If so, "recycle" this information with your local media.
- How can you tie into seasons and holidays? Think at least 4 months ahead and be prepared to release the most unique Fall cocktail, seasonal dishes using local ingredients, activities that reflect that month (like free yoga on International Yoga Day), or tips from your romance concierge for Valentine's Day.

Creative Contests and Angles
- Create a program specifically designed to garner media attention and brand engagement, such as a contest, giveaway, or stunt.

Awards
- Has your hotel recently received an award?

> A note about awards: Some awards come at a significant expense but may be worth pursuing if the prestige of the award is important to your target audience. Other lesser-known awards can be dubious, and paying for entry may not give you your desired outcome, so proceed with caution.

Community Outreach
- Have you recently supported a local book drive, animal shelter, school park renovation, soup kitchen, or other community organization? Even cooking pizzas for the local fire department can make for good local PR. It is also good for the culture of your brand, for employee loyalty, and for guest loyalty.

No matter your story, it is critical to have a wealth of gorgeous lifestyle and architectural photography, with and without people, to which you have full rights to offer to support any press. A vibrant and compelling photo or video can be the reason your hotel is selected by the editor as much as the story itself.

AMPLIFY AND ENGAGE

Attention spans are growing ever shorter. Simply sending out a press release and letting journalists handle the rest won't garner the results you are hoping for in most cases. As a part of your PR plan, incorporate some longer-range amplification and engagement steps.

How you tell your story will influence its amplification and engagement potential. Whether you tell your story via a press release, through images, or via video, like everything in the digital age, ensure it is optimized.

It is key to remember that PR is now two way—so answering and engaging with comments and posts as a hotel representative needs to be a part of any plan. If you generate conversations about how unique or interesting your hotel or destination is, don't miss the opportunity to create a personal and authentic tone by personally engaging with comments and responses. Credible and authentic engagement continues to drive conversion so don't skip this critical step.

MEASURE AND ANALYZE RESULTS

In the past, the value of utilizing a distribution service or a PR agency to land your narrative as a feature in a publication was measured by the AVE (Advertising Value Equivalent). The AVE measures the cost of the media space, or time, devoted to your story based on advertising value. The formula is simple: if you had paid for the media exposure, what would it have cost you? For example, if you were featured in an article that was 10 column inches long in a medium whose rate was $100 per column inch, the AVE is 10 x $100 = $1000.

An argument can be made that AVE is more valuable than a paid advertisement because of the credibility factor, so some include one more factor—between 3 and 12—that accounts for the multiplier of credibility. In the same example, in a highly credible source AVE would be 10 x $100 x 12 = $12,000.

In Barcelona in 2010, a delegation at the International Association for Measurement and Evaluation of Communication (AMEC) developed seven principles for a more modern and robust framework for effective PR and communication measurement. This new framework, the Barcelona Principles, shifted the focus from activities to outcomes:

1. Goal setting and measurement are fundamental to communication and public relations.

2. Measuring communication outcomes is recommended versus only measuring outputs.
3. The effect on organizational performance can and should be measured where possible.
4. Measurement and evaluation require both qualitative and quantitative methods.
5. AVEs are not the value of communication.
6. Social media can and should be measured consistently with other media channels.
7. Measurement and evaluation should be transparent, consistent, and valid.

AVE has not disappeared but has merely been reduced in relevance.

Other common metrics for measuring PR include:

- Followers, likes/comments, shares, mentions, click-throughs, hashtags, survey results, review ratings, and ranking changes
- Traffic: Was there a measurable increase of visitors to your site or visitors to your specific landing page during the period surrounding the event or promotion?
- Virality: How much was your content viewed and shared?
- Sentiment Analysis: What kind of emotional response was driven by your PR campaign?
- Share of Voice (SOV): To what degree is your audience seeing your message in a particular market compared to those of your competitors? The formula is: SOV = your mentions / total market mentions.

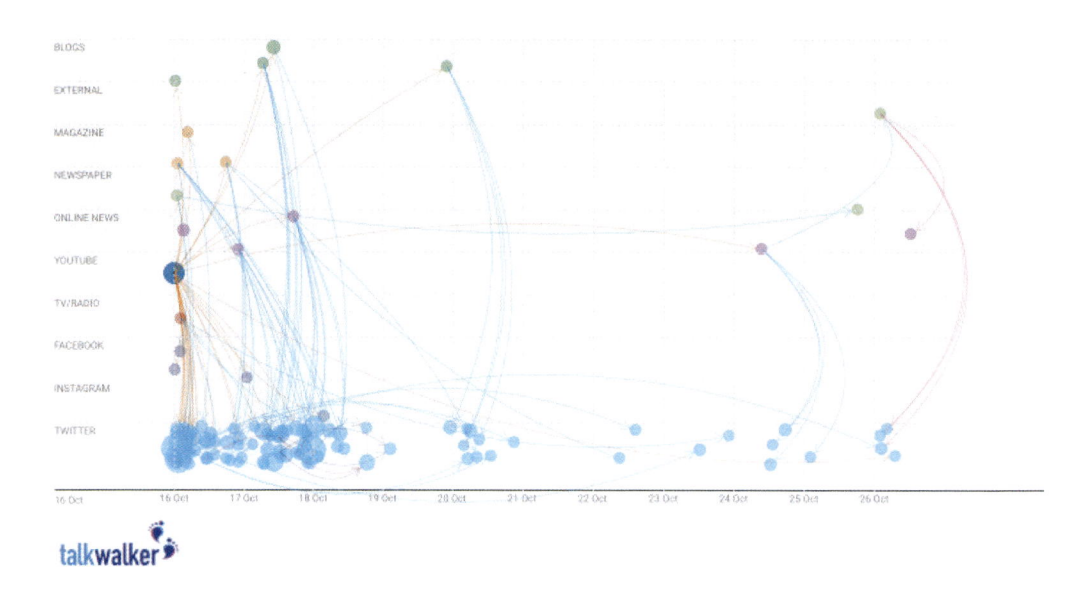

A virality map can illustrate how widely your content was viewed and shared.[101]

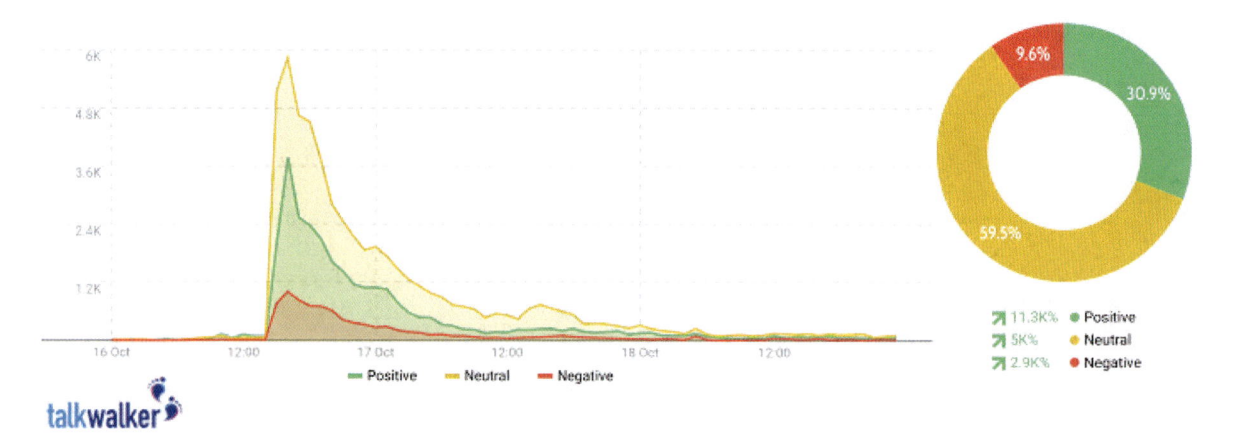

A sentiment study will show a positive or negative outcome.[102]

An effective way to contribute to SOV is by utilizing influencers. Influencers are not just brand ambassadors for reviews. Yes, they may generate a review for your hotel, but they must be utilized as news outlets to increase the percentage of mentions for specific initiatives. Without influencers, you lose serious credibility in making yourself seem newsworthy, especially when aligning with specific community themes or events.

When aligning with a larger community theme or event, measure success by thinking about share of voice (SOV). SOV is measured mentions generated by your hotel during a specific period (like during an event period such Pride Month in June in much of the world). Benchmark your success by comparing your SOV, or mentions, against other hotels that also created programming during the same specific period.

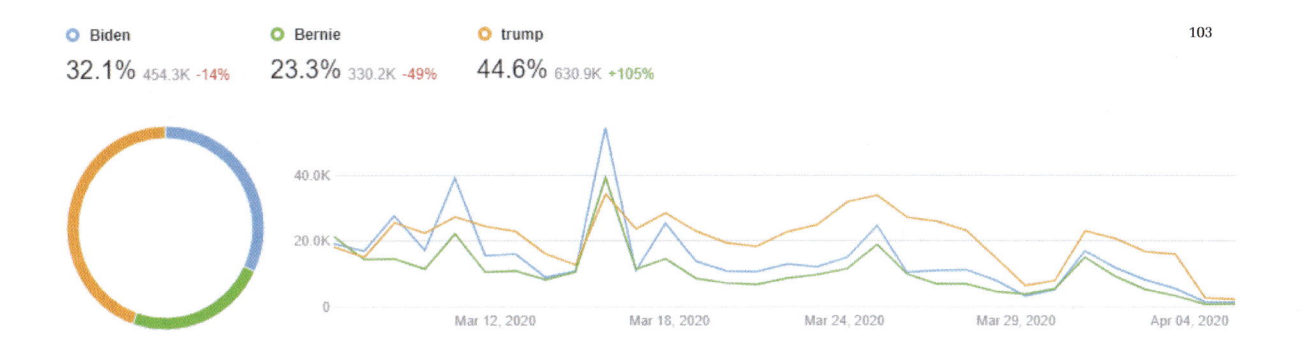

103

CRISIS MANAGEMENT AND PUBLIC RELATIONS

Every company or property is vulnerable to a crisis. If 2020 taught us anything, it is the importance of being prepared for the unforeseeable crisis. Public relations plays a key role in crisis management—small or large. Take proactive steps today to be prepared for the inevitable future event. There are a few critical components to any crisis management plan from a PR standpoint.

- Anticipate and plan for a potential crisis. Talk with your executive team about what could happen and what precautions you can put in place to minimize the negative outcomes.
- Understand—in advance—the role that your brand, management company, and ownership will play in any crisis communication.
- Assign a designated spokesperson, and ensure all employees know who it is. That is the person who will interface with the media or any external contacts. All questions should be referred to the designated spokesperson.
- Buy yourself some time with a "holding statement." This is a press release that lets interested parties know that you are aware of the situation and are working on it.
- Ensure that all stakeholders are included in any internal communications plan. Keep everyone internally on the same page as efficiently as possible. Plan—in advance of a crisis—the frequency and the channels you will use to communicate ongoing information.
- Make it clear what information should and should not be shared via individual social media accounts. While you can't necessarily dictate what gets shared, you can make your expectations of privacy clear.
- Assume the crisis will last longer and continue to communicate to all stakeholders—internal and external.
- After a crisis, always review the organization's response and outcomes. What could be improved?

A helpful PR crisis communication checklist is downloadable at https://tinyurl.com/Crisis-CommunicationsChecklist.

A Field Guide for Navigating Today's Digital Landscape

SAMPLE CHDM EXAM QUESTIONS

1. Which of the following are true about a crisis communication plan?
   a. It helps a hotel prepare for the unforeseeable crisis
   b. It should include a designated spokesperson
   c. It will prevent potential lawsuits
   d. It ensures all stakeholders are kept up to date
   e. A, B, & C
   f. A, B, & D
   g. All of the above

2. Which of the following is NOT a typical public relations measurement?
   a. SOV (Share of Voice)
   c. EMB (Earned Media Value
   c. CTR (Click Through Rate)
   d. Sentiment Analysis
   e. Virility

3. What is the biggest change that the International Association for Measurement and Evaluation of Communication made with the 2015 Barcelona Principles?
   a. Measuring communication outcomes is recommended versus only measuring outputs
   b. Social media cannot be measured the same way as other medias
   c. The value of impressions should be considered above all else
   d. Share of Voice should now be the predominant measurement tool
   e. All of the above

Answers
1 = f
2 = c
3 = a

Chapter 16: Reviews & Reputation Marketing

KEY POINTS
- The evolution of user-generated content and online reviews
- Key components driving review ratings and ranking
- Best practices for responding to reviews
- The benefits of review aggregators and sentiment analysis
- Value and risks of user-generated content on websites

SUMMARY

Online reviews drive business because consumers find reviews written by peers the most credible of all media sources. Positive reviews, management responses, up-to-date content, and photos are the primary factors that contribute to an effective reputation marketing strategy. According to a report by TripBarometer, 70% of travelers seek social recommendations before booking, and 86% won't book without reading reviews first. Effectively managing your online reputation impacts every touchpoint of the buyer's path to purchase.

Successful reputation optimization is a key form of branding. Online reviews are powerful social proof of how well your brand is living up to your brand promises. The reviews your guests share about your business are a reflection of your mission, your culture, and your values, which comprise your branding. If there is a gap between what you say about your brand and what your guests say about their experience, the reviews will serve to point you directly to where to place your attention.

The most common myth in the hospitality industry is that reputation management is just about composing written responses to reviews. This is a minimum standard. On its own it cannot achieve significant change or revenue growth.

Instead of simply handling a problem and apologizing for it, identify and fix the root cause of the problem. Most times a change in communication, process, or mindset is all that is needed to make significant lifts in guest satisfaction, and therefore increase sales conversions and ADR without any significant expense.

To elevate your team to deliver higher levels of guest satisfaction and loyalty, you must embrace feedback. Celebrate and expand on the positives, and use insights from the negatives and neutral comments—even the lack of enthusiastic comments can be telling—to explore with your team where to implement tiny touches of continuous improvement that enhance the guest experience.

Elevating your public reputation requires leadership, teamwork from every employee, and diligent collaboration between operations and

Users are looking for reviews & other guidance at every stage of their research journey [104]

- 70% seek social recommendations before booking — DREAMING
- 57% book attractions while on vacation — EXPERIENCING
- 4 in 5 book with providers who they've had a *prior* positive experience with — BOOKING
- 86% won't book without reading reviews *first* — PLANNING

Source: TripBarometer 2018 Study

A Field Guide for Navigating Today's Digital Landscape

sales and marketing. Leadership involvement is key, but the executive office cannot deliver the experience; line staff do. Companies who can challenge and support their teams with a creative and collaborative work environment are the ones whose teams are empowered to inspire their guests to leave enthusiastic reviews.

THE EVOLUTION OF USER-GENERATED CONTENT AND ONLINE REVIEWS

Prior to 2000, hotels capitalized on increasing demand on the internet by creating websites, taking advantage of third-party intermediary sites, and providing the content that they wanted the public to see. The internet was often perceived as a digital brochure for a property. Hotels and brands controlled the content, photos, branding, and message on their websites. Several professional review sites did exist at that time—born from offline guidebooks such as Frommers and Lonely Planet—and while these could expose some less-than-brochure-perfect properties, generally the business owner had content control.

At the turn of the millennium, things began to change with the emergence of user-generated content. Hotels and other industries could no longer maintain total control over their digital presence because users—guests—were now able to post their own perceptions online.

Initially, most user-generated reviews were presented as simple additional features on existing websites. Since the hotel or brand controlled the content, these reviews could be moderated, edited, or skewed to show a property in a positive light. Most third-party booking engines and OTAs began to allow comments, and in some cases also created rating systems for properties.

Then came Tripadvisor. The site, which wasn't a booking engine, launched in 2000 and quickly became a popular venue where the general traveling public could become hotel reviewers by sharing their experiences and photos with anyone who was interested. Over the past 21 years, the site has amassed more than 880 million reviews and opinions; it now attracts hundreds of million unique visitors every month.

Early on, as the practice of sharing details and opinions about hotel properties became increasingly widespread, there was cynicism surrounding anonymous reviews. What prevented disgruntled employees or competitors from writing negative reviews? What kept hotel owners from writing positive reviews about themselves? Such cynicism has lessened somewhat, and today statistics show consumers trust peer recommendations significantly more than traditional advertising.

It is important to monitor review sites as well as reviews on OTAs and search engines. The review landscape is in constant flux, but four main players have come to dominate a crowded field in recent years: Google, Booking.com, Tripadvisor, and Expedia. In addition, it has become common for hotel brands to include reviews on their hotel websites.

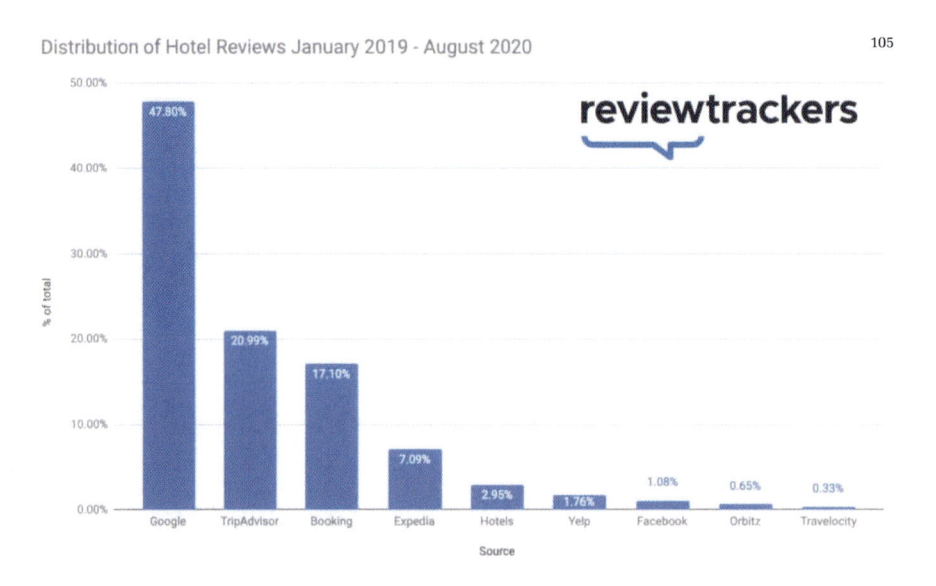

Distribution of Hotel Reviews January 2019 - August 2020 [105]

reviewtrackers

Source	% of total
Google	47.80%
TripAdvisor	20.99%
Booking	17.10%
Expedia	7.09%
Hotels	2.95%
Yelp	1.76%
Facebook	1.08%
Orbitz	0.65%
Travelocity	0.33%

"Reputation marketing" has become a far more apt description of managing reviews and responses for multiple reasons. Ratings continue to play a stronger role in SEO for organic hotel listings. Preferred placement in the SERPs consider ratings, and higher placements continue to contribute to increased web traffic. Positive reviews add credibility and authority when displayed on a property or brand website. And authentic, management responses to a variety of reviews drives trust on behalf of consumers. A superior customer experience is more relevant than ever in this age of digital transparency.

COMMON COMPONENTS OF REVIEW SITES

Most review sites are similar in approach. They list basic content—address, summary of property details, and photographs, often provided by the hotel owner/operator—and they provide an opportunity for visitors to write reviews and rate the hotel. Most review sites have some sort of popularity ranking of properties within a market and filtering capabilities for the user. Many sites default the display of reviews to the most recent ones, while others will show reviews more tailored to the user (e.g., reviews from travelers from your country or in your language). Lastly, most sites also allow a management response to a review.

How a property ranks in customer satisfaction on review sites can have a powerful impact on the number of visitors to the business profile page as well as to the hotel's own website—and their placement within the search engine organic results pages.

Ranking criteria is site specific, based on algorithms known only by the review site employees. But in general, success is built upon the Five Rs: Ratio, Rating, Recency, Relevancy, and Response.

1. RATIO: number of reviews relative to the size of the property

2. RATING: user-generated score/rating of the property

3. RECENCY: number of recent reviews

4. RELEVANCY: clout/authority of the person writing the reviews (usually determined by quantity of reviews)

5. RESPONSE: frequency and quality of management responses to reviews (on sites where applicable)

While these five factors are important, Tripadvisor and other sites increasingly tailor the display sort to customer behavior or specific preference attributes, thus decreasing the importance of the actual "rank" in a market and increasing the importance of focusing efforts on overall reputation marketing.

Fraudulent behavior on the part of the property harms its ranking. For example, if a hotel is influencing guests to write positive reviews by offering a financial incentive, or if an employee of one hotel is writing negative reviews about a competitor—and this behavior is reported and verified—Tripadvisor can penalize your hotel with a drop in ranking.

If Tripadvisor determines there is cause to believe a business is manipulating the reviews, the site will flag that business with a banner identifying the reviews as suspicious. To avoid damaging your business reputation in this way, learn what constitutes manipulation on the review sites—and ensure everyone at your property is familiar with those rules as well. Not all the rules are obvious, and they can change over time. For example, while many hospitality professionals understand that incentivizing guests is not allowed, they may not realize that selectively soliciting reviews from travelers who have written positive guest surveys is also considered manipulating the results. Be sure to periodically check the management center on each review site for information.

Search engines jumped on the review bandwagon once hotel mapping became prevalent. Search results on Google began returning local business results with an opportunity to read or write reviews; most search engines now allow reviews and provide some ranking and filtering capabilities. Location-based sites encourage visitors to visit a property and then share tips to be viewed by others.

Guest surveys are like online reviews in that they collect the opinions of actual guests; however, there is generally a lag time in reporting.

Review site postings are instant; feedback is often quick, giving a savvy manager real-time information that can be used to take immediate action. From a marketing standpoint, a survey response sent to the general manager does not have the potential to attract new business compared to an online review that may be read by thousands of people.

A good rule of thumb is that if your guest surveys are not at least 90% positive, continue with private surveys while identifying any problems and creating opportunities for more positive feedback. Once you have 90% or higher in positive survey results, instead of sending out surveys, direct your post-stay review links directly to Tripadvisor (or Google if you prefer) where they can help pull revenue to your business.

ROI ON REVIEWS

The exact attribution rate of any review site has not been determined, but a Cornell University study found that a larger number of positive reviews correlates with increased bookings and the ability to raise rates. Trends suggest that the following factors increase conversion and ADR:

- hotels ranked at the top of the market
- positive review scores
- appropriate management responses to reviews—both positive and negative
- multiple property photos showing the hotel in a positive and realistic light
- videos showing hotel in a positive light
- detailed hotel information provided

TripAdvisor has significant influence **on bookings**

And is visited prior to booking by...

- 77% of all **Travel** bookers
- 82% of all **Hotels** bookers
- 78% of all **OTA** bookers
- 75% of all **Airline** bookers
- 79% of all **Car Rental** bookers
- 75% of all **Cruise** bookers

Source: Jumpshot

The benefit of increased conversion due to a strong reputation can be seen not only in electronic bookings, but also in bookings of groups and corporate accounts through traditional sales and marketing efforts where consumer confidence is elevated by the social proof of past guest testimonials.

Paid advertising is possible on review sites. Business listings, links directly to your brand.com or independent website, or display, graphic, or video ads are all available. Like any advertising decision, a strategy guiding the targeted ROI, measurability, and overall effectiveness should be determined beforehand. Best practices suggest that an easy link from a review site to a property website or booking engine shows a positive ROI; however, some review communities shun any traditional marketing approaches. If strengthening your direct business is important to your revenue strategy, then adding a business listing (with contact information and a link to your website) may help.

If your hotel is part of a major brand, check first to see if there are any corporate relationships between sites such as Tripadvisor and the brand, and what is included in those agreements, such as business listings, metasearch, display advertising, etc.

WHO IS RESPONSIBLE FOR MANAGING REVIEWS?

Responding promptly and politely to reviews—especially negative reviews—can create a positive impact. Responding with genuine hospitality, compassion, and ownership of the experience—even going so far as sharing what changes you have made to your procedures or communications based on the insightful feedback given—can create a powerful and lasting impression on your brand image that will draw more guests to book with you.

How you respond to a negative review says more about your hotel than the review itself. It's generally recommended that reviews be responded to at the hotel level. The hotel staff is in the best position to understand any situations or issues that may have occurred, and thus can best respond with appropriate context to a review. However, reputation management crosses disciplines and is often "touched" at both the property and above-property levels.

Review management also has a strong property operations component. Friction points need to be relayed to leadership and the operations team at the hotel for resolution with the customer, and for finding creative solutions to prevent these issues from occurring in the future. This should be done quickly so the solution can be addressed in the online response, making it a far more effective marketing tool.

Above-property ecommerce, digital, or social media managers are often responsible for the overall coordination and accountability of reviews. Sites like Tripadvisor and the OTAs often fall in the realm of above-property team members—from hotel information, listing, ranking, and advertising perspectives—who may oversee an entire portfolio ensuring that all hotels are responding in an appropriate and timely fashion. These team members may also uncover recurring issues across numerous reviews and work with the hotels to resolve them. The location of the person who composes the response doesn't matter. What matters is that when responding to a complaint, the response must be a true reflection of the actions that have been taken to address the issue.

The hotel's search engine optimization (SEO) lead—whether on property, above property, or a vendor—will also have an interest in the reviews and management responses because user-generated content can influence hotel rankings in the search engines.

Some brands now include responses and response times in their QA assessments. This shows that brands recognize the impact reviews and responses have on revenue, as well as the value of this process to the guest experience and future intent to return.

In the end, it is best to understand all impacts that reviews may have on the hotel and ensure accountability for all aspects of review management.

BEST PRACTICES: RESPONDING TO REVIEWS

Not all sites displaying customer reviews allow management responses. But when you can, do—hotels that provide a management response to reviews are 21 percent more likely to receive a booking inquiry via that site. A Cornell study also found that hotels that respond to up to 40 percent of their reviews observe a 2.2x average lift in revenue.

Some of the major sites that allow public responses include:

- Booking.com
- Tripadvisor
- Yelp
- Expedia.com
- Google My Business
- Travelocity
- Facebook
- Trip.com (the largest OTA in China which also has the largest share of online reviews)
- And others…Trivago, Rakuten, HolidayCheck, HRS, and more

When responding to reviews:

- Research the situation before responding to make sure you have the story straight and understand what action needs to be taken in the future to prevent recurrence.
- Make it a priority to respond to negative reviews—reply to all of them. If handled well, this can increase your esteem in the eyes of the readers. In fact, 84% of users surveyed by Tripadvisor agree that an appropriate management response to a bad review "improves my impression of the hotel."
- Thank the reviewer for their feedback.
- Use your name. A person is responding, not a bot, and the use of your name conveys that sentiment.
- Be sincere and genuine. Do not use generic canned responses.
- Apologize for the negative guest experience.
- Explain steps you will take to prevent the negative experience from happening again.
- Do not offer compensation online. This can make readers believe that complaining can bring financial reward.
- Wrap up by acknowledging any positive comments and ask for an opportunity to show them the improved guest experience.
- Invite the guest to contact you offline.
- Have someone else read responses for tone and intent prior to posting.

- For every negative review that receives a response, also respond to a positive review.
- Aim for a 40 percent response rate (data from a 2016 Cornell study indicate diminishing returns on response rates beyond this). It is not necessary to publicly respond to every positive review, but it is good form to privately thank all positive reviewers.
- Respond quickly—within 24 hours whenever possible. However, it is sometimes better to wait another day than to get the details wrong in your research of the events or planning your recovery.
- Follow your brand's requirements for responses (for example, some require a response within 48 hours).
- On some platforms you can update an old response and replace it with a new response when new information is available.

Future guests often search only for the negative reviews to see what the issues of a hotel are, so even old reviews and responses are guiding people's opinion of your hotel today and into the future. You can and should go back to old complaints, especially 1- or 2-star reviews that were unanswered or vaguely answered. Now you can address them beautifully, saying what has changed or been fixed since then. This is great follow up for issues that take time to fix—such as a redesigned restaurant menu with more vegetarian and vegan items, extended room service hours, more flexible check-out times, or policies around how much you authorize for incidentals. Past guests feel respected when you can share that you have truly heard them, and future guests see that you are indeed focused on evolving the guest experience to meet guests' changing needs.

When new serious complaints arise, quickly respond saying you are so sorry their experience was a disappointment, thank them for making you aware, and let them know that you are investigating the issue and will update with a complete response tomorrow. Give your name, telephone number, and email, and invite the guest to reach out to you directly if they wish. Once you have properly researched the situation, you can go back with a full response.

> One study shows that potential guests visiting review sites read management responses more carefully than the actual online review.[106]

When writing a response to a review, keep in mind that you aren't communicating only with the person who wrote the review—you are responding for the benefit of everyone else who may one day read it. Indeed, a management response could be viewed by hundreds, or even thousands, of potential customers, so a response should be treated similarly to an advertisement. A responsible marketer would never place an ad without reviewing the content, and having it proofread for errors and messaging. The same is true for management responses to reviews. Each response may drive a potential guest to your hotel or drive them away to a competitor.

One of the biggest mistakes you can make when responding to reviews is being defensive and diminishing what the customer is telling you about their experience. Criticizing the guest—or somehow holding them responsible for their poor experience—makes you look arrogant or uncaring, which is not only disappointing to the reviewer but to other readers as well. According to a Tripadvisor survey, 64% of users say an aggressive/defensive management response to a bad review "makes me less likely to book that hotel."

While it may be unfair to book a Disney Resort and then complain that there are too many kids, pointing a finger at the guest for "not visiting the website before booking" runs the risk of turning other potential guests off. Being humble and kind yet authentic can help clarify for travelers if your hotel is the right match for them, so approach replies with caution. It can be a difficult task not to take negative reviews personally. Just keep in mind that the reward can be very high. You can make a powerful impact, generating demand for your hotel by harnessing the power of reviews to communicate your property's message to lessen any potential disappointment and increase satisfaction.

BEST PRACTICES: GENERATING MORE POSITIVE AND FEWER NEGATIVE REVIEWS

Every hotel has a desire to make every guest happy. Review scores are a measure of your success in that area and the ratings should be monitored and shared daily with your team just like Occupancy, ADR, or RevPAR. With the ubiquity of online reviews, a focus on guest happiness and continuous improvement is critical to meeting the goal of generating more positive reviews and fewer negative reviews.

Generating More Positive Reviews
- Observe the behaviors that inspire positive comments at your hotel—and at your competitors'. Look for ways to consistently integrate similar experiences into every guest's stay.
- Be authentic in the descriptions and depictions of your property so you only attract those who genuinely prefer your type of hotel.
- Graciously request reviews in your post-stay email, giving a link to the review site(s) to make it easy for guests to respond.

Generating Fewer Negative Reviews
- Immediately find creative solutions to problems mentioned in reviews. Do not wait until you have many complaints about the same issue.
- Assure staff members that they will not get in trouble for looking for creative solutions to resolve problems and make guests happy.
- Create the opportunity to resolve guests' issues while still on property. Have staff members in all positions smile, make eye contact, and ask guests how their stay is going. Even if they don't have a problem, they will perceive better care and be more likely to give a positive review.
- Ensure feedback opportunities are in place at the hotel and follow up with unhappy guests while they are still in-house. Do not let a guest leave dissatisfied without efforts to make their stay a pleasant one.

BEST PRACTICES: ELIMINATING PAST REVIEWS

Is it possible to remove negative reviews? The policies for sites vary, but in general it's difficult to do. At Tripadvisor, for example, reviews will only be removed if:

- there is a change in the property's ownership
- there is a change in the property's brand
- the property has undergone major (not simply cosmetic) renovations
- the review violates Tripadvisor guidelines and/or is proven to be fraudulent
- the negative review is being used to "blackmail" a property into providing goods or services (blackmail must be reported immediately when it happens and not after the guest has posted the review)
- the guest who wrote the review requests that it be removed

In general, the best practices for downplaying a bad review are 1) provide a management response promptly and politely, and 2) ensure that many positive reviews are posted after it. The most recent reviews usually show up first. In most cases, reviews on the third page or beyond will not be read. Keep in mind that a small number of older negative reviews may not hurt your overall business, especially if more recent reviews trend positive.

TRIPADVISOR'S CERTIFICATE OF EXCELLENCE, TRAVELERS CHOICE AWARDS, AND BEST OF THE BEST

Since 2010, Tripadvisor has award the Tripadvisor Certificate of Excellence to recognize businesses that are focused on delivering great service. In 2015, Tripadvisor also announced the Certificate of Excellence Hall of Fame to hotels that earn the award for five consecutive years.

In 2020, Tripadvisor renamed the Certificate of Excellence Award to the Tripadvisor Travelers Choice Award for the top 10% of hotels. At the same time the Travelers' Choice Award was renamed the Traveler's Choice Award "Best of the Best" and recognizes the top 25 hotels in various regions and market segments.

Tripadvisor provides free award "widgets" that hotels can place on their own websites, in email signatures, or use on on-property signage or collateral, letting guests know the hotel has been recognized.

While this can be positive marketing for the hotel, do NOT link an award widget from the hotel website back to the hotel's Tripadvisor listing! Best practice dictates not "linking away" potential customers from your site to another site where they may become easily distracted with many other hotel choices. More importantly, this negatively impacts your hotel's website by providing Tripadvisor with potentially thousands of "inbound" links to their site, giving them additional SEO "juice" over your hotel's site in the search engine ranki

REVIEW AGGREGATORS

There are thousands of hotel and travel review sites. Keeping up with the comments being broadcast about a hotel is a time challenge. As a result, there are several companies that will collect every review written about a property and place them on a single dashboard. In addition to monitoring review sites, these aggregators will also collect comments about an individual hotel and competitors on blogs, YouTube, and other social media outlets.

Sentiment analysis helps make sense of the "noise" of many reviews, helping a hotelier truly understand the online conversations about their property. Aggregators, using sentiment analysis, can sort reviews into positive and negative around keywords. For example, "front desk" may show a 69% positive sentiment meaning that 69% of the guests who included a comment about the front desk had an overall favorable opinion of the property.

A single review may be complimentary or damaging, but should be taken for what it is, one opinion. Hotels that do very well on review sites tend to put importance on the individual perspective; however, the value of aggregators is that they allow a property to recognize patterns. If one guest complains about noise, they might have loud neighbors.

That does not mean you can't have someone investigate to see if a solution exists. You can think of ways to prepare to deal with the situation better in the future through improved guest management or additional insulation between connecting rooms, for example. If 25 guests complain about noise, there is likely a larger problem. Aggregators can tabulate the number of reviews received from sites to give you a broader picture of your guest review landscape.

Alerts can also be set to notify management of a potentially negative or harmful review as soon as it is posted. Most aggregators will allow you to select certain keywords that will trigger an immediate email notification—"bed bugs," for example.

Generally, third-party aggregators charge a monthly fee for their services. A free alternative to an aggregator is Google Alerts. Though far more cumbersome, alerts can be established, with daily or weekly emails sent to you based on keywords. You can select your property name in several variations, as well as competitors' names, and a daily collection of those keyword appearances can be collected. The analytics are missing, but for the budget conscious property this is a viable option. Many hotel brands have internal or proprietary review aggregation tools. First understand what such tools capture before purchasing additional third-party tools.

HOTEL/BRAND WEBSITES AND USER-GENERATED CONTENT

Allowing user-generated content on an individual hotel website is becoming more prevalent and most major brands now collect customer reviews to be published on their own hotel websites. Some brands are adding a feed from Tripadvisor directly to their websites as a testimonial source, along with a widget to collect more reviews, while others are allowing guests to create reviews directly on their hotel websites or through guest satisfaction survey portals.

Keep in mind that both the third-party review sites as well as brand.com reviews need to be managed and acted upon.

When weighing the pros and cons of each option, remember that reviews created directly on a hotel's website do not help increase your ranking on larger travel review sites. Though, they might be seen as more trustworthy if reviewers are verified as actual guests—something not every third-party site is able to do (Expedia and Booking.com can and do verify, but Tripadvisor does not). On the flip side, using Tripadvisor-sourced reviews on your website allows you to leverage the popularity of Tripadvisor to generate additional demand for your hotel.

Consumer reviews add credibility, so if your reviews are positive overall, adding them to a hotel website might make sense. The flip side is that a negative review on your own website also has credibility and will likely influence purchasing decisions. However, a single negative review in a sea of positive reviews can actually add legitimacy to the overall collection of reviews.

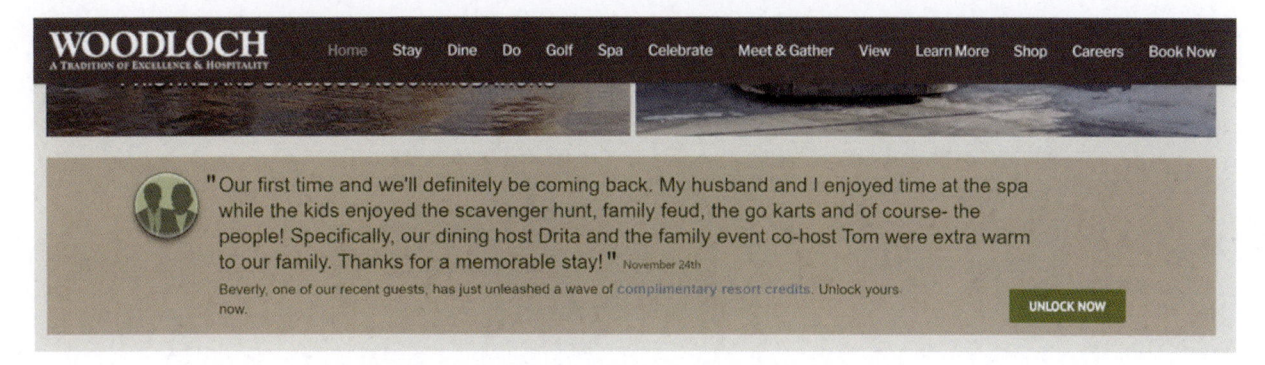

Example of on-site reviews from Woodloch Resort

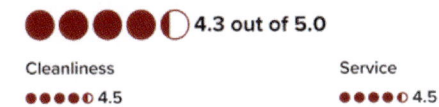

Example of on-site reviews from Marriott Phoenix Resort Tempe at The Buttes

Another pro on the side of hosting user-generated content directly on the hotel website is the SEO value. Recent and relevant content is appealing for search engines and can have a positive impact on your search ranking.

CONCLUSION

Review sites continue to grow in relevance due to credibility and authority of the content and can help or hinder conversion rates for hotels. Hotels must have a robust review strategy that includes:

- A plan for reading, analyzing, and sharing review results
- Responding effectively to reviews in a timely manner
- Reviewing and sharing competitor review information
- Modifying behaviors, policies, and products based on guest feedback to lessen complaints and inspire positive reviews
- Updating current and authentic information, as well as photos and video on top review sites and anywhere people may look for information about your hotel
- Creating opportunities to increase the number of positive reviews received and minimize negative reviews
- Leveraging technology to aggregate reviews, improving the efficiency of review responses, and more easily identifying trends through sentiment analysis
- Analyzing and taking advantage of marketing opportunities that review sites create

Chapter 17: Social Media

KEY POINTS
- The importance of social media for hotels
- Best practices for social media listening and monitoring
- How social media algorithms have evolved and what changes mean for marketers
- Best practices for publishing and posting—in general and by platform
- Nine time-honored metrics for measuring social media results
- Insights into the target audiences of top social sites to help hotel marketers identify the best match(s) for their goals

SOCIAL MEDIA TODAY

The age of social media has given rise to hyper-aware consumers. No longer limited to what is delivered to them by brands, consumers can now virtually tap into a worldwide network of fellow consumers to gather information, opinions, reviews of real-life experience, and more.

Consumers today are more aware of ads and sponsor-driven content; they have developed better "filters" to weed out the content they don't want, and are better equipped to search out the relevant, engaging content they do want. More than 80% of internet users worldwide use social networks for just that. What began as a way for people to stay in touch evolved into platforms for sharing stories, images, political viewpoints, recipes, and more. For almost every interest there is a social platform or social group.

Social media usage has seen exponential growth since its inception. In 2019, many predicted that time spent on social channels would plateau or decline, but a multitude of factors in 2020 (from the Covid-19 pandemic to political upheaval around the world) changed that projection.

The *Digital 2021* report[108] from We Are Social and Hootsuite highlights many eye-opening statistics including:

- 53.6% of the world's population are active social media users. That is up 13% year over year.
- 44.8% of internet users search for information about brands on social media.
- 73.5% of internet users follow brands or research brands and products on social media.

[109]

JAN 2021 — DIGITAL AROUND THE WORLD
ESSENTIAL HEADLINES FOR MOBILE, INTERNET, AND SOCIAL MEDIA USE
INTERNET USER NUMBERS NO LONGER INCLUDE DATA SOURCED FROM SOCIAL MEDIA PLATFORMS, SO VALUES ARE NOT COMPARABLE WITH PREVIOUS REPORTS

	TOTAL POPULATION	UNIQUE MOBILE PHONE USERS	INTERNET USERS*	ACTIVE SOCIAL MEDIA USERS*
	7.83 BILLION	5.22 BILLION	4.66 BILLION	4.20 BILLION
	URBANISATION: 56.4%	vs. POPULATION: 66.6%	vs. POPULATION: 59.5%	vs. POPULATION: 53.6%

It is expected that the social media habits that developed in 2020 will continue. The data from eMarketer on the U.S. market provides an example.

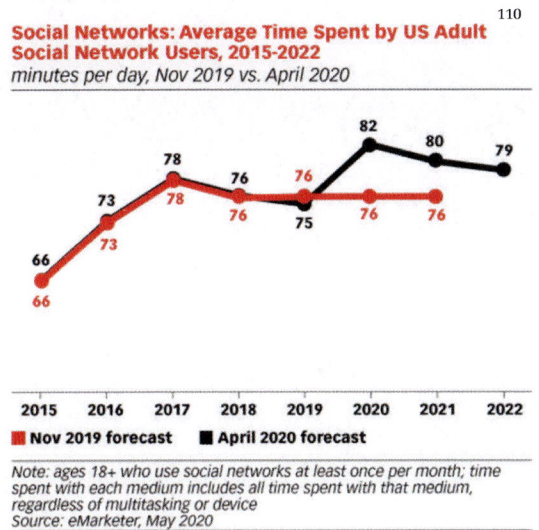

Social Networks: Average Time Spent by US Adult Social Network Users, 2015-2022[110]
minutes per day, Nov 2019 vs. April 2020

Year	Nov 2019 forecast	April 2020 forecast
2015	66	66
2016	73	73
2017	78	78
2018	76	76
2019	76	75
2020	76	82
2021	76	80
2022		79

Note: ages 18+ who use social networks at least once per month; time spent with each medium includes all time spent with that medium, regardless of multitasking or device
Source: eMarketer, May 2020
255186   www.eMarketer.com

For hoteliers, social media offers a tool for responding to customer inquiries and complaints. Used wisely it can turn your happy customers into advocates. Social media influencers can promote your hotel's story—with credibility—to their followers.

In fact, social media influencers have become such a force in the hotel marketing arena that a chapter is dedicated to them in this edition. While influencers are mentioned in this chapter, see Chapter 18 for more depth and detail.

WHY SOCIAL MEDIA?

Social media creates an opportunity for brands (hotels) to tell their story and create engagement and interaction between the brand and their customers. Social media transforms conventional one-way messaging into a two-way conversation. Anyone can create and share content—and almost everyone does.

As social beings, we are drawn to interesting stories. When we find a compelling story, we instinctively want to share it. We share because we like feeling connected. Whether it's with our friends on Facebook or the expanse of the "Twittersphere," social media is a 21st-century expression of human interaction.

Traditionally hotel marketers fed information to consumers that they wanted them to have. We had considerably more control over what was published about our brand, but far less organic reach. Today, marketers still push out information, but now our customers share their thoughts and stories around our brands with their networks.

Social media drives word of mouth much differently. Before social media, word of mouth was limited to people to whom you spoke directly. Social media has no such limitation—you can communicate with anyone, anywhere, about anything—significantly increasing the speed at which information is shared. Word of mouth has always been an important factor in the traveler's decision-making process, and that still holds true today.

While marketing in the traditional sense is very much about brand and product awareness, social media goes beyond that to actual engagement with consumers. Creating a community based on deep contact and one-to-one relationships where everyone has a voice, can turn consumers into loyal fans and even brand evangelists. As consumers rely more and more on their peers for endorsements and word-of-mouth referrals to make decisions, it is this type of engagement that creates powerful relationships that are more likely to generate sales—and repeat business—in the long term.

At the same time, consumers are interested in rich visuals on social networks like Facebook, Tripadvisor, and even Google—all of which have been redesigned to be more visually clear and appealing. Rich visuals make a story more compelling and interesting. Video, dramatic images, captions, or sound all contribute to the messaging marketers are creating on these platforms.

Social is the top channel for reporting and responding to customer service issues among millennials, and the number two channel across all age groups. Needless to say, it is critical that hotel marketers have a social media strategy.

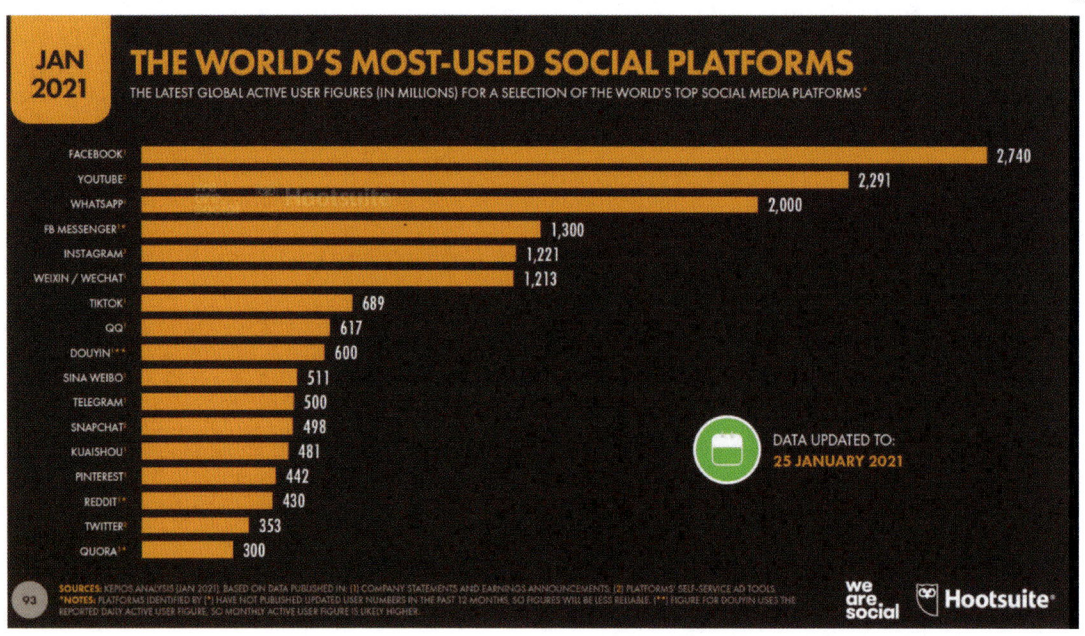

JAN 2021
THE WORLD'S MOST-USED SOCIAL PLATFORMS
THE LATEST GLOBAL ACTIVE USER FIGURES (IN MILLIONS) FOR A SELECTION OF THE WORLD'S TOP SOCIAL MEDIA PLATFORMS*

Platform	Users (millions)
FACEBOOK¹	2,740
YOUTUBE²	2,291
WHATSAPP¹	2,000
FB MESSENGER¹*	1,300
INSTAGRAM²	1,221
WEIXIN / WECHAT¹	1,213
TIKTOK¹	689
QQ¹	617
DOUYIN¹**	600
SINA WEIBO¹	511
TELEGRAM¹	500
SNAPCHAT²	498
KUAISHOU¹	481
PINTEREST¹	442
REDDIT¹*	430
TWITTER²	353
QUORA¹*	300

DATA UPDATED TO: 25 JANUARY 2021

SOURCES: KEPIOS ANALYSIS (JAN 2021), BASED ON DATA PUBLISHED IN: (1) COMPANY STATEMENTS AND EARNINGS ANNOUNCEMENTS; (2) PLATFORMS' SELF-SERVICE AD TOOLS. NOTES: PLATFORMS IDENTIFIED BY (*) HAVE NOT PUBLISHED UPDATED USER NUMBERS IN THE PAST 12 MONTHS, SO FIGURES WILL BE LESS RELIABLE. (**) FIGURE FOR DOUYIN USES THE REPORTED DAILY ACTIVE USER FIGURE, SO MONTHLY ACTIVE USER FIGURE IS LIKELY HIGHER.

we are social • Hootsuite

The Uses of Social Media in Marketing Strategy

For hotel marketers, it is extremely important that, no matter where you focus your marketing efforts, you make your activities shareable on social media, and make your activities interesting enough for people to want to share them. In addition, since sharing is by its nature a two-way street, it is important for you to share interesting items that others have produced that are relevant to your hotel's story and your customers.

The uses for social media in your marketing strategy are many.

- Brand Awareness: Social allows you to present a visual and detailed representation of your brand to potential customers who have never seen you in real life.
- Customer Service: Social media allows you to monitor and positively influence the way potential and existing customers perceive your brand. By monitoring reviews, and providing feedback or action when needed, you can elevate guest relations and increase loyalty with customers like never before.
- Website Traffic: Social media can generate awareness of and credibility for your website, maximize conversion and traffic flow, establish you as an expert in your market, and increase organic search engine rankings.
- Offer Distribution: In collaboration with revenue management, social media is an ideal channel for driving special rates, offers, promotions, and packages to a large audience quickly.
- Content Distribution: Social media is an incredible source of content. Think of it as a worldwide pool of photographers and writers creating content for your hotel. You just need to curate it into snackable chunks and re-amplify it into the community.
- Research: Tracking the social conversations of your competitors has never been easier. You can see what customers are saying and sharing about all your competitors—and, of course, vice versa. Additionally, you can use social media to spot trends, see where people are spending their time, and learn what they're looking at and talking about. The reviews your audience writes and the photos they take give you great insight into what they value. They literally show you why they've chosen your hotel over the competition.
- Customer Engagement: This was never more evident than when the Covid-19 pandemic struck and savvy hoteliers used social media to communicate the steps being taken to ensure guest safety, what was happening in the local area, and how they were prepared for visitors.
- Sales and Lead Generation: In its early days, the actual business value of social media was often in question. Today, you can not only make sales on social media

platforms, but you can drive conversions, increase organic search results for your website, and impact several KPIs directly and indirectly. Advanced tracking and attribution modeling has made it easier to connect social activity to actual bookings. Remember that social media is a fantastic source of leads. Lead magnets might include photo contests, loyalty program signups, virtual tours, and targeted photography for inspiration to name just a few.

SOCIAL MEDIA LISTENING AND MONITORING

Social media listening means analyzing the conversations and trends happening around your brand, and around your industry as a whole—and using those insights to make better marketing decisions.[112]

Social media monitoring is more specific. You monitor social media to discover and respond to specific comments (from an in-house guest for example).

There are multiple applications for hotels when it comes to both listening to and monitoring social media.

- Reputation Management: Keep an eye on the sentiment and nature of conversations around your brand name.
- Audience Research: Create buyer personas. Identify where your audience is (geographically and internet-wise) and what they are talking about.
- Trend Research: Identify what's hot in your niche and online.
- Competitor Research: Determine your share of voice as well as your competitors' strengths and weaknesses.
- Product Research: Identify what customers want from your and your competitors' products.
- Increasing Brand Awareness: Get involved in niche-specific conversations and communities.
- Link Building: Find unlinked mentions and potential opportunities for link building to support your off-page SEO.
- Customer Care: Find and respond to customer care queries on social media.
- Influencer Marketing: Identify influencers in your niche.

This list is certainly not comprehensive but gives you a clear sense of the myriad opportunities that exist today around discovery and research using social media listening and monitoring.

There are many tools available to assist in your efforts. Start with each social media channel. Adjust your settings to be notified of mentions important to your property or brand.

Social media listening aggregators can help you make sense of all the data. Most of these tools collect data around brand mentions or any search term or content piece around which you are trying to collect data. Examples include Revinate and ReviewPro (which were created specifically for hotels), and Sprout Social, Awario, Buzzsumo, and Agorapulse—to name just a few.

THE EVOLUTION OF SOCIAL MEDIA PLATFORM ALGORITHMS

In the earliest days of social media, the idea was to collect friends or followers and whatever you post would show up on the news feeds of those contacts. As time passed, too much clutter was appearing in news feeds, so social algorithms were introduced to help the most relevant information appear.

How was this relevancy determined? Initially, the more likes and views your post had, the more exposure you were able to get. If you had more friends or followers, you were deemed more popular, so your posts appeared more often.

Facebook began delivering more personalized results based on your interests. If you showed an inclination for certain posts, more of those post types would appear in your news feed. From 2011-2015, Facebook experimented with several factors including relevancy, video content, and link-friendly posts. At the same time, it began penalizing commercialized posts.

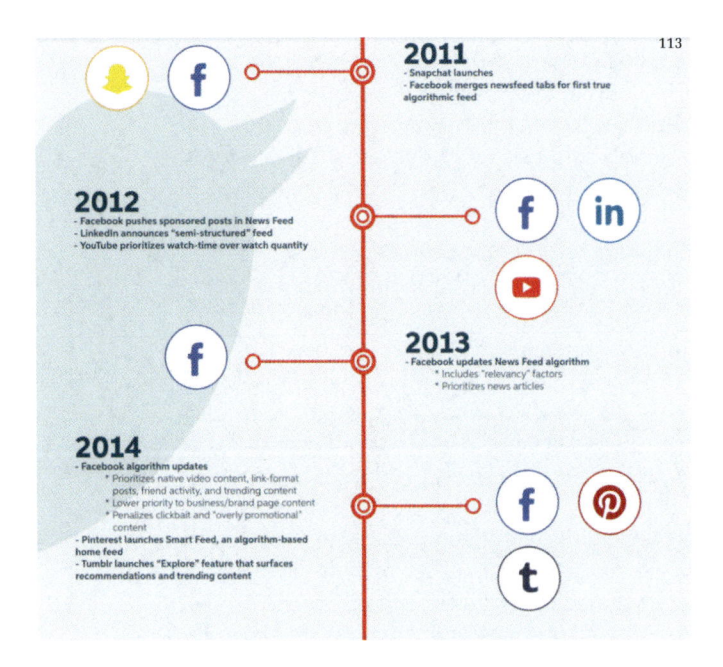

2011 [113]
- Snapchat launches
- Facebook merges newsfeed tabs for first true algorithmic feed

2012
- Facebook pushes sponsored posts in News Feed
- LinkedIn announces "semi-structured" feed
- YouTube prioritizes watch-time over watch quantity

2013
- Facebook updates News Feed algorithm
  * Includes "relevancy" factors
  * Prioritizes news articles

2014
- Facebook algorithm updates
  * Prioritizes native video content, link-format posts, friend activity, and trending content
  * Lower priority to business/brand page content
  * Penalizes clickbait and "overly promotional" content
- Pinterest launches Smart Feed, an algorithm-based home feed
- Tumblr launches "Explore" feature that surfaces recommendations and trending content

2015 [115]
- Facebook updates
  * Begins fight against fake news
  * Rebalances the algorithm to relax Pages limitations in News Feed
  * Time spent viewing and actions taken affect ranking on News Feed
- Pinterest updates
  * Machine learning determines "pinnability" on home feed
  * Real-time input improves home-feed algorithm

2016
- Facebook updates
  * Facebook Live content prioritized
  * Friend updates prioritized
  * New ranking factor predicts most "informative" content
  * Content ranked based on probability of relevance and engagement
- LinkedIn updates
  * Relevance ranked in feed
- Twitter updates
  * Optional algorithmic timeline launches
- Instagram updates
  * Algorithmic timeline launched
- Tumblr updates
  * Ads display on dashboard

Beginning in 2015 and continuing today, all the social channel algorithms became more sophisticated and intentional. For example, Facebook prioritized Facebook Live posts and friend updates. The most informative content—based on relevance and engagement—began to appear most frequently. Like Google's work around SEO, faster web page load time in the news feed became a priority in 2017, and the fight against fake news began.

Two engineers from Twitter, Nicolas Koumchatzky and Anton Andryeyev, attempted to explain their ranking system: "With ranking, we add an extra twist. Right after gathering all tweets, each is scored by a relevance model. The model's score predicts how interesting and engaging a tweet would be specifically to you. A set of highest-scoring tweets is then shown at the top of your timeline, with the remainder shown directly below. Depending on the number of candidate tweets we have available for you and the amount of time since your last visit, we may choose to also show you a dedicated 'in case you missed it' module. This module meant to contain only a small handful of the very most relevant tweets ordered by their relevance score, whereas the ranked timeline contains relevant tweets ordered by time. The intent is to let you see the best tweets at a glance first before delving into the lengthier time-ordered sections." [114]

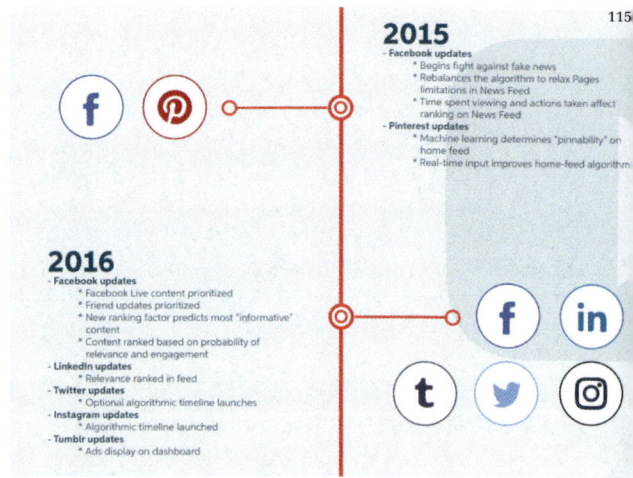

Trusted sources mattered more, and likes were no longer enough. To show up, you had to deliver content that was shared, which eventually evolved into content that was commented upon. At this printing, for most social sites, comments are the strongest indicator of the most relevant content, so social channels give the highest rewards or exposure to posters who collect the most comments.

The United States' 2016 presidential race ushered in the onset of fake accounts—Russian bots posed and posted erroneous news articles—and Cambridge Analytica scraped more private user behavioral data than was allowed. Trust in social channel content began to diminish and the social channels began their slow but deliberate efforts to reduce fake news, protect user data, and, most importantly, make their channels more addictive.

Some form of this is true for all social algorithms. They want to always return to you the results that keep you engaged—so that you spend more and more time on their platform.

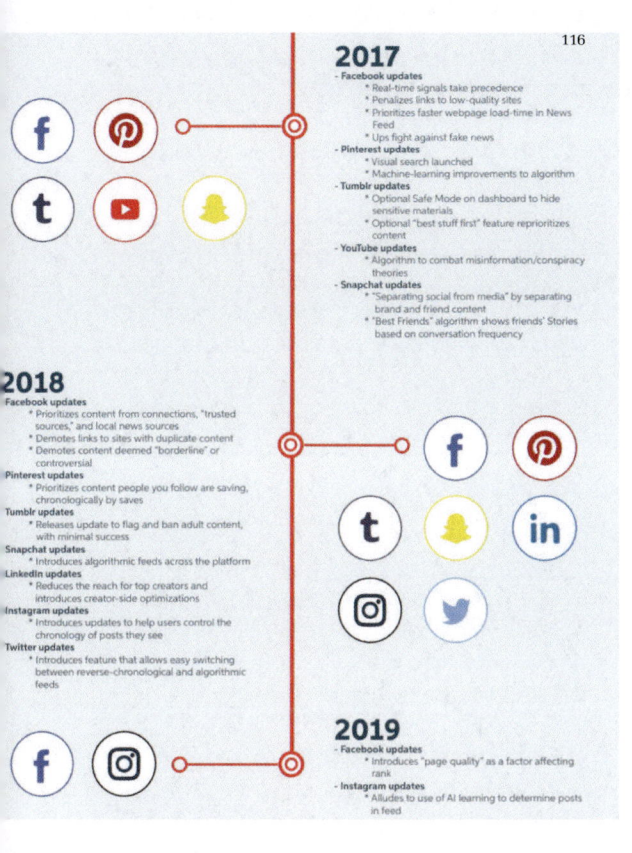

2017
- Facebook updates
  * Real-time signals take precedence
  * Penalizes links to low-quality sites
  * Prioritizes faster webpage load-time in News Feed
  * Ups fight against fake news
- Pinterest updates
  * Visual search launched
  * Machine-learning improvements to algorithm
- Tumblr updates
  * Optional Safe Mode on dashboard to hide sensitive materials
  * Optional "best stuff first" feature reprioritizes content
- YouTube updates
  * Algorithm to combat misinformation/conspiracy theories
- Snapchat updates
  * "Separating social from media" by separating brand and friend content
  * "Best Friends" algorithm shows friends' Stories based on conversation frequency

2018
- Facebook updates
  * Prioritizes content from connections, "trusted sources," and local news sources
  * Demotes links to sites with duplicate content
  * Demotes content deemed "borderline" or controversial
- Pinterest updates
  * Prioritizes content people you follow are saving, chronologically by saves
- Tumblr updates
  * Releases update to flag and ban adult content, with minimal success
- Snapchat updates
  * Introduces algorithmic feeds across the platform
- LinkedIn updates
  * Reduces the reach for top creators and introduces creator-side optimizations
- Instagram updates
  * Introduces updates to help users control the chronology of posts they see
- Twitter updates
  * Introduces feature that allows easy switching between reverse-chronological and algorithmic feeds

2019
- Facebook updates
  * Introduces "page quality" as a factor affecting rank
- Instagram updates
  * Alludes to use of AI learning to determine posts in feed

116

BEST PRACTICES FOR PUBLISHING ON SOCIAL MEDIA

Social media publishing is the process of planning, creating, scheduling, and distributing content across various social media platforms.

Best Practices: Listen to Wow
Like responding to reviews, creating a system to uncover and quickly respond to brand mentions, compliments, and concerns, and answer questions or simply engage in the ongoing story of your brand with customers, is critical today. Use a listening tool to keep track of who is talking about you, and have staff trained in appropriate responses dedicated to engaging.

Use social listening tools to create opportunities for "wow" experiences for your guests. Outrigger Hotels searches for opportunities to surprise their in-house guests with gifts based on their social posts. If a guest mentions they are traveling to the property for an anniversary or special event, the hotel will send a special gift and encourage their guest to share it on their social channels. One guest was ill, so the hotel sent a bowl of soup to their room. That guest happened to have more than 54,000 followers who saw their post about the delivery.

Best Practices: Start Each Post with a Goal in Mind
Every post should support your overall marketing strategy and align with your messaging. Have a goal for everything you publish on social media. What specific target audience are you trying to reach? What point in their journey are you addressing? What do you want your viewers to do? What opinion do you want them to form?

Best Practices: Define and Use your Brand Voice
Start by researching your audience's demographics, needs, pain points, and interests. Make note of the words and phrases they use when talking about subjects relevant to your brand. Consider the values and culture your company wants to communicate. Then establish brand voice guidelines that outline the words, tone, and style you'll use to appeal to your audience. This is helpful even if you are the only one who posts, but chances are good you may have several people who help with your social efforts, so it is critical for everyone to use the same voice.

Best Practices: Write for the Platform
In social media channels, your message competes fiercely with others for your readers' attention. That is why it is important to use plain language and craft your message so the information you present is easy to understand.

Platforms vary in terms of what their audiences enjoy; therefore, the algorithms prioritize different types of posts. Research the platform and use what works best on it. For example, video gets the most engagement on Facebook, so make text-only Facebook posts less than 50 characters. On the other hand, text-only posts on LinkedIn get 1000% more views than image or video posts.

Social media content generally has a more informal tone than other communications, but it varies by channel. Your goal is to have an engaging, conversational tone that resonates with each platform's audience.

Best Practices: Make the Most of Visual Storytelling
For hotels, visual storytelling on social media is an ideal way to connect with potential guests

in a very real, personal way. More than just a TV ad or a "brochure" website, social media gives you the chance to tell your hotel's story in a visually compelling manner, and show off your rooms and amenities, as well as your people and your guests, with impactful visuals, quickly and easily, across multiple channels.

- Ensure content encourages emotional connections and interactions—stories engage—they don't just share facts and data.
- Maintain consistency (imagery, colors) throughout all platforms. Ensure your brand profile is complete on any platform, fill in the About information, and be sure there is visual consistency in terms of colors and imagery style.
- Always consider video—and if you do, remember that the majority are watching your video with the sound off or on their phone—so include captions and remember sizing.
- Consider livestreaming—engagement is high currently.
- Always be prepared to interact with your audience. You can create an amazing post that garners engagement but be sure to comment back, answer questions, and in general interact with your audience.

Hotel Giraffe does a great job encouraging engagement by asking you to tag your "Galentine."

Best Practices: Use Emojis on Facebook and Instagram

Text alone does not always imply tone. Emojis can help. Use emojis that mean something to your audience. Review posts from influencers or other brands in your space to familiarize yourself with your audience's emoji language. Reference Emojipedia to find, copy, and paste relevant emojis into your social media posts.

> According to an Emojipedia analysis, the top 10 emojis used on Twitter across 2020 were:
> 1. 😂 Face with Tears of Joy
> 2. 😭 Loudly Crying Face
> 3. 🥺 Pleading Face
> 4. ❤️ Red Heart
> 5. 🤣 Rolling on the Floor Laughing
> 6. ✨ Sparkles
> 7. 😍 Smiling Face with Heart-Eyes
> 8. 🙏 Folded Hands
> 9. 🥰 Smiling Face with Hearts
> 10. 😊 Smiling Face with Smiling Eyes

emojipedia.com

Best Practices: Use Relevant Hashtags

Adding hashtags to social posts is a critical element for success on most social sites. Hashtags make your content searchable, and you may attract new followers if you have hashtags that others are searching for—as long as your content is relevant. Don't be misleading just to capitalize on a trending hashtag. To boost brand awareness with popular hashtags, use a free tool like "Hashtagify" for Twitter or "Keyword Tool for Instagram Hashtags."

Best Practices: Tag Partners and Add Links

Add a link within your post that takes your reader to more valuable content or another piece of the story. A link that supports your post adds credibility—as long as it is relevant. The exception to this best practice is on Instagram: since links don't work on Instagram, put the link in your bio and refer Instagram users there.

Tagging a partner, typically by using the @ in front of their username, grows your exposure and notifies your partner that you are including them, which ought to encourage them to also share with their audience.

Linking and tagging increase your credibility—which should always be a goal on social.

Best Practices: Add a Call to Action

End posts with a call to action that is aligned with your overall strategy. If you want to drive people to your website, add "Reserve Now!" or "Click for more information." If you want engagement, use "What's your take?" or "Tell us what you think." Remember the significance of comments to the social algorithms. Asking for comments is the best way to increase your comments!

BEST PRACTICES BY PLATFORM

When it comes to social media, the single biggest mistake brands make is failing to strategically align their product with their target audience on the sites that most closely match their targeted demographic.

Which platform should you use? What should your messaging be? As covered in Chapter 3 (Hotel Digital Marketing Strategy), your targeted segments and their needs should be considered before you dive into the world of social media marketing. Each platform has a different demographic and approach, so before you begin, understand both your targets and what each platform offers.

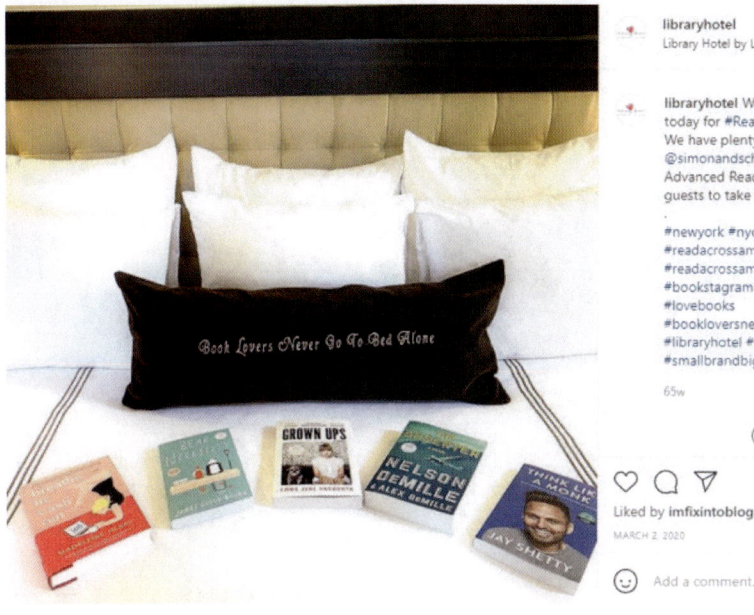

A great example of a call to action from the Library Hotel

A Field Guide for Navigating Today's Digital Landscape

SOCIAL PLATFORM FEATURES & OPPORTUNITIES FOR MARKETERS

It is important to understand what a social media platform offers to both consumers and marketers. Expand on this chart to add additional platforms you are considering.

	Facebook	Instagram	Snapchat	TikTok	Twitter
Newsfeed	X	X			X
Ads?	X	X			X
Stories	X	X	X		X
Ads?	X	X	X		
Short-Video Feed		X	X	X	
Ads?				X	
Direct Messages	X	X	X	X	X
Ads?	X				
Livestreaming	X	X	X	X	X
Ads?	X		X		
Augmented Reality	X	X	X	X	
Ads?	X	X	X	X	
Long-Form Videos/Shows	X	X	X		
Ads?	X	X	X		
Influencer Integration	X	X	X	X	
Ads?	X	X	X	X	
Ecommerce Capability	X	X	X	X	
Online Storefronts?	X	X	X		
Shoppable Ads?	X	X	X	X	
Shoppable Video Streams?	X	X	X	X	

BEST PRACTICES FOR FACEBOOK

Facebook is the largest and most well-known social network. More than 160 million businesses use Facebook each month[117], and 49% of Facebook users report liking a brand's page to show their support of that brand.[118]

- Make use of the cover photo feature. Your cover photo is a great way to establish your brand in a big, bold way. And given its prominence on your page—and the simplicity of updating it—you can change it regularly to tie in to promotions or give seasonal views of your property.

- Complete all About information and provide correct details for contact and location information.

- Take advantage of the Facebook app infrastructure. There are more than 7 million apps and websites that integrate with Facebook. Using apps is a great way for you to leverage the Facebook platform while telling your story the way you want to tell it—and the way that engages your customers most effectively. With apps, you can customize your Facebook experience to your hotel's brand, display multi-media, promote loyalty programs and offers, enable booking, and more.

- Be responsive. More and more, people are using social media as a support platform. If you have guests and prospects asking questions on your wall or through Facebook Messenger, write back promptly—and politely!

- Study your community. Analyze and better understand your Facebook audience and their interests—align Facebook content to better resonate with your community. Use Facebook Polls to get input and opinions.
- Be human and authentic. Be approachable and honest. Personalize the page so it is consistent with your brand/property.
- Get existing customers and prospects to be fans by emailing to your opt-in list, blogging about your page, sending out tweets, linking it to your email signature, and posting a link or badge on your website.
- Use Facebook's built-in analytics to track valuable metrics such as page views, wall posts, discussion threads, and photo views.
- There are advertising options that target specific demographics. See Chapter 23 for details on the paid media side of social media.
- DO NOT constantly change your "profile" picture. This is the image users see in their news feed every time you're active on Facebook—it should be something recognizable and familiar, so that everyone knows right away who you are.

BEST PRACTICES FOR YOUTUBE

YouTube revolutionized online video sharing with its introduction in 2005. Quickly bought by Google, YouTube has over 2 billion monthly logged-in users watching over a billion hours of video and generating billions of views—every day.[119] It's considered the second most popular social site worldwide.

- Ensure videos are posted on channels that make sense for your personality, style, features, and amenities. Some brands have successfully created their own YouTube channels to syndicate their content as part of a broader marketing strategy.
- Consider the global audience. YouTube is localized in more than 100 countries and 80 languages worldwide.[120] Include videos that have global appeal to attract worldwide travelers. The beautiful thing about imagery is that it requires no language translation.
- Share videos other than your own. You might not have the resources to create new videos every week, but that doesn't mean your YouTube channel page should sit idle. Consider the types of videos your guests and followers might like; showcase local events and other travel videos.
- "How to" videos get the lion's share of attention of YouTube. Consider what you can do to develop relevant "how to" videos, "How to host a hybrid meeting" or "How to find the best local spots in London" for example.
- Listen, monitoring all mentions of topics relevant to your brand/property to better understand customer sentiment. Use YouTube Insights and comment/discussion sections to monitor customer concerns or misconceptions of the brand/property.
- Link channel videos on other social mediums. Integrate other social media properties, for instance by adding your YouTube content to your Facebook page, to better unite social media efforts and raise the relevancy of your content in search.
- Maximize SEO opportunities. Title and tag videos and channel appropriately to maximize their SEO value for consumer searches. Be sure to brand yourself by displaying brand/property information, URL, email, and phone number in every video, and post links to your videos on social networks.
- Tag videos with relevant keywords.
- DO NOT share completely unrelated videos. While it's tempting to share the latest hilarious video you see making its way through social media, be careful not to dilute your message: stay on brand and give your visitors only the videos that relate to your property's image and identity.

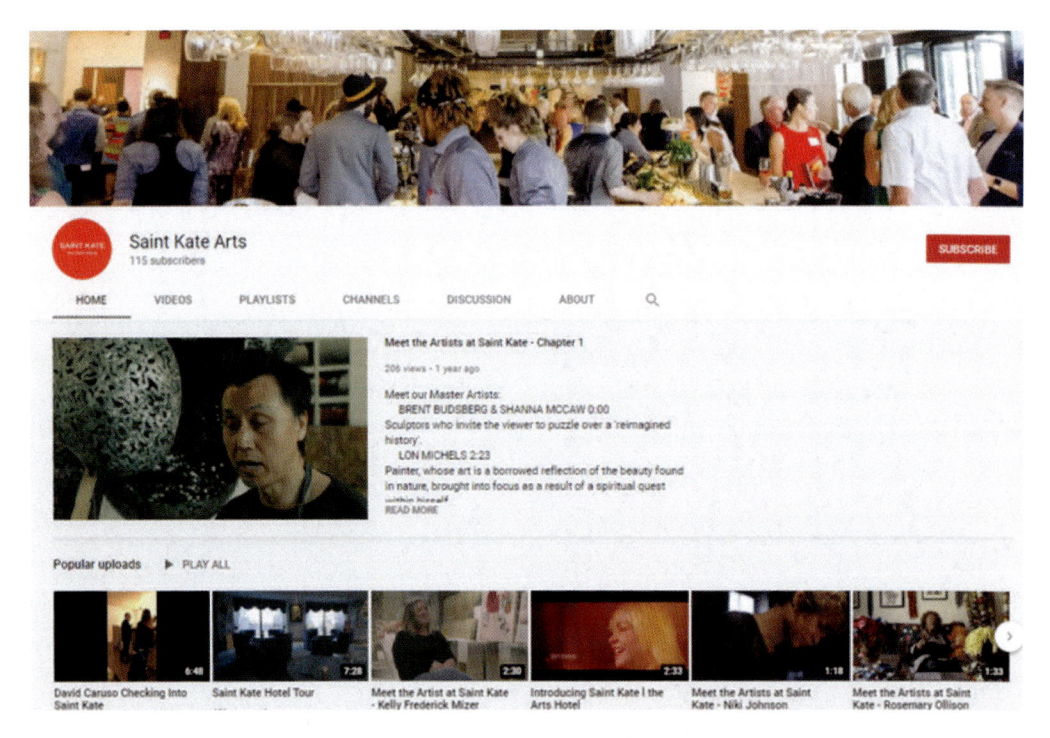

The Saint Kate Arts hotel offers videos of their art installations and events on their YouTube channel. It is visual, well targeted to their audience, and on brand.

BEST PRACTICES FOR INSTAGRAM

Instagram is one of the most visual platforms. "Travel inspiration" is consistently a top use reported by Instagram users. Most Instagram users are between 18 to 29 years of age with 32% of Instagram users being college students.[121]

It was created to enable the sharing of pictures and videos, both publicly and privately.

Since its creation in 2010, more than 40 billion photos have been shared. On average, 95 million photos are uploaded daily on Instagram.[122]

Instagram was acquired by Facebook in 2012.

- Show the human side of your property. Take people behind the scenes for an insider look, create stories about your history, or highlight special employees.
- Show off the surrounding area. Let people know the look and feel of your neighborhood.
- Collaborate with influencers. If you have targeted niches, make sure you have contacted influencers in that niche to help showcase what you can add (see Chapter 18 for more insights).
- Make your property Instagram-able. Have areas around your property "staged" and ready for selfies to be snapped and shared.
- Don't forget hashtags. Trending and location hashtags are best.
- Consider partnerships for IGTV video content. Find a local partner (e.g., restaurant, attraction, or event) that can help you create an interesting IGTV channel.

BEST PRACTICES FOR LINKEDIN

LinkedIn is a professional networking service founded in 2002. It tops the list for most trustworthy networking sites with more 750 million members and more than 57 million company pages in 200 countries worldwide.[123]

- Use the blue space at the top of your profile page for branding photos.
- Ask your employees to share your content. LinkedIn is one of the few social media platforms that is business focused. Asking your employees to share your posted content is acceptable.
- Add value for your audience with your posts. Provide links to important information or articles that your audience may find helpful.

- Decision makers are on LinkedIn more than any other platform which is ideal for B2B businesses like hotels.
- Don't forget hashtags. While not as relevant as on Instagram, a few hashtags—around content and location—can be helpful on LinkedIn.
- Add images and other media to profiles.
- You can add links to your websites, to blog posts, or to area information in the features section of your business or personal profile page.

BEST PRACTICES FOR SNAPCHAT

Snapchat was created in 2011 as a private messaging app that gave users the ability to create "snaps" or messages that would self-destruct (be automatically deleted) after being viewed. Today, 60% of Snapchat users are 18-34 years old and create and share approximately 3 billion snaps every day.[124]

There is no limit to creativity, as Snapchat content is considered informal and fun.

- Make your profile public. Make everyone your friend.
- Personalize your Filters and Lenses. For example, a special branded filter can frame the moments at a wedding and make the event even more special.
- Responses on Snapchat are immediate and real-time, which means interaction with customers needs to be prompt. Customers' inquiries should be handled immediately.
- Marketing on Snapchat is all about unleashing creativity. Therefore, have more than one administrator post content. This will bring more diverse content that is more likely to keep the customers interested.[125]
- Make it snappy. Snaps should be brief and easy to watch in about 10 seconds.
- Link individual snaps together to create a Snapchat Story. Stories should last only 1-2 minutes.
- Go vertical. Snapchat is used via mobile phone, so vertical content is easiest to view.
- Fill your space. Make sure images take up the whole frame.
- Go for contrast—with white text on a dark background, for example.
- Make liberal use of emojis.
- Engage followers with snaps about contests, coupon codes, employee bios, etc.
- Cross-promote your Snapchat content on other social media channels like Facebook and Twitter to bring more views and engagement on Snapchat.

When it comes to content for Snapchat, collaboration with social media influencers can deliver content to a wider audience, emphasize brand personality, drive purchase decisions, and ultimately increase sales. See Chapter 18 for more on working with influencers.

Additional content ideas include:

- Virtual tours of your restaurant, meeting rooms, or neighborhood
- Live updates from an event held on or near your property
- Behind-the-scenes shots
- Themed campaigns where followers can submit their own content

BEST PRACTICES FOR TWITTER

Twitter's quick bursts of information are ideally suited to our time-crunched, on-the-go, society. Twitter has embraced more visual storytelling features as well, including header photos, photo streaming/swiping on mobile apps, and photo filters for mobile uploads.

Founded in 2006 as an experiment, Twitter quickly became a messaging addiction for many. Today close to 460,000 new Twitter accounts are registered every day. Twitter users post 140 million tweets daily which adds up to a billion tweets in a week.[126]

- Use your background. Use an image that says something about your property, or that shows off what you have to offer. Consider the way your background image "splits," with your timeline in the middle. Why not have a photo of your hotel on the left and photos of your pool, business center, and restaurant on the right?
- Re-tweet. As with other social sites, sharing is a huge part of Twitter. Follow local businesses and other Twitter users that may be relevant to your guests, and retweet anything you think has value. Add photos to your tweets. To engage visually,

augment your tweets with photos—of your property, of your guests enjoying themselves, of your chef's latest creation.

- Use hashtags. Hashtags are used before a relevant keyword or phrase to categorize tweets and help them show more easily in search. They are a great way to join an existing conversation or even start your own. It is also important not to overuse them. Hashtags are intended to add value to your tweets, so use them sparingly and respectfully. A good rule of thumb is to use no more than two per tweet.

- Keep tweets short to allow room for your followers to give you credit when they "retweet" and share with their friends. Always include a link within the message, ideally at the beginning, since it will increase the likelihood that followers will click on it. Twitter also allows an image to be added to each tweet.

- DO NOT worry if your tweets don't get a response. Avoid focusing on measuring retweets; instead, focus on making your content engaging and relevant to your followers.

- #dontmakeyourhashtagafullsentence. They are simply too hard to read and no one will ever hashtag that again, and therefore no conversation will happen.

Marriott Bonvoy uses Twitter to inspire and share their story through visuals, hashtags, and links.

SOCIAL MEDIA MEASUREMENT

There are a variety of social media marketing tools and an almost infinite stream of data available. Remember though, there's no magic potion to turn your social media activities into dollars. The social sphere is and always will be a rapidly evolving marketplace. Understand the role of social media in the shopping journey so that you can keep your eye on how it's helping you achieve your larger marketing objectives. What should you measure and why? Following are nine time-honored metrics.[127]

1. Share of Voice
The number of mentions of your brand versus competing brands on the social web. Your share of voice can be a good indicator of the consumer awareness of your brand as compared to your competitive set. It essentially shows how much of the social conversation your brand has earned or is currently earning.

2. Brand Volume
The total number of brand mentions over a given period of time. If this number isn't growing, your campaign probably isn't working. Tracking brand volume week-over-week and month-over-month can be a good way to measure the overall health of your social presence.

3. Engagement
The overall number of times a user talks to your brand on social sites. You can push out all the content in the world, but if no one cares to reply or discuss it, what's the point? Social media is a conversation, after all. The more highly engaged your followers and fans are, the more likely they are to be brand-loyalists, or to become influencers and evangelize your products or services on their own personal networks.

How to calculate engagement rate? Engagement rate is the number of engagements on a post divided by the reach of that post. For example, if your Facebook Live video had 50 reactions, 50 comments, and 50 shares with a reach of 750, the engagement rate equation would be 150/750 = .20 (20%).

4. Interaction Per Post
The number of likes, replies, or comments you receive on a given post, tweet, or update. Like the engagement metric, the more times a user

makes the effort to comment or reply, the more likely it is that they will grow to care about your brand and what you have to say.

5. Sentiment Analysis
The process of determining how people talk about your brand on social media and how they actually feel about your brand, products, or company. Although P.T. Barnum famously said, "There's no such thing as bad publicity," it's a problem if your hotel is consistently being trashed on social media. Also, if the sentiment is mostly neutral, that could be a sign your marketing is not making a big enough impact, and no one cares enough to have a strong opinion either positively or negatively.

6. Social Click Through Rate
The number of times a user clicks on a link to one of your owned web properties (e.g., your hotel's website) shared via social media. Typically, one of the goals of a social media campaign is to drive traffic to a brand's website, microsite, or other owned media, thereby creating consumer awareness and subsequently bookings. The growth in the number of click throughs can be one of the indicators of a successful, engaging campaign.

7. Key Influencer Mentions
The number of mentions by users you've designated as "key influencers" due to their substantial and loyal social media following. Having influencers discuss your brand and serve as a brand ambassador is an extremely powerful way to organically extend your reach within key communities. While having anyone mention your brand on social media can be proof your tactics are working, mentions by key influencers are considered more valuable since they have a deeper reach or more pull/influence with your target demographic or communities.

8. Platform Reach
The number of social platforms that your hotel appears on, or the social "reach" across various online networks. Your brand might be a hot topic of discussion on various forums, but your Twitter mentions are low. Whether this is a problem depends on the social networks your targets use. After all, having a popular Pinterest page, which has a predominantly female user-base, doesn't really help if your brand is trying to target teenage males.

9. Mobile Mentions
The number of mentions of your hotel on mobile social sites. Social media is an increasingly mobile form of communication. Posting updates while on the go is part of nearly everyone's lifestyle, thanks to smartphones and tablets. If consumers aren't bringing your brand with them via mobile apps, this could be a sign you are getting left behind. It is especially important if your campaign involves mobile coupons, QR codes, or anything else that's tied into the Android or iPhone operating systems.

Additionally, each platform has specific measurements available. For example, on Facebook you can track:

- Key areas: fans, engagement, impressions, brand awareness, reach, engaged users
- Fans: new organic, new paid, fans lost, net fans
- Engagement: reactions, clicks, comments, private messages, shares, total engagement
- Impressions: organic impressions, paid impressions, viral impressions, total impressions
- Brand awareness score: # of mentions of your page and shares of your content for the selected period

SAMPLE CHDM EXAM QUESTIONS

1. Which factor does Twitter take into consideration when determining if your tweet will appear on your followers' news feeds?
    a. The tweet itself: its recency, presence of media (image or video), and total interactions
    b. The tweet's author: the follower's past interactions with the author, the strength of their connection, the origin of their relationship
    c. The follower: tweets the follower found engaging in the past, how often and how heavily they use Twitter
    d. A & B
    e. All of the above
    f. None of the above

2. When creating a social media strategy, which of the following is essential?
    a. Specifying price points when posting special offers
    b. Identifying the target audience(s)
    c. Keeping social strategies and objectives separate from the overall sales and marketing strategy
    d. Changing your social media voice based on the campaign
    e. Having your LinkedIn postings mirror your Facebook postings

3. Engagement rate can be calculated by:
    a. The number of engagements on a post divided by the reach of that post
    c. The number of people who click through to your website
    c. The number of likes on your post
    d. All of the above
    e. None of the above

Answers
1 = e
2 = b
3 = a

NOTES

Chapter 18: Influencers

> **KEY POINTS**
> - The definition, evolution, and types of influencers
> - Best practices for working with influencers including setting goals, finding good matches, compensating, and measuring success

As younger consumers stopped watching TV and turned to mobile apps, digital ad blocking reached an all-time high, so finding and capitalizing on social media influencers became a new opportunity for hotel marketers. The early days of trading a free room for a social post to reach a mini celebrity's followers have given way to more sophisticated targeting of niche market micro-influencers who have proven capable of delivering a strong ROI to hotels. This chapter explores the evolution of influencer marketing and shares success stories and best practices around finding and measuring influencers.

WHAT IS AN INFLUENCER?

An influencer is someone who has the power to affect the purchasing decisions of others because of their (real or perceived) authority, knowledge, position, or relationship with their audience.

In hospitality, we have worked with influencers for years in the form of travel agents and travel writers. Prior to social media, hotels would often host travel agent fam (familiarization) trips to showcase a new property or renovation. The intent was to encourage those agents and travel writers to influence travel buyers to choose your property.

However, it wasn't until social media and the explosion of the Kardashians that influencers for all industries emerged. The emergence of influencers as we know them today started when Kim Kardashian, an American media personality, had 60 million social media followers while the superstar singer Katy Perry had over 100 million. With fewer followers, Kim Kardashian was more of an influencer because every time she tweeted or posted, 25% of her followers on average would retweet or repost, giving her one of the broadest reaches in the social world.

Then along came Kylie Jenner, Kim's younger sister. While Kylie was a paid Snapchat influencer, she tweeted "Sooo does anyone else not open Snapchat anymore? Or is it just me…ugh this is so sad." The following day, Snapchat experienced a $1.3 billion drop in value. This event really made brands understand the impact that influencers can have on revenues.

Forbes — Money | Innovation | Lifestyle | Leadership | Consumer | Industry | Billionaires

Snapchat's $1.3 Billion Drop In Value Is Linked To A Kardashian

Megan C. Hills, Contributor
Feb 23, 2018, 08:07am • 30,370 views • #NewTech

WHY THE RISE IN BRAND USES OF INFLUENCERS?

There has been a steady growth in the use of influencers since 2016.

Estimated Influencer Marketing Growth (YOY) [128]

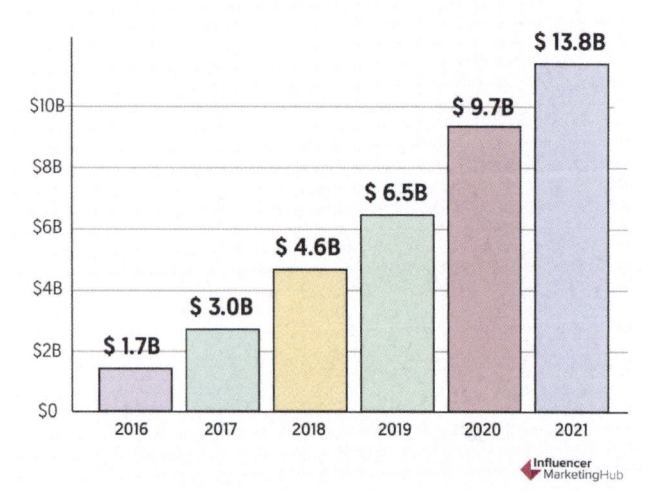

According to Influencer Marketing Hub, the influencer marketing industry will be $13.8 billion in 2021. What factors have contributed to this meteoric rise? The year 2015 was the first year more time was spent on mobile apps than on television. According to Flurry Analytics, in the second quarter of 2015, TV viewership averaged 168 minutes a day and time spent inside mobile apps increased from 139 minutes to 198 minutes.[129] This trend began to cost advertisers as there were audiences that they couldn't reach using traditional advertising methods. Investment in social media marketing—and in influencers—began to rise significantly.

Cost of ad blocking in the United States from 2016 to 2020 [130]
(in million U.S. dollars)

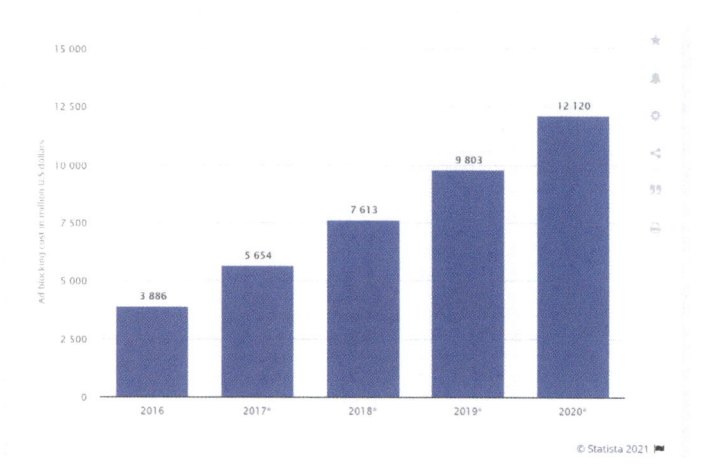

This led to the second reason influencers increased in their appeal: ad blocking became a widely accepted practice for consumers. According to Global WebIndex's 2019 data, nearly 47% of internet users globally use ad blockers, which cost U.S. companies alone an estimated $12 billion in 2020 according to Statista.com.

TV ads were down and digital ads were being blocked. At the same time, according to Nielsen, only 33% of consumers trust ads, while 90% trust peer recommendations. Even more significant for marketers, 71% of consumers would buy based on social media referrals.[131]

Marketers across many industries began seeking new methods to increase product awareness and improve the likability of their products. They began by paying celebrities to post recommendations about their products on the celebrities' social channels. Each industry had its own celebrities—the Kardashians ruled fashion, and NASA led the science industry.

Some companies of all sizes began working with influential people in specific niches—primarily due to cost. These influencers would often accept free products instead of cash in exchange for social posts about product preferences.

As the use of these influencers grew, the public began to grow a bit distrustful. For example, in the U.S. in 2017, the Federal Trade Commission (FTC) took notice and began requiring influencers to make it clear in their social posts if they were being compensated in any way to promote a product. All required disclosures—and the dos and don'ts around legal influencer marketing—were outlined in "Disclosures 101 for Social Media Influencers."[132] This guide remains a valuable tool for hotel digital marketers today.

Disclosure is a global issue. In September of 2020, the United Kingdom's ("UK") Committee of Advertising Practice ("CAP") reviewed the Instagram accounts of 122 UK-based social media influencers to determine whether content was being properly flagged as advertising in accordance with applicable social media influencer laws. In March 2021, the UK Advertising Standards Authority ("ASA") released its report on the subject social media influencers' content. ASA found that many of the social media influencers were violating UK advertising rules by failing to adequately disclose advertising content. The report serves as a good reminder to social media influencers outside of the U.K. that they must follow with social media influencer laws or face the consequences.

The following are among the requirements and best practices outlined in "Disclosures 101 for Social Media Influencers:[113]
- Disclose when you have any financial, employment, personal, or family relationship with a brand.
- Financial relationships aren't limited to money. Disclose the relationship if you got anything of value to mention a product. If a brand gives you free or discounted products or other perks and then you mention one of its products, make a disclosure even if you weren't asked to mention that product. Don't assume your followers already know about your brand relationships.
- Make disclosures even if you think your evaluations are unbiased.
- Keep in mind that tags, likes, pins, and similar ways of showing you like a brand or product are endorsements.
- If posting from abroad, U.S. law applies if it's reasonably foreseeable that the post will affect U.S. consumers. Foreign laws might also apply.
- If you have no brand relationship and are just telling people about a product you bought and happen to like, you don't need to declare that you don't have a brand relationship.
- Place your disclosure so that it is hard to miss.

Once it became widely known that paid influencers had to disclose their brand relationships, trust among consumers seemed to return and influencers again began to flourish—and expand. The number of platforms and agencies specializing in influencers has grown steadily since 2015, but as a percentage it grew more after the FTC's involvement in 2017.

These agencies and apps have curated a diverse collection of influencers—and use cases. No longer are celebrities the only source of influence. Today, influencers come in a wide array of popularity, media presence, and areas of expertise.

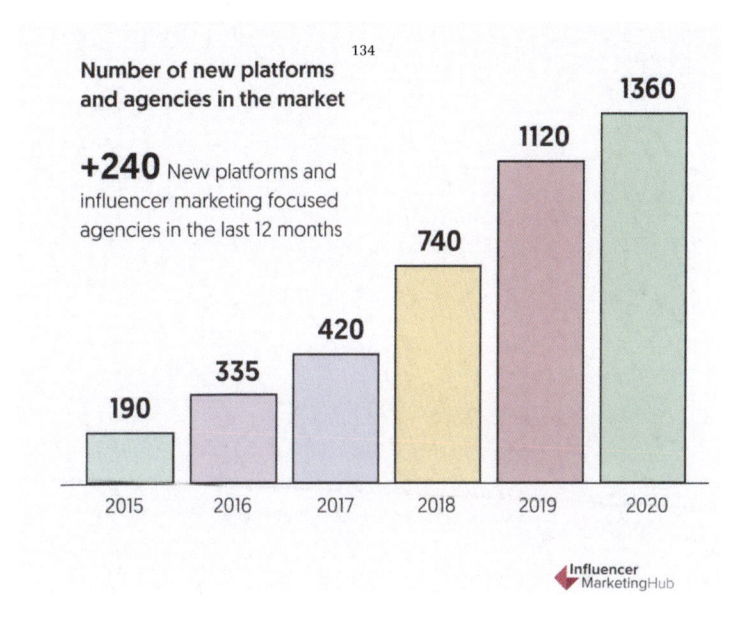

[134]

Number of new platforms and agencies in the market

+240 New platforms and influencer marketing focused agencies in the last 12 months

2015	2016	2017	2018	2019	2020
190	335	420	740	1120	1360

Influencer MarketingHub

TYPES OF INFLUENCERS TODAY

There are several ways of categorizing influencers. The most popular are:
- By followers
- By content type
- By influence level

By Followers

The most commonly used classifications of influencers—based on the number of their followers—are outlined in the chart "Average engagement rate of selected influencers 2020."

Average engagement rate of selected influencers 2020 [135]

Overall Benchmarks

Average engagement rate benchmarks across six key channel sizes on each of the major social media platforms.

	👥	Instagram	YouTube	TikTok
Micro < 15K		3.86%	1.63%	17.96%
Regular 15K-50K		2.39%	0.51%	9.75%
Rising 50K-100K		1.87%	0.46%	8.37%
Mid 100K-500K		1.62%	0.43%	6.67%
Macro 500K-1M		1.36%	0.44%	6.20%
Mega 1M+		1.21%	0.37%	4.96%

*data is based on influencers selected and added to influencer lists by Upfluence software users

upfluence

This chart outlines engagement rate benchmarks across the six key channel sizes on each of three major social media platforms: Instagram, YouTube, and TikTok.

By Content Type

You can also categorize influencers based on where their content can be found, and in what format. The most popular categories in this area are:

- Bloggers and micro-bloggers
- YouTubers
- Podcasters
- Social posters only

By Influence Level

Influencers can also be categorized by influencer level:

1. Celebrities
2. Key opinion leaders (e.g., journalists, academics, industry experts, professional advisors)
3. People with above-average influence on their audience

Influencer Campaign channel utilization [136]

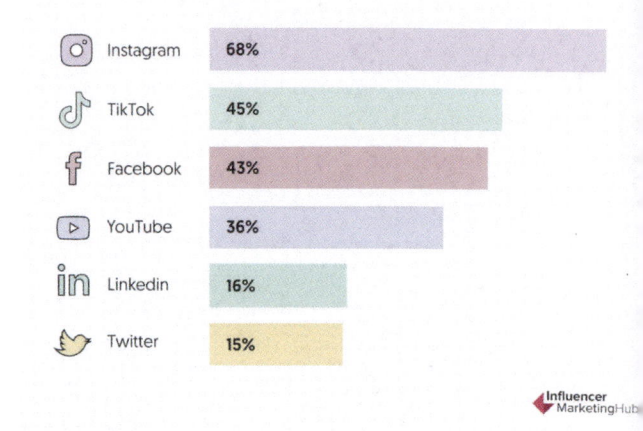

Platform	%
Instagram	68%
TikTok	45%
Facebook	43%
YouTube	36%
Linkedin	16%
Twitter	15%

Influencer MarketingHub

BEST PRACTICES: DETERMINE YOUR GOALS

As mentioned earlier in this book, everything a digital marketer does should be for a reason. Before you engage with an influencer, be clear in your goals for the partnership. Common goals for hotels working with influencers include the following:

- Create awareness of the hotel with a new audience
- Create awareness of a new amenity (for example, a spa) or package (for example, a ski weekend) in a particular niche audience
- Grow your mailing list or social media followers from a particular audience
- Increase engagement on your social channels
- Sell more rooms, F&B, spa appointments, or weddings

BEST PRACTICES: IDENTIFY AND EVALUATE INFLUENCERS

Once you have determined your goals, search for the right influencer(s) to help you accomplish them.

Travel writers/bloggers are the most obvious influencers for hotels. While travel bloggers specifically target people interested in learning about hotels, destinations, restaurants, and attractions, bloggers with influence in other areas such as fashion, design, lifestyle, music, and art can also draw attention to your hotel if it caters to those audiences.

Hotels often receive requests from self-proclaimed influencers asking for a free stay in exchange for a post to their followers. Rather than settling for what comes to you, take a more targeted approach to finding the right influencers based on your goals and your target audience demographics.

To determine the fit and value of a particular influencer for your property, do the following:

- Determine how many followers an influencer has on their blog, Instagram, TikTok, YouTube, Facebook, Twitter, Pinterest, and/or other digital platforms.
- Monitor the influencer's posts to ensure they are relevant to your brand and appropriate for your target audience. Attracting the wrong audience can have a negative impact on your online reputation, while consistently reaching the right audience greatly and economically improves awareness just where it can help your business the most.
- Be sure the look and feel of the writing and graphics are a good fit for your company's brand. Does the influencer already share content similar to your brand? How have past travel articles, videos, and posts been executed?
- Determine the influencer's connection to travel. Do they have a travel section in their online presence? If not, how will people find articles and videos about your hotel?

There are several tools—available for a fee— that will help you evaluate influencers. The most popular are Awario, Klear, Buzzsumo, HYPER, Buzzstream, and Traackr. Most of these tools are also social listening or social monitoring tools, and some enable you to build relationships directly with influencers from inside their app. You can also engage agencies to help with your influencer strategy as most digital agencies have a specific PR/influence division committed solely to this function.

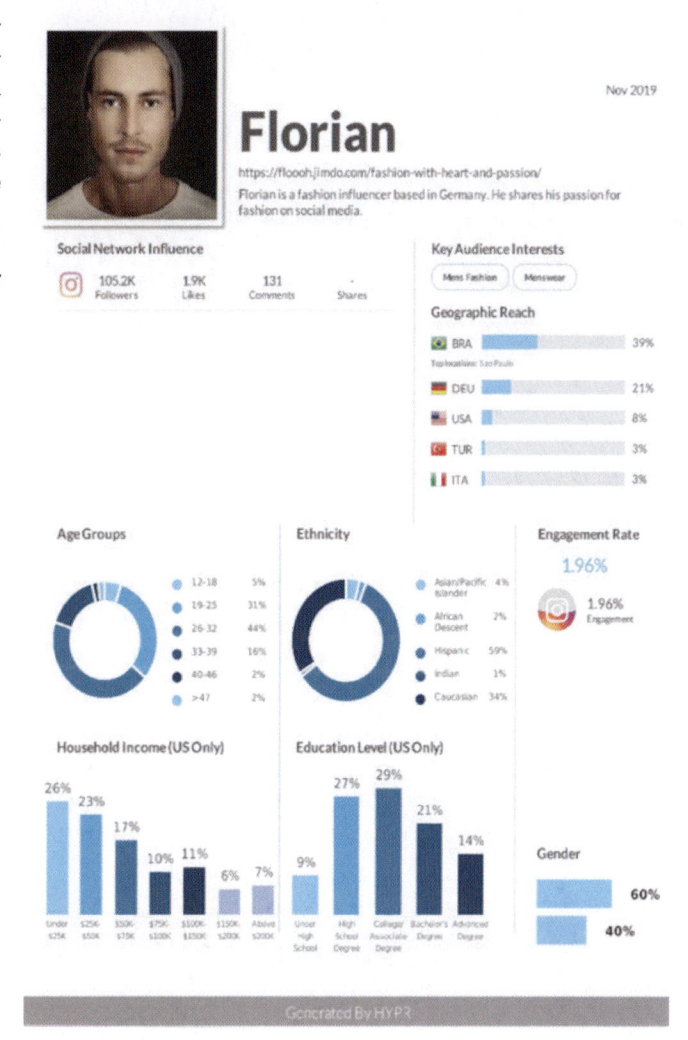

hyper.com influencer stats

BEST PRACTICES: BUDGET AND TRACK ROI

Your projected ROI should drive your budget. For hotels, micro-influencers currently deliver the best ROI.

- On average, micro-influencers cost 1.5x less than macro-influencers and 7x less than celebrity influencers on Facebook, Instagram, and YouTube.
- Micro-influencers generally drive 7x more engagement than macro-influencers.
- Micro-influencers deliver 30% better ROI per $1 spent than macro-influencers and 20% better ROI than celebrity influencers.[137]

The cost of an influencer is typically determined by a combination of factors including the social media platform they use, their following, their engagement rate, the product you're selling, whether you work directly with the influencer or with an agency, and the extent of the campaign.

There are guidelines and tools available to help marketers calculate how much to pay influencers. A few helpful resources include:

- Instagram Money Calculator: https://influencermarketinghub.com/instagram-money-calculator/
- TikTok Money Calculator: https://influencermarketinghub.com/tiktok-money-calculator/
- YouTube Money Calculator: https://influencermarketinghub.com/youtube-money-calculator/
- How Much Does Social Media Influencer Marketing Cost? https://buffer.com/resources/influencer-marketing-cost

BEST PRACTICES: CREATE BRAND AMBASSADORS OR CUSTOMER ADVOCATES

Never forget your own loyal guests. Chances are great you have guests staying at your property right now who have large social media followings. Make sure to provide "influencer" photo opportunities on property to encourage social sharing from your inhouse guests.

Outrigger Hotels has a "surprise and wow" system where they monitor social media for property mentions by present and past guests, and then send them a gift—to their guest room or to their home. For example, a guest posted that they weren't feeling well, and the hotel responded by sending them soup. The guest posted about it with a photo and shared it with their 54k followers!

User-generated content sharing companies like Flip.To, Olapic, and Stackla provide services for hotels to enable their guests to tell their brand story and share on the property website, or on their own social networks. These tools can help build relationships with inhouse guests by enabling photo sharing incentive programs—and some track new bookings while growing traffic, leads, and tracked potential guests through the conversion funnel. Touch points throughout the traveler journey let guests share their authentic stories about the hotel to their own social networks.

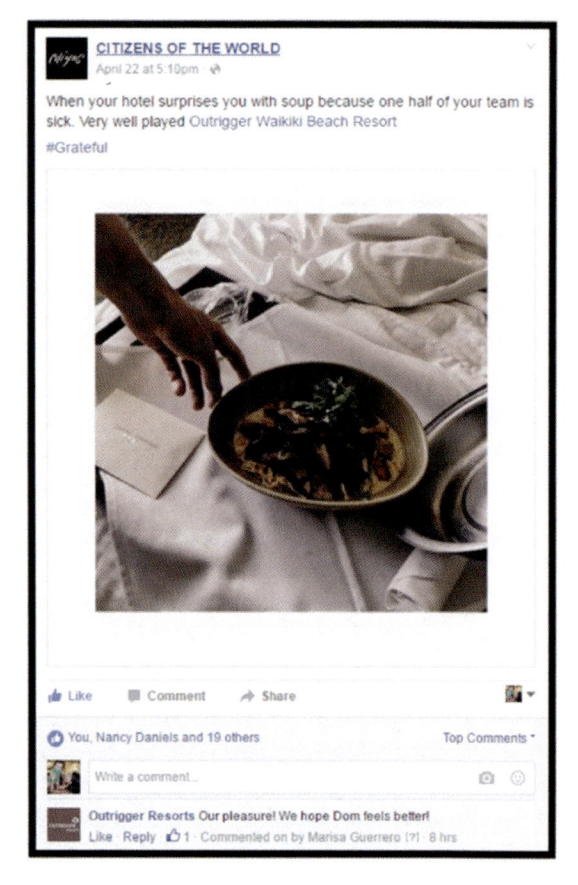

For example, The Crane Resort in Barbados captured a library of guest stories through an advocacy platform—stories that reveal the property's character from the guests' point of view. Using touch points throughout the traveler journey, guests were able to share their authentic stories about the hotel to travelers worldwide. By using photo sharing and incentive programs, the resort expanded its reach by a quarter of a million in five months, while driving more than 23,000 unique site visitors, 2,100 warm leads, and 21 booked room nights through the platform.[138]

"Staying at The Crane is always the most relaxing week of the year." — MARK M.

BEST PRACTICES: CREATE A WRITTEN AGREEMENT

When partnering with an influencer, be sure to create a written agreement that is specific about what payment the influencer will receive whether it is a complimentary stay, food and beverage, spa services, money, or something else.

Just as important, be clear about the hotel's expectations of the influencer. Specify items like how many social posts the influencer commits to, and over what period. Outline the expected reach of those posts, retweets, and shares.

Think about including performance goals such as a number of contest entries, Facebook likes, social engagements, or actual bookings that the influencer should generate.

BEST PRACTICES: ENGAGE WITH INFLUENCERS

Don't dismiss the traditional "fam" trip—bringing influencers to your hotel and showing them the experience firsthand is still an effective strategy. Partner with attractions and venues outside of your property to ensure a robust stay.

Encourage influencers to communicate what they love about your guest experience. It can be much more effective—and less expensive—than trying to communicate that message directly yourself.

BEST PRACTICES: MEASURE INFLUENCER CAMPAIGNS

Align your goals with specific key performance indicators. The most common measurement statistics for influencers are:

- social reach
- engagement
- shares
- video views
- comments
- page growth
- conversions

Example Goal	Recommended Measurements
Create awareness of the hotel with a new audience	Impressions, views, video views, reach
Increase engagement on your social channels	Likes, comments, direct messages, platform audience growth, shares, contest entries, web page visits
Sell more rooms, F&B, spa appointments, or weddings	eBook downloads, form completions, inquiries, bookings, loyalty membership growth, event attendance

CASE STUDY: Premier Inn and TikTok

A leading U.K. economy hotel touts the value of getting a good night sleep, and so they are proud of their trademark pillows—which they also sell. They worked with a TikTok influencer (@charconnor) who posted a video to her audience about how much she loved her pillow. The video received 90,000 views and inspired others to create a similar video. Since the video was shared, the hotel company sold over 6,000 pillows, a 65% increase.[139]

CASE STUDY: Marriott and Snapchat

Marriott partnered with four Snapchat users to engage with their audiences for select destination cities and generally engage with them during their travels to Marriott hotels. The four destinations chosen by the Snapchat audiences were Berlin, Seoul, Dubai, and New York. As Snapchat content only stays available for 24 hours, Marriott also partnered with Naritiv to make the content available on their other channels, so that a larger audience could use the content for travel planning. The end goal for this promotion was to increase membership in Bonvoy, their loyalty program.

CASE STUDY: Visit Irving and a Progressive Dinner with a Purpose

Visit Irving's overarching goals of a unique event involving influencers were to dispel rumors that the local Toyota Music Factory had closed, and to familiarize the Dallas-Fort Worth (Texas) area with the entertainment complex and its unique offerings.

Secondarily, they also wanted to:
- Collect photos and content from the event for social media and their websites.
- Showcase individual Toyota Music Factory tenants.
- Network with local bloggers and build relationships to partner on brand work in the future.

The key message for this campaign was that the Toyota Music Factory's many dining establishments and watering holes were alive, well, and delicious. By co-hosting a progressive dine around/pub crawl with social media as the primary media component, Visit Irving would effectively and efficiently spread the word about the incredible venues that remained open at the Toyota Music Factory. Each restaurant partner agreed to provide small bites/samples for tasting, beverage options, and full-sized portions to be photographed.

The target audience for the event was local foodie Instagram influencers—and their thousands of followers. They identified the top 20 foodie influencers, sent invitations, and offered them free transportation via the event app in Uber. "Passports" were provided to be stamped at each venue so that attendees would be sure to visit all the restaurants.

Each influencer was asked to provide two of the following:
- One Instagram story about the entire event using swipe up link to the Toyota Music Factory
- Minimum of one Instagram post for each venue within two weeks of the event
- Blog inclusion (if applicable)
- Usage rights to photographs

With cameras clicking, the influencer attendees created excitement everywhere they went, and conferred instant celebrity on the food and drink they sampled. The resulting images were all over the internet just hours later, reaching thousands of local foodie followers. With the help of 16 influencers, the message reached 500K+ consumers through Instagram and blogs.

Mouthwatering food and drink shots, appropriately hashtagged, appeared in mass and elicited strong engagement from the targeted audience. Instagram posts were saved for Visit Irving's Instagram content. Beyond the immediate successes, Visit Irving and the Toyota Music Factory acquired highly curated online content and more than 50 high-res photos to use and repurpose throughout the year.

TASTE OF THE TOYOTA MUSIC FACTORY
INSTAGRAM POSTS

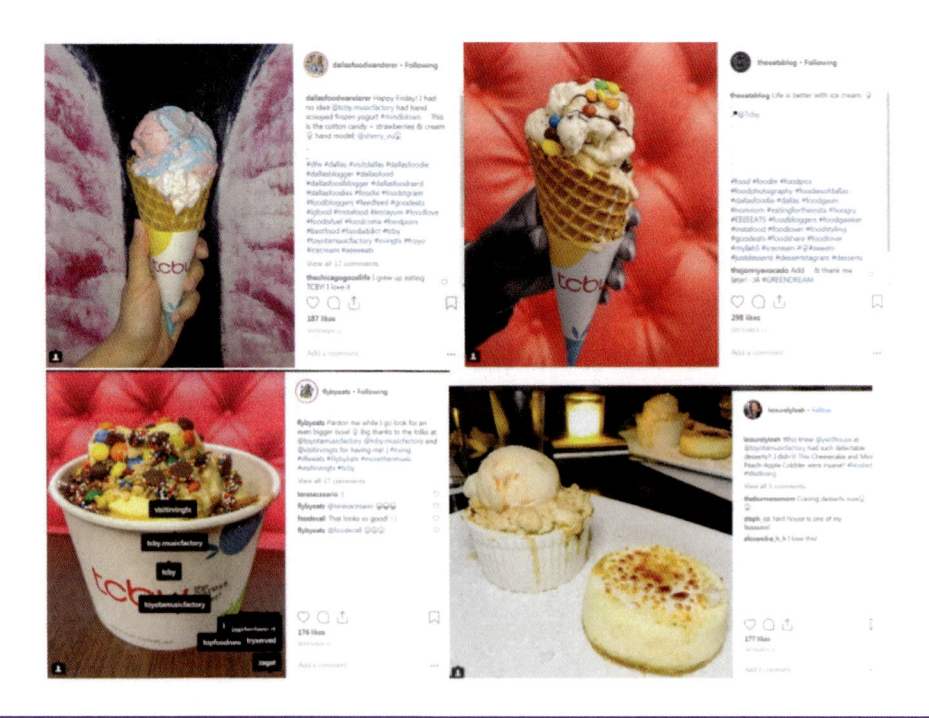

SAMPLE CHDM EXAM QUESTIONS

1. Which factors contributed to the growth of influencer marketing? (select all that apply)
    a. The decrease in time spent watching TV
    b. The increase in time spent on mobile apps
    c. The increase in consumer use of ad blocking software
    d. The lower fees celebrities began accepting for social posts
    e. All of the above

2. Which are typical classifications of influencers? (select all that apply)
    a. Number of followers
    b. Age range of influencer
    c. Content type
    d. Level of influence
    e. All of the above

3. Micro-influencers generally drive 10x more engagement than macro-influencers.
    a. True
    b. False

Answers
1 = a, b, & c
2 = a, c, & d
3 = b

NOTES

PART FOUR: PAID MEDIA

PART FOUR: PAID MEDIA

KEY POINTS

- Paid advertising has several elements that drive viewers to your desired destination, typically your website. Paid search, display advertising, metasearch, and social are the four primary forms of digital advertising.
- All types of media utilize various forms of keyword or data-based targeting and require analytics to gauge results. This includes the ability to target individuals based on their past and present behaviors, demographics, purchase history, and relationship with a hotel.
- Display media and social media allow for the addition of visual components to the delivery of advertisements including photos, images, logos, animation, and/or videos.
- A hotel or brand can extend its reach to attract potential guests through affiliate marketing, creating partnerships with companies that offer complementary or non-competing services.

Driving traffic to your website or any web destination will involve either organic optimization, earned media (see Part 3), or paid advertising. There are four very common methods of paid advertising.

1. Search engine marketing, often referred to as SEM, paid search, or pay per click (PPC), is keyword marketing on search engines like Google, Bing, Yahoo, Baidu, Yandex, etc.
2. Display advertising includes "traditional" ad spend and purchasing ads on a specific publisher's site, targeted/retargeted display, programmatic, or native advertising.
3. Metasearch sites are shopping comparison sites that allow consumers to compare hotels' prices between suppliers and OTAs.
4. Social media advertising is available on all social media platforms.

When it comes to paid media there are important financial models and key terms with which digital marketers should be familiar. It is important to understand the models so you can determine which works for your goals and will enable you to set up success metrics, most commonly return on ad spend (ROAS) or return on investment (ROI).

Financial Models & Key Acronyms

- ROAS – Return on Ad Spend
- ROI – Return on Investment
- CPC – Cost Per Click (Clicks)
- PPC – Pay Per Click (Clicks)
- CPM – Cost/Thousand Impressions (Views)
- CPA – Cost Per Acquisition/Action (Transaction)
- VTR – View Through Rate (for video)
- Subscription – Flat fee for period of time

Source: Hotel Digital Marketing Essentials course materials

Chapter 19: Paid Search

> **KEY POINTS**
> - Most people utilize search to start their travel journey, and Google is by far the dominant search engine they use, but other search engines should not be ignored by marketers.
> - The first step to a successful paid search strategy is to ensure your website is optimized for organic search (see Chapter 9). Paid search will complement those efforts.
> - It is important to reach guests at every stage of the travel planning journey to influence and shape decisions that lead to a booking. Before you conduct keyword research and launch campaigns, think about your KPIs and how you will reach users throughout every step of their journey, from planning to booking.
> - Consistently measure and test the effectiveness of your campaigns and fine tune them while considering your available budget.
> - Avoid analyzing the performance of your paid search campaigns in a silo. Looking at the ROI of every keyword is not the right approach and can lead to pausing keywords and campaigns that reach users at the top of the funnel.

SUMMARY

Paid search, or search engine marketing (SEM), should be an integral part of any digital marketing strategy. With 93% of internet users starting on a search engine (usually Google)[140], this is often the first exposure searchers will have to your website. If your website is your digital front door, search is the map that will send them there.

SEM is a great way to improve your ranking on the SERP (search engine results page) and allows delivery of a concise marketing message to a highly relevant marketing segment with measurable results. A balanced strategy that includes paid search in addition to SEO, display advertising, social media advertising, native advertising, metasearch marketing, and email marketing yields the best results over the long term. This is often referred to as an "omnichannel" approach or strategy.

Paid search, due to the inherent immediacy of its results and control of the message, lends itself to the tactical promotion of specific rates, packages, and promotions. With an understanding of booking lead times, paid search campaigns can be executed with precision and coordination with the revenue management strategy of your hotel. The strategic use of paid search can supplement a solid SEO program.

On the next page is a SERP delivered in 2020. Google often changes its SERP, so it is important to consistently familiarize and refamiliarize yourself with the display on a regular basis.

While Google is the dominant search engine in many parts of the world, marketers should still pay attention to other search engines as they are sometimes less expensive and convert as well or better than Google, albeit with less traffic. Microsoft Bing still has a good portion of desktop users and is the default search engine for the Microsoft Edge browser (the default browser for most PCs), and powers AOL, Yahoo, many car navigation systems, and voice assistants. In addition, in some geographies, Google is not the dominant player. Specifically, in China, where Google is not allowed, the local search engine Baidu dominates. In Russia, Google competes neck and neck with Yandex, and there are other countries that have local players that may be worth working with.

Ultimately paid search is a means for achieving first page SERP placement. Google (and other search engines) uses a PPC or bidding model. You determine which keyword(s) you want to purchase and set a bid amount. Then, based on any other bids for that keyword(s) and the Google algorithm, you will be assigned a placement on the page. You may get the first result at the top of the page or the last result at the bottom of the page based on the Google algorithm. Your paid search strategy can be directed to various levels (by keyword, keyword groups, etc.), while placement and rotation of your ad

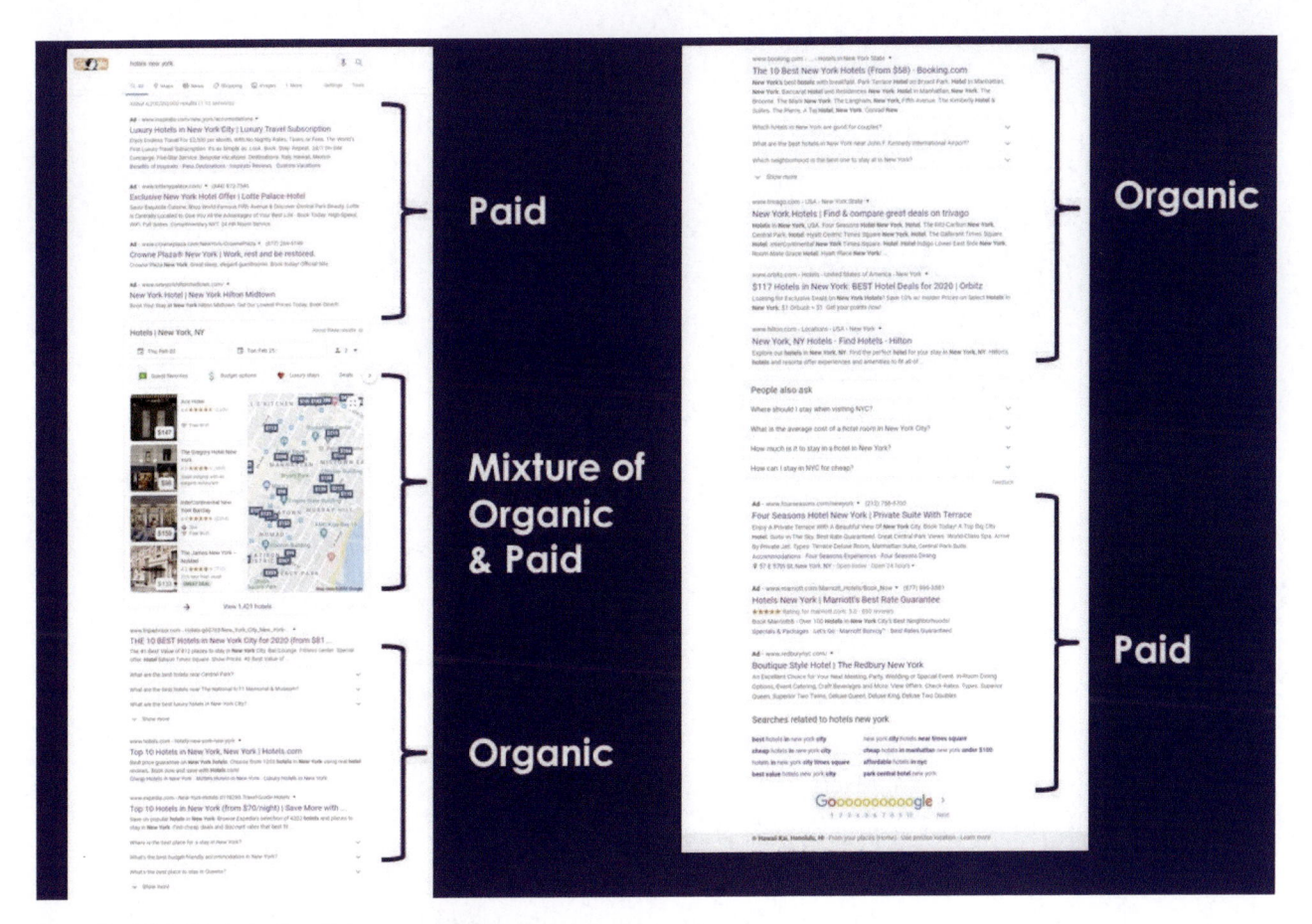

Source: Hotel Digital Marketing Essentials course materials

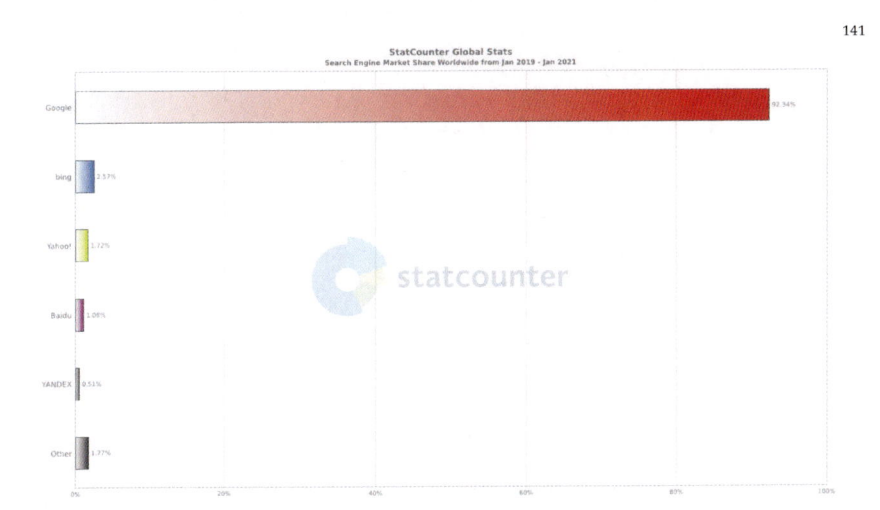

141

is based on your maximum bid amounts and allocated budget. Paid search listings allow for nearly complete control of the message and title in contrast to organic listings where these are determined by the search engine.

A Field Guide for Navigating Today's Digital Landscape   163

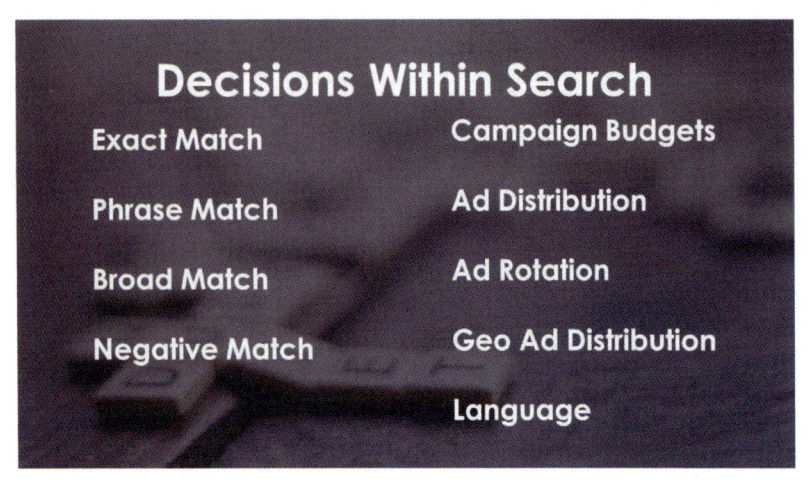

Decisions Within Search

- Exact Match
- Phrase Match
- Broad Match
- Negative Match
- Campaign Budgets
- Ad Distribution
- Ad Rotation
- Geo Ad Distribution
- Language

Source: Hotel Digital Marketing Essentials course materials

DIFFERENTIATORS OF PAID SEARCH

Paid search advertising is popular because it is easy to measure the return on investment (ROI) and return on ad spend (ROAS). If you spend $10, you know your ROAS because you can likely track the transaction from the click through to the actual booking. The platforms utilized to manage paid search campaigns allow for adjustments to your bids, ads/messaging, keywords, and ad extensions that take immediate effect. Paid search engines, like Google, factor a relevancy score into the process which impacts the cost to the advertiser, ultimately impacting your ranking, or placement, and the effectiveness of your ads.

[Example ad layout showing:
- Headline
- Display URL
- Description
- Ad Extensions

Ad · www.marriott.com/Marriott_Hotels/Book_Now
Marriott | Chicago Downtown Magnificent
Book at Marriott.com for the best prices. Guaranteed. Pay When You Stay. Mobile Check-In. Free Wi-Fi for Members. Room & Bed Preferences. Best Rate Guarantee.
Specials & Packages — Get our special offers & packages only available at Marriott.com.
Book Marriott Chicago — You'll get the best prices when you book at Marriott.com.

Ad · www.virginhotels.com/ · (312) 940-4400
Virgin Hotels Chicago | Official Site
How Low Can We Go? Indulge In Your Chicago Needs With Our Lowest Rates & Exclusive Offers. Book Direct & Pay Less For More! Unmatched Amenities, No Urban Fees, & No Hidden Fees. Book Direct To Save. Chicago Loop Hotel.
Fresh and Foodie — From Our Lobby To The Rooftop We Are Ready To Please All
Get Comfortable — Our Rooms and Suites Offer More Than You Can Imagine.
Park It Right Here — Parking Is Hard in Chicago. Book Our Exclusive Pkg To Save $20
Find Your Scene — Explore The City Right Outside Our Doors. Don't Miss A Beat]

Source: Hotel Digital Marketing Essentials course materials

Developments in the technology interfaces between search engines and central reservations systems (CRS) allow for dynamic content, such as specific rates, to be pulled directly from a hotel's CRS. This extends the capabilities of the CRS as a channel management tool and allows paid search to be even more tactically precise. This is best facilitated via the application programming interfaces (API), third-party paid search management tools, or web services being developed by technology providers on both sides of the equation.

BEST PRACTICES: KEYWORD RESEARCH & ANALYSIS

Any marketing program or campaign should start with clearly outlined goals and objectives and should be complementary to the overall digital marketing strategy. By ensuring this at the outset, the results will be more quantifiable, and for paid search specifically, it is critical for the development of an appropriate keyword strategy and for writing ad copy.

Begin by making a list of words and phrases that describe your hotel by its location and unique selling points (USP). Where is your hotel located? What would the consumer have in mind when looking for a hotel in your location? It can be helpful to ask yourself why the consumer would be traveling to the destination. Consider including modifying words like the city, state, or country, as well as the neighborhood and surrounding landmarks.

The major search engines have access to a huge amount of data about which keywords people search for every day. For instance, Google has a keyword tool within its Google Ads (previously known as AdWords) interface that provides additional keyword suggestions based on a list of keywords you might enter. By leveraging the tool, you can understand not only the potential of your keywords but also related terms that you might want to use in your paid search campaign.

This same tool can be utilized to estimate the required budget. Each keyword or keyword group will provide an estimate of the number of impressions you will receive, and from this you can anticipate the budget required to fund your campaign. There is also a plethora of third-party tools that can help in identifying keywords and keywords opportunities (e.g., Moz, SEMRush, Ahrefs, and many more).

Include long- and short-tail keywords as part of your strategy. See Chapter 9 for additional information on these keyword types.

Organize your keywords into related or similarly themed groups. These will become "Ad Groups" in your final campaign setup. By approaching the keywords in this way, you can optimize the use of ad copy and descriptions. Many campaign management tools utilize this concept to organize the keywords and manage budget. Otherwise, you will need to identify a keyword, then a description, then a headline, repeatedly.

If you can group similar words, you can write less copy, and the smaller sample will enable you to test your headlines a little more easily. Tightly themed ad groups also help to ensure that the most relevant ad copy is being served for all keywords within the group. As a rule of thumb, groups of 10 to 15 keywords work well.

Brand Keywords vs. Acquisition Keywords (Generic Keywords, Unbranded Keywords)

In search, we often talk about branded and unbranded terms. Branded terms use your brand/hotel name to help people more easily find you. An example would be "Bob's Beachside Hotel." If that is your hotel's name and you are purchasing this term in search, it is considered brand keywords. It is likely you would have gotten some of that traffic regardless of buying the search term, especially if you have an effective SEO strategy.

One can argue that while there is value in purchasing brand terms, there is limited incrementality to the bookings you get from these ads. Since people are actively searching for your property, the likelihood would be that your ROAS would be very good with these sorts of terms. But remember to consider how much is realistically incremental and would not have been picked up with organic search.

When you buy unbranded or acquisition terms, for example "London Hotel," your ROAS would not be as good as with branded terms, but most of the bookings would likely be incremental (unlikely to have been booked without the ad).

Keyword Matching

Keyword matching is a method the search engines use to serve ads based on keywords that might be similar to what you selected or similar to what the consumer has utilized. Understanding this allows you to determine how broad or narrow you want to set your campaign.

It is important to understand the difference between a "keyword" and a "search query." A keyword is the word or phrase you choose to bid on in paid search. A search query is a word or phrase that a consumer types into the search box of the search engine. Matching helps you refine your keyword list so you don't have to bid on and manage every possible keyword combination. While the details of use vary by search engine, there are some general concepts that apply to all of them.

- EXACT MATCH: Your ad will show when someone searches for your keyword or close variations of your keyword. This includes but is not limited to misspellings, singular or plural forms, stemming, abbreviations, synonyms, and paraphrases. Exact match allows for you to show up for keyword variations you may not have thought to bid on.

- PHRASE MATCH: Your ad will appear on searches that include the words in your keyword phrase, in the same specific order, but the query can also include other words before or after the word or phrase you are bidding on.

- BROAD MATCH: Casts the widest net and is the most difficult to control. When using broad match, your ad is shown on queries containing similar phrases and relevant variations of the keyword. This will generate a lot of activity, some less relevant.

- MODIFIED BROAD MATCH: This match type is offered by most search engines and is a more targeted approach than simple broad match. By utilizing a plus sign (+) in front of a word within a broad match keyword, you ensure that your keyword will only match to queries that contain each word that you've marked with a plus sign. Searched keywords can be added before, after, and in between the search term you are bidding on.

- NEGATIVE MATCH: Used to ensure that your ad does not show for any query that includes the terms you specify. Think about phrases containing words like "free" or "cheap," inappropriate content, customer reviews, news-related terms (like robbery, bedbugs, fraud, etc.), competitors' brand names, etc. Do you want to show up in these searches or not?

- **DAILY CAMPAIGN BUDGETS:** These are set for each individual campaign to determine how much you want to spend on average per day. It is possible to be charged slightly more or less each day on your set campaign budget. In the end you will never be charged more than your set budget in the month, and in any given day you will not spend more than 2 times the daily budget.
- **AD DISTRIBUTION:** Allows you to control whether your ads appear only on SERP or also on display network sites like news and blogs, mobile apps, etc. You will want to consider that users on other websites may or may not be as likely to click as those directly searching on a search engine.
- **AD ROTATION:** The way you would like your ads delivered on the search network and display network. You can have them rotate ads indefinitely, or in an optimized rotation.
- **GEOGRAPHICAL AD DISTRIBUTION:** Allows you to pinpoint where you want your ads to be displayed based on the physical location of the consumer, or the location that they are searching for. This can be particularly useful if you understand the major feeder markets for your hotel, or if a campaign is intended to focus on a specific market.
- **LANGUAGE:** Language settings allow you to target the consumer based on the language they have specified in their internet browser settings. This is a key consideration as your campaign can be more effective if you also have keywords translated into the preferred language of your target audience. It is important to also have translated ad copy as well as translated landing pages used in the ad copy.

BEST PRACTICES: CAMPAIGN SET-UP

The implementation of a successful paid search campaign involves several elements.

Ad Copy & Headline

Your ad copy and headline should be brief, and, in conjunction with the keyword utilized, provide a compelling reason to click through to the landing page. It must be succinct due to the character limitations imposed by the search engine. It should communicate your unique selling proposition (USP), what you are promoting, and encourage a call to action in a small amount of space. Think about the following issues when you create your copy.

- Include keywords in your ad copy whenever possible as this will assist in continuity and relevance.
- Why should someone click on your ad? Consider your USP and use this as the ad headline or the call to action.
- Create a sense of urgency and a call to action (like "Book Now!") to trigger the desired action (which is to click through).
- Include rate, percent off, or value adds if applicable as these are strong compelling messages.
- Consult search engine guidelines for rules about ads to ensure you don't violate any editorial policies or have ads disapproved by the engines.

Keyword Group

Develop the ad copy to correspond with the ad groups created to ensure that the ad copy is relevant to what users may be searching for.

Consider the Competition

Some simple searches of your keywords should show you what your competition is doing and what you are competing against. The intent here is not to copy the competition but to position your ads and messaging well. Be aware that your ads will display alongside these. Knowing what your competition is doing can help you modify your ad copy to stand out and help you decide whether to bid on certain keywords at all.

BEST PRACTICES: MEASURING YOUR CAMPAIGN PERFORMANCE

Paid search metrics for hotels include four key metrics in addition to revenue, ADR (Average Daily Rate), room nights, and market share:

1. CONVERSIONS: when a person who clicked your ad completes an action on your website, such as booking a room, buying something, signing up for an email list, or requesting more information

2. CONVERSION RATE: the percentage of clicks that resulted in a conversion
3. COST PER CONVERSION: total conversions divided by total cost
4. ROAS (RETURN ON AD SPEND): measures how profitable your advertising is

Calculating ROAS

Using Google's Keyword Planner, you can work backwards to determine potential results and return on ad spend.

This display shows that in this specific period you could expect 9K clicks and 240K impressions. If you bid $3 max CPC, the cost would be $16K. The click through rate would be 3.8%, and the CPC (the actual cost per click) would be $1.82 with an average position of 1.6.

Clicks	Impressions	Cost	CTR	Avg. CPC	Avg. Position
9K	240K	$16K	3.8%	$1.82	1.6

You can use this estimate from Google to extrapolate the potential results:

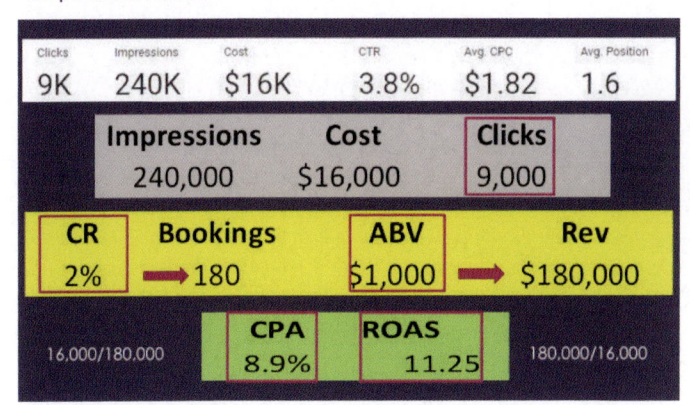

Clicks	Impressions	Cost	CTR	Avg. CPC	Avg. Position
9K	240K	$16K	3.8%	$1.82	1.6

Impressions	Cost	Clicks
240,000	$16,000	9,000

CR	Bookings	ABV	Rev
2%	→ 180	$1,000	→ $180,000

	CPA	ROAS	
16,000/180,000	8.9%	11.25	180,000/16,000

The numbers in yellow should be calculated on a property's historical performance. In this case, the hotel's website CR (conversion rate) is 2%. Two percent conversion of the 9,000 clicks leads to 180 bookings. The hotel's ABV (average booking rate) is $1,000, so they can expect $180,000 in revenue, giving them an effective CPA (cost per acquisition) of 8.9%. This is a percentage of revenue, or a ROAS of 11.25 : 1.

In this example, if you consider a travel agent commission is 10% and the cost of an OTA booking is somewhere between 15%-30%, the cost to acquire this customer at 8.9% is quite good.

Additional cross-industry metrics include:

- IMPRESSIONS: how often your ad is shown—each appearance of your ad equals one impression
- IMPRESSION SHARE: the percentage of impressions you received divided by the estimated number of impressions you were eligible to receive based on your targeting, bid, and other factors
- CLICKS: the number of times a user interacts with your ad by clicking on it
- COST: total cost that you have spent with each search engine or campaign
- AVERAGE COST PER CLICK (CPC): how much you paid for each click on your ad; can be calculated by dividing cost by the number of clicks
- CLICK THROUGH RATE: expressed as a percentage, this metric is the number of clicks divided by the number of impressions
- AVERAGE AD POSITION: a statistic that describes how your ad typically ranks against other ads; this rank determines in which order ads appear on the page (position one is the first ad on the page)

BEST PRACTICES: CAMPAIGN, BID, AND BUDGET MANAGEMENT

Managing your paid search campaign involves fine tuning your keyword strategy, ad messaging, bids, and available budget. By manipulating these elements, the budget can be managed to allow you exposure all day or during the key hours you want to be displaying. Keep in mind that when the daily budget is depleted you will no longer be rotating and have no presence until the new budget period begins. The optimization of the campaign will come through changing ad copy and the keywords being utilized—in and of itself this process is a series of tests to find the correct balance of exposure and return.

Quality score affects your cost per click and ad position and therefore is a key component of the management of the optimal campaign. As a way of rating paid search keyword relevance, quality score ranks relevance on a scale from 1 to 10, with 1 being the worst and 10 being the best. The components of quality score are your CTR (click through rate), ad relevance, landing page quality and relevance, and expected impact from the use of extensions and ad formats. It is important because it is used to:

- determine the actual cost per click (CPC) that you pay
- estimate first page bids
- determine if a keyword is eligible for the ad auction
- rank your ad against other advertisers in the auction

Quality score will directly impact what you pay for a click, where you appear on the list of ads, and therefore how effectively your budget will be consumed.

BEST PRACTICES: TESTING

Testing is an indispensable component of any marketing strategy. A challenge for certain channels, like email or direct mail, is that they take more time to test in setup and to receive test results. PPC tests can take less time depending on the volume we are able to drive. While nearly every element of paid search can be tested, following are some of the most common tests.

Keywords
Which keywords draw more quality traffic to your page? Also important is to measure if those visitors are staying and converting.

Headlines
Changing one word in a headline can alter performance dramatically. Not unlike headlines in direct mail, certain words seem to compel action, like "new," "limited," or "free." The usage of rates, discounts, or other numerical ad components can also significantly improve your ad's performance. Again, it's important not only to measure traffic but the results of the traffic.

Once you find the headline that works the best, that becomes your control. Then test other headlines to see if they can beat it. Do the same with ad copy. A/B testing or split testing is a method of testing marketing strategy—a base-line control sample is compared to a variety of single-variable test samples to improve response or conversion rates. You can change the settings to rotate ads indefinitely to ensure clean results.

Landing Pages
Having a relevant landing page is extremely important. Often fantastic ads will be created only to drop the visitor off on a page that is not related to the ad, this will lead to a very high bounce rate. So, if your ad says "Great Rates for the Chicago Marathon" you should land them on a page that references that, or deep link into a search for marathon rates. If you land them on your home page that has no reference to the ad, you are likely to lose them.

You can often create multiple landing pages and see which has a higher conversion rate. More images? Fewer images? Placement of your call to action?

Testing can be an arduous process, but it is worthwhile as paid results can be expensive. To maximize your investment, always test and change your purchases or copy based on results.

The data gathered from a test can be applied to all elements of the digital marketing strategy, but specifically it is most useful when developing organic optimization of keywords and even website content.

SAMPLE CHDM EXAM QUESTIONS

1. Regarding keywords, which type of match ensures that your ad does not show for any query that includes the terms you specify?
   a. Exact Match
   b. Phrase Match
   c. Negative Match
   d. Broad Match

2. If you have a good ad, you don't need a good landing page.
   a. True
   b. False

3. If you spend $10,000 on an ad and it drives 25,000 visitors, what is the cost per click?
   a. $.40
   b. $2.50
   c. $.20
   d. 1.25

Answers
1 = c
2 = b
3 = b

NOTES

Chapter 20: Display Media

> **KEY POINTS**
> - Display advertising and paid search advertising work best in an omnichannel campaign that should also include other consumer touch points like social media, email marketing, and so on.
> - Programmatic display uses several data sources to target a user more effectively.
> - Measure performance based on media metrics specific to hotels.

HOW ONLINE BEHAVIORAL ADVERTISING WORKS[142]

A basic premise in marketing is the more you understand your customers' preferences, the more effectively you can advertise and ultimately sell your product or service. Marketers are constantly trying to answer questions such as: What do customers like to see? What do they want to hear? What do they like to do? What prompts them to buy?

Recommending relevant advertising based on past browsing activity is commonly referred to as "online behavioral advertising." This practice is also called "behavioral targeting" or "interest based advertising." Because online behavioral advertising is based on the users' inferred or declared interests from the cumulative browsing patterns across a variety of websites and pages, it differs from contextual advertising, which is based on the correlation between an advertisement and the content that directly surrounds it.

Consider this example of the distinction between online behavioral advertising and contextual advertising. Imagine you are an advertiser, trying to promote a French vacation package. Your best bet is to advertise your vacation offer to users who display interest in travelling to France. You could try to reach them on a website that reviews and recommends vacations in France (contextual advertising). However, you may also want to display your vacation package to users who have visited sites previously that involved travel to France through advertising on a subsequent, unrelated website, for instance one about their favorite baseball team (online behavioral advertising).

A great amount of behavioral targeting today relies on cookies. Cookies allow publishers to track website visits and user behavior. A lot of the targeting we can do today is done by aggregating third-party cookies, meaning we can target based on broad search history. By 2023 Google will eliminate third-party cookies. A lot of marketers and consultants are scrambling now to figure out target marketing in a cookie-less world, and many predict that we will go back to more contextual advertising. This change will also impact programmatic advertising.

What is a cookie?	What is a pixel?
A cookie is a small piece of text sent to and **stored in your browser** by a website you visit. Cookies help websites remember information about your visit.	A pixel is a tag or a block of code placed within your site's code that allows you to collect data about user behavior and is **stored on a server**.
Example: When you go back to a site and you are already logged in. It is also used for retargeting.	Example: A Facebook pixel that can be put on pages of your website, and when the pixel "fires," it tells Facebook to show them ads of a product they saw on your website.

PROGRAMMATIC ADVERTISING

Programmatic advertising helps automate the decision-making process of media buying by targeting specific audiences and demographics.

Programmatic display advertising platforms track consumer behavior through cookies placed on users' browsers. These cookies collect insights on users' behavior, and the data allows display platforms to deliver the right messaging to the consumer at the right time to convince them to buy your product.

For example, a travel-specific display network may have information about a consumer with a tendency to book luxury rooms who may be traveling to Chicago in two weeks. This creates an opportunity for luxury hotels in Chicago to advertise to this consumer. Alternatively, if your hotel's prime target audience is "college-educated women aged 30-40 in the Southeast U.S.," display networks will enable you to deploy ads to that audience with precision.

WHY PROGRAMMATIC DISPLAY?

There are millions of different combinations of target audiences—by age, geography, education, reading habits, personal hobbies, etc. Targeting specific audiences with this much detail is not feasible through manual optimization and would likely lead to a significant waste of advertising dollars. That's why programmatic advertising platforms use sophisticated algorithms, machine learning, and artificial intelligence to precisely target niche audiences at the most opportune time to drive high conversion rates.[143]

Additionally, programmatic advertising platforms utilize machine learning to improve over time based on your current advertising performance and changing market dynamics.

CAMPAIGN DELIVERY

Programmatic based media can appear in a variety of digital environments, such as news sites, blogs, social networks, video sites, and mobile/tablet-based apps. Programmatic media is delivered to these environments via an ad server which allows an advertiser or agency to centrally manage the setup, trafficking, and reporting of their campaigns.

An ad server is simply a web server backed by a database, which stores advertisements and delivers them to visitors to websites where advertising is enabled. Ad servers also perform important tasks like counting the number of impressions, clicks, and interactions for an ad campaign, as well as providing detailed reports that can help the advertiser determine the ROAS for ads on a particular website, platform, or network.

PROGRAMMATIC DISPLAY NETWORKS

The most common programmatic display networks for the hospitality industry include:

1. Google Display Network
2. Google Marketing Platform – Display and Video 360
3. ADARA
4. Sojern

Google Display Network

The Google Display Network can help you reach people while they're browsing their favorite websites, watching a YouTube video, checking their Gmail account, or using mobile devices and apps. Google Display Network will put your ads in front of a user before they start searching for what you offer, which can be key for your overall advertising strategy. You can also remind people of what they're interested in, as in the case of remarketing to people who previously visited your site or app.

It is designed to help you find the right audience for your ads. Following are examples of how you can approach targeting.

- Find new customers or engage your existing customers using audiences: Similar audiences and in-market audiences allow you to target people who are most likely to be interested in your products, helping you find new prospective customers. You can also use data, like remarketing lists, to help you re-engage people who previously visited your site.

- Drive more conversions using automation: Automated targeting helps you get more conversions by finding high-performing audiences based on your existing audiences and landing page. By automatically optimizing over time, Google Ads can learn which audiences work for you. Automated bidding automatically adjusts your bid to help you meet your return on investment. Smart display campaigns combine the best of automated targeting, bidding, and creative to maximize your conversions on Google Ads.

Display allows marketers to engage users with different ad formats, including:

- Responsive display ads: Creating ads on the Google Display Network is partially automated with responsive ads. To create them, enter ad text, then add images and logo, and Google will optimize the ad to improve performance. Both new and advanced users benefit from responsive ads because they show as "native" ads, and blend into the font and feel of the publisher's site.
- Uploaded image ads: For more control, you can create and upload ads as images in different sizes or HTML5.
- Engagement ads: Run engaging image and video ads on YouTube and across the Display Network.
- Gmail ads: Show expandable ads on the top tabs of people's inboxes.

Google Marketing Platform – Display and Video 360 (previously Doubleclick)

Display and Video360 is Google's Enterprise level advertising platform which offers advertisers access to audience insights and targeting. According to Google, "Specialized options for keywords, demographics, and remarketing help you engage the right audiences. Manage your audiences in the same product where you execute media buys. Apply existing audience lists to your media plan, discover and create new audience segments, and reach the right people across screens by tapping into Google's unique understanding of intent. Apply machine learning to automate steps like bidding and optimization, helping you respond to customers' needs faster. Fueled by powerful machine learning algorithms, Display and Video360's automated bidding strategy drives performance at scale to help you reach your goals."

ADARA

According to ADARA, "ADARA offers people-based insights to increase marketing efficiency, foster growth, and maximize the value of your customer portfolio. The value-based understanding of your customers is fueled by travel patterns, trends, and behaviors representative of 750+ million monthly unique traveler profiles across more than 200 of the world's top travel brands. ADARA offers a full suite of media solutions and uses predictive targeting to deliver on brand and performance goals. You can activate ADARA's traveler intelligence across your media plan to deliver on campaign objectives at scale."

Sojern

According to Sojern, "Sojern's platform is focused on travel, taking a true omnichannel approach that starts with building awareness. Your property is put in front of people who are in-market to travel to your destination but may still be doing research. When these travelers are ready to book, Sojern drives them directly to your website where they complete the booking transaction. Sojern leverages the power of programmatic ad-buying technology across a wide-range of media channels including mobile, social, native, video, and the open web."

KEY ELEMENTS OF IMPLEMENTING PROGRAMMATIC DISPLAY ADVERTISING

There are four important steps to take when implementing programmatic display advertising:

- Setting your goals
- Understanding your audience
- Segmentation and targeting
- Measuring performance

Setting Your Goals

A successful paid media campaign starts with your business goals. Depending on your business needs, map your digital media strategy by leveraging customer data to grow loyalty and business, using audience targeting and applying personalization strategies and continuous testing. Fine-tune based on the results and performance of your campaigns.

As you are setting goals, it is important to consider that display campaigns can be divided into two major categories: prospecting and retargeting.

Prospecting campaigns are focused on finding new customers for your hotel or business. Display campaigns are an ideal method of prospecting for new customers as the display

Source: Milestone Inc.

networks enable you to enter detailed information about your audience profiles. Integrating your audience list (your email database, website data, etc.) enables the display networks to create audiences like your current audience, which means there is a greater likelihood of conversion.

Typically, prospecting campaigns are focused on the top of the funnel or the "awareness stage," hence they result in lower ROI. While this may be the case, it is still critical to allocate advertising funds to prospecting campaigns, otherwise you may not be attracting new customers to your property.

Retargeting campaigns focus on consumers who have already visited your website. These consumers have already expressed an interest in your company or product, and have proven intent; therefore, targeting them will result in higher ROI. These consumers are typically at the lower end of the funnel in the conversion stages. If ROI is the primary focus, retargeting campaigns work well to drive higher ROI. All major programmatic display advertising platforms provide opportunities for allocating marketing funds towards prospecting and retargeting. The actual split of funds between the two types of campaigns will depend on your goals.

Understanding Your Audience

The core underlying strength of programmatic display strategies comes from precise targeting of your audience at scale. Prior to setting up display campaigns, it is critical for you to understand your audiences. In addition to the guest profile data in your hotel systems, there is a lot of data about your audiences available from social media channels such as Facebook or Google Analytics.

Segmentation & Targeting

The next key element to implementing programmatic display advertising is segmenting your audience based on data and customer behavior. You must leverage the wealth of data and intelligence that is available—both from your own CRM data as well as from available advertising platforms—to create campaigns that are highly targeted based on customer behaviors and target demographics.

Typical segmentations include:

- Search history
- Geo-targeting
- Social interactions
- Psychographic attributes
- Incomes
- Likes and dislikes
- Hobbies

Use your knowledge of your customer base to create targeted campaigns that focus on "like" consumers and provide offers to drive bookings to your website.

If your primary goal is to gain and retain a significant share of customers who are loyal to your brand, then your marketing strategies and tactics will be slightly different than if you are focused solely on acquiring new customers.

Before focusing on acquiring new customers, it is critical to create an action plan to retain

A Field Guide for Navigating Today's Digital Landscape

brand-loyal customers. Own 100% of the share of impressions for your branded terms by allocating and maximizing budget for branded campaigns and consistent omnichannel personalized campaigns across devices. Deploy your marketing channel strategy based on CRM data, retargeting specific customers such as those who have visited your site but did not book.

Once you have gained a significant share of current and loyal customers, you can deploy strategies like in-market campaigns, business-focused and destination-specific "things to do," and FAQ campaigns across multiple online channels to attract new visitors with unbranded yet targeted campaigns.

Measuring Performance

Display campaigns can be measured on their effectiveness using several KPIs. Examples of KPIs include:

- Advertising Metrics
  - Impressions (Views): How many people viewed the ad
  - Cost Per Thousand (CPM) Impressions: Cost/Impressions x 1000
  - Clicks: Number of people who click on the ad
  - Click Thru Rate (CTR): Number of clicks/number of impressions served
  - Cost Per Action/Acquisition (CPA) or Cost Per Booking: Cost/Actions
  - Return on Ad Spend (ROAS): Revenue/Spend

- Revenue Metrics
  - Total Room Nights Booked
  - Total Revenue
  - Assisted Revenue: Revenue booked via other channels after an interaction with the display ad
  - Conversion Rate: Percentage of people who convert (book) compared to all users exposed to the ad
  - Average Daily Rate (ADR): Revenue/Number of nights
  - Check Availability Rate: Percentage of people who enter the booking engine to check availability

IMPORTANT TERMINOLOGY TO KNOW

The following definitions are taken from the IAB Wiki—Glossary of Interactive Advertising Terms.[144]

- **AUDIENCE TARGETING:** A method that enables advertisers to show an ad specifically to visitors based on their shared behavioral, demographic, geographic, and/or technographic attributes.
- **BEHAVIORAL TARGETING:** Using previous online user activity (e.g., pages visited, content viewed, searches, clicks, and purchases) to generate a segment that is used to match advertising creative to users (sometimes also called Behavioral Profiling, Interest-based Advertising, or online behavioral advertising).
- **CONTEXTUAL TARGETING:** Targeting content that deals with topics, as determined by a contextual scanning technology.
- **RETARGETING:** A method that enables advertisers to show an ad specifically to visitors who previously were exposed to or interacted with the advertisers' creative.
- **DEMOGRAPHIC TARGETING:** A method that enables advertisers to show an ad specifically to visitors based on demographic information such as age, gender, and income which may come from site registration data or an inference-based mechanism.
- **GEOGRAPHIC TARGETING:** A method that enables advertisers to show an ad specifically to visitors based on zip code, area code, city, DMA, and state and/or country derived from user-declared registration information or inference-based mechanism.
- **KEYWORD TARGETING:** Targeting content that contains keywords.
- **SEARCH RETARGETING:** A method that enables advertisers to show an ad specifically to visitors based on one or more searches or search click events.
- **SEMANTIC TARGETING:** A type of contextual targeting that also incorporates semantic techniques to understand page meaning and/or sentiment.
- **SITE RETARGETING:** A method that enables advertisers to show an ad specifically to previous site visitors when they are on third-party websites.

- **TIME-BASED TARGETING:** A method that enables advertisers to show an ad specifically to visitors only on certain days of the week or times of the day (also known as Day Parting).

NATIVE ADVERTISING

As defined by one of the largest native advertising networks (Outbrain), "Native advertising is the use of paid ads that match the look, feel and function of the media format in which they appear. Native ads are often found in social media feeds, or as recommended content on a web page. Unlike display ads or banner ads, native ads don't really look like ads. They look like part of the editorial flow of the page. The key to native advertising is that it is non-disruptive—it exposes the reader to advertising content without sticking out like a sore thumb."

An example of a native ad campaign from Hilton

Native advertising can be compared to advertorials in the print media world. One of the most controversial points of native advertising is whether the user understands that it is an ad; sometimes the notice that it is paid placement is not clearly marked or understood by the end user.

SAMPLE CHDM EXAM QUESTIONS

1. What is the difference between a cookie and a pixel?
   a. A cookie is stored in a browser and pixel is stored on a server
   b. A pixel is stored in a browser and a cookie is stored on a server
   c. A cookie cannot be removed
   d. All of the above

2. Which metric is the number of clicks divided by the number of impressions?
   a. Impression Share
   b. Click Through Rate
   c. Average Ad Position
   d. None of the above

3. What is an ad that looks and feels like it is part of a news site?
   a. Search Ad
   b. Display Ad
   c. Programmatic Ad
   d. Native Ad

Answers
1 = a
2 = b
3 = d

NOTE

_____
_____
_____
_____
_____
_____
_____
_____
_____
_____

Chapter 21: Affiliate Marketing

Affiliate marketing is a performance-based advertising channel in which the advertiser rewards the publisher (affiliate) with a pre-determined commission for each lead or conversion that the publisher drives. Affiliates typically use online advertising methods (paid search, email, content, retargeting, display, etc.), which allow hotels and brands to extend their digital reach to attract potential guests. Typical affiliates include cash-back sites (Rakuten), coupon/deals sites (Retailmenot.com), shopping apps (Ibotta), credit card rewards (Capital One) and blogs (travel sites). Some affiliates offer a merchant's own website-enhancing technologies.

Many hotel brands offer affiliate programs geared toward driving direct traffic to their websites under a revenue share model. In the hospitality sector, affiliates predominantly operate on a commission model where the hotel/brand pays a percentage of revenue for every consumed booking delivered by an affiliate partner (typically a base of 3-10%). Other compensation methods include CPC (cost per click), CPA (cost per action), or CPM (cost per thousand views) depending on the type of promotional placement offered.

AFFILIATE NETWORKS

Affiliate networks offer a platform for advertisers to connect and partner with hundreds of affiliate publishers all from one centralized tool. Typically, the affiliate network allows merchants to quickly scale their programs by providing turn-key reporting, tracking, payment and refund processing, program management, and access to a large database of publishers. For the affiliates, networks offer easy registration for a merchant program and a central database of affiliate programs organized by category and popularity. Some of the biggest affiliate networks include Rakuten, Linkshare, CJ Affiliate, ShareASale, Performance Horizon, and Impact.

Hotel advertisers can upload display banners and text links which publishers can then extract from the affiliate platform and place on their websites. All tracking elements are included in the creative to record each click or transaction.

Hotel advertisers can leverage the affiliate network to regularly connect with the hundreds of partners via email newsletters to inform interested publishers about the latest seasonal promotion or incentive the brand is offering.

Advertisers can also purchase flat-rate media with the publishers for additional exposure. This includes home page placements, travel category placements, email blasts, and more.

Many advertisers are now working with influencers and influencer networks through affiliate platforms to allow for a centralized set-up. The influencer agrees to the terms and conditions set within the platform, and reporting and payment happens within the network.

Hotel brands should consider this tactic as a part of their broader digital strategy offered through performance marketing. Across the globe, affiliate marketing has been proven successful in driving increased website traffic and revenues in a cost-efficient manner. Affiliate marketing is also a great tool to manage partners at scale and enable strategic partnerships that may not be otherwise available through direct deals.

Chapter 22: Metasearch

Metasearch sites are shopping comparison sites that allow consumers to compare hotels' prices between suppliers and OTAs. Metasearch has proven to be a key component of direct bookings, as it drives traffic to your website—providing first-party cookies—and provides your hotel with guests' information.

Tripadvisor, Kayak, and Trivago were the originators of this model but in the past several years, Google has taken the lead when it comes to metasearch. Often when searchers looking for hotels on Google they are driven down the metasearch path.

A very important aspect of metasearch is its "pay for play" model, meaning if you are not paying to participate you will not show up in the metasearch results. While metasearch companies often present themselves to consumers as the best way to comparison shop, it is only showing consumers those companies that have agreed to pay them for the leads. So, if someone wants to book your hotel and is on a metasearch site, but you are not participating, your hotel will not appear as an option to the consumer.

METASEARCH MODELS

In the beginning, metasearch was built on a CPC (cost per click) bidding model. Since its inception, the metasearch companies have tested and added other products like commission models on bookings. During the Covid-19 pandemic when hotel marketing budgets were more constrained than normal, most of the meta companies added a commission model, as many hotels were willing to advertise for "guaranteed" bookings. Since the advertising models change often, they are not outlined in depth here. Do research into each one carefully before participating.

CONNECTING TO METASEARCH PARTNERS

It is important to note that in most cases hotels cannot connect directly to the metasearch partners. The connection needs to be made through the process set up by your brand, or, if you are independent property, through one of the approved technology providers (usually your booking engine, CRS, PMS, or channel manager).

THE "BIG 5" METASEARCH CHANNELS

The "Big 5" metasearch channels today are Google, Tripadvisor, Trivago, Kayak, and Bing. These five channels are common players in most global markets but may have variances by location. [Special Note: Depending on your target market, be sure to check for regional players like Qunar in China.]

> Metasearch continues to grow in importance for hotels, especially in relation to the "book direct" movement. HSMAI's Navigating Metasearch on-demand course will help you:
> - Understand how metasearch works
> - Confidently navigate the metasearch marketing landscape
> - Create campaign goals and strategies using metasearch to achieve them
> - Realistically plan your metasearch budget
>
> Learn more at https://hsmaiacademy.org/.

Google	• The 800lb Gorilla • Multiple commercial models including CPC, PPS, PPB, and more • Most volume + best conversions (usually)
Tripadvisor	• Best for longer sales cycle • Make sure guest review scores are positive • Consider pairing with Business Advantage (Business Listing)
trivago	• Considered the best channel for European travelers (pre-COVID). • Tends to have lower conversion, but lower CPC • Just introduced CPA/PPS model (10/2020)
KAYAK	• Has been doing meta since 2005 • Booking.com family • Tends to have higher conversions, but higher CPCs • Low traffic volume
Bing	• Copied Google Model • Converts well with very low CPC but lower volume • Often overlooked • Powers search for AOL, Yahoo, MSN, etc. and most car nav systems

Source: Hotel Digital Marketing Essentials Course

Google

As of July 2021, the Google commercial models include Cost Per Click (CPC), Pay Per Booking (PPB), and Pay Per Stay (PPS). The latter option (PPS) is based on a commissionable revenue from consumed stays (net after cancellations), while PPB is based on gross bookings. It is important to note that each of the "PP" models are ultimately reverse-engineered into what's known as an eCPC, or "effective," cost per click.

For example, if you have a $300 booking, and Google gets a 10% commission, that is $30. Now let's say you had a 5% conversion rate, meaning it took 20 clicks to get a booking: $30 divided by 20 clicks = a $1.50 eCPC. This is then ranked against the CPCs offered by other advertisers bidding for the same point of sale.

In 2021, Google began offering free organic metasearch listings which opened a world of possibilities for big and small hotels alike. This, combined with the traditional paid metasearch results, means a hotel can occupy two points of sale—but so can everyone else.

Tripadvisor

Tripadvisor gained much of its notoriety as a source for hotel guest reviews and user-generated content (UGC). The platform was one of the early implementers of assisted booking technology, called Instant Book, to help facilitate the metasearch booking process.

While Tripadvisor has had some ups and downs over the years, it has a strong niche market for travelers looking for and/or planning getaway vacations. Tripadvisor is ideal for hotels and resorts that want guests to "look at all the pretty pictures," and continues to be a great resource not only for guest reviews but also for researching a destination (and asking "What are the best restaurants and/or attractions near my hotel?").

Tripadvisor should always be a standard part of marketing programs for high-end luxury properties and resorts, and for destination marketing professionals.

Trivago

Often, when hotel marketers think of the metasearch channel Trivago, they think of European travelers. This mentality has been a little misleading in past years as the platform also engaged in aggressive television marketing that appealed to U.S. travelers.

The international traveler demographic took a huge hit during the Covid-19 pandemic, as did Trivago's television marketing budget. The company has started to reengage with display advertising as well as new TV ads focusing on vacation rentals.

Historically, Trivago has had the advantage of having one of the lowest CPC metrics in the industry. While this was often paired with a lower conversion rate, it still could drive strong ROI due to low costs. This is a good channel to watch as an indicator for travel trends from other markets.

Kayak

Giving credit where credit is due, Kayak has been running travel metasearch programs longer than any other major site on this list. It started in 2004 alongside a former competitor called Sidestep, which Kayak eventually acquired.

Kayak is now part of Priceline, which enables the platform to feature many of Priceline's special rate programs such as Pricebreakers within its search results. Kayak's site also features a wide array of in-line and pop-up ad opportunities.

Kayak's acquisition of HotelsCombined also positioned it well for increased international awareness. And while Kayak has a history of excellent conversion rates, it has lacked the volume seen by other channels. A key area of strength right now stems from alternative lodging options, including B&Bs and even campgrounds/RV resorts. Plus, Kayak has many "children" sites around the world (see "South America" below) that can be very influential in the right markets.

Bing

Think of Bing as Google without the volume. It is practically identical to Google in terms of its offerings. Differentiators include the fact that its guest reviews and ratings are almost exclusively powered by Tripadvisor, and—because most vehicle navigation software programs are powered by Microsoft—when consumers ask their car's GPS to find a hotel near them, they are being delivered results from Bing.

Both of these factors make Bing worthy of your consideration. On top of that, Bing performs very well. You could effectively "own" your presence there on a very small budget.

REGIONAL VARIANCES IN METASEARCH

South America

While Kayak itself is not a primary channel, many of the Kayak "children" are. These sites include Mundi, Momondo, and DetectaHotel, all of which are part of the Kayak/Booking Holding family. Other relevant metasearch channels include Voopter and Skyscanner; however, these are generally more focused on flights.

The Brazilian hotel market in particular consists of more than 80% independent hotels with a wide array of electronic distribution systems. This can make integrations challenging, and rates and availability often don't work via two-way interfaces. It's also a common practice for consumers to pay for travel in installments—over a 12-month period, for example—which can further complicate guarantee and cancellation policies within the metasearch points of sale as they may not all offer this feature.

Europe

Europe tends to be a very diverse region for all travel programs, and metasearch is no exception. Trivago had long been the dominant player in the market prior to the Covid-19 pandemic. Tripadvisor also has a strong presence, but more in the travel-planning stage rather than in rate shopping.

Europe also saw a sharp increase in the percentage of traffic booking directly during the pandemic. Many consumers wanted the ability to speak directly with the hotel to have questions answered prior to travel.

Google dominates this market but is getting some competition from a lesser-known search engine called Ecosia, which demonstrates its commitment to ecological and carbon-friendly practices by planting a tree for every search. While Ecosia doesn't yet have a metasearch point-of-sale component, it does follow more traditional paid search and SEO formats.

Asia Pacific

Metasearch within the APAC market changed drastically during the pandemic. The use of such engines has been heavily reduced due to the lack of international travel and the heavy regulation of domestic travel.

Pre-pandemic, Google, Tripadvisor, Qunar (Trip.com), and Kayak were the largest metasearch players, although you have to keep in mind that Google has limited access from within China. The one channel that does hold some prominence is Tripadvisor, due largely to consumers wanting to know if a particular hotel is safe—or for that matter even open. Beyond metasearch channels, much of the deal-searching within China is driven by livestream shows run by different online celebrities and/or channels.

THE LONG TAIL

The list other metasearch channels could span additional pages. Sites like Hotelvoy, Hotelscan, Yandex, Allstay, and more have very region-specific audiences. Google will almost always be the dominant player in the room, but only focusing on that platform will mean you're ignoring 25-40% of your market's potential traffic.

The best solutions come from understanding consumer buying behavior for each channel and how that may or may not be relevant to your hotel and/or market. By combining this with a proper cross-channel optimization strategy, you can cast a wider net without losing focus on the bigger fish.

BEST PRACTICES

- If you're not already doing so, make sure you have a point of sale on Google's free organic meta (AKA FBL, Free Booking Links). This is a must-do minimum, even if you do absolutely nothing else.
- If you're running campaigns, make sure you have unique tracking to identify paid versus organic on Google.
- Identify your regional demographics and pair them up with channels best suited to your feeder markets.
- Track those first-party cookies! Not everyone books, and with third-party cookies on their way out, these are going to be extremely valuable.
- Run campaigns, even if they are modest ones. Meta CPCs are increasing. Running a baseline campaign can be very inexpensive but will provide you with valuable historical data and help you identify key trends.

SAMPLE CHDM EXAM QUESTIONS

1. Which of the following is not an advertising model for meta?
   a. CPC
   b. CPA
   c. CPM
   d. PPS

2. The OTA with the greatest market share is:
   a. Google
   b. Tripadvisor
   c. Kayak
   d. Bing

3. Metasearch is free and unbiased.
   a. True
   b. False

Answers
1 = a
2 = b
3 = b

Chapter 23: Paid Social Media

Social media is distinctly different from all other forms of digital advertising. Social media-based ad placements are designed to integrate with the actual content and therefore the consumer experience within the site. This form of ad placement is referred to as an "in-stream" placement and, unlike traditional digital media placements, offers the ability for a consumer to both share, like, dislike, and comment on the ad unit. For this reason, it is often considered a best practice to create ad units which are not just content based but also informational and entertaining in nature to drive consumer interactions.

Examples of social media websites include Facebook, Instagram, Twitter, YouTube, and TikTok. See Chapter 17 for more information on social platforms. Each channel has its own unique opportunities and challenges. By far the most popular social channels for hotels are Facebook and Instagram. Hotels generally see high levels of engagement as well as some revenue and leads through these channels.

Social media ads are inherently mobile friendly in nature. They are often preferred by marketers when the desire is to target a consumer while they are on a mobile device.

The approach to social media advertising is like any other ad campaign:

- Set expectations and goals.
- Determine the right audience.
- Create the ad.
- Budget for the initiative.
- Test and measure performance.

SET EXPECTATIONS & GOALS

What is the desired outcome for your social media advertising campaign? Do you want to focus on new guest acquisition? Do you want to create brand awareness? Do you want to drive ancillary revenue on property (spa bookings, dining reservations, etc.)? Are you trying to increase your loyal customer base? Or, do you have a different goal?

Once you have determined your objectives, then you can determine the best way to reach your goals. There are multiple options for setting goals for social media advertising, including:

- Drive clicks/traffic to website
- Drive clicks/traffic to social company page
- Boost the visibility of a specific post promoting an event or promotion
- Convert views to bookings
- Increase social channel followers

For example, your desired outcome may be to promote a holiday weekend package. You can drive people from your social ad directly to the landing page of your website promoting that package, or you can drive them to a products page on your social channel which encourages them to follow or like your page to qualify for future promotions. One method increases bookings, and one method increases your targeted list and helps build a bigger audience for future marketing efforts.

DETERMINE THE RIGHT AUDIENCE

Social channels provide a multitude of targeting options. Most channels offer you the ability to target new customers or communicate to your existing followers—or target an audience that has similarities with the audience that is already a follower of your brand. This is typically referred to as targeting "like" audiences. A few audience targeting examples you should consider follow.

Location
Is your hotel primarily visited by people from a certain location? For example, do you run a small hotel in the Adirondack Mountains that draws primarily from the New York City area? Or perhaps most of the guests at your hotel in wine country come from Los Angeles?

Demographics
Does your hotel target a particular age group? Gender? College graduates? Married couples? Depending on your location, Facebook offers

a range of demographic attributes to choose from.

Interests
What are the demand generators near you? Great sights, attractions, or even restaurants? Why are your current guests coming to visit your area? Make sure to target for those interests. What are your guests' hobbies? Are you looking for soccer players, knitting enthusiasts, or backcountry skiers?

Connections
Who is already connected with your brand? Do you want to reach the people who have an established affinity for your hotel? Or do you want to specifically exclude them to focus on finding new people to (for example) like your page?

Create the Ad
Each platform offers different ad types and ad requirements. We cover some best practices in the specific areas of Facebook, Instagram, and LinkedIn later in this chapter but the same rules apply for all ad creation. Be sure the visual component is compelling, use your keywords in your ad copy, and ensure you are communicating messaging that will most likely appeal to your target audiences. Every ad should have a call to action.

Budget for the Initiative
Most platforms allow you to determine a daily budget and a duration for your ad to run. You can also choose a total budget and duration, and then the daily budget will be automatically calculated. Most platforms offer suggestions on the probable response rate so you are able to determine if the amount of spend is going to reach the return you want.

Test and Measure Performance
Most platforms provide robust tracking for your ad performance. If you have set up your goals correctly, most of the platforms will analyze exactly how close you are to meeting or exceeding your expectations, and you can adjust your budget or extend your promotion based on your success.

While every social media platform has unique offerings based on their users' behaviors, we will go into a bit more detail for three of the more popular platforms to show the similarities and differences.

Facebook
Social media, and Facebook in particular, is very good at touching customers wherever they are in the travel cycle.

Setting Goals for Facebook Ads
Based on your objectives, your approach to Facebook ads will vary greatly. So first, define your desired outcome or goal. Once you are clear on your goals, there are many marketing opportunities depending on your goal.[145]

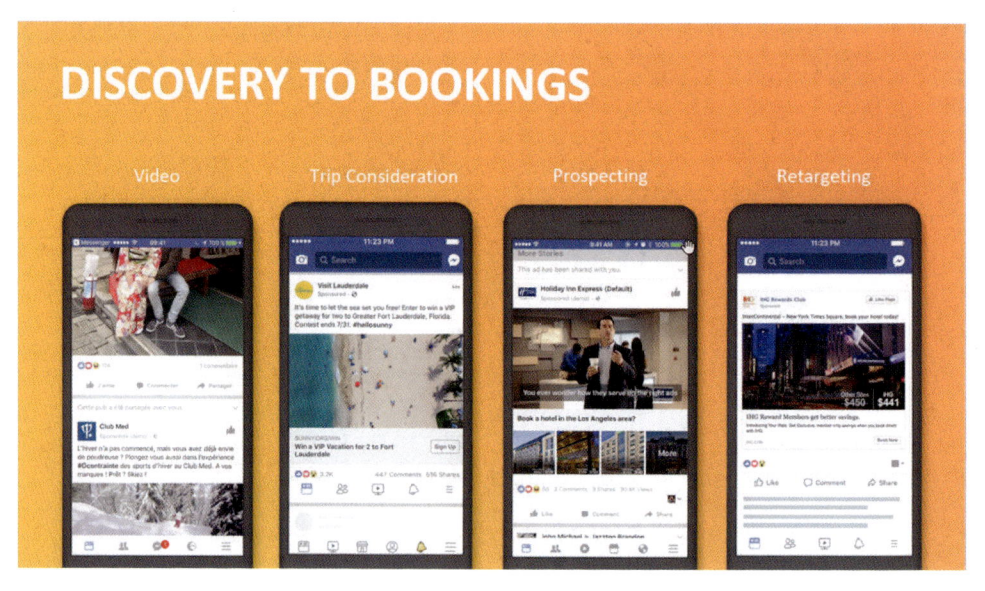

Source: Facebook

Traveler Goal	Tool	Placement	Objective	Creative	Optimization
Find trip inspiration	Stories, video, trip consideration	Instagram Feed, Instagram Stories, Facebook Stories	Video Views, Awareness, Conversion	Vertical Video <15s, Single Image, Collection	Landing Page Views, Reach, Ad Recall Lift
Plan (whether they have a destination in mind or not)	Trip consideration	Automatic placements	Website conversion	Single Image, Carousel, Collection	Offsite Conversions, Landing Page Views
Plan and book a room (with a destination in mind)	Hotel Ads for Prospecting	Automatic placements	Catalog Sales	Carousel, Collection	Return on Ad Spend, Offsite Conversions
Book a room (from your site visitors)	Hotel Ads for Retargeting	Automatic placements	Catalog Sales	Carousel, Collection	Return on Ad Spend, Offsite Conversions
Book a room from a sale/ promotion	Trip consideration	Automatic placements	Website conversions	Carousel, Collection, Vertical Video <15s	Return on Ad Spend, Offsite Conversions
Install a hotel app	Trip consideration	Automatic placements	App installs	Vertical Video <15s	App installs
Discover ancillaries, amenities	Hotel Ads for Retargeting	For more details see https://www.facebook.com/business/help/			
Engage post- booking	Messenger				

Following is a sample ad with the simple goal of increasing page likes—or page promotion.

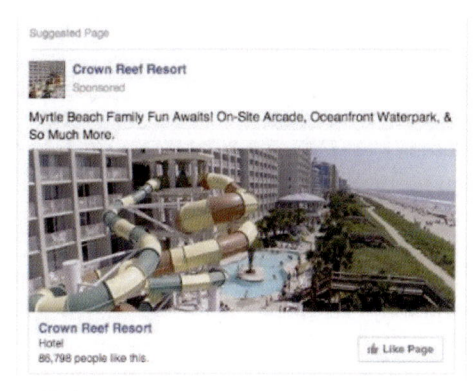

146

This ad for Crown Reef Resort puts their 4-story oceanfront waterpark front, a unique and popular amenity that they offer, front and center.

TIP: Use high quality images that showcase unique property amenities or upgraded rooms and features.

Source: Fuel

Increasing likes on your page may seem fantastic on its own, but you must be sure to think strategically about your target audience. They will only continue to engage with you organically if you are reaching the right consumer for your property. If you simply buy "likes" or entice likes from people who have no real interest in your property, you will have low engagement rates which will harm your organic reach.

Determining Your Audience
Facebook offers a wide range of audience options. You first must choose between all of Facebook or only those members of Facebook who have previously interacted with your page. Within each, you can then narrow your focus by selecting age and gender, interests, education level, and more.

Facebook recommends specific best practices for targeting audiences for hotels. One best practice is to target your ads to people based on their travel dates and location:

- People with specific travel dates or booking windows
- People looking to travel on the weekends
- People with travel dates or with no travel dates
- People searching for specific destinations

To reach people who are interested in traveling, consider targeting:

- People with high travel intent signals (e.g., time spent on a site or the number of searches on a site)
- People traveling alone, in groups or with kids
- People who searched for or booked flights recently but haven't booked hotels
- High value audiences (e.g., loyalty members)

Also, consider excluding people who don't meet certain qualifications:

- People whose travel dates have passed
- People who have flights with the same departure and return date and won't need a hotel

One of the most interesting features in Facebook advertising is the ability to target lookalike audiences. You can import a mailing list of your best customers for example and ask Facebook to create a lookalike audience based on who is a current customer. You can then further adjust the demographics of that lookalike audience. It is a fantastic tool if your end goal is to grow your customer base.

Creating Ads for Facebook
Facebook offers multiple ad options—a single image, a video, a carousel (or several images), or a slideshow (which becomes a video with up to 10 images).

Write a compelling headline. Make sure it appeals to your target audience. If you are searching for new customers, make sure your headline matches what your research tells you might be appealing about your property to that audience. If you are retargeting existing customers, remind them why they like you.

Typically, you only have up to 25 characters for your headline. Headlines are a great way to test your ads—create two ads that are the same in every way but change the headline and see which draws better engagement.

Next write the body or text of the ad. Typically you have up to 90 characters for the text. That is not a lot of space so choose your text wisely. Keywords are important here too—and can make the ads compelling.

Finally have a call to action (CTA) based on your goals. "Book Now," "Contact Us," "Learn More," and "Download" are just a few of the CTA options you have available. This CTA should be a logical next step based on your ad and your audience. If your audience knows you, "Book Now" might be a reasonable CTA, especially if you are promoting a specific event. If you are trying to create awareness, a simple "Learn More" might be your best option.

As you create your ad, always test to see how it will appear on a desktop and on a mobile device. You may choose to target only mobile or desktop with ads.

Budgeting for Facebook Ads
Facebook allows you to allocate a daily budget and set a time limit for how long an ad will run. Based on the criteria that you set, Facebook will also let you know the projected results you can expect so you can adjust your daily bid, duration, or placement based on their predictive analysis.

Measuring the Performance of Facebook Ads
Check progress frequently on your results page in Facebook. You can see if your ad is resonating, or if you need to adjust the creative or perhaps change your audience. You can make modifications to an ad in process if you feel it is required.

Always connect your end results back to your original intent. If you were testing your ad, which elements performed better? Make note to use that format again in the future.

The typical data you will see includes:

- Number of people reached
- Number of engagements
- A breakdown of engagement metrics by action taken (comments, share, views)
- Demographic breakdowns by age, gender, location, and interest.
- How much you spent

You can sort this data in a wide variety of views—by the hour or by the day for instance. You can also compare performances of ads over different time periods. In general Facebook makes it easy for you to evaluate when your ads are most effective.

Facebook Pixels

Facebook offers the ability to retarget easily by creating a Facebook pixel. Place this pixel on your website and then Facebook can track which visitors went from your ad to your website but perhaps did not convert. This information allows you to see who has some interest but for any reason didn't convert. You can then create additional content and advertising to appeal to that specific audience—which has historically shown a very positive ROI for hotel marketers.

INSTAGRAM

As Facebook is the parent company of Instagram, most of the advertising information is the same. However, Instagram behaviors are different from Facebook so you have to take an Instagram-specific approach. Instagram is a much more visual platform and placing traditional ads will not be as effective. You will need to use visuals much more than text to tell your story.

You can run ads in three ways on Instagram:

1. Run ads directly from Instagram
2. Create ads from your Facebook page
3. Create ad campaigns in Ads Manager (in Facebook)

You will need to set up a business profile in Instagram and ensure that it is linked to your Facebook account. You can currently only add the following call-to-action buttons to your business profile:

- Buy/Get Tickets
- Start Order
- Book (Book an appointment)
- Reserve (Make a reservation)

Similar to Facebook, you can boost your individual Instagram posts in addition to creating ads.

What about video? Instagram launched IGTV which is a quickly evolving platform. Currently you can promote your IGTV channel (which hosts your pre-recorded vertical videos) via sharing on stories or on your Facebook channel—not through promoted ads. However, this area is changing quickly so be sure to check as this could be a valuable resource for hoteliers soon.

Instagram Insights allows you to see analytics for your Instagram Business Account. There is a tremendous amount of data that can be mined from Instagram Insights, and it covers three main areas: activity, content, and audience. Some of the data points available are outlined here:

Activity

- Profile Visits: the number of users that have visited your Instagram profile
- Website Clicks: the number of users who have clicked on the website link in your bio
- Email: the number of times users have tapped on Email on your profile
- Call: the number of times users have tapped on Call on your profile
- Reach: the number of unique accounts that have seen any of your posts
- Impressions: the total number of times that all your posts have been seen

Content

- Comments: the number of comments on your post
- Engagement: the number of unique accounts that liked, commented or saved your post
- Follows: the number of accounts that started following you because of your post
- Get Directions: the number of users who tapped Get Directions because of your post
- Impressions: the total number of times your post has been seen
- The Gender, Age and Location of the audience who viewed the post

Audience

- Gender: the percentage split of your followers
- Age Range: the age brackets of your followers
- Top Locations: the locations of your followers based on City and Countries
- Followers: the most active times of your followers, by hour of the day and days of the week

LINKEDIN

Not surprising, LinkedIn advertising follows along the same lines as the others. Set your goals, identify your audience, create your ad, and track results. However, while Instagram favors visuals, LinkedIn favors text—or content. In general, LinkedIn is a great way to reach more of a B2B audience: meeting and event planners and wedding planners for instance.

In terms of setting goals—be aware that there are several ways to advertise on LinkedIn.

LinkedIn Sponsored Content

While Instagram wants you to tell a story visually, LinkedIn sponsored content lets you use your words. You can write articles, share white papers, or use any content that your audience might find interesting.

There are a few LinkedIn best practice recommendations for sponsored content:

- Analyze industry news instead of just sharing it. Offering insights and key takeaways will keep your content from feeling generic and help establish thought leadership in your field.
- Add content curation to your plan. Share information that is useful and relevant to your audience without creating it all yourself. Always credit your source.
- Repurpose your own content. Remember to check your blog, website, and social media channels instead of creating new content every time.
- Use rich media (like video, audio, or other element) by incorporating YouTube, Vimeo, and SlideShare videos. They play right in the LinkedIn feed, so your audience can engage organically.
- Include human interest stories that connect to your brand, and you will help your audience establish an emotional connection.

Sponsored InMail

You can contact your potential audience via LinkedIn InMail. You can take a more personal approach by appearing to have sent an individual email, speaking directly to that prospect with this approach.

Best practices for sponsored InMail follow traditional prospecting email guidelines. Make it personal, make it relevant, make it interesting. Write for your audience. If you are targeting influencers, create value for them to share your content. If you are writing to decision makers, ask for next steps in your call to action.

LinkedIn suggests that the best performing subject lines use some of the following key words: thanks; exclusive invitation; connect; job opportunities; or join us.

LinkedIn Text Ads, Carousel Ads, Video Ads, Dynamic Ads

These ads will show up in newsfeeds and will be noted as sponsored.

Dynamic Ads are personalized ads tailored to each member based on each member's own LinkedIn profile data including profile photo, company name, and job title.

Advertisers only need to build their creative and write their ad copy once, and LinkedIn will automatically personalize their campaign for each person in their audience.

With that in mind, you can determine what your goal is and what avenue you should pursue based on those goals.

Your Audience

You can select your target audience in the following categories in the LinkedIn environment:

- Experience—function, title, seniority, years of experience
- Company—name, industry, size, followers, connections
- Education—schools, degrees, fields of study
- Interests—skills, groups
- Identity—location, age, gender

Like lookalike audiences in Facebook, LinkedIn also offers advanced targeting via their audience expansion option. You can also use matched audiences to customize LinkedIn audiences with your own business data so that you can re-engage website visitors with website retargeting, nurture prospects with contact targeting, and run account-based marketing campaigns with account targeting.

Enable lead gen forms to capture more qualified leads. This feature pulls LinkedIn profile data (like job title, company name, and contact details) into a form that members can submit with one click.

Measure and Optimize

LinkedIn provides analytics like other networks. You can track traffic, engagement, and conversions. You can see how your targeted audience is behaving and compare your results over different time periods.

improve your ad relevance score (based on indicators that LinkedIn members find the ads interesting, such as clicks, comments, and shares), which will help you win more bids.

- Use direct sponsored content to test different creative and targeting combinations. This ad type is only shown to the campaign target audience, never on your LinkedIn Page.

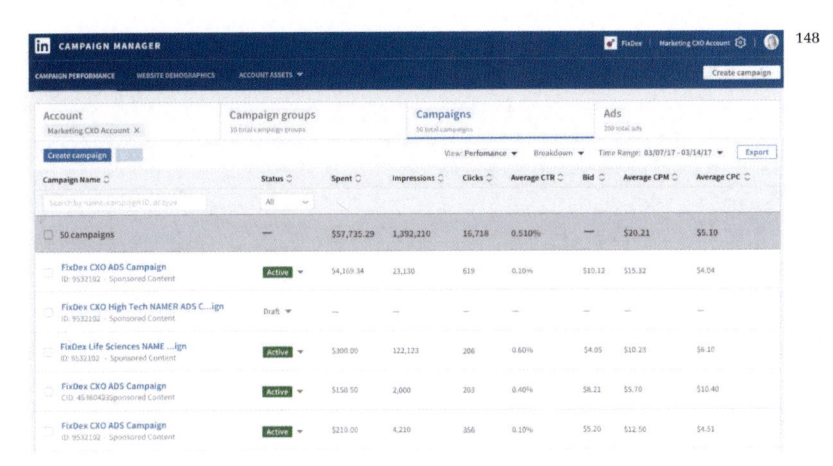

[148]

Install the LinkedIn Insight Tag on your website, so you can track conversions and enable demographic reporting on your website visitors.

You should also optimize for mobile. Make your landing pages easy places to view, navigate, and submit information from a smartphone.

BEST PRACTICES: ALWAYS BE TESTING[149]

- Run A/B tests to compare multiple messages or versions of your ad creative. You'll see which one resonates most with your target audience.
- Use A/B testing to optimize targeting too. Create a campaign, duplicate it, and alter the targeting criteria slightly. Run both campaigns to learn which audiences are more receptive to your content.
- Include 2-4 ads in each campaign. Campaigns with more ads usually reach more people in your target audience.
- Every 1-2 weeks, pause the ad with the lowest engagement and replace it with new ad creative. Over time, this will

SAMPLE CHDM EXAM QUESTIONS

1. Facebook advertising is only relevant for low funnel advertising.
    a. True
    b. False

2. Which of the following is a valid goal for social media advertising?
    a. Drive clicks/traffic to website
    b. Drive clicks/traffic to social company page
    c. Boost the visibility of a specific post promoting an event or promotion
    d. Convert to a booking
    e. Increase social channel followers
    f. All of the above

3. Which segment are you least likely to connect with through LinkedIn?
    a. Meeting Planners
    b. Event Planners
    c. Business Travelers
    d. Leisure Travelers

Answers
1 = b
2 = f
3 = d

Chapter 24: OTA Paid Media

Many of the online travel agencies (OTAs) have paid media models where you can purchase "media assets" that will try to drive bookings (in some cases within the "walled garden" of the OTA). These are helpful in need periods and should be considered carefully. Keep in mind that the cost of acquisition needs to be calculated (your margin plus the media cost divided by your revenue).

Note that some brands restrict the type of OTA paid media a hotel can participate in—for example, mobile and/or last-minute deals—so it is always important to understand your brand's directives as they relate to OTA advertising.

Most OTA campaigns are known as "link-in" campaigns. That means your ad will be linked to a page on the OTA and the booking will be on that OTA. While not common, some OTAs offer "link-off" campaigns that enable you to link the ad directly to your hotel's website.

BUDGETING FOR OTA PAID MEDIA

Advertising with OTAs can often help hotels achieve their goals, but a word of caution, DO THE MATH. Remember: your hotel pays an OTA anywhere from 10%-30% in commission, so any advertising you do that is "link-in" (where the booking happens on the OTA), means that you pay commission plus the advertising cost. This should be included in your analysis and budget. The "OTA Math" graphic illustrates this issue.

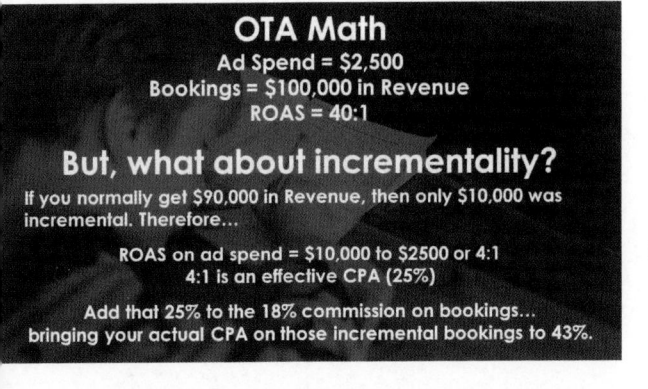

OTA Math
Ad Spend = $2,500
Bookings = $100,000 in Revenue
ROAS = 40:1

But, what about incrementality?
If you normally get $90,000 in Revenue, then only $10,000 was incremental. Therefore...

ROAS on ad spend = $10,000 to $2500 or 4:1
4:1 is an effective CPA (25%)

Add that 25% to the 18% commission on bookings... bringing your actual CPA on those incremental bookings to 43%.

Source: Hotel Digital Marketing Essentials course materials

At times an OTA may offer a "link-off" campaign where they allow you to use their media assets to send traffic to your website. When these are offered, view and assess them as you would any other marketing effort based on the cost and how it relates to your goal (traffic, ROAS, email sign-up, etc.).

As of this printing, the following sections outline the paid media options from Expedia, Booking.com, Priceline, and Trip.com.

EXPEDIA GROUP MEDIA SOLUTIONS PAID MEDIA OPTIONS

Expedia Group Media Solutions includes Expedia, Hotels.com, Vrbo, Travelocity, and more.

- TravelAds Sponsored Listings connect hotel advertisers with highly qualified travel shoppers across Expedia Group's global portfolio of travel brands. By allowing advertisers to customize their messaging and target travel shoppers based on their needs, hotels can stand out in a competitive marketplace and drive more room nights. The pay-per-click model is a flexible and efficient way for hotels to maximize bookings and revenue by reaching the right traveler at the right time.

- Accelerator gives hotels the option to temporarily increase compensation for select dates to help influence your visibility in the Expedia Group marketplace.

- Display Advertising includes native and standard ad placements across Expedia Group's portfolio of global travel brands. Displays ads are integrated seamlessly throughout the entire travel shopper journey and booking funnel. They can also be purchased as a sponsorship or takeover that allow the hotel to be the official brand sponsor for select site-wide and holiday sales.

- Passport Audience Extension Ads allow a hotel to follow the shopper through the travel shopping journey with targeted display ads based on Expedia Group's first party travel intent and booking data anywhere on the internet.

- Co-Op Campaigns are a collective display advertising effort made by multiple brands with common marketing goals. Hotels can collaborate with like-minded partners including CVBs, DMOs, other hotels or a collection of hotels to extend and amplify marketing spend together.
- Email marketing solutions are available through dedicated emails to an Expedia targeted audience or through a featured display ad placement on specific Expedia brand newsletters.

BOOKING.COM PAID MEDIA OPTIONS

- Preferred Program is status-based program that hotels qualify for, and they must maintain the criteria. There is an increase in commission to participate. Preferred properties get extra visibility in search results next to a thumbs up sign that indicates they have met the criteria.
- Visibility Booster allows an accommodation to improve visibility on need dates to drive increased business on those specific days or periods.

PRICELINE/AGODA (PART OF BOOKING.COM GROUP) PAID MEDIA OPTIONS

Priceline and Agoda have many advertising opportunities including sponsored banner ads, sponsored listings, promotions, email ads, and more. See detailed information at:

- https://partnerhub.agoda.com/hotel-solutions/agoda-display-network/
- https://www.priceline.com/advertise/

TRIP.COM (FORMERLY CTRIP) PAID MEDIA OPTIONS

- Pay for preferred placement to attract Chinese consumers
- Display Advertising
- Trip Moments - participation in Trip.com social channels
- VIP Club, WeChat, Weibo, etc.

SAMPLE CHDM EXAM QUESTIONS

1. Cost of acquisition for rooms sold on an OTA can be calculated as margin plus media cost divided by revenue.
    a. True
    b. False

2. All brands restrict the type of OTA paid media a hotel can buy.
    a. True
    b. False

3. What is it called when the booking happens on the OTA?
    a. Link Off
    b. Link In
    c. Link Up

Answers
1 = a
2 = b
3 = b

NOTES

PART FIVE: DIGITAL INTERMEDIARIES

Chapter 25: Online Travel Agencies (OTAs)

KEY POINTS
- History of the OTA segment and characteristics of the primary OTA models
- Understand what makes OTAs a compelling choice for consumers
- Best practices in working with OTAs to deliver a long-term, sustainable ROI
- How to think about content marketing and user experience on an OTA

SUMMARY

As a part of an overall digital marketing strategy, it is important to understand how online travel agencies (OTAs) work. They are often a preferred research and booking point for consumers and should therefore be considered when you are determining how to reach consumers.

Look at the OTA business holistically. In some instances, they are a fantastic marketing and distribution partner, and in other instances they may be a hotel's competitor for direct bookings. Determining which OTAs will provide incremental revenues at long-term, sustainable cost requires a thorough understanding of the models and specific OTA marketing efforts. (See Chapter 24 for the opportunities for paid media when it comes to OTAs.)

Consolidation in the OTA segment has resulted in a virtual duopoly of Expedia Group and Booking.com in the U.S. and Europe, while Asia still has several regional sites looking to expand beyond their primary countries.

OTAs are large contributors to hotel booking mix. Over the years the growth rates in OTAs have outpaced brand.com. However, over the past several years hotels have been battling for a larger share of bookings. The book direct "movement" was probably best illustrated by Hilton's "stop clicking around campaign" launched in 2016, and many hotels followed with aggressive book direct campaigns. Not to be outdone, the OTAs and metasearch sites pushed back with their own messaging.

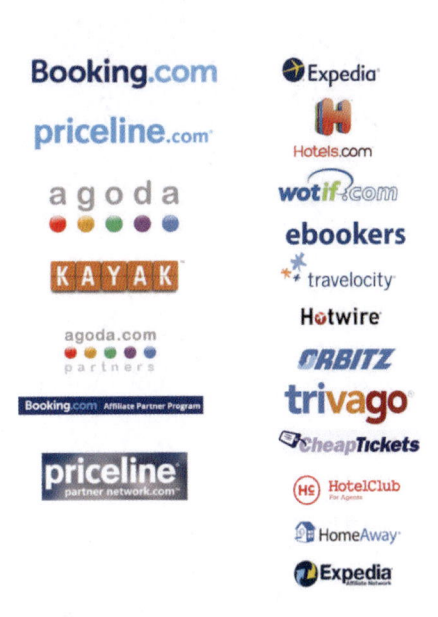

Many OTA brands fall under the Booking.com and Expedia umbrellas.

A "book direct" ad from Hilton

According to *Demystifying the Digital Marketplace*[150], brand.com across the industry is still almost twice the source of business for hotels compared to OTAs (20% vs. 12%), although those percentages can vary widely depending on location, brand, and size of hotel. Independents often see OTAs outpacing direct bookings.

A Field Guide for Navigating Today's Digital Landscape

A BRIEF HISTORY

As the overall internet has evolved over the years, OTAs have proliferated as relevant research and booking channels. For a more complete history of the channel, Skift produced the *Definitive Oral History of Online Travel*[151]. Following are some of the highlights of this segment's growth.

- In the 1980s, American Airlines subsidiary Sabre developed eAAsySabre to allow consumers to make flight, hotel, or car reservations through early internet service providers like Compuserve and AOL.
- In 1991, Hotel Reservations Network and Travelscape pioneered the wholesale model of buying blocks of rooms and reselling them through other channels, which became the "merchant model."
- In 1996, Sabre launched Travelocity.com, the first website to allow consumers to book directly and purchase airline tickets online without using a travel agent.
- Later that year, Microsoft launched the online travel booking site MSFT Expedia Travel Services, which later was shortened to Expedia.com.
- In 1997, Booking.com was founded in Amsterdam as booking.nl, and Priceline.com was launched in the U.S.
- Ctrip (now Trip.com) and eLong in China were both founded in 1999.
- Hotwire launched in 2000 and Orbitz in 2001.
- In 2001, Hotel Reservations Network was acquired by USA Networks (which then became InterActiveCorp or IAC). Hotel Reservations soon thereafter changed its name to Hotels.com, and later in 2001, IAC acquired a controlling stake in Expedia.com.
- In 2003, IAC acquired the opaque travel site Hotwire, and in 2005, IAC spun-off its travel businesses—Expedia, Hotels.com, Hotwire, corporate travel site Egencia, and Tripadvisor—into what is today known as Expedia Group, Inc.
- In 2004, early-stage team members from Orbitz, Travelocity, and Expedia co-founded Kayak.com as the first travel metasearch site.
- In 2005, The Priceline Group acquired the European hotel booking website Booking.com, and metasearch site Trivago was launched.
- In 2007, Kayak bought metasearch competitor SideStep.com, which it shut down in 2011.
- In 2008, Expedia acquired the Italian OTA site Venere.com, giving them the backend system to launch the retail model in Europe in addition to their legacy merchant model.
- In 2010 and 2011, the growth of specialty metasearch engines continued with the launch of Hipmunk and Room 77. In 2011, Expedia spun off Tripadvisor.
- In 2012, Expedia bought Trivago, which it then took public in 2016. Also in 2012, Kayak went public and four months later was acquired by the Priceline group.
- In 2014, Tripadvisor launched its instant booking feature, enabling consumers to book directly with hotels, which was paired with a metasearch component which Tripadvisor had launched years before. Over the years, Tripadvisor acquired dozens of niche online travel companies, including Oyster.com, FlipKey, GateGuru, Viator, and Jetsetter, as well as restaurant review/reservation sites.
- In 2015 and 2016, the OTA market entered a phase of consolidation, with Expedia acquiring Travelocity and Orbitz. With these transactions, Priceline and Expedia control 90+% of the OTA marketplace, creating a duopoly for booking channel OTAs in the U.S. and Europe. In late 2016, CTrip (now Trip.com) acquired the metasearch site Skyscanner.
- In 2018, The Priceline Group changed its name to Booking Holdings.
- In 2019, Airbnb acquired last-minute booking site HotelTonight.
- In 2020, with the Covid-19 pandemic, Expedia began to retrench, closing some business units like their offline activities business and short-term rental business. At the same time Booking.com continued its effort to build a package product. After past economic shocks hotels have often taken greater market share as the recovery begins. As of the writing of this book, it is to be determined what will happen post-pandemic.
- In 2020, Airbnb went public, at a valuation of $86.5 billion. This was more than the combined market capitalization of Hilton, Marriott, and Intercontinental Hotels Group, which were together worth $84.1 billion on the same day.

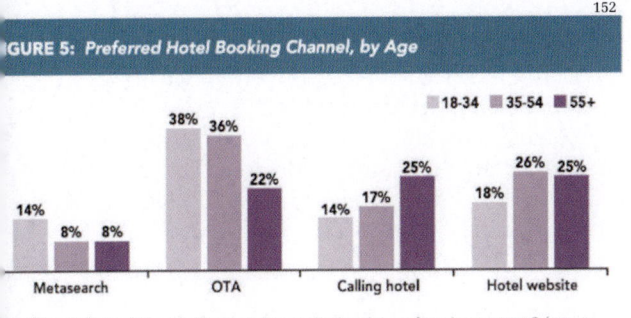

FIGURE 5: *Preferred Hotel Booking Channel, by Age*

	18-34	35-54	55+
Metasearch	14%	8%	8%
OTA	38%	36%	22%
Calling hotel	14%	17%	25%
Hotel website	18%	26%	25%

Question: Please indicate which method you typically use to book each type of travel component. Select one response per row.
Base: U.S. travelers who purchased lodging (2015 N=1,437)
Source: Phocuswright's U.S. Consumer Travel Report Eighth Edition
© 2017 Phocuswright Inc. All Rights Reserved.

OTA MODELS

It is critical to understand the OTA business models to take full advantage of these channels for your hotel. There are four primary OTA business models: retail (or agency), merchant, opaque, and auction/unknown price.

Retail Model

Much like a traditional travel agent, the consumer books through an intermediary and pays the hotel directly on checkout. The hotel then pays the intermediary a commission (or margin), typically 10-20%. This model is also sometimes referred to as the "published" or "agency" model. Room revenue for retail OTA bookings is captured on the hotel income statement as a gross rate, or what the consumer paid. In an example with a room revenue of $200 and a commission rate of 20%, the income statement would look like this:

Room revenue = $200

Commission paid (@ 20%) = $40

Net room revenue = $160

Typically, this model also operates more like a traditional reservation where the guest can cancel until the day of the reservation (or with a longer lead time if the hotel utilizes a stronger cancellation policy), which often results in high cancellation rates. Marketers and revenue teams need to monitor these cancellation rates as they plan their sellout strategies, as markets with long lead times or days to arrival (DTA) can be impacted by retail model cancellations. Of course, this has been exacerbated by the Covid-19 pandemic, as hotels offered (rightfully so) more liberal cancellation polices to give consumers more confidence to make the booking.

Merchant Model

The merchant model was created by former wholesale tour operators and later adopted by OTAs, most notably Expedia. Initially, OTAs would negotiate room blocks just like wholesalers and guarantee payment for those rooms, but today that practice has largely gone away. Here, the traveler pays the OTA by credit card directly upon booking, so the OTA becomes the "merchant of record" hence the model's name. The OTA charges the traveler a room rate, which is a combination of the hotel's net rate and the OTA's commission (or margin). The net rate is the actual revenue the hotel receives for the room while the margin is the negotiated fee that the OTA charges for its service. Typically, in this model, the guest will pay the OTA up front on their credit card and, after the traveler's stay, the OTA pays the hotel the net rate.

Under the merchant model, a hotel provides OTAs net rates that are typically 10 to 30 percent below published levels. This discount is usually consistent with the retail model commission rate. The OTA will then offer the hotel on its site to make the room rate equal to the published rate. To maintain rate integrity, many hotels require that the room rate charged by OTAs equals the hotels' officially published rate, also known as rate parity. Rate parity has become a very big issue in the industry, both from an operational perspective and trying to control it, and from a legal perspective as several jurisdictions, the European Union in particular, have struck down parity requirements as illegal.

A variation of the merchant model is the package model. In the package model, the consumer is offered a bundled price where the hotel rate is combined with a rate for another travel product such as an airline ticket or car rental. OTAs often require a deeper discount (an additional 10% or more is fairly standard) for package rates versus hotel-room-only rates. Packages are typically booked farther in advance, for longer lengths of stay, and are often chosen by guests that will have higher incremental spend.

Room revenue for merchant OTA booking is captured on the hotel income statement as a net rate. The amount the OTA pays the hotel does not include the OTA margin, which some call a hidden marketing expense as it does not show up on the income statement directly. In our example with a room rate of $200, the net room revenue is still $160 but the commission paid at 20% ($40) is kept by the OTA up front. No marketing expense shows up on the hotel's P&L.

Since merchant model reservations are pre-paid, typically their cancellation rates are much lower than the retail model.

Opaque Model

Opaque refers to the fact that the hotel's rate is not known to the guest. This can take several forms:

- Package Rate: The rate is packaged with other items (usually air) so that the hotel's rate cannot be seen by the guest. OTAs often request package rates so that they can offer lower rates for bundled packages. The benefit to the hotel is that the hotel can offer lower rates for package bookings without undercutting its room-only sell rate.
- Unknown Hotel: Guests are given the opportunity to book hotels based on star rating and general area. The rate is shown but the hotel is not. The benefit to the hotel is that it can offer a lower rate than its current rate in the market for incremental business. Since the guest does not know it is your hotel, it can be considered incremental—business you would not likely have gotten without participating. See the example from Hotwire.

Most hotels use these channels to yield last-minute revenue when they are not going to fill, or over future slow period dates. Hotels must be mindful of using these channels and ensure that they are truly opaque. If not, this will undercut their direct booking efforts. While the decision to offer this sort of rate is usually the realm of revenue management it is very important for hotel digital marketers to understand what rates are in the market and how they compare to what you are offering direct. The general rule of thumb is that you should never offer lower rates in the market than you have on your own website, but opaque allows you to get around that without the negative impact (if it is truly opaque).

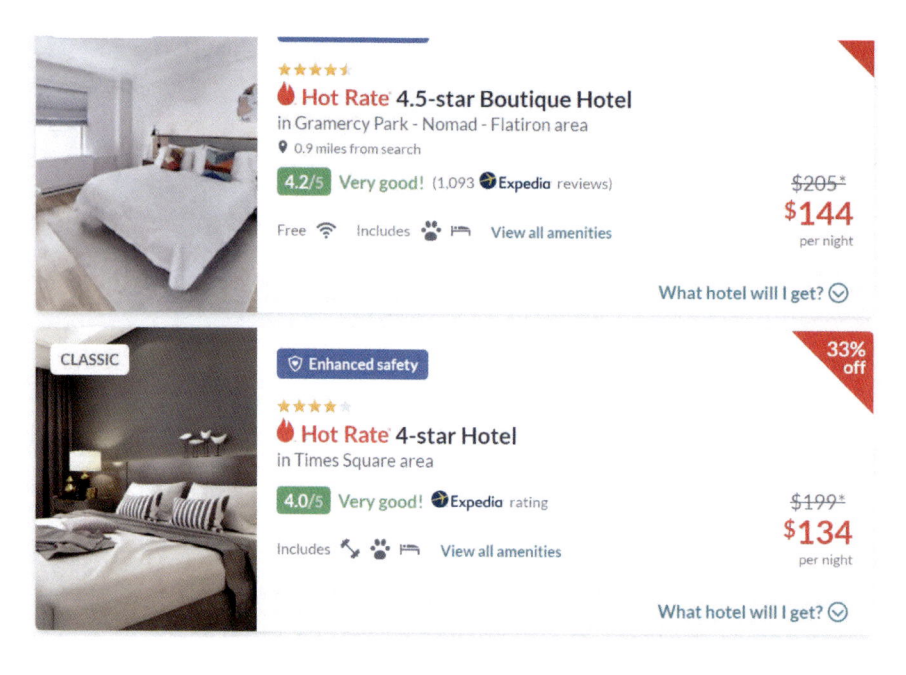

An "unknown hotel" opaque offering from Hotwire

Auction/Unknown Price Model

Priceline popularized the auction model allowing guests to make an offer for a specific hotel. If the offer was "accepted" the guest would be booked in that hotel. In reality, Priceline had net rates and set sell points, but the actual rate (until the offer was accepted) was opaque to the consumer.

This model is no longer available on Priceline, and has not been seen in use recently. But, Priceline did not leave the opaque business entirely. Its latest opaque offering is called Pricebreakers where consumers search by location and travel dates then are shown three hotel choices. Pricebreakers makes the final choice of hotel, which is shown to the consumer right after they book. This model is probably more akin to unknown hotel.

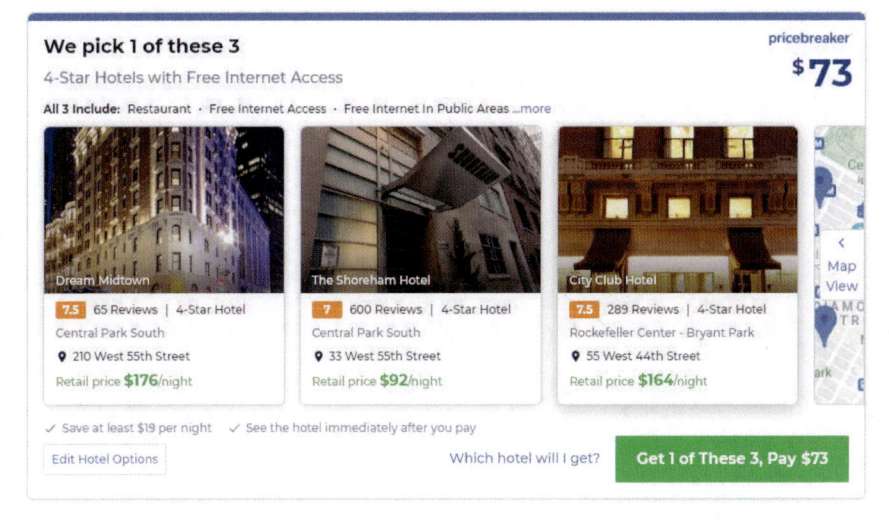

Pricebreakers is Priceline's newest opaque offering

MARGIN VS. MARKUP

When working with resellers, you will often hear the terms margin and markup, so it is important to understand the difference. What is the difference between margin and mark-up?

"The difference between margin and markup is that margin is sales minus the cost of goods sold, while markup is the amount by which the cost of a product is increased in order to derive the selling price. A mistake in the use of these terms can lead to price setting that is substantially too high or low, resulting in lost sales or lost profits, respectively."[153]

Margin is sales minus the cost of goods sold, so how does that translate into hotel rooms? If the sell rate for a room is $100 and the net rate given to a reseller is $80, the reseller's margin is $20 or 20%.

Markup is the amount by which the cost of a product is increased in order to derive the selling price. Using our hotel example, a markup of $20 from the $80 cost yields the $100 price. Or, stated as a percentage, the markup percentage is 25% (20/80).

PARITY

There are many reasons that third-party rates may be out of parity with your own website. It may be a connectivity issue. Or, it may be the third party is adjusting rates based on perceived parity issues. But more often than not, parity violations happen when the hotel gives a net rate, package rate, or opaque rate to a contracted wholesaler, and the wholesaler then gives those rates to bad actors who undercut parity. This is extremely difficult to manage, but it can be managed.

Manage Parity
- Ensure contracts are clear regarding onward distribution.
- Require electronic connectivity.
- Utilize dynamic rates.
- Have a clear escalation procedure.
- Monitor rates.

Police Violations
- Identify the root source of the issue.
- Escalate your response per your agreement.
- If you can't get to a resolution, close inventory for that wholesaler. Unless you are willing to shut off violators you will never resolve the issue.

CONSUMER PERCEPTIONS AND BEHAVIOR

OTAs are popular because they simplify the search and selection process for travel consumers. Instead of researching multiple individual hotel or brand websites, a shopper can go to one OTA site and search many hotels in a specific location for a particular date, all at one time. The name, location, availability, and price of each hotel appears in an easy-to-read format to aid decision making. Robust content including hotel details, high resolution photos, and traveler reviews are also key components to aid comparison shopping on OTAs.

Some OTAs offer the ability to search multiple travel products including flights, car rentals, vacation packages, and cruises, which make them a very viable "one stop shop" for many brand-agnostic shoppers. This ease of shopping is enhanced as the OTAs can segment their traffic and conduct A/B (or multivariate) tests, as well as ethnographic consumer research. Given their broader reach beyond just one vertical (hotels) or brand, they are typically able to innovate much faster than brands can.

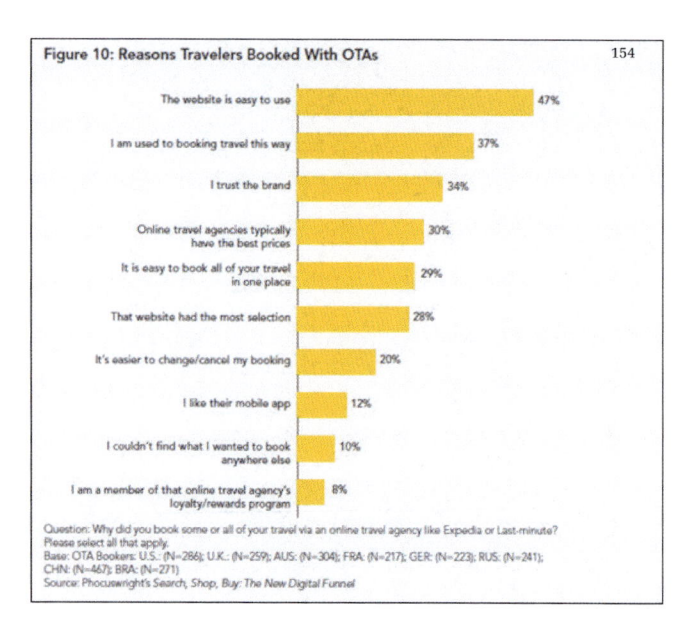

Figure 10: Reasons Travelers Booked With OTAs [154]

Reason	%
The website is easy to use	47%
I am used to booking travel this way	37%
I trust the brand	34%
Online travel agencies typically have the best prices	30%
It is easy to book all of your travel in one place	29%
That website had the most selection	28%
It's easier to change/cancel my booking	20%
I like their mobile app	12%
I couldn't find what I wanted to book anywhere else	10%
I am a member of that online travel agency's loyalty/rewards program	8%

Question: Why did you book some or all of your travel via an online travel agency like Expedia or Last-minute? Please select all that apply.
Base: OTA Bookers: U.S.: (N=286); U.K.: (N=259); AUS: (N=304); FRA: (N=217); GER: (N=223); RUS: (N=241); CHN: (N=467); BRA: (N=271)
Source: Phocuswright's Search, Shop, Buy: The New Digital Funnel

Fueling this strategy to test and learn is the OTAs' relentless passion for consumer marketing. Even a small uptick in conversion on an OTA site can mean millions in bookings and revenue for large OTAs. OTAs can take that revenue and put it back into their marketing strategies and technology. To put this in perspective, in 2019 Expedia and Booking.com spent $11 billion dollars on marketing[155] and Expedia spent $1.6 billion on technology.[156] These significant resources and powerful marketing abilities allow them to optimize spend and cost of customer acquisition, typically far more effectively than hotels can.

Many OTAs also include loyalty marketing as part of their acquisition and retention strategy. Offering perks for VIP customers, additional discounts, or "buy X rooms get one free" are all ways that OTAs try to lock in the consumer and build loyalty to their sites. Often these benefits are being funded by the OTA's marketing budget, but in some cases are offered by the hotel or supplier directly. Hotels participating in VIP programs should do so with a clear ROI in mind and a strategy to create loyalty with that guest on future visits.

For hotel only rates, most OTAs offer a best rate guarantee. This means if a customer finds a lower rate for the same booking, the OTA will match the lower rate found and often provide additional compensation. Similarly, most major hotel chains also offer a best rate guarantee, and this is a best practice for all hotels, as it gives confidence to the consumer. But as previously mentioned, hotels need to have systems in place to manage and police parity violations.

Some OTAs will use practices that are not in the best interest of the hotels. Examples of these practices include:

- promoting a toll-free "800" number, which some guests mistakenly believe is a direct line to the hotel
- bidding on brand terms on Google
- creating URLs with the brand name in them, further confusing customers and leading them to believe that they are booking directly with the hotel, not with an intermediary
- reducing agreed-upon sell rates, or utilizing third parties to undercut agreed-upon parity

As part of their digital search strategy, hotel marketers must stay on top of these practices and raise red flags to their OTA, brand, and marketing partners as appropriate. Like parity, if you do not monitor and police it, it is unlikely that these practices will stop. Sometimes the only way to find out where inventory is coming from is to make test bookings with suspicious sites to find out how they are accessing inventory, and then have serious, direct conversations with the partner responsible for that inventory about not allowing the offending OTA access to rates and availability. This often takes the combined effort of the revenue and digital marketing teams.

THE IMPORTANCE OF STRATEGY

Given the current dynamic with many players vying to be the guide of choice for the consumer through the travel shopping journey, a hotel must not only ensure its content is well represented across all channels, but that its rates and availability are also accurate. Attracting travelers to any single hotel in a place where tens of thousands are visible is one of the most challenging jobs for the hotel marketer. And it is not just about making the available information accurate and timely, but it must be equally compelling and relevant. The travel search process involves multiple steps of inspiration, planning, searching, validating, and sharing before the shopper even gets to booking and experiencing, making it even more crucial for marketers to ensure they are represented well on OTAs.

OTAs can bring great benefits to a hotel:

- INCREMENTAL/NEW CUSTOMERS: OTAs can help hotels extend their reach and visibility to millions of consumers domestically and all around the world. These customers can help build RevPAR, GOPAR, and market share. OTAs can be an effective channel for hotels to acquire new customers and turn them into loyal customers by signing them up for loyalty programs, and some brands have taken aggressive strategies to grow their loyalty bases via deep partnerships with OTAs. And as mentioned in the loyalty chapter, this is not limited to the big brands. Through effective email, social media, and other mechanisms hotels can gain preference and loyalty.
- MARKETING: OTAs deploy a wide variety of online and offline marketing efforts to inspire travelers around the world and to connect these travelers directly to hotels. These marketing efforts are even more beneficial for hotels with smaller budgets to reach audiences that they would otherwise not be able to reach.
- PAY FOR PERFORMANCE: OTAs are a pay for performance marketing vehicle as hotels only pay the OTA for actual bookings. Hotels that are listed on OTAs benefit from the "billboard effect" (which is often hotly debated). It gives a boost in reservations through the hotel's own distribution channels (including its website) due to the hotel being listed on the OTA website.
- CUSTOMER DIFFERENTIATION: Online travel agents can bring unique types of customers with regard to booking window, days to arrival (DTA), length of stay (LOS), and price point. OTAs can help hotels across the entire booking curve (short-term, mid-term, and long-range) as well as provide promotional opportunities to fill need dates and complement the hotel's own revenue strategy.
- DATA AND INSIGHT: The global OTAs and many regional OTAs offer valuable market data and insight either by way of self-service tools or local account managers commonly referred to as market managers. Increasingly the OTAs offer rate, conversion rate, market dynamics, and other insights on their hotel-facing portals.

Sort order on an OTA is based on a variety of factors including offer strength (a benchmark of your hotel price relative to value), quality score (a measure of how attractive your property is to travelers), and commission (similar to other marketplaces or auction models, the commission you are paying the OTA will influence your rank). Some OTAs also offer avenues to improve your ranking or placement via paying an additional override commission. Hotels should weigh these options carefully as they evaluate the overall ROI of the channel. Staying on top of your scores, commission rate, and conversion rate compared to the competitors in your market are key aspects to having a winning strategy with an OTA.

BEST PRACTICES FOR DIGITAL MARKETING THROUGH OTAS[157]

While the daily room allocation and rate offering for the OTAs typically falls under the responsibility of the revenue manager, the digital marketer has a key role to play in this booking channel. It is important to advocate for the direct channel. Often the "easy" approach is to reduce the rates OTAs offer to drive volume, but it is important that these rates are also offered through the direct channel. As has been mentioned throughout this book, it is important for the revenue team and digital team work together on this.

Know the models inside and out, and understand your pricing

Work in tandem with your revenue management counterparts to understand the points of differentiation, their costs, how (and when) revenue will be recognized, and the payment terms. Understand that for your market or competitive set some sites or models have strengths which you should look to capitalize on when you need to drive occupancy, rate, or both. If a consumer pays $200 for your room, exactly how much of the $200 will the hotel see? Will you incur any connectivity or channel management costs to get your rates and inventory to the OTA?

Read and adhere to contracts

If you do not have a clear understanding of the terms, then ask for additional clarification or do not participate. Each OTA model is different, and the contract may have certain requirements that you should know about. OTAs generally have language around how they will market the hotel; if you have a trademark you want protected, then ensure the rules of engagement and marketing are clear in the contract.

Understand the nature of any opaque offering

If it is not truly opaque, the consequences of offering a significantly lower rate are far reaching as regular guests might book the hotel at a deep discount rather than at the best available rate. Ensure your hotel is opaque and not getting too much of its share in the opaque site's comp set as it can impact not just your nightly RevPAR but your overall brand value proposition.

Get to know your market manager

An OTA market manager is analyzing trends across markets, and working with him or her to identify opportunities or just understand key market trends is an essential part of any marketing strategy.

- You'll stay on top of their promotions and the market segments they specialize in. You'll understand if and how they align with your customer mix targets. For instance, Booking.com has a significant presence in the European market, Expedia can deliver package guests with long lead times, and Hotel Tonight is focused on guests arriving tonight.
- A market manager is more likely to help your hotel if they know you and you have established some credibility with them. For instance, if your property received many negative reviews prior to a renovation, the market manager may be able to remove them once the property is upgraded.
- Ask for more opportunities, placement, and advertising. With your revenue management team, develop your need-date strategy and determine ways that online sites can help you fill them. Often there are win-win initiatives that can be implemented. Placement on a results page is important and will have a direct impact to the volume of business you receive from an OTA.

Be willing to test strategies

Once you've identified need dates and talked it over with your revenue management counterpart, be willing to try things out of the box. Online sites can often provide immediate feedback on specific rate, advertising, promotion, or channel strategies. So test, learn, and test again.

Analyze your results

How is your property performing via your hotel's website? How is your property comparing against the comp set in the OTA? You can garner a lot if information through the OTAs and you should use this to help improve your overall performance, both on OTAs and through your direct channel.

Be strategic in your use of OTAs as a part of your marketing strategy

Every OTA wants to inspire customers to book more travel. Converting more business through these sites is usually not just in the site's best interest but the hotel's as well. Understanding how to use these partners effectively can help grow RevPAR and market share. That said, understand the overall costs of the OTA and weigh that versus your other marketing costs to ensure you are delivering the right mix of business for your property.

Align your OTA participation with your current customer base or need segments

If you are a predominantly weekend leisure hotel, you may not want to affiliate your property with an OTA primarily targeting weekend business. Or if you are a corporate Monday through Thursday hotel, a weekend leisure stay may be exactly what you need to win. Also, attracting international travelers can be a boon for your RevPAR but make sure your operations teams are set up to succeed with guests who may not be fluent in your local language.

Offer compelling and consistent content

Just like anything on the web, content matters. If you are participating with an OTA, be sure your content is accurate. Have high quality photos—as many as are allowed. Note that other third-party databases may be feeding content to an OTA. Ensure that your content and photos are updated in the primary data aggregators like the GDS, IcePortal, and Leonardo. Content can be pulled from several sources, some of it beyond your control, so take precautions to ensure that the data you can control is accurate and compelling.

Connect with guests

Also make sure you monitor your OTA traveler post-stay reviews as many OTAs allow you to write a management response. More and more OTAs provide channels for guests to connect with hotels before and during their stay, so ensure your teams are equipped to answer those queries as well.

Win over guests for future stays

One of the greatest opportunities hotels have is to convert OTA-booked guests into direct bookers for their next visit. Have programs in place that encourage your guests to opt-in to your email, social media, and loyalty program (if you have one), with the goal of ensuring their next booking will be direct.

BEST PRACTICES: CONTENT AND USER EXPERIENCE

Content and user experience are key variables that can drive online consumers to one site over another. However, it is important to keep in mind that because travel shoppers visit so many sites and are touched by so many promotional contacts in the research process up to a booking, a presence on multiple sites and at multiple consumer touch points is likely to be a good strategy for your hotel.

- OFFER COMPELLING CONTENT: Make your content compelling and relevant, whether it is on your own website or on OTA sites where you have a presence. Investing in great visual and written content is a highly effective differentiator given the number of hotel websites from which a traveler can choose. Content is a form of merchandising and should be developed with that in mind.

- CREATE BIAS FOR YOUR PREFERRED CHANNELS: You can't make travel shoppers choose one channel over another, but you can put out breadcrumbs along their path that are so compelling that they will choose your route because it is appealing and helps them accomplish their goals better than the alternatives. This doesn't mean only using your own website. By collaborating with others, you can get travelers to choose sites on which you can deepen your relationship with them as you lead them to your booking engine, whether that is on your own website or embedded in an external one.

- TEST AND MONITOR: Whatever you do online, you should track results in all places possible. If you partner with a website (social, transactional, or informational) to promote your hotel, be sure you can track the results from it, whether it is a booking or other form of interaction. If you decide to test a new option, try to remove other factors that would muddy the results.

- DISTINGUISH YOURSELF: It is helpful to think about how your brand (independent or chain) differs from the others. On a national or international basis, there is a tendency to dilute a brand's uniqueness with messages that resonate with so many consumer profiles that they fail to distinguish the brand for any particular customer cohort. Ensure that your content sets you apart with the audience(s) that matter most to you.

- SEEK SUSTAINABLE PROFIT: As much as every hotel would love the simplicity of one-step promotions that deliver immediate revenue, few consumers buy without having some kind of relationship first, so while a booking usually requires multiple interactions, it's important to understand which channels deliver a sustainable ROI.

CONCLUSION

OTAs currently generate on average about 12% of all bookings and roughly 40% of all online bookings. Third-party sites use a range of models to generate bookings for their partners and use that revenue to develop exceptional technology systems and marketing strategies. Many brand-agnostic customers turn to OTAs for their research and booking, so it's incumbent upon the hotel marketer to develop strategies and use best practices when working with OTAs.

When considering a relationship with any OTA, it is important to understand your brand's position, or if you are an independent hotel, you may want to seek a partner who can help you navigate OTA deals and requirements. Ensuring you have content that supports your hotel's positioning is key, and merchandising your property is as important on OTA sites as it is your own. Lastly, OTAs are typically the fastest growing segment for customers looking for a hotel, so it is paramount to constantly monitor and manage the percentage of bookings that come from third-party partners.

SAMPLE CHDM EXAM QUESTIONS

1. What type of rate is it when the guest pays the hotel and the hotel sends commission to the OTA?
   a. Retail Rate
   b. Merchant Rate
   c. Opaque Rate
   d. Secret Rate

2. What should you do when considering using an OTA as part of a marketing strategy?
   a. Understand the available OTA models offered in the marketplace
   b. Build a relationship with the OTA marketing manager
   c. Align your OTA participation with your current customer base or need segments
   d. Take the time and opportunity to test various marketing strategies using OTAs
   e. All of the above

3. If the sell rate for a room is $150 and the margin is 18%, what is the markup?
   a. 18%
   b. 15%
   c. 22%
   d. 32%
   e. Not enough information to calculate

Answers
1 = a
2 = e
3 = c

NOTES

_____
_____
_____
_____
_____
_____

Chapter 26: Group Intermediaries

KEY POINTS
- What is a group intermediary and why are group intermediaries important?
- How should a hotel optimize its presence on group intermediaries?
- How can digital marketers craft campaigns to attract business through group intermediaries?

The Knot, Maritz, Connect, Cvent, and HotelPlanner are all group intermediaries.

SUMMARY

Before the introduction of online sourcing technology, meeting planners often struggled with finding the right venue to meet their event needs, and hotels found it difficult to target their marketing dollars to book incremental group business. Today, meeting planners have shifted from the traditional means of venue sourcing and adopted online methods to save time and money.

As a result of this shift, hotels are receiving more group business than ever before via online group channels. However, this also means that hotels must work to build a stronger online presence on these platforms through eye-catching profiles and increased digital marketing efforts.

A group intermediary is a company or Software-as-a-Service (SaaS) platform that connects event and meeting planners with venues, and vice versa. Similar to other online marketplaces like Amazon or Expedia, group intermediaries provide a way for meeting and event planners to easily compare venues and send and receive RFPs. They benefit hotels and venues by increasing qualified demand for group business and allowing hotels and venues to manage that demand more efficiently.

THE IMPORTANCE OF GROUP INTERMEDIARIES

Cvent, a group intermediary, surveyed over 800 planners in a wide-ranging study on sourcing behaviors. It found that the top sourcing channel for planners was through online sourcing tools or group intermediaries. Today, Cvent claims over 200,000 active users of its platform.

Group intermediaries have changed the meetings and events business by unifying venue sourcing into a few platforms on which planners now rely. They've been able to do so because it used to be particularly time-consuming for a planner to research venues at scale. While one-to-one relationships remain an important part in the decision-making process, the increased volume and velocity of meeting requests—paired with gains in technology—have made it easier to use online tools to make faster decisions.

Hotel websites are typically focused on transient leisure and business travelers, treating group business as an afterthought, and in some cases ignoring it entirely. That also makes it difficult for search engines like Google to return relevant pages to a meeting planner.

Group intermediaries allow planners to search through databases of venues whose profiles only display information relevant to a planner. In a few clicks, they can find pertinent details about a hotel including the square footage of meeting space, what those spaces look like, and the number of sleeping rooms available. Meeting planners now have access to tools that allow them to research and act (like send an RFP) at once. This would not have been possible in the not-too-distant past.

For hotels, it means creating and maintaining a presence where planners are researching because the competition is not just across the street anymore. Hotels are each competing with a universe of choices. In the meeting planner's consideration set may also be a property across town, in another state or country, or a unique independent boutique the planner hadn't heard of before. And who is the planner going to choose? The hotel that is marketing itself everywhere and telling a great story, or the one whose profile is empty and whose ads do not catch the planner's eye?

This means hotels cannot rely on having a basic presence (profile) on group intermediaries. They must aggressively pursue opportunities that ensure their property's advertising is displayed where the planners are. Furthermore, the property must identify itself as unique, showcasing what differentiates it from the competition. The only platform that allows for that kind of specific targeting is a group intermediary.

Planners have turned to group intermediaries for efficiency. Instead of a planner creating separate RFPs for each property from which they want a proposal, they can create a single electronic RFP that they send to multiple properties with a single click. Rather than creating spreadsheets to compare venues' pricing and proposals, group intermediaries automate the response process and allow planners to collect and analyze their responses in a single, easy-to-access location. They centralize all the communications between planners and venues, ensuring that miscommunications are limited and responsibilities adhered to.

For the hotel, the tools assist with responding quickly, managing lead flow, and using analytics to optimize response behaviors.

SHOULD YOU INCORPORATE GROUP INTERMEDIARIES INTO YOUR MARKETING STRATEGY?

If the group market is an existing segment, or targeted segment, there may be some marketing opportunities in this area. As established above, planners are no longer reaching out directly to venues to source their meetings and events, but are instead turning to group intermediaries.

Hotels must demonstrate to meeting planners that they are willing to participate in the client's preferred channel. By not participating in the channel, the venue's chance of consideration is significantly diminished.

Like paid advertising on search sites, advertising on a group intermediary channel allows venues to gain a leg up on competition by placing their venue front and center in the planner's search process. Hotels can target planners by showcasing their unique qualities and differentiators.

BEST PRACTICES: BUILDING A GROUP INTERMEDIARY PRESENCE

With more and more planners turning to online sourcing platforms, it's crucial that a hotel's online presence on group intermediaries is as strong as on their own website. Unfortunately, many hoteliers don't invest in their group intermediary profile like they do their own website. This is problematic because, to many planners, a hotel's profile on a sourcing platform is the only web presence about that venue that they'll see before moving to the next step in the consideration process.

Your presence on online sourcing channels begins with your hotel's profile content. To ensure your listing on these sites can be found easily and is interesting, take the time to follow these best practices.

Fish where fish are.
Today there are multiple group intermediary sites—and most have some sort of specialized niche. For example, TheKnot.com focuses on

weddings. HotelPlanner has some expertise with college, sports, and government bookers.

If you have certain audiences you are targeting, make sure you have a presence on the group intermediary that specializes in that market. If you do NOT want an intermediary's market, it is best not to have a presence on its site. Otherwise, you will waste searchers' time, and your salespeople's time in responding to RFPs or leads that are not right for your property.

Make it complete.
This profile should be an event planner's one-stop shop for all things group related. By limiting the amount of information on your profile, you are encouraging the planner to move on and look elsewhere. Keep their attention by offering as much information as possible and being accurate in your listing.

This task can be simpler than you think if you focus on relevant information and keep your target audience in mind. First and foremost, ensure the content about your hotel is accurate and up to date. Include the relevant information that a meeting planner would care most about (meeting space, airport transportation, F&B minimums, etc.) and ensure your content reads easily. Always add menus and meeting space floor plans. If applicable, include safety precautions that the property is taking (during the Covid-19 pandemic for example).

If relevant, adding information about local attractions can be helpful, but go beyond just listing the names of points of interest. Instead, include a short description, the address, and website of some of the top attractions that drive demand to your location. Always remember that meeting planners are likely scanning dozens of listings, or using filters to hone in on their key needs, so make sure your listing is complete.

Make it visual.
Your online profile must be visually enticing. The image gallery is one of the most visited portions of your profile, and the main image is the first and last thing a planner notices. Make sure the images are of good quality, sized correctly, and accentuate your property's best features.

Additionally, pay special attention to every image you include. Think about your audience and what they would want to see on an onsite tour. Would you spend time showing them the hotel room bathroom or would you spend more time in each meeting room? Would you show them only one room setup or several? Do you have inspirational images merchandising your hotel effectively for meeting planners that want a memorable event? Answering questions like these will help you organize your ideal image gallery.

Make it valuable.
Now that planners are paying more attention to your profile, add a little something extra that will encourage them to take the next step. Although your property may provide everything their event needs, they may not believe right away that yours will offer the best deal—unless you tell them so.

Including planner-specific deals directly on your profile is an important part of spreading the word about new promotions or incentives available at your property. Even if you are not running specific promotions consider highlighting your property's key differentiators. Simply stating that your property is willing to negotiate any contract over 200 attendees, or F&B minimums are negotiable with a large enough sleeping block, can be enough to convert a planner's initial consideration into a genuine lead for your sales team.

Make it unique.
The last step of managing a successful profile is getting noticed. To stand out from the several hundred other properties in your area, your listing should offer something unique and different. Among the photos of hotel rooms and static square footage statistics, your profile can more easily catch a planner's eye by doing something different. If your hotel's greatest selling feature is the picturesque landscape, incorporate that as a visual element. No picturesque landscape? Turn it into an opportunity to use creativity to inspire meeting planners to give your hotel a second look.

Like your property website, the URL to your profile should be leveraged as a sales tool. Whether that's including the link in social media posts, saving it to your email signature, or pulling it up during a face-to-face meeting, the most important thing is not to neglect it.

BEST PRACTICES: DIGITAL GROUP MARKETING CAMPAIGNS

Today's digital group marketing campaigns often involve a multitude of moving parts. From brand awareness to lead generation, campaigns should be multi-faceted, trackable, and have clear expectations of results. Consider these actions when implementing a digital group marketing campaign.

Understand your opportunities.

Fully understanding the promotional vehicles at your disposal and matching that with your goals is key to evaluating what campaigns you may wish to undertake. Intermediaries often have levels of promotion, offering additional exposure or content depending on your investment level, and traditional display advertisements or other CPM or CPC models are often offered to lure advertising dollars. Fully evaluate your options before moving ahead with your plan.

Have a plan.

As with all campaigns, know what your key performance indicators (KPIs) are at the beginning of your campaign, and what your expected outcomes are. Are you improving your branding and want impressions, or need specific leads? Do you have a specific ROI in mind? Remember that group sales funnels and booking lead times will impact your ability to measure ROI. Chart a course and refer to it regularly to measure your performance from beginning to end as a need to adjust your strategy may often arise.

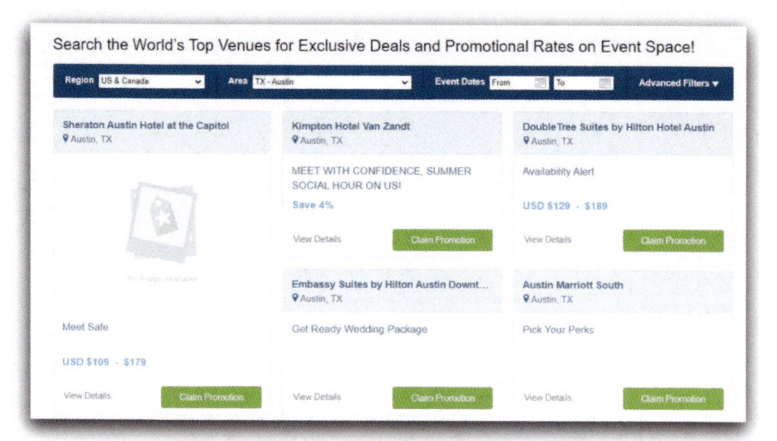

An example of "paid media" inside of Cvent

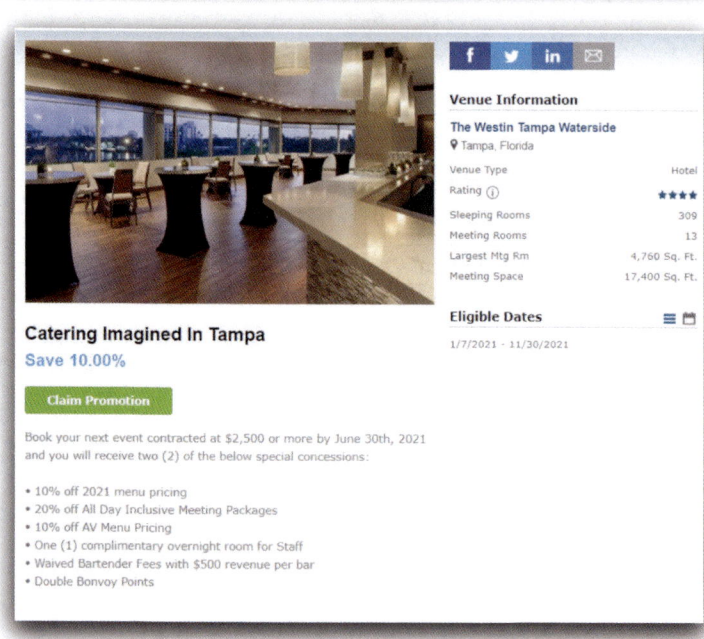

A view of what planners see when they claim the promotion to the left.

Lead with the big idea.
Advertising campaigns are often run in order to push awareness of a new group promotion or offering. Even if a promotion contains a lot of caveats and details, some small piece of it can be woven into all advertising elements.

For image-based advertisements, include a short amount of relevant teaser text. In a more content-based placement, use the extra words to provide more of the key highlights of your offering.

Of course, this isn't to say that the ads should only represent the big idea. Don't forget about your own company's branding as well. Often, these ads only capture a quick glance.

With each eye-catching opportunity, you want to make sure the planner knows who you are and what you are offering. These two details are essential to helping a planner determine if the advertisement is relevant to them. And if that isn't enough to convince them, a good tag line doesn't hurt.

Create clear calls to action.
When the planner is ready to learn more about your offer, be sure your campaign allows them to do so easily and without confusion. For example, including phrases such as "learn more" or "book now" will encourage viewers to click on your ad versus simply seeing the placement as branding. In some cases, a planner may need to take additional steps to claim an offer, which makes it important to be clear about what is expected.

Whether that is mentioning a code within their RFP details or submitting an RFP within a certain date range, the clearer your messaging is, the more effective your campaign will be. Eliminating confusing variables within the advertisements will also lead to additional success. For example, if one of the images in your ad campaign says "click here" but does not link anywhere, the planner is more likely to stop the process and move on to another hotel.

Lastly, request a mock-up or proof of your advertisement before it goes live. This will help you stay one step ahead of your campaign instead of being forced to change elements at the last minute. The best way to make sure your ads follow this rule is to view and test them yourself.

Keep it visual.
One of the biggest trends in hotel marketing right now is the visual experience. Almost every new website update or social media platform incorporates more visual elements, and for good reason. Humans process images 60,000 times faster than words. When your advertisements may only have a moment to make an impression, it's important to keep this fact in mind.

Keep a look out for image-based advertising opportunities. Most advertising campaigns require a visual component, but if it's optional take time to analyze whether it makes sense to add imagery to it. These opportunities can be the best way to feature your hotel and impress your potential clients. If your hotel needs to update its visual gallery, make sure you allocate time and financial resources to take some new, updated pictures of your property or destination.

Provide a seamless experience.
A common mistake in digital marketing campaigns is a broken buying path. For example, the advertisement says there is a "pick your incentive" program with your hotel, but the landing page outlines no details about the incentive. Promotions change, and with that, so should the advertisements. The planner experience must be fluid, with an advertisement leading to additional relevant details directing them to submit an RFP.

Once your campaign launches, click through the advertisements as if you were the meeting planner to get a feel for their process. This practice will help ensure you are utilizing all placements correctly and effectively. And if your campaign will be running over a long period of time, make a note to check on it every month or so to ensure everything is still accurate, up to date, and functioning correctly.

Track your success.
Implementation should not be the end of your group marketing campaign. While it's easy to click the completed check box and move on, tracking the overall success of the campaign by comparing its performance to your group business goals is a key criterion for success.

Know what your KPIs are at the beginning of your campaign and refer to them regularly to measure your performance from beginning to end. No matter how well executed your campaign is, there will always be room for improvement. The trick is to stay ahead of the game and never rest on your successes.

Each group intermediary has metrics available to you. For example, some of the measurements available through Cvent include:

- Turndown Rate
- Proposed ADR
- Conversion Rate
- Average Response Time
- Planner Declined Rate
- Awarded Group ADR
- RFP Market Share
- RevPAR
- Awarded Room Nights

Regularly check lead volume and conversion rates in addition to your offers and content. Solicit feedback from meeting planners who book your hotel. Make test bookings — how easy is it for attendees to use the tools provided to book your rooms? Just like the strategies and tactics digital marketers put into place for websites and transient channels, it is incumbent upon them to manage and measure these channels as well to drive value for the hotel.

CONCLUSION

Meeting and event planners are notoriously short on time, which is why most planners have made the switch to group intermediaries to handle the RFP process. By investing time and resources into group intermediaries, hotels can build a stronger online presence, run more effective digital marketing campaigns, and ultimately receive more group business leads because hotels can place themselves in front of meeting planners more easily. With the volume of analytics available on these sites, you can more fully understand why you lost out on business, where it went, and what share your property is receiving. You can use all these analytics to make better display, listing, content, imagery, and pricing decisions.

SAMPLE CHDM EXAM QUESTIONS

1. Turndown Rate, Proposed ADR, Conversion Rate, and Average Response Time are all examples of what?
   a. Digital marketing opportunities
   b. Key performance indicators
   c. Keywords for group intermediary profiles
   d. None of the above

2. Regardless of your target audience, you should maintain a presence on all popular group intermediaries.
   a. True
   b. False

3. What key item should you include in your group intermediary profile?
   a. Meeting room layouts
   b. Menus
   c. Images of your function space
   d. Nearby activities with descriptions
   e. Property description
   f. All of the above

Answers
1 = b
2 = b
3 = f

NOTES

_____

_____

_____

_____

_____

_____

_____

_____

PART SIX: TRENDING TOPICS

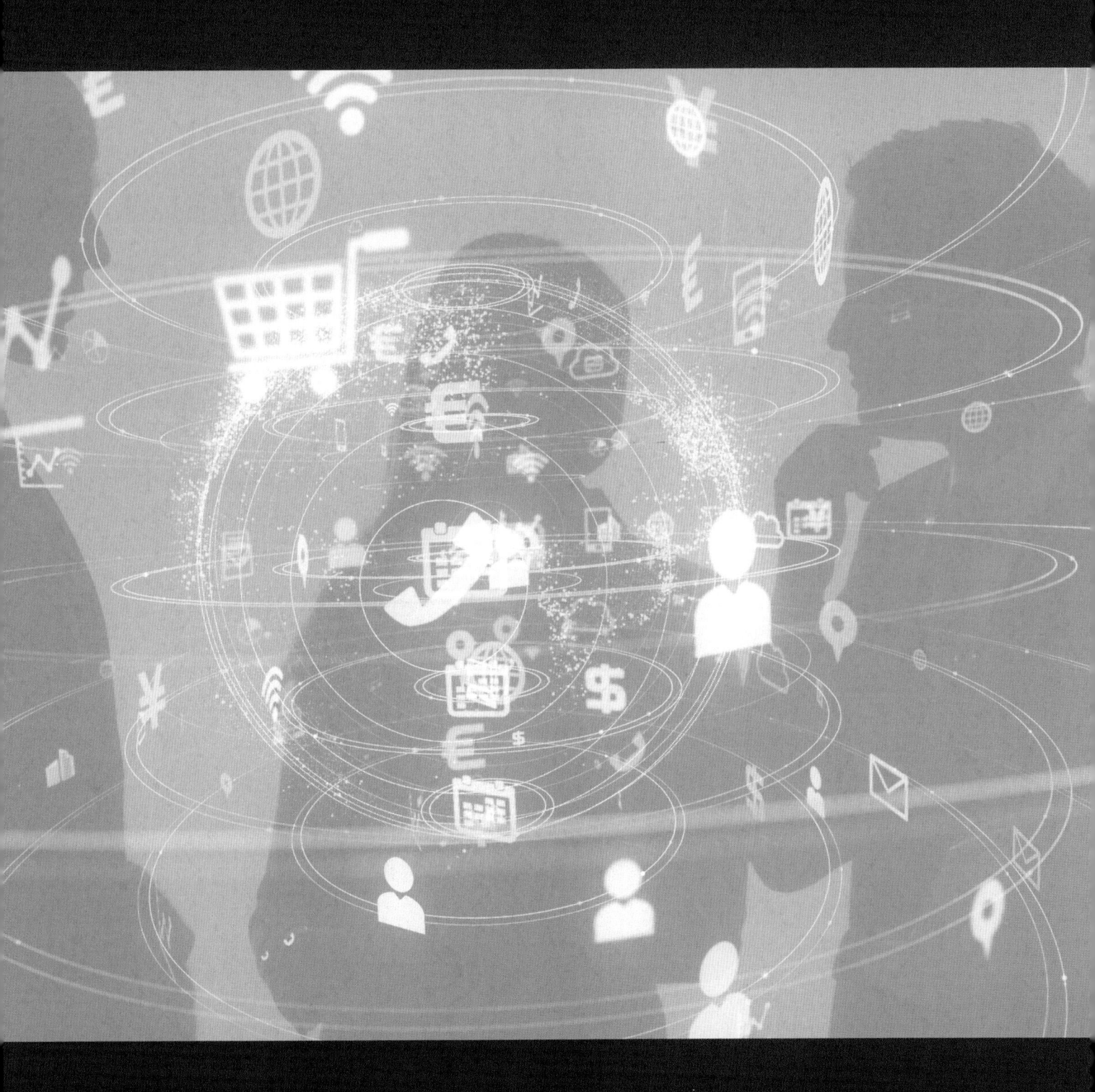

Chapter 27: Virtual Reality & Augmented Reality

> **KEY POINTS**
> - Difference between augmented reality (AR) and virtual reality (VR)
> - Current VR applications to enhance traveler experiences
> - Best use cases for AR in hospitality

SUMMARY

The technology that drives virtual reality, augmented reality, and the ability to view multiple directions on any screen is developing quickly. How hospitality enterprises can leverage this technology is limited only by the imagination—and the budgets—of its developers.

As for right now, using this technology is not as elusive or cost prohibitive as it might first appear, yet it has not been adopted by most of the traveling population past the stage of novelty. But unless a particular set of circumstances exists, so much more should be done in digital marketing before you explore the world of VR and AR marketing.

VIRTUAL REALITY

Offered by almost every manufacturer of smartphones to date, VR (virtual reality) viewers are rapidly becoming a legitimate engagement platform for many brands. But are they as valuable to the hospitality industry as VR advocates suggest?

Virtual reality is "an artificial environment which is experienced through sensory stimuli (such as sights and sounds) provided by a computer and in which one's actions partially determine what happens in the environment; also the technology used to create or access a virtual reality."[158]

Clinical definition aside, VR is at its core an artificially created environment. This artificial environment can be a location previously recorded with 360 cameras that allows the user to view in a virtual way the experiences recorded by the camera, but the user cannot 'interact' in that environment in real time unless the experience is truly generated to be interactive.

This can be produced in two ways: computer generated graphics, such as immersive technology like Oculus Quest currently owned by Facebook; or "live" 360 broadcasts like Periscope by Twitter. The term "interaction" is quite dissimilar in these two examples. One refers in part to the amount of technology needed to create both, and the second to the options available to interact with what is being shared. Oculus requires not only the unique equipment it has developed, but a minimum level of computing power to render the complexities of the engagement.

With Periscope TV 360 a variety of cameras can be used to display both the image and sound associated with the location of the camera, but your interaction is limited to simply changing the POV (Point Of View) shared by the camera. Ironically, the latter holds the greatest potential for VR in hospitality.

VIRTUAL REALITY IN USE TODAY

Google Street Maps
The ability to provide a spherical view of a particular location is one of the most adopted forms of VR use, both with flat-screen navigation as well as using Google Cardboard for a more immersive experience.

Google Street View
This is content generated by users and shared with the same technology as Google's Street Maps. But unlike Street Maps, the user recorded the 360 still image and placed it on Google's Map app. Also available is Google's Cardboard Camera app that allows you to capture sounds while recording the 360 image.

A notable feature of all these apps is the ability to create your own content and then share it based on the location where it was taken, allowing anyone looking for a view of that location to access it from Google's search function. You can also create connecting 360 images that allow the viewer to proceed from one location to a connected second location. For example, you can create a picture of your hotel's entrance with a connection to your lobby then move onwards to a meeting room—all for free, and findable on Google for your location.

Google's Museum View
This is a notable 360 development by Google that allows the user to experience in 360 view the great museums of the world.

Google Expedition
This application of VR takes children on field trips around the world in 360 view. With the entry cost already low and usable by owning a smartphone, the cost to do more robust engagements such as live meetings, with platforms like Liveit Now which allow live streaming in 360, is falling quickly.

Vr.YouTube.com
YouTube has an entire channel devoted to virtual reality and its offerings are robust. Destinations and hotels are featured—viewers can get up close and personal without leaving their home or office.

Virtual 360 tours can be viewed on any desktop and the user can navigate by pointing the mouse through doors or down hallways. But more sophisticated virtual reality tours are enhanced with head gear like the Oculus Quest, Oculus Go, PlayStation VR, and Lenovo Mirage Solo.

Oculus Quest   Oculus Go   PlayStation VR   Lenovo Mirage Solo

Virtual reality tours are enhanced with head gear like these.

Best Western began using virtual reality as a training tool in the customer service world. It allows agents to experience multiple guests standing in line and learn how to deliver service virtually before facing actual guests.

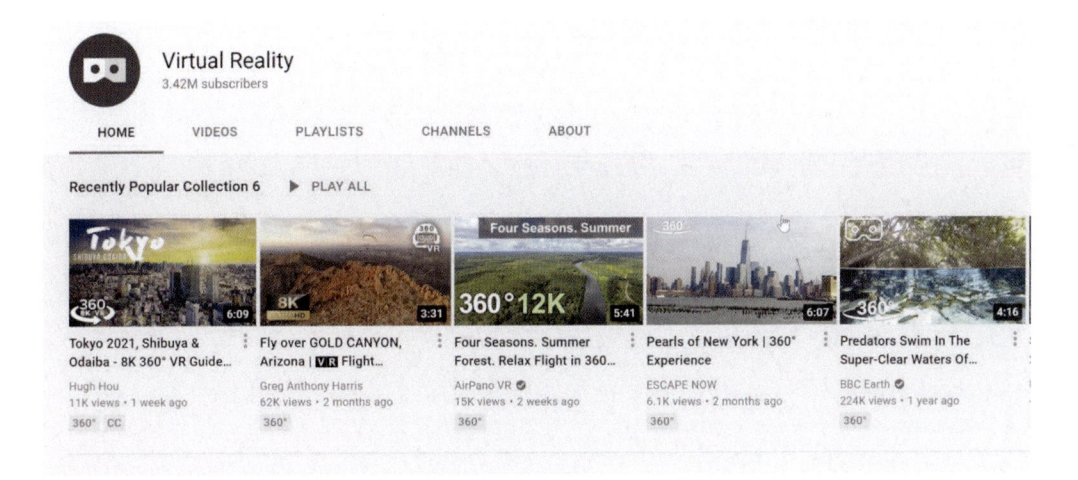

YouTube's Virtual Reality Channel | https://vr.youtube.com/watch/

VR IMPLICATIONS FOR HOSPITALITY
The Covid-19 pandemic and the stay-at-home period forced advances for hospitality in the virtual reality space. With their customers suddenly unable to travel, dozens of destinations and hotels created virtual experiences. On the low-tech end, virtual 360 property tours became the norm. On the higher tech end, the Oculus Quest headgear gave stunning virtual tours at some of the most amazing destinations and hotel properties around the world.

Virtual reality is still in the infancy stage in hotels. While other industries have found more use cases, we have only seen the beginning of this technology in the hospitality sector.

AUGMENTED REALITY
Holding the brightest promise for hospitality, AR (augmented reality) has become the rising star of visual interaction. Augmented reality is "a live direct or indirect view of a physical, real-world environment whose elements are aug-

mented by computer-generated sensory input such as sound, video, graphics, or GPS data."[159]

The differences between VR and AR are based on the devices you need to experience each, and the actual experience. VR is 100% virtual, while AR incorporates the real world and enhances it. VR requires a headset to fully experience it while AR can be experienced with any smartphone.

One example of AR in action today is Yelp's Monocle feature on its mobile app. This radar-like app uses your phone's camera to indicate locations around you with their Yelp listings. There are also AR apps that can do things like help you find the stars in the sky or where you parked your car, provide language translations of anything written, or give you movie times and let you buy tickets through a poster for that movie. Another notable AR tool is Amazon's visual product finder which, when opened within the Amazon app, will identify what you are pointing at with your camera and show you if you can buy it with a one-click purchase.

AR IMPLICATIONS FOR HOSPITALITY

Augmented reality is already in use in hospitality. Some applications like WallaMe allow you to leave AR messages at locations to be discovered by others using the app. An artist or docent can virtually stand beside a piece of artwork and explain its creation.

Let's not forget how the whole world went a little crazy for a few weeks when it was introduced to the biggest launch of an AR platform with Pokemon Go. As developers continue to work on wearable technology like Google Glass, AR will remain in the world viewed through our handheld devices. Menus could be in your native language, visual directions can be provided, reviews and displays can be on the outside of businesses—creating a kind of hyper-reality. Currently its strongest potential uses are for:

- guest engagement
- guest education
- guest travel enhancement
- guest communication
- destination exposure

Two Use Cases

Marriott partnered with LIFEWTR and provided a unique AR experience for its guests. Guests scanned a custom bottle tag on LIFEWTR bottles found at participating Marriott hotels. They were then prompted to open the Facebook in-app camera and the AR experience began. Guests could customize their rooms virtually with an augmented reality art gallery on their phones, featuring artwork from 18 different LIFEWTR artists. They could then share photos of their rooms with followers across social channels within the app.

Mohonk Mountain House was celebrating its 150th anniversary and faced a unique challenge. An iconic resort, it provides fond childhood memories for thousands of past guests—but they wanted to update their image. Augmented reality allowed them to marry the two. Physically, they kept the artwork in the hallways the same, but they provided an augmented reality experience for their guests that they could access with their smartphones that would provide details and history on each piece. It provided an enhanced guest experience and positioned the property as more modern.

We see today glimpses of what AR and VR may become. Imagine advanced rides at theme parks that immerse riders in a sensory controlled environment if even for a brief few minutes. Will that become an adapted way of exploring travel? Will we attend concerts or sporting events via a VR viewer? All possibilities are not too far from current technologies.

SAMPLE CHDM EXAM QUESTIONS

1. The only difference between virtual and augmented reality is the equipment you need to experience each.
   a. True
   b. False

2. What is a good use case of augmented reality in hotels? (select all that apply)
   a. Guest engagement
   b. Guest education
   c. Expedited responses for billing inquiries
   d. Keyless check in
   e. Express check out

Answers
1 = b
2 = a & b

NOTES

Chapter 28: Artificial Intelligence & Machine Learning

> **KEY POINTS**
> - The definition of big data
> - The differences among descriptive, diagnostic, predictive, and prescriptive analytics
> - Best practices around artificial intelligence (AI) and machine learning in hotel marketing

SUMMARY

Artificial intelligence and machine learning have brought exciting advancements to our world: self-driving cars, digital assistants, chat bots, automation of resume screening, and automated credit scoring to name just a few. Like most new technology in the hospitality industry, there has been a lot of discussion around AI, but not a lot of action—due to a knowledge gap when it comes to analytics and the limitations of legacy operating systems.

The hospitality industry was not alone. In McKinsey's 2019 survey[160] of global executives, only "58% of respondents report that their organizations have embedded at least one AI capability into a process or product." When the Covid-19 pandemic forced many companies to adopt a "digital first" mindset—where you approach every new opportunity or problem with the assumption that the solution should be as digital as possible[161]—more progress was made.

This chapter—with a combination of theoretical information and tangible examples of current best practices—will help hotel marketers understand how to make the best use of AI and machine learning technologies. It also addresses some of the barriers to success for analytics-dependent initiatives, and provides direction for how to overcome them.

Data, analytics, and algorithms form the foundation on which AI and machine learning are built, so we will start there.

WHAT IS BIG DATA?

A commonly accepted definition of big data is "when volume, velocity and variety of data exceeds an organization's storage or compute capacity for accurate and timely decision-making."

An early example of big data is when the volume of data that Google—then called Backrub—collected crashed the Stanford servers (see Chapter 2 for the full story). As you can imagine, the ensuing 23 years have created a bit more data—an overwhelming amount of data on several levels.

Today, there is such a volume of information that it takes too long for humans to make sense of it all—which has led us to data scientists to help us analyze and parse it.

WHAT ARE ANALYTICS?

Analytics is a term used so broadly that it is easy to confuse which analytics are best suited to address which business questions. This is likely part of the problem that marketers face in identifying the right solution for their business problems, leading most to believe incorrectly that AI and machine learning will be a silver bullet for any business pain.

There are four overarching categories of analytics.

1. DESCRIPTIVE ANALYTICS answer the question "what happened." They provide a snapshot of historical data that describes the past, including things like year-over-year changes, number or quantity of sales, and total revenue or costs. This is also known as business intelligence.
2. DIAGNOSTIC ANALYTICS answer the question "why did it happen," looking at processes or causes instead of the result. Techniques like drill-down, data discovery, statistics, correlations, or data mining are examples of diagnostic analytics.

3. PREDICTIVE ANALYTICS answer the question "what could happen in the future," providing a forward-looking analysis or prediction. Common techniques include forecasting, statistics, data mining, predictive modeling, machine learning, and artificial intelligence.
4. PRESCRIPTIVE ANALYTICS answer the question "what should we do about it," providing an action or recommendation, considering business opportunities and constraints. Techniques like optimization, simulation, game theory, decision-analysis methods, machine learning, and artificial intelligence are in this category.

Within predictive analytics (what could happen in the future), there are three key models that are relevant for marketers:

- Cluster Models: These algorithms are used for audience segmentation based on past brand engagement, past purchases, and demographic data.
- Propensity Models: These evaluate a consumer's likelihood to do something, such as convert, act on an offer, or disengage.
- Recommendations Filtering: This model evaluates past purchase history to understand where there might be additional sales opportunities.[162]

WHAT ARE ALGORITHMS?

An algorithm is a very specific set of instructions for performing a concrete task. Algorithms are commonly applied in solving everyday problems (like a recipe), in mathematics and scientific calculations, and in computer programming.

Machine learning algorithms are high level instructions about how to build a model from a set of historical data. Data is fed into the algorithm which searches a very large set of models to find the one that fits the data best. Best fit means the model generates the most accurate output, based on the stated goal.

This search for a best fit model is a fairly black box process, and algorithms "out of the box" are designed to optimize the accuracy of their prediction or output. In all cases, these algorithms train on existing historical data, and apply what is learned from that data to new observations. The accuracy of future predictions is evaluated—passing or failing—and the model is adjusted as time goes on to be more and more accurate.

While this "learning" over time can be extremely valuable, it is important for marketers to understand that the models will do EXACTLY what they are asked in the most accurate way possible. They won't give you anything you don't explicitly ask for. This can have unintended consequences if a scenario critical to the "right" solution is not explicitly identified as part of the goal of the algorithm.

For example, the navigation app Waze is designed to provide the optimal (fastest) route to users based on GPS coordinates, road layout, and current traffic conditions. The app, along with similar mapping tools, is essential navigational support for many drivers. During the California wildfires in 2017, people fleeing the wildfires naturally turned to Waze to help them navigate the most efficient route out ahead of the rapidly spreading wildfires. Unfortunately, the app ended up navigating many users directly into roads that were engulfed in flames. The learning algorithm was designed to find the fastest route, and these empty roads appeared extremely efficient. No one had thought to program the app to avoid hazards that didn't create traffic congestion.

A machine learning algorithm will not give you anything you don't ask for, even at the expense of the users' safety[163].

WHAT IS ARTIFICIAL INTELLIGENCE AND MACHINE LEARNING?

Artificial intelligence (AI) and machine learning are predictive and prescriptive analytical techniques. AI refers to the theory and development of computer systems able to perform tasks that normally require human intelligence. For example:

- See—recognize new images
- Hear—understand and react to speech
- Move—perform task-oriented movement with a real-time reaction
- Reason—recognize patterns and make decisions about them

Machine learning is a branch of AI and computer science which focuses on using data and algorithms to imitate the way that humans learn, gradually improving its accuracy—without being explicitly programmed.[164] At its most basic, machine learning is powerful math and prediction.[165]

Machine learning involves testing, passing, and failing. A passing algorithm moves on to the next test, while a failed one does not. That is how the computers "learn." For machine learning, it takes a lot of failing to get to the best answer. So, if there is a high cost to failure, be aware.

> Identifying the difference between Chihuahuas and muffins is an easy task for a toddler but poses a challenging task for machine learning.
>
> When you "teach" a computer, you feed it a lot of data–in this case telling it which image is a dog and which is a muffin. Eventually the computer starts to determine that it is highly likely that the first one is a muffin, and the second is a dog.

AI and machine learning are not new—in fact, most of the techniques that underpin AI and machine learning are decades old, if not older. What is new is that we finally have the computing power to apply algorithms to massive volumes and varieties of data at the speed of business.

WHY DO MARKETERS NEED TO UNDERSTAND DATA, ANALYTICS, AND ALGORITHMS TO USE AI?

Marketers should have a basic understanding of the differences among these categories, and be able to identify which category of analytics is best suited to answer their question. This helps ensure that the right resources—both human and technology—are invested to solve the question. It also ensures that the business purposefully balances its focus on historical performance with identifying and targeting future opportunities.

An analyst should be able to perform analyses in the descriptive and diagnostic categories easily (provided they have the right tools and access to data). As questions become more predictive, a more advanced modeler might be required, and the organization will likely need to invest in a statistical analysis application (e.g., SPS, SAS, or open-source code like R).

Prescriptive analytics are extremely complicated mathematical algorithms, requiring highly specialized skills sets. Since these techniques provide ongoing decision support, organizations will typically acquire them in products or solutions delivered by a vendor (e.g., revenue management system, lead scoring, or recommendation engine).

HOW CAN AI AND MACHINE LEARNING HELP MARKETERS AND HOTELS?

The value of AI is in its ability to automate more complex, but routine, tasks ordinarily performed by humans. Machine learning is particularly useful for complex problems where outcomes can be widely varied and ever changing.

Consider the following practical use cases:

- Website Performance: Your website is your digital storefront, and with rising distribution costs in hospitality, driving more direct bookings should be a key part of the marketing strategy. A/B testing on websites is crucial to continually improve the performance of the website. Machine learning can help more effectively deploy and analyze test-and-learn initiatives, so that you never sacrifice performance even during unsuccessful treatments.
- Chatbots: Chatbots use natural language processing and machine learning algorithms to replicate human interactions. They are being leveraged on websites and as virtual concierge via text messages. Chatbots have been shown to be very effective in engaging guests while reducing the labor associated with responding to messages and texts.

- Optimizing Marketing Spend: Improve the allocation of marketing resources through recommendation engines. Recommendation engines are probably the most well-known and widely used applications of machine learning in marketing, particularly in retail (Amazon) or entertainment (Netflix). Machine learning algorithms can detect hidden patterns in complex data at a very low level of granularity, which makes it ideal to identify and target recommendations, and get better at it over time. Recommendation engines also support personalization initiatives, as they help to surface relevant content to guests.
- Attribution: Attribution and optimizing market spend go hand in hand. Unless you understand how channels, partners, etc. are producing, it is quite difficult to optimize marketing spend. If marketers understand which interactions are producing conversions, they can more effectively allocate spend across channels. Attribution is widely researched and practiced across industries, mostly using traditional analytics (as opposed to AI and machine learning).
- Campaign Performance: By supporting test-and-learn initiatives, evaluating response rates, and understanding the impact of preferences and past behavior, AI and machine learning algorithms can improve campaign performance by increasing response rates and decreasing costs.
- Customer Relationship Management: AI and machine learning are used in modeling customer value, preferences, and behavior. This supports activities like next best offer, reducing churn, and identifying cross-sell and upsell opportunities.

FOUR STRATEGIES FOR AI & MACHINE LEARNING

According to AI developer Jacob Bergdohl, AI can help any business solution through either automation or augmentation. Bergdahl has created four strategy descriptors to help clarify the practical uses of AI to solve business problems that might be helpful in determining use cases for hotels.

Automation and augmentation are at opposite ends of the spectrum when it comes to the benefits of AI and machine learning. Automation is when a machine takes over a human task that involves making a decision or taking an action. Augmentation is when a machine helps a human make a decision or complete a task.

Based on the complexity of the work and the data, you can determine the best mix of automation and augmentation in your strategies for implementing AI and machine learning. Four strategies are described in the next pages:

1. Efficiency Strategy
2. Effectiveness Strategy
3. Expert Strategy
4. Innovation Strategy

Personalization

Some of the most widely and effectively used applications of AI and machine learning in business today are found in the marketing discipline. Marketing was the first, and arguably most, impacted by digital transformation—first with ecommerce, then the evolution of the social web, and now with mobile and location. With consumers creating a greater volume, variety, and velocity of data, marketing was forced into the center of the big data tsunami, and analytical applications that could create insights from all this data became paramount.

Personalization of marketing depends on understanding customer behaviors. Predictive analytics can be especially useful to marketers in this area such as with:
- Customer value predictions
- Promotional behavior for next-best offer predictions or response modeling
- Web analytics to predict what to surface next and follow up on
- Location-based analytics to understand where the customer is and what you'd like them to do next
- Automation of routine communication (chatbot, digital assistants)

Because personalization is such a broad category, with such a wide scope, it is difficult to define success and extremely challenging to control scope. Almost more than any initiative supported by analytics, success in personalization depends more on the strategy and the data, as opposed to the quality of the algorithms themselves, which puts the onus back on the marketer as opposed to the technology solution.

In other words, the challenge is not getting the personalized offer to the guest, but rather deciding what the "personalization" is. This makes creativity, backed by effective test-and-learn programs, essential. From a data perspective, it can be challenging to effectively capture, process, and then serve up guest-specific data. Full personalization requires an intensive data effort, which many companies are reluctant to "go all in on," so to speak.

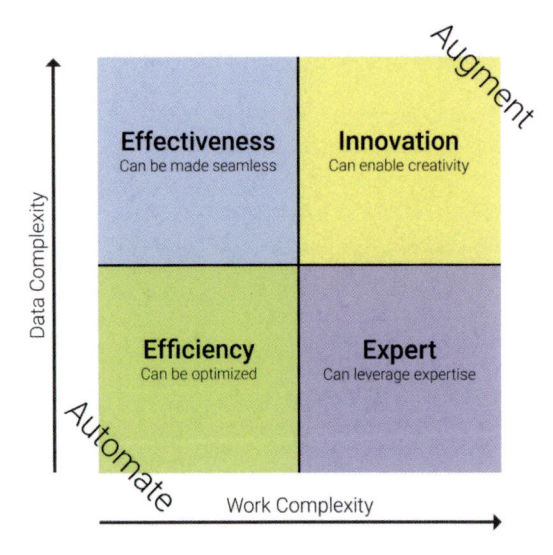

Automation and augmentation on a scale that encompasses four strategies[166]

The Efficiency Strategy

In the efficiency strategy, activities are optimized through automation. This strategy is especially effective for repetitive, routine tasks that may have multiple steps but don't require decision-making—like running a report or doing inventory—and for taking existing business rules and automating them.

An example of the efficiency strategy in action is automating the conversion of a table of data into a chart so that it is easier to understand. While analytics may be embedded in the process, it is just a computer following a series of pre-programmed steps that happen the same way every time. It does not require decision making or any sort of human judgement.

In the hotel world, you might use the efficiency strategy to flag arriving VIP guests and trigger the order of a specific gift basket—based on a collection of data points from past stays, social media activity, etc.

See the case study on page 223 for another example of automating a highly manual process with multiple complex steps and multiple systems—and a lot of opportunity for human error. End-to-end automation of this type of process reduces error, speeds up time to completion, and eliminates the need for resources dedicated to a manual task.

The Effectiveness Strategy

With the effectiveness strategy, the goal is to make humans more effective by either eliminating or simplifying scheduling, communicating, or monitoring.[167] Conversational chatbots—an automated way to answer consumers' questions—are an example of the effectiveness strategy in action.

For a hotel, a chatbot can act as an online concierge that enhances the consumer experience. It simplifies communication because consumers don't have to wait on the phone or in the concierge line to get the answers to simple questions. For example, what amenities does the hotel offer? What time does the restaurant close? What attractions are close to the hotel? To get started, input a hotel's most frequently asked questions into the chatbot engine. Often this information is already available on the hotel's website.

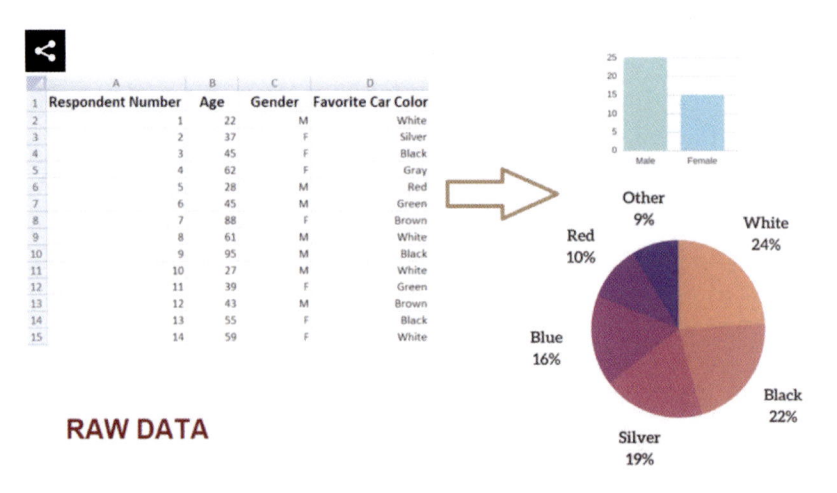

The efficiency strategy can be used to turn a table into a chart that makes it easier to understand. Source: Hotel Digital Marketing Essentials course materials.

RAW DATA

Descriptive Statistics

> A well-executed chatbot can enhance the consumer experience for the increasingly sophisticated younger generation that prefers to type on their phones instead of calling the hotel.

If the chatbot engine is built with artificial intelligence, it can interpret different variations of natural speech language and provide answers to similar queries even if they are not asked exactly the same way. When the chatbot is not able to answer the question, it can guide the consumer to a live online attendant or to make a phone call. Each time the chatbot is not able to answer a question, it learns and gets smarter.

The Expert Strategy

The expert strategy is more closely associated with augmentation than automation—it empowers human decision-making using prescriptive analytics. It takes decision-making up a notch and makes complex jobs more manageable. In this strategy, humans always have the final say.[168]

An expert strategy in the hotel marketing world could be used to optimize bids for paid ads—recommending the best platform, time, and ad to serve for the best results. In the end, the marketer makes the final decision.

Another interesting application is a recommendation engine and using it for psychographic targeting of customers. Based on psychographics and what millions of tests have determined is more appealing to a particular audience, you could change the images, headlines, and text of your emails to be more appealing to each customer based on what you know about their personality.

The Innovation Strategy

The innovation strategy is all about augmenting humans to enable creativity.[170] A hotel marketer might employ this strategy by using data to find a new market and design a unique approach to targeting and generating awareness through machine-created rich media.

> Recruiters conducting interviews with job aspirants can be augmented by an AI that proposes follow-up questions in real-time. Meanwhile, writers could be augmented by an AI that not only advises them on their vocabulary and grammar but even notifies them when some topic needs to be explained more clearly[171]

BEST PRACTICE: CLEARLY DEFINE THE DESIRED OUTCOMES

Like anything in marketing or in life, success with AI and machine learning depends on having a clear vision and strategy to achieve that vision. Start with the desired outcomes or goals, and then determine which components involved in achieving them can be supported by automation or augmentation.

Business leaders have two responsibilities in any analytics initiative. Especially when it comes to supporting the implementation of AI and machine learning-driven solutions in their businesses, they must clearly define how the output will be used and understand the data inputs.

Dear Mrs Smith,
Feeling the strain? Go overseas to a remarkable destination. Hassle free.

Dear Mrs Smith,
Feeling the stress? Go abroad to a beautiful destination. Hassle free

An introvert might find certain images appealing while an extrovert would not, so your email images could change based on your customer's personality.[169]

AI and machine learning algorithms will do exactly what they are told to do, with no nuance, so make sure you clearly define expectations. Given the investment of time and resources required to implement AI or machine learning, clarity around exactly how the outcomes will be used in the eventual business workflow will save time and rework later in the process. This decision should be led by the business, not the developers, or the implementation will ultimately be unsuccessful. Be prepared to take input from stakeholders and the technical teams to improve the solution but stay clear and firm on the goals and success metrics.

BEST PRACTICE: WATCH FOR PRIVACY AND FAIRNESS VIOLATIONS

The data scientist who builds your solutions doesn't know your business as well as you, and the algorithms themselves won't identify any potential issues, unless asked specifically to find them. It is business leaders' responsibility to know their business, their data, and their industry well enough to identify any undesirable outcomes, and work with the developers to mitigate them.

There are two primary areas to watch out for:

- Privacy violations
- Fairness violations

Beware Privacy Violations

Data privacy is a serious concern, and regulations in this area are increasing. All organizations must carefully watch for potential privacy violations.

Hotels gather a lot of potentially sensitive consumer data and want to be able to use the data (appropriately) for personalization initiatives to improve service and drive conversions. Before beginning an initiative as data intensive as AI or machine learning, be certain that your guests' data is protected, and be certain that the output of one of these algorithms won't inadvertently surface information that should be kept private.

Remember that even anonymized data sets might not be fully anonymous—consider the New York Times' ability to identify specific individuals in a location database[172], Netflix cancelling its contest for a better recommendation engine when it was found that individual users could be identified in the anonymized training data set[173], and the fitness tracker app Strava revealing the location of secret U.S. military bases[174] when it produced a heat map of global fitness activity.

Consider Fairness Violations

The notion that machine learning algorithms base their outputs on your historical data, and that they will not give you anything you don't explicitly ask for, brings up an important consideration for business leaders. If there are inherent biases in your data, or conditions that exist in the environment that could create bias, it is up to the business leader to identify these and ask for a model adjustment.

Business leaders are in the best position to uncover these potential fairness violations, not the data or the data scientist. While you as a leader may not know, or even need to know, the inner workings of the algorithms or models, you had better know the implications of the historical data they train on.

You may recall the example of Amazon's recruiting algorithms that identified and rejected female candidates at a higher rate than equally qualified male counterparts[175], or the Goldman Sachs and Apple credit cards that gave higher limits to men with equivalent scores than to women[176]. These biases were identified only after the algorithms were implemented. Examples like these are rampant and will only continue if proper safeguards are not put in place.

The algorithms and the data scientists that create them do not know enough about the business to catch every potential bias. It is up to business leaders to know the data and the desired outcomes.

Unfortunately (strictly from the perspective of a data scientist), safeguards involve constraining the model in some way, which can result in a less accurate prediction. This tradeoff between accuracy and fairness will be a regular topic of conversation as AI and machine learning projects proliferate. Be prepared to have the conversations in your organization.

Given the complexity of potential interactions in a data set, it might not be possible to imagine all the possible biases introduced by the data. At times it might be easier to consider the potential bias in the outputs instead. This could be an effective way of communicating additional constraints needed to guide the model to a fairer outcome.

Keep in mind that protecting from bias doesn't always mean removing fields like gender or race from the algorithm. If there is bias in your data, the algorithm can use other fields as a proxy for the missing fields and produce biased results anyway. Including these fields helps the developers put checks and balances on the model to prevent bias. Be careful about asking developers to remove fields without explaining specifically what you are worried about.

BEST PRACTICE: PLAN FOR BARRIERS TO SUCCESS

Clearly there is opportunity for, and the desire on the part of, marketing leaders to take advantage of data, analytics, and technology to support business strategy and operations. So why haven't more companies gone down this path? There are four primary barriers that get in the way of hospitality organizations fully embracing analytics, including AI and machine learning:

1. Legacy operating systems
2. Lack of internal support and strong partnerships
3. Communication challenges among stakeholders
4. Lack of education

Legacy Operating Systems

Most hospitality organizations are burdened by legacy systems that are so embedded in internal processes that it is extremely difficult to replace them. These systems tend to be the primary data collection sources, and the execution arm that operationalizes analytical results. This means that when business leaders want to take on an initiative like personalization or automated pricing, they quickly find that the internal systems don't collect and store data at the level of detail to support the required analytical processes. Even if they do, the systems can't operationalize the analytical outputs.

This quickly turns a small analytical project with high ROI and a relatively quick implementation path into a multi-million-dollar, multi-year initiative with significant risk to the organization. Understandably, business leaders have trouble justifying this type of investment.

Rather than giving up, be creative. Are there smaller parts of the vision that can be accomplished within system constraints? Is there value in implementing 30%, 40%, or 50% of your desired functionality? If you can get started, you can show value. If you can show value, you can eventually get the internal support for the larger infrastructure projects that get you to full vision.

Data infrastructure is a crucial component in analytics, and even more so for AI and machine learning initiatives. Clean, credible, and easily accessible data are required for algorithms to produce effective results, but most hospitality data is anything but clean, credible, and easily accessible.

Regardless of the state of legacy systems, internal resources, or budgets, every hotel organization would benefit from starting a data governance initiative:

- Focus on establishing practices that ensure collection of credible data, and ensure the organization is aligned on definitions and source of key data points and key metrics.
- Build a plan for where and how data will be captured, organized, and accessed.
- Think through any bias or privacy concerns.

These initiatives take much longer than anyone anticipates, and they are essential to the success of any analytics project. They can also be started with nothing more than time and attention from key internal resources.

Lack of Internal Support and Strong Partnerships

Marketing leaders typically don't have strong internal partners to help explore analytical or technical solutions. Very few hotel organizations have a dedicated analytics team. Some organizations have analysts imbedded in their business units, but these team members are not intended to be a resource for sourcing analytical solutions.

IT departments traditionally hold responsibility for sourcing technology solutions, but they are most often focused on "plumbing"—ensuring the in-room technology is working and keeping the selling systems up and running. These days, they are consumed with cyber-security issues, which have caused many organizations to be even more conservative with investments at the risk of inadvertently opening the possibility of a breach.

This means that marketing leaders have no one to turn to internally for education and support of their strategic and operational initiatives. Your vendor partners can help—ask them for case studies or benefits templates that support a more effective conversation with your colleagues in IT and other departments. Also ask for insights into how marketers in organizations like yours communicated the value of similar initiatives.

In an ideal world, marketing would present a business problem or need to IT (or analytics) which would determine whether it can be solved internally or requires a vendor partner. IT wouldn't drive the solution strategy, but would be a strategic partner to ensure that the solution meets the technical and business needs of marketing. The point is, there needs to be a tight partnership, with each side bringing their area of expertise to support the others.

Communication Challenges Among Stakeholders

Another common barrier to success is that marketers, IT, and analytics do not necessarily speak the same language, and therefore do not know how to effectively ask questions or interpret the answers they get. The resulting gap in understanding means that analytics may deliver results that don't really answer the question the marketer asked, and the marketer doesn't quite know how to interpret them. Or IT may spend time and money implementing a solution that never really gains traction with marketing. Clearly, these gaps waste valuable resources internally and block the organization from moving forward.

Some IT and analytics organizations have a team designed to serve as translators between the technical resources and the business (be it marketing, sales, revenue optimization, or some other aspect of the business). These team members are technical, but they also understand, or are responsible for learning, the business. They manage the relationship between the business and the technical functions and are tasked with translating the business requirements into analytical or technical requirements—and vice versa. These roles are valuable, as they reduce the amount of rework and improve user-stickiness of business solutions. These integration resources can explain business needs and critique proposals on behalf of the internal business client, which make the design process extremely efficient.

Lack of Education

Analytics and technology are complex and technical disciplines, and marketers should not be expected to become experts at a detailed, technical level—it's not a good use of their time! However, to take advantage of these opportunities to move the business forward, marketers do need to have a practical understanding of what these solutions are, how and where they can benefit the business, and what it takes to successfully implement them.

CONCLUSION

The benefits of AI and machine learning include automation of routine processes, deeper insights into consumer value and consumer behavior, and more intelligent marketing, sales, and revenue management support. However, these algorithms are very complex, require specialized skills sets and many iterations to develop, and can have unintended consequences if not implemented properly.

Business leaders need to understand the differences among broad categories of analytics, which are best suited to solve what kinds of problems, and the benefits they should expect from implementation. They should focus on:

1. Asking the right questions. Give equal weight to understanding the past and planning for the future.
2. Understanding how analytics will support the strategy. Develop the strategy first, and then find ways for analytics to help in the refining and execution of the business strategy.
3. Knowing their data. At a deep level, understand what it means, what's missing, and where there might be inherent biases or privacy concerns. This will make you a much better partner to the internal or external resources that are developing your solution—particularly if it uses AI and machine learning.

CASE STUDY: AUTOMATION IN ACTION

The Challenge

Achieving speed and accuracy in rate loading has always been a challenge for the hotel industry. Most hotel brands have a complex, manual rate loading process involving multiple touchpoints, teams, and systems, which can lead to costly delays and errors. In addition, it often takes up to 30 days for brands to load rates, meaning that corporate customers can't book a brand's hotels during that time. Moreover, once rates are loaded, corporate customers and their travel management companies must conduct expensive rate audits to ensure that the loaded rates are accurate.

Choice, like many other hotel companies, wanted to improve its rate loading speed. "We wanted to upgrade our ability to load rates in a reasonable amount of time, with greater accuracy," says Chad Fletcher, VP of global sales at Choice. "With feedback we received from customers, we saw firsthand the opportunity to quicken the rate loading process to help facilitate deals."

Abhijit Patel, VP of marketing and distribution strategy at Choice, agrees. "We listened to hotels and corporate clients and determined that, through automation, we could improve accuracy and speed and seize additional revenue opportunities."

Choice saw improving rate loading as an opportunity to double down on this commitment to corporate customers and use quick, seamless, and accurate rate loading as a competitive differentiator.

The Solution

Working with ZS, Choice implemented IPA, which allows computer software, or a robot, to mimic the work that humans had previously done. Rate loading was a very good candidate for automation through IPA because it involves legacy systems, structured data, and repetitive but rules-based tasks.

By automating significant portions of the rate loading process, IPA decreased manual effort so rates could be loaded faster, and with no errors. "Since everything with rate loading is a process, and you're repeating the process hundreds of thousands of times a year, IPA was definitely the right thing to do," Patel says. "It allows you to monitor performance in real time to show what's working and what's not, using a combination of automation and strong analytics."

The Impact

Through implementing IPA, Choice's average rate loading time decreased from 14 days to two days. Moreover, because rates are available for booking much earlier than before, Choice expects to realize a significant increase in revenue in shifting manual staffing effort for rate loading to higher-value activities.

IPA has both increased customer satisfaction and helped the company get an edge over its competitors, Fletcher says. "Corporate travel managers are telling us that speed and accuracy for rate loading have improved, and there's more clarity around the process. We follow up with them when it's completed, in a more consistent way, and they're not getting that with the competition." Moreover, IPA has allowed Choice to be more flexible in serving corporate customers during the pandemic. Choice was one of the first hotel brands to roll over its rates from 2020 to 2021 automatically while allowing corporate customers to negotiate deeper discounts where it made sense.

Choice is also finding other opportunities to deploy IPA, including responding to RFPs on behalf of franchisees. "We're combining IPA with AI for better pricing, and looking at using it in other areas of the company to shift away from manual processes to help improve efficiency by 10 to 20%," Patel says.

Overall, IPA helped Choice reinforce its value proposition to corporate travel managers to make their lives easier.[177]

SAMPLE CHDM EXAM QUESTIONS

1. Predictive analytics answers the question "what happened?".
   a. True
   b. False

2. Which are potential use cases for AI and machine learning in hospitality? (select all that apply)
   a. Augmented reality
   b. Chatbots
   c. Affiliate marketing
   d. Optimizing marketing spend
   e. All of the above

3. Which category of analytics answers the question "what should we do about it?"?
   a. Descriptive
   b. Diagnostic
   c. Predictive
   d. Prescriptive

Answers
1 = b
2 = b & d
3 = d

Chapter 29: Chatbots

KEY POINTS
- There are two types of chatbots—conversational (rule-based) and transactional.
- Like AI, chatbots can be used either to automate or augment business processes.
- Chatbots, used correctly, can enhance the customer experience and save human resources for needed human interactions.
- The addition of stronger AI enables chatbots to help us market and grow revenues.

SUMMARY

"Bots" or computer robots have been around almost since the dawn of the computer, and have evolved into practical and necessary business solutions. Today, at their most basic level, chatbots can answer simple questions for our customers, freeing up human resources for more complex interactions. Chatbots are evolving in their level of sophistication and have begun to truly augment the marketing process by analyzing requests and offering solutions tailored to the needs of our guests with lightning speed.

CHATBOTS DEFINED

People want to communicate anytime, anywhere, and they want relevant and useful answers quickly. Chatbots are an automated way for a consumer to communicate with your hotel and get the answers to their queries quickly without human interaction. Although this may sound counterintuitive to the personal touch most hotels strive for, a well-executed chatbot can enhance the consumer experience for the increasingly sophisticated younger generation that prefers to type on their phones instead of calling the hotel.

Additionally, chatbots may be able to help hotels engage in customer delight by answering their queries at once. They also offer the opportunity to realign resources that were previously used to answer questions to further enhance customer service and interactions.

Facebook launched a chatbot platform for businesses, and several major hospitality players such as Booking.com and Expedia now offer chatbot platforms on their websites.

HOW CHATBOTS WORK

At the most basic level, imagine a database of frequently asked questions and their answers. The simplest of chatbots asks a question and presents the viewer with different options, like in Figure 1:

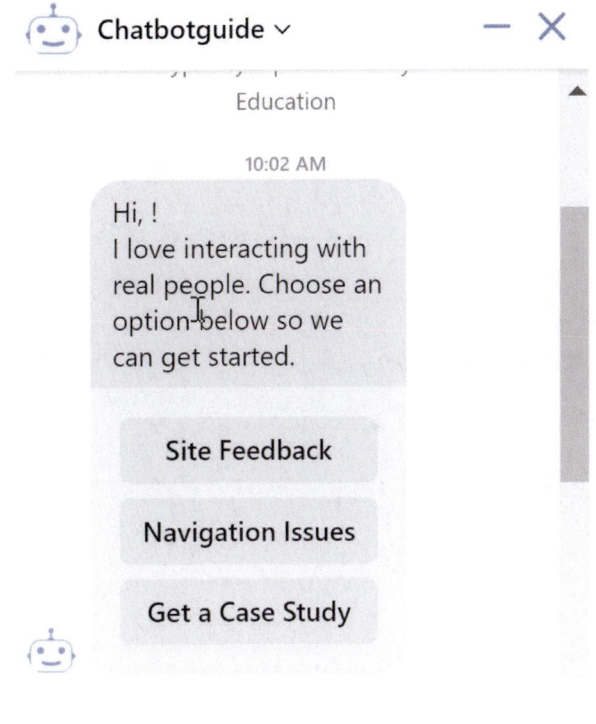

Figure 1

Chatbots can also be programmed to recognize certain behaviors of visitors and respond accordingly. Like in Figure 2, the chatbot recognized the customer was still present on the site after several minutes.

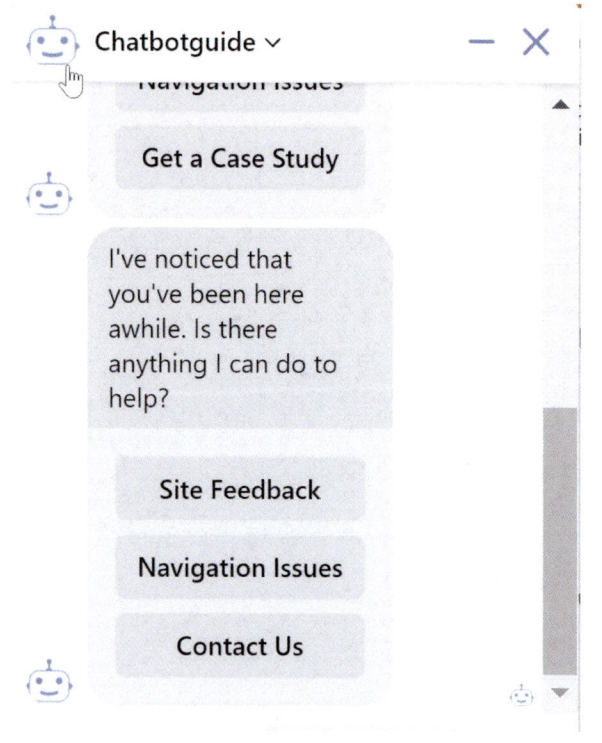

Figure 2

Chatbots can allow the customer to ask any question they want. In this case, the chatbot relies on keywords in the question and serves up the appropriate answer. Take the example of a database that is set up to answer the question "What time is check out?" with the answer "Checkout time is 11:00 am." A consumer might type any of the following:

- "Checkout time"
- "What's checkout time"
- "When is check out?"
- "How late can I check out?"

The chatbot will look for keywords—in this case, "check out"—and then return the answer "11:00 am is check out time."

Another level of complexity is when the guest speaks instead of typing. With different accents and intonations, they might ask:

- "Tell me when I have to check out"
- "What time do I need to leave?"
- "What's the latest I can leave my room and not get charged?"
- "What time is y'all's check out?"

At this point, NLP (natural language processing) needs to be incorporated into the chatbot program. NLP teaches the program to recognize different language patterns, accents, and slang words, so that the chatbot can respond with "check out time is 11:00 am."

If the consumer asked or typed "Can you give me a late checkout," for this type of rules-based question, a chatbot would not be able to help. When the chatbot is not able to answer a guest's question, the hotel should guide them to a phone number to reach a live attendant.

However, each time the chatbot is not able to answer the question, it can learn what it was not able to answer and get smarter through the use of even a weak artificial intelligence. AI powering a transactional chatbot can collect previous data points about the customer asking questions and potentially use the customer interaction/question as a potential upsell opportunity, as in this example exchange:

- Customer: "Can I get a late checkout today?"
- Chatbot: "What time would you like to check out?"
- Customer: "Around 2 pm"
- Chatbot: After checking availability, it can calculate a late checkout charge and offer the guest this: "Yes, you can check out as late as 2 pm for an additional charge of $45. Shall I extend your check out time?"

This technology exists today. The potential is tremendous for setting up systems to answer a multitude of guest inquiries currently handled by front desk agents or hotel salespeople.

But first, you must be clear about the functions you want the chatbot to perform.

TYPES OF CHATBOTS

There are two main types of chatbots.

Conversational or Rule-Based Chatbots

Conversational or rule-based chatbots can provide information about the amenities at the hotel, hours of operation of outlets, information about attractions close to the hotel, and more. Often this information is already available on the hotel website and can easily be programmed into the chatbot based on a rules environment.

The chatbot essentially acts as an online concierge or sales rep on your website. This approach will represent the first widespread implementation of chatbot technology, with the main function being to enhance the consumer experience. Consumers won't have to wait on the phone or in the concierge line to get simple answers.

When building a conversational engine, start with the most frequently asked questions, or conversational topics, that customers regularly raise. Cover at least 80% of the conversations by providing answers to the top 20% of questions. Create a system that can seamlessly engage live agents when the conversational bot cannot answer. Leverage the human interactions to capture these "non-supported" questions and train the engine by feeding answers to questions that were not answered automatically.

Transactional Chatbots

This is the holy grail of chatbots when it comes to marketing. With this, a consumer could book a room at your hotel or inquire about the prices at your hotel through the chatbot. This type of chatbot needs integration with your booking engine, and is the direction major OTAs and brands are heading—being able to provide a booking through a chatbot query like "book me a hotel room at Hotel Elite in Boston on the 29th of January at the lowest available rate."

There are multiple steps involved with a transaction chatbot and the requirements are much more complex. Currently, text messaging chatbots are being used as a concierge/customer service platform. However, with advanced AI, these platforms have begun to evolve because they can target customers at the right time with the right messaging via the right channel. See the case study in the sidebar for a use case.

The future opportunities are limitless for AI-integrated chatbots. As NLP becomes more advanced, and more data is collected and parsed about customer behaviors, we will be able to tailor more marketing messages and deliver right time/right message/right customer/right platform more consistently.

CASE STUDY: GO MOMENT/IVY OFFER

The Challenge: Hotels needed an efficient way to increase revenue from the few guests on-site during the Covid-19 pandemic. Additionally, they needed to increase loyalty and repeat business.

The Solution: Ivy Offer®—a messaging based conversational guest services solution that dynamically presents hotel guests with offers such as extended stay, late checkouts, and F&B offers—was deployed at 10 hotels between September 2020 and January 2021. The hypothesis was that certain guests would extend their stay if they received a personalized offer at the right time via the right channel.

Two areas were chosen for the case study test: late checkout, and extended stay deals prior to a guest's checkout. Guests received these appropriately timed offers on their phones and read 98% them within 3 minutes.

If a guest responded favorably to the question "How is your stay?", they were offered a discount on extending. If they requested a late check out, there were offered an extended checkout for an additional fee.

The Results: A property using Ivy Offer that had 250 rooms saw an average of over $25,890 in added annualized revenue. This came from a targeted conversion rate of up to 6%, and $100 incremental profit per accepted guest offer.

SAMPLE CHDM EXAM QUESTIONS

1. What are the different types of chatbots? (select all that apply)
   a. Conversational
   b. Rule-Based
   c. Transactional
   d. Organic
   e. Paid

2. Why is NLP (Natural Language Processing) technology helpful for chatbots?
   a. It allows the guest's questions to have multiple steps
   b. It allows the guest's questions to be phrased using different accents
   c. It can understand abbreviations in speech, or even slang words
   d. It allows the chatbot to target the guest on the right platform
   e. B and C
   f. All of the above

Answers
1 = a, b, & c
2 = e

PART SEVEN: MEASUREMENT AND MANAGING DIGITAL PERFORMANCE

Chapter 30: Website Analytics

> **KEY POINTS**
> - It is important to examine, measure, manage, and optimize your website's performance.
> - While reporting is important, reporting without action is meaningless.
> - Website analytics will enable you to improve the performance of your site–from content to technology.

SUMMARY

Both the beauty and the challenge of digital marketing is that almost everything is trackable and measurable. We can generate reports (often automated) on most aspects of marketing and website performance. The challenge is that reporting is meaningless unless it leads to some action. This is why we talk about website **analytics** and not website reporting.

As digital marketers are faced with mountains data, it is increasingly vital to focus on the most significant and relevant information available to make decisions and act.

WE ARE SURROUNDED BY DATA

As with most analytics reporting systems, the core process revolves around data collection, configuration, processing, reporting, and analysis and action.

- **DATA COLLECTION:** Collect user interactions from your website, from your mobile app, and any digitally connected environment like your PMS system.
- **CONFIGURATION:** The analytics tool applies your configuration settings—such as any filters you might want to introduce—to the raw data it has collected. Once the data is processed, it is housed in a database.
- **PROCESSING:** Once the interactions from a user have been collected according to your configuration in the database, the next step is processing the data. This is the "transformation" step that turns your raw data into something useful that you will be able to look at and share to make future decisions.
- **REPORTING:** Typically, you will use a web interface to access your data. However, most brands will use proprietary reporting systems that have simply pulled the data from the analytics tool and put it in a format that is brand specific.
- **ANALYSIS & ACTION:** Use the reports to create actionable next steps.

Website analytics focuses on four main areas—audience data, audience behavior, audience acquisition, and ecommerce data—each containing a tremendous amount of data points, some of which are listed in the table.

Audience Data	Audience Behavior	Audience Acquisition	eCommerce
· visits/sessions	· landing pages	· traffic sources	· shopping behavior
· new vs. returning	· exit pages	· traffic performance	· product performance
· country, state, city	· frequently visited pages	· direct	· promotion performance
· browser type	· length of time spent	· organic	· conversion funnels
· device (mobile/ desktop)	· number of pages per visit	· paid	· ADR, room nights, revenue
· age range	· bounce rate	· social	
· gender	· site speed	· referring websites	
· interests			

The following table illustrates some of the core metrics and definitions that are utilized in website analytics. While this list not exhaustive, it identifies some of the most common metrics that are available in most tools and that apply to marketing challenges.

Metric	Goal Served	Rationale
Visits, Unique Visitors	Marketing effectiveness, brand awareness	Visits, sessions, unique visitors, and similar metrics count the volume of traffic a site receives. They help marketers identify when customers come to the site and whether various marketing activities increase awareness of the hotel's brand.
Bounce Rate	Guest interest, engagement	The percentage of visitors who leave the site after viewing only one page. Provides insight into guest interest in marketing offers. Pages with high bounce rates fail to engage customers and point marketers to ineffective messaging, poor customer experience, or both.
Referrers, Traffic Sources	Identify valuable traffic sources	Visitors who followed a link from another site. Highlights guest interests and potential marketing opportunities for your hotel's team.
Search, Search Terms	Guest interest, traffic sources, marketing effectiveness, brand awareness	Most analytics tools provide easy access to the search terms guests used prior to coming to your site. Reviewing these terms helps marketers understand what their guests care about and how to speak to guests in their own words. For instance, few guests ever search for "accommodations" no matter how often hotels may use the term internally. Similarly, changes in how often guests search for a hotel's name, brand, or location may point to the effectiveness and reach of marketing activities.
Top Content, Top Pages, Most Viewed Pages	Guest interest, engagement	Whether called top content, top pages, or most viewed pages, the concept is the same: where are your guests spending their time on your site? Marketers can then use these pages to promote the hotel's benefit to the greatest number of site visitors.
Search Conversion	Purchase intent	Guests who enter the booking engine typically signal purchase intent or an interest in comparative rate shopping. High abandonment rates from the booking engine may result from poor user experience, limited content, ineffective value proposition, high rates or, often, the combination of these factors.
Website Conversion	Business results	Conversion rate—as is typically defined in the hotel industry—measures the percentage of visits or unique visitors resulting in a reservation. Reservations represent the ultimate measure of marketing success for many hotels.
Reservations, Revenue, Cost per Conversion	Business results	The number of bookings, room nights, and revenue produced by your website should be tracked on a monthly basis and analyzed on a year-over-year basis due to seasonality. If possible, cost per conversion should be tracked from referral sources to determine the best marketing strategies.
Entry, Consumption, Analysis	Website optimization	Website clickstream analysis helps to better understand visitor behavior and improve the user experience. The website should be organized to efficiently and effectively guide the customer journey. Web analytics tools track the visitor flow including: 1) Entry-top entrance pages for visitors, where visitors come from, the best sources for visitors; 2) Consumption-count of pages with the greatest number of visitors, how long they stay, how deep they go, what they do, what they 'consume;' 3) Exit-last page view, most common last page views, where visitors left, why they left

Currently the two most popular analytics tools are Google Analytics and Adobe Analytics (formerly Omniture). Regardless of which tool you use, there are many similarities.

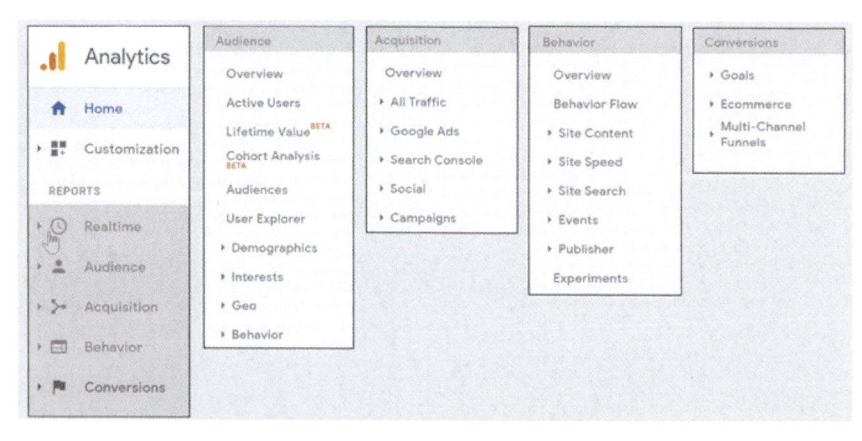

Google Analytics reporting categories and their subcategories as of June 2021

Breaking down the categories of Google Analytics reporting, there are many types of data available to you:

- REAL-TIME: Allows you to monitor activity on your website as it occurs, giving you a live snapshot of what is currently happening; helpful for everything from site performance issues to monitoring campaigns in real time
- AUDIENCE: Allows you to understand insights about who is visiting your site including things like location, device, browser, demographics, and more
- ACQUISITION: Allows you to examine data which reveals the sources of traffic, keywords, and campaigns that drove traffic to your site; breaks out traffic by direct, referring, or search, each with its own report. The Search report reveals the keywords—organic and paid—that drove traffic. There are also reports for each campaign (for example, paid search, email, display, and social media) and the results for each ad being run for paid search campaigns. The traffic results can be linked with booking information to determine the efficacy and success of each channel.
- BEHAVIOR: Shares insights on your website usability from the visitor perspective by tracking behavior flow, site content, navigation, speed, and search. Content reports reveal the pages being viewed along with their exit rates, entry rates, and bounce rates. The navigation summary sub-report analyzes the path taken by visitors in the site and highlights trouble spots. There is also an in-page analytics section that overlays a specific page from the website with key metrics for each link on that page, indicating which links drive sales, traffic, and conversions.
- CONVERSIONS: Allows you to track conversion at both a high level (e.g., conversions and revenue over a period of time) down to a detailed level (e.g., conversions by rate types and room types). It also allows you to track revenue generated by specific campaigns and efforts. So, for example, if you ran a display campaign you can track how much revenue was generated by that campaign. Keep in mind that this is complicated by attribution modelling which will be reviewed in Chapter 31.

CONVERSION RATE

Probably the most asked question in website reporting and analytics is, "What is your conversion rate?"

There are several ways to look at conversion, the most common of which are search conversion, booking engine conversion, and website conversion. Each one tells you something different.

Search Conversion

This metric tells how effective your site is at driving people to the booking engine. How many visitors (sessions, users, unique visitors) who came to your website resulted in a booking engine search?

- To calculate, divide the number of booking engine searches by sessions (30,000 searches /100,000 sessions = 30% search conversion rate).

Booking Engine Conversion

This metric tells you how effective the booking engine is at converting. How many of those who searched on the booking engine actually booked?

- To calculate, divide the number of bookings by searches in the booking engine (1,500 bookings/30,000 searches = 5% booking engine conversion rate).

Website Conversion

This gives you a big picture of how well your website converts visitors to bookers. How many website visitors (visits, sessions, users, unique visitors) booked?

- To calculate, divide the number of bookings by sessions (1,500 bookings/100,000 sessions = 1.5% website conversion rate).

When comparing conversion rates with other people, companies, or sites, be sure the conversion is calculated the same. For example, make sure you aren't comparing Booking Engine Conversion to Website Conversion. Or, make sure both calculations use the same divisor (like sessions, not visits). Otherwise, the comparison will not be apples-to-apples.

A best practice is to set your own benchmark and work to improve upon it, as opposed to trying to compare to another's. If you are part of a group or a brand with consistent and accurate benchmarks, you should be able to compare against your sister properties and the overall brand conversion numbers.

BEST PRACTICES: ANALYTICS IMPLEMENTATION

Mark Twain said, "Data is like garbage. You'd better know what you are going to do with it before you collect it." In the case of data and analytics tracking, make sure to start by identifying the strategic goals for your marketing efforts. Tracking just for the sake of tracking makes no sense. Ensure you understand the goals important to your organization before you start measuring.

Determine which conversion actions support those strategic goals. While reservations likely remain your most important conversions, email signups, loyalty enrollment, RFP requests, and other key visitor actions represent useful business outcomes. Determine which actions matter most and include them in your analysis.

Work with your analytics team or vendor to configure your defined conversion actions within your reporting tool. Include segmentation to evaluate where your most valuable traffic comes from. Additionally, review the core metrics and definitions that are utilized in website analytics (page 231) for measures and the goals with which they best align.

Identify the segments producing greatest conversion for each conversion action. Start with your most important conversion action, measuring activity during peak and shoulder periods to determine your core segments. Note any variation in your conversion patterns monthly with year-over-year comparisons and look for possible causes. Repeat this step for each conversion action as you move forward.

Set improvement targets. Once you understand both your conversion rate and the segments driving those conversions, set a clear, measurable target for improvement. Ultimately, the point of any analytics efforts is to produce improved business results.

Evaluate changes in metrics based on outcomes from your action plan. Share these results across your organization to build support for ongoing efforts.

SAMPLE CHDM EXAM QUESTIONS

1. Which calculation is for website conversion rate?
   a. Number of booking engine searches/sessions
   b. Number of bookings/booking engine searches
   c. Number of bookings/website sessions
   d. Number of booking engine searches/cost per click

2. Which of the following cannot be found in web analytics?
   a. Visitor geography
   b. Revenue by room type
   c. Exit pages
   d. Visitors who booked on OTAs

3. Which two of the following are the most utilized analytics tools?
   a. Google Analytics
   b. Webtrends
   c. Adobe Analytics
   d. Tableau

Answers
1 = a
2 = d
3 = a & c

NOTES

Chapter 31: Marketing Analytics & Attribution Modeling

KEY POINTS
- Identifying and assigning credit to sources of business has become more challenging as the buyer's journey to purchase has evolved into a multichannel process.
- There are numerous attribution models. By default, many continue to use last-click/last-interaction attribution.
- Choose one model and use it consistently but find methods to account for different contributions.
- Work with publishers and agencies to ensure you understand and agree on the attribution model you will use to determine success.

SUMMARY

Measuring the effectiveness of marketing campaigns is critical to any successful digital strategy. The multichannel and multi-device customer journey makes it harder to determine the effectiveness of any one channel. Different attribution modeling schemes can be used to report results, but regardless of the approach used, be sure to report and track the impact of all channels that influenced the reservation and not just the last click.

ANALYTICS

"You cannot manage what you cannot measure," is an adage most marketers live by. It's critical to measure the effectiveness of each marketing initiative and constantly monitor the ROI/ROAS you are achieving from those channels. As covered in earlier chapters, there are different KPIs that can be used to measure the effectiveness of campaigns and their ROI/ROAS.

- ROAS: Return on Ad Spend. Usually presented in the form of a ratio. For example, if you spend $10,000 on an ad and get $100,000 in booking revenue, that is a 10:1 Return on Ad Spend. For every dollar you spent, you earned ten back. If you reverse the formula, it becomes the cost as a percentage of revenue, in this example 10%.
- ROI: Return on Investment. While this is often used interchangeably with ROAS, ROI should be a fully loaded number including all costs, not just ad spend.

Despite the ability to clearly track and measure your performance, the typical customer journey poses some challenges for measuring the true return on your marketing efforts.

THE MARKETER'S DILEMMA

As discussed throughout this book, the customer journey is complicated, with micro-moments filled with digital messaging coming from different devices and different media. So with all the digital touchpoints, how do you figure out which ones influenced or resulted in a conversion? This has been an area of great debate in digital marketing.

Let's look at an example.

Day 1: Visitor clicks PPC ad on Google

Day 2: Visitor click on social media ad

Day 4: Visitor clicks on display ad

Day 8: Visitor searches google

Originator
Assist
Assist
Convert

An example of the marketer's dilemma

In this example, the guest has clicked on a Google pay-per-click ad, a social ad, a display ad, and an organic listing...and makes a booking. Which ad/listing gets the credit?

In theory we should be using big data, advanced analytics, and machine learning to give us a report that accurately assigns value to each ad. Unfortunately, until recently, this has only been a dream. And last-click attribution has been the default for most companies. But there are several other attribution methods available. Following are the attribution models available on Google Analytics.[178]

- Last Interaction Attribution Model: The last touchpoint receives 100% of the credit for the sale.
- Last Non-Direct Click Attribution Model: All direct traffic is ignored, and 100% of the credit for the sale goes to the last channel that the customer clicked through from before converting.
- Last Google Ads Click Attribution Model: The last Google Ads click receives 100% of the credit for the sale.
- First Interaction Attribution Model: The first touchpoint receives 100% of the credit for the sale.
- Linear Attribution Model: Each touchpoint in the conversion path shares equal credit for the sale.
- Time Decay Attribution Model: The touchpoints closest in time to the sale or conversion get most of the credit.
- Position-Based Attribution Model: 40% credit is assigned to each first and last interaction, and the remaining 20% credit is distributed evenly to the middle interactions.

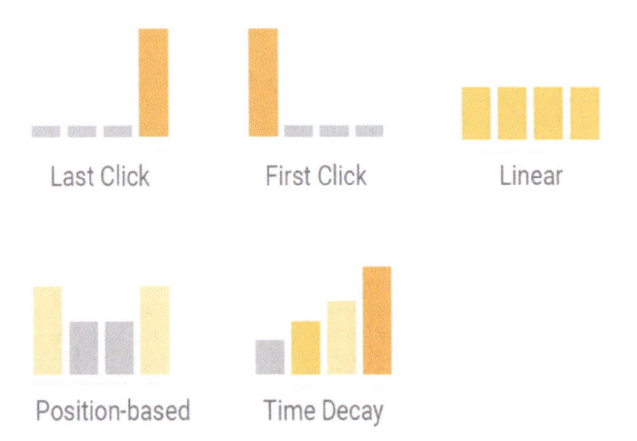

Visual representation of attribution models

Recently analytics platforms have been developing more advanced approaches to attribution. For example, Google's Data Driven Attribution Model, distributes credit based on past data and user behavior. While this is somewhat limited, it is the hope of digital marketers everywhere that this type of attribution becomes more reliable and prevalent.

MEDIA ATTRIBUTION

As addressed in the Part 4: Paid Media, there are various ad models—CPA, CPC, CPM, etc. Often advertisers or vendors will apply their own attribution models to show their value. When looking at advertiser attribution models it is important to understand them, as some models can be very generous in taking credit for transactions. Take into consideration:

- Look-Back Window: A look back window determines how long you will give credit. For example, if the look-back window is 30 days, the publisher would get credit for up to 30 days after the ad has been seen or clicked on by the user. The longer the look-back window, the more generous the attribution.
- Click Through: This means that the ad was actually clicked.
- View Through: This means that the ad was served. It does not mean it was clicked, and it does not even mean it was actually seen by the person. It means it was simply served on a page visited.

Let's look at another example, this time of a display retargeting campaign, which means it is targeting people who have already been to your website.

ATTRIBUTION MODEL A	ATTRIBUTION MODEL B
100% attribution on any reservation	20% on assist, 100% on conversion
View Throughs	Click Throughs
60 Day Look-Back Window	14 Day Look-Back Window

Attribution Model A means that it will take 100% credit for anyone who was served a retargeting ad and booked within 60 days of being served that ad. Attribution Model B means that it will give 20% credit for anyone who clicked on the ad and purchased 14 days after the click, and 100% credit for anyone who clicked on the ad and made a direct purchase.

Clearly, Model A throws a wider net and will be able to claim more revenue and bookings than Model B even though it is the same exact campaign.

A concept that is important to consider in attribution is **incrementality**. Simply stated, would you have gotten the booking regardless of running the ad campaign? If the answer is "no" then the business is incremental. If the answer is "yes," then it is not. Usually, there is no obvious answer to what is incremental and what is not, but you can use the data and your intuition to guide you and your attribution model.

Advertisers and vendors will almost always use more generous attribution models, which is why it is important to decide what your attribution model is and apply it consistently across publishers, vendors, and your owned efforts.

BEST PRACTICES: USE AN ATTRIBUTION MODEL CONSISTENTLY

As a marketer, be consistent in your approach. Don't let advertisers or agencies dictate your attribution models. Determine what you will use and apply it consistently, even if you (or your agency) must recalculate the math. This allows you to compare campaigns like to like.

BEST PRACTICES: CALCULATE ROI/ROAS AND EFFECTIVENESS BY STAGES OF THE CUSTOMER JOURNEY

Not every campaign is intended to end in a transaction. Some campaigns may be run to generate awareness, capture emails, join loyalty programs, etc. When setting up your measurement make sure that you keep these goals in mind.

SAMPLE CHDM EXAM QUESTIONS

1. Analytics and attribution allow us to assign credit to ads with 100% accuracy.
   a. True
   b. False

2. What is a shorter look-back window?
   a. a more generous attribution model
   b. a less generous attribution mode
   c. the same as a view through
   d. the same as a click through

3. Which is NOT an attribution model?
   a. Last Click/Last Interaction
   b. Time Decay
   c. Random Elemental
   d. Data Driven

Answers
1 = b
2 = a
3 = c

NOTES
_____
_____
_____
_____
_____
_____
_____
_____
_____
_____
_____
_____

Chapter 32: Digital Marketing Organizational Structure

> **KEY POINTS**
> - To understand how to assemble and deploy an effective digital marketing team
> - To understand the most common digital marketing roles in hotels
> - To ensure goals are aligned throughout the organization
> - To understand commonly used organizational structures and the benefits and challenges of each

SUMMARY

Managing a team or working with an agency to drive digital marketing results is a daunting endeavor—no matter if it is for an individual hotel, a group of hotels, or a brand. A digital marketer needs to be at once strategic, analytical, creative, and a technology master.

And to be the leader of a digital marketing team? A successful leader responsible for the digital marketing function must consider not only the direct marketing results, but how they translate into enterprise profitability through the most efficient deployment of available technology and resources.

No other discipline in the hospitality industry has evolved as quickly, or continually, as digital marketing. Keeping up with trends and best practices, spotting revenue opportunities, and avoiding digital pitfalls—all while trying to explain to a hotel owner why your hotel is not showing up first on Google—seems an almost impossible task. And in truth, it is a challenging one.

This chapter looks at the varied demands on the digital marketer, explores solutions and best practices around hiring for the right skill set, and suggests ways to structure the department to address the organization's needs most efficiently.

TYPICAL DIGITAL MARKETING ROLES AND REQUIRED SKILLSETS

There is no one or "right" way to staff a digital marketing team. Typical digital team member roles and their preferred skill sets are outlined here.

Title	Description	Key Skills Required
Digital Marketing Director, VP, EVP, SVP	This position is responsible for driving and executing an effective digital marketing and media strategy for an individual or cluster of hotels (and related outlets). Develops, implements, and organizes online marketing campaigns to acquire new customers, increase hotel revenues, market share, and brand awareness while in parallel providing home office support to hotels—measuring and reporting on brand and property performance, managing digital agencies and media partnerships, and liaising with internal and external stakeholders.	• Strategy • Creativity • Budgeting • Analytics • Communication/Presentation Skills • Finance • Hotel/Travel Industry Knowledge • SEO expertise • Understanding of OTA Impact
Digital Marketing Manager	Primarily responsible for digital advertising strategy execution, email marketing, and content management of the company website. Maintains up-to-date and error free content on website and oversees website development projects. Maintains paid search ads and display advertising, and consistently evaluates new digital opportunities in partnership with the digital marketing agency. Analyzes results and makes recommendations for changes to creative campaigns and budget.	• Digital Advertising Strategy and Implementation • Email Marketing • Content Management • Analytics • Budgeting • SEO & OTA Understanding
Director of Loyalty, CRM	Creates and delivers communications to drive engagement with and revenue from loyalty members and stakeholders. Marketing channels include email marketing, SMS messaging, direct mail, social media, and other channels as needed. Leverages CRM databases including building segmentation flowcharts for marketing communications and maintaining direct marketing contact strategy rulesets. Identifies emerging marketing and competitive trends, including direct competitor analyses and tracking. Meets financial objectives by overseeing and managing annual budgets.	• Strategy Creation • CRM Technology • Analytics • Email Marketing • Social Media • Database Management • Paid Advertising • Budgeting
Social Media Manager	Oversees hotel's interactions with the targeted audiences through content strategies on social media platforms. Responsibilities include social posts, customer feedback, analyzing engagement data, identifying trends in customer interactions, and planning digital campaigns to grow their community. Also responsible for managing influencer marketing campaigns, as well as liaising with the brand to ensure brand social compliance.	• Social Media • Email Marketing • Paid Advertising • Analytics • Creativity
Analytics Manger	Responsible for monitoring and reporting on the performance of all marketing campaigns and websites. Must be skilled in problem solving, advertising models, attribution database management, and data mining.	• Analytics • Database Management • Business Intelligence Tools • Attribution Modeling • Google Analytics (or other analytics tools)
Corporate eCommerce Manager or Director	Responsible for developing strategic practices that result in increased market share and the achievement of each assigned hotel's top line budget through a focus on e-distribution and other online marketing tactics. Outlines how to capture online marketing opportunities and develops methods to capture direct and semi-direct online channels to drive revenues. Responsible for partnering closely with leadership to develop and research higher-level, more complex marketing opportunities and strategies.	• Paid Advertising • OTA Understanding • Analytics • Communications • Creativity • Budgeting • Brand or vanity web development

Content Manager	Responsible for executing all aspects of social media and email marketing with goals to build a more engaged and growing audience to increase brand awareness, attract new customers, and deepen customer engagement. They work to ensure that assigned websites, social media, email, and digital assets forms align with the branding and marketing messages created and evaluated by the team for effectiveness and efficiency.	• Written Communication • Social Media • Email Marketing • Graphics • Video • SEO/ Keyword Research
Public Relations Manager/ Director	Leads the marketing communications efforts to drive brand awareness, generates inbound and outbound traffic and report results through the distribution of press releases, organizing fam trips, and coordinating with influencers. Responsible for a crisis communication plan in the event of any potential negative disasters—nature- or man-made.	• Public Relations • Communication • Social Media • Press Management • Crisis Management • Event Management and Promotion

While this list is not finite, it does illustrate the most common roles and responsibilities for digital marketing team members. Other roles that may be found under the digital marketing umbrella include Copywriter, Director of Photography, Video Production, and SEO Expert.

COMMUNICATION AND TEAMWORK

The responsibility for digital marketing cannot fall on one person alone. Every hotel needs a team that contributes to and understands the decisions made and the strategies developed. Achieving optimal results requires not only strategies and their implementation, but also understanding and buy-in throughout the revenue impacting departments.

The following table outlines typical interfaces by department within a hotel or management company.

Position/Department	Role and Responsibilities in Digital Marketing Space
Digital Marketing (could be one or multiple roles from listing above)	This person is typically the main driver of all things digital and is responsible for providing relevant data to all stakeholders around brand promotions, web needs, email marketing, paid advertising, OTA advertising, group intermediaries, and analytics of results.
General Manager	The GM should have a fundamental understanding of how digital works and provide feedback and direction on overall digital strategy. The GM is also responsible for budget/resource allocation and should ensure that each department is providing the necessary information to allow digital marketing to operate effectively.
Revenue Management	The revenue manager is responsible for conveying critical data—pace, pick up, variances to the budget, forecasting, rates, and promotions. They should ensure that all special package rates offered are bookable through appropriate channels—via brand.com, OTAs, etc.
Director of Sales	The director of sales is responsible for group forecasting and providing detailed input to the digital marketing team around specific need periods and group customer segmentation. This position has solid insight into what is happening in the group world that may impact keyword and link strategies. They also need to fully understand and be part of the strategic direction of the hotel. Support and communication of the digital strategy and direction to the entire sales team is needed.
Front Office Manager	The FOM needs to understand the specific digital marketing offers and promotions—and must ensure that data input is complete and thorough in order to assist in data mining and analytics. This role should also ensure the fulfillment of special packages promoted, and ensure company and revenue source tracking is collected and accurate.
Sales Managers	This individual or group should be aware of corporate and destination partnership opportunities and communicate those to the digital marketing team. They should also recommend special promotions and packages based on their customer needs as well as competitor insights.
Director of Catering	This department should ensure that all food and beverage and meeting space information is provided to the digital marketing team to ensure they keep online sites updated. They may also be involved in special menus, packaging, and promotions.
Director of Finance	The director of finance often sees the end result and so including them in regular discussions can help ensure that promotions and digital marketing efforts realize both top and bottom line results.

ORGANIZATIONAL STRUCTURE

There is no one-size-fits-all structure for effective digital marketing deployment. The ideal structure will be based on a number of key elements:

- The company's overall organizational structure
- The company's culture
- The talents in existing leadership
- The company goals
- The makeup of the company portfolio (branded v. independent, full service v. select)

Common options for digital marketing deployment include:

1. On-property team
2. Centralized corporate or clustered team
3. Outsourced agencies
4. Some combination of the above

For branded hotels, there is generally some level of digital marketing support for the basics—brand.com website, GDS accessibility, email, and some social functionality. Some brands also offer additional paid support for digital resources, similar to hiring an outside agency except they are more familiar with the requirements and best practices of the brand.

On-Property Team

Brands typically offer some digital marketing services as a part of their franchise agreement—maintenance of a branded website,

GDS connectivity, and even some online advertising. On-site, marketing has traditionally been handled for branded properties by a director of sales and marketing (DOSM). Many properties who go the do-it-yourself route will add an ecommerce manager to assist with specific property needs that may not be supported by the brand. That ecommerce manager might provide extended social media management, respond to reviews, provide updates for meta, OTA, and other travel sites, as well as manage some paid advertising.

The benefit of this structure is that the property has the highest level of control over its resources. The staff is onsite, they are the close to the specific needs of the property, it is easier for them to stay in touch with need periods, they are knowledgeable about any service or physical plant changes, and they are focused on driving revenue for a single property. If this is the approach you choose, this role should be tightly integrated with revenue management and sales to ensure opportunities are regularly addressed.

The biggest danger or downside to this approach is staff turnover. Digital marketing and ecommerce encompass a multitude of details—and missing any of them can cause long-term financial damages. If you go with an on-property team, ensure you have a well-documented calendar of due dates and auto-renewal triggers so that any short-term impact of staff turnover can be minimized.

Another downside is finding the right talent and skillset to fill the role. Many hotels are inclined to find someone talented in one area—social media for instance—and then put them in charge of PR, email, and analytics. The same social or creative person may not have the aptitude for the analytics, and the result can be a waste of resources without measurement.

Finally, keeping up with the evolution of digital technology and trends is often overlooked when the resource is a single person onsite. The day-to-day demands tend to prevent them from recognizing larger changes in the digital landscape.

Centralized Corporate or Clustered Team

Another popular approach is to have a corporate or regional team dedicated to supporting a set number of properties in the digital space. There are a few ways that these clusters or regions may be structured.

- By Geography—There may be a person or team who supports all properties within a management company that are located within one geographic region.
- By Brand—Since each brand has such vastly different digital marketing support and requirements, some companies organize their clusters by brand.
- By Hotel Type—For companies with a mix of full service and focused service properties, this division may make sense. Focused service properties will have more brand support than full service because of the additional outlets like meeting space, spa, or restaurant on the full-service side. Having people on the team with expertise in areas outside of guest rooms is a logical division of responsibilities. Also, if a management company has independent properties without any brand support, those properties will have far higher support needs than a focused service branded group.
- By Digital Media Type—Some organizations (primarily branded managed properties) may have specific roles to support all their properties. For example, they may have a social media expert and a paid ads expert, each of whom will only perform those singular functions, but for multiple properties.

There are multiple benefits to the centralized corporate or clustered approach. Economies of scale allow for more targeted expertise—meaning you will probably be able to attract and pay for experienced digital marketers if they have multiple property responsibilities. They will be accountable for a specific number of properties, so their attention can still be focused on aggressively driving revenue.

Turnover, while always costly, is less severe in this case because you typically have more defined systems in place, and another cluster or regional staffer may be able to fill in while a replacement is sought. There is also likely a corporate leader of the group who can ensure that new technology is explored and best practices from outside of their own organization are discovered and implemented.

Another benefit is that this corporate or clustered team is likely very in tune with the corporate culture and values of the company overall. There should be fewer disconnects with this set up than with a completely outsourced agency.

The downside to this approach is that the person supporting a property is often not on property. They tend to be less in touch with the daily changes, shifts in need periods, and service and physical plant changes. They are not always able to be included in specific property revenue management or sales meetings so they may miss some opportunities and updates.

The other significant downside of this approach is that it sometimes results in less accountability. The individual or team often will have a dotted line to the general manager, but they report to the corporate office. That means their priorities will always be company over property. This can result in misunderstandings, miscommunications, and stalled productivity.

Outsourced Agencies

From a structural standpoint, this is fairly similar to the corporate or clustered approach.

The upside is that the property or company is able to tap into high-level, expert resources without investing in the human resources required of an onsite person. The level of expertise is often very high as there are multiple people assigned to a single property, based on skill sets. Each week you might get a few hours from a very savvy social marketer, several more hours from an SEO expert, and an hour or two from a paid ads guru.

Turnover is not an issue because that falls on the shoulders of the agency. The hotel need not see a decrease in services because someone quit—the agency will simply shift another resource over.

Keeping up with technology trends and new best practices is another upside—as digital marketing is the agency's entire business. They are not distracted by revenue management or housekeeping staffing issues—they can focus solely on digital marketing.

There are multiple downsides to this approach however. Not only are they not on property, but they are also not part of the company so they are not as in touch with any changes—cultural, physical plant, need periods, etc. Additionally, many agencies focus on multiple verticals, so they may be digital marketing whizzes, but completely unfamiliar with the unique demands of hotels. Finally, you have the least amount of control with this approach. You are one of multiple clients and the sense of urgency you have around your individual property may not necessarily be shared by your agency.

A Hybrid Approach

In this scenario, an on-property person—or corporate person—may be responsible for a segment of digital marketing management, but they may outsource other components.

For example, the onsite person may be responsible for the overall strategy, planning, and budgeting of all things digital marketing, but they hire an outside agency for support with their paid ads campaigns. They may have a separate vendor for reputation management—someone who responds to reviews and distributes a roll-up report to management. The onsite person may be responsible for social media, but they may also hire a PR agency to help with press releases, influencer marketing, big events, and crisis management.

This approach often evolves organically—or accidentally. The onsite or corporate person may be handling everything, and, as they become overwhelmed, they hire one agency for help in one area. They see measurable results from this approach so they try it in another area. Alternatively, some organizations plan this from the start—the onsite person is a specialist in managing vendor relationships. Or the hotel or company may hire a consultant to set up all of the agency interactions initially and then turn it over to an in-house person or team.

The benefit to this approach is targeted expertise. You can hire an agency that is extremely skilled in one area—like reputation management, metasearch, or other paid advertising.

The downside is that your success is very directly tied to the success of your vendor. If that company undergoes any changes, the impact to your property may not be obvious right away, depending on the structure of reporting. Again, your control is somewhat limited because you are not the only customer of any of these vendors. In fact, you are probably only a small piece.

COMMONALITIES OF ORGANIZATION STRUCTURES

Regardless of your organizational structure, there are a few best practices around the management of digital marketing resources that apply to all.

Leadership

Many organizations are creating a new role—Commercial Director or Head of Commercial—who oversees sales, marketing, and revenue management. The recognition that leadership needs to encompass more than a basic knowledge in all three areas is important for the evolution of our industry.

If your organization is not the size that can afford this approach, the end result can still be achieved as long as you have the leaders in each area—sales, marketing, and revenue management—fully cross-trained and engaged with the objectives of each fellow leader. A cross-department understanding is essential for any organization to be truly effective at maximizing their revenue.

Goal Alignment

A primary reason for the creation of the Commercial Director role is to ensure goal alignment between the three departments of sales, marketing, and revenue management. Understanding key objectives and aligning the goals of sellers, revenue managers, and digital marketers begins to ensure that the revenue potential and overall profitability is realized.

The need for goal alignment extends beyond the individual property and into management companies and ownership groups that may have portfolios of competing brands.

For example, if sales has a quota of group business to be booked each quarter, and it is based on room night production versus last year, they may have a conflict with revenue management who is trying to meet their own goal of increasing ADR. Ensuring that digital marketing, sales, and revenue management have some common goals that align allows for stronger teamwork and ultimately higher revenues. Misaligned goals can lead to decreased productivity, interdepartmental tensions, and missed communications.

If the role of commercial director doesn't exist in your company, it is incumbent upon sales, marketing, and revenue management to work together to ensure ongoing communication around overall hotel revenue goals and strategies.

Well-Documented Systems and Requirements

In every single scenario, there is a need for clearly documented systems and requirements. This includes the basics like passwords, auto renewal dates for subscriptions, and budgeting allocation. And it also includes the broader concept of strategy implementation. Are the day-to-day tactics—ad placements, social posts, email blasts—reflective and supportive of the hotel's overall strategy? Are you targeting the right customers at the right time with the right messaging? Does your front desk know what marketing promotions are being offered so that they are capable of fulfilling them and ensuring your guests have a positive experience?

Accountability

This is certainly tied in with the previous category of well documented systems, but it goes a little further. Clear expectations around areas of ownership of results are vital. If the strategy of the hotel is to reduce dependency on the OTAs, the individual(s) in charge of digital in any capacity—onsite, clustered, or managing an agency relationship—should be measuring and reporting back on the milestones reached around that goal.

Communication

A portion of every digital marketer's job is communication. They need to be able to communicate strategies across departments, to upper management, and to ownership. They also need to communicate how those strategies will be brought to life in the day-to-day tactics, how results are measured, and the progress the property is making toward accomplishing those results.

Guest Centricity

While there will always be changing technology, one constant that can be counted upon is that decisions made that benefit guest satisfaction and loyalty will generally be longer term winners. We are first and foremost in the hospitality business and any goals or tactics we have should be run through the guest filter first. If our approach is counter to continued guest happiness, we have likely taken a wrong turn and been lured by the shiny object syndrome that is so relevant in our fast-paced world full of technology.

CONCLUSION

Due to rapid and continual evolution in technology, which leads to ongoing changes in the digital marketing space, the role of the digital marketer will never be a stagnant one. The role of the individual, or team, and the structure should be regularly reviewed to ensure that the goals are aligned with not only the organization but with the advancements in technology. What worked last year might not necessarily be ideal for next year, or the year after.

SAMPLE CHDM EXAM QUESTIONS

1. Which responsibility(ies) does a Director of Sales have when it comes to digital marketing? (check all that apply)
   a. SEO
   b. Relevant keyword input
   c. Link building responsibilities
   d. Paid ad creation
   e. None of the above

2. Which is a benefit of having a cluster or corporate support team for digital marketing?
   a. Less disruption if there is turnover
   b. More in touch with specific need periods
   c. SEO expertise
   d. Stronger educational background
   e. None of the above

3. Which of the following roles would NOT necessarily have expertise in social media?
   a. eCommerce Director
   b. Content Manager
   c. Director of Loyalty, CRM
   d. Analytics Manager
   e. Social Media Manager

Answers
1 = b & c
2 = a
3 = d

NOTES

_____

_____

_____

_____

_____

_____

_____

Chapter 33: Vendor Relationship Management

> **KEY POINTS**
> - Vendor management allows hotels to choose the right way to scale resources quickly and easily.
> - Most hotels use a combination of inhouse and outsourced service providers to achieve their digital marketing and distribution objectives.
> - Vendor management allows hotel marketers to achieve the greatest value for their property by ensuring the right mix of vendor and inhouse resources.

SUMMARY

As technology continues to evolve at a breakneck pace, inevitably most hotel properties and brands will need to engage an outside vendor. If you work for a large brand with a capable team, you may use vendors to assist with various tasks and objectives that require short-term scale for implementation. If you work with a smaller brand or independent hotel, you may use vendors as an extension of your team to perform daily or weekly duties. Since vendors and vendor relationships are so vital to the success of the digital marketer it is important that these relationships be optimized.

WHAT IS VENDOR MANAGEMENT?

Due to the wide variety of skills and resources needed to market a hotel today, most hoteliers rely on one or more vendors to help them achieve their digital marketing objectives. For instance, a given hotel might ask vendors to supply at least some of the following:

- Strategy consulting
- Web development
- An internet booking engine (IBE)
- Content development
- Graphic design
- Photography and videography
- Organic search engine optimization
- Paid search engine marketing
- Display media and remarketing campaigns
- OTA distribution and channel management
- Metasearch connectivity and marketing support
- Social media marketing
- Email and database marketing
- Mobile marketing
- Analytics support

Some hotels choose a single vendor for all these services to streamline their management overhead while others choose multiple vendors in hopes of finding "best of breed" for each required discipline. No single approach—no single vendor, for that matter—guarantees success or failure. But failing to plan for how to work with your vendors often makes it difficult to achieve your objectives effectively, efficiently, or both.

Vendor management is the process of finding and managing the right vendor, or set of vendors, to help achieve a property's objectives, deliver excellent results, make the best use of the internal team's time and efforts, and do all of this for a reasonable cost.

INHOUSE OR OUTSOURCE?

The first question facing many hotel digital marketers revolves around whether to use a vendor at all. Are you more likely to succeed by finding a vendor to help you meet your hotel's digital marketing needs? Or are you better off in the long run to build your digital marketing capabilities inhouse?

No one answer works for every property or hotel company. You must assess your own situation and determine the best solution for your unique needs. However, first acknowledge that the decision to use inhouse or outsourced resources is not an "either/or" decision. Most successful hotel marketers rely on a blended approach, choosing to develop talent inhouse in some areas, and using vendors to supplement and enhance their internal capabilities.

Additionally, you can shift your approach as your needs change over time. Businesses frequently choose to use outsourced vendors while they build their internal capabilities, then gradually move those functions inhouse. Alternatively, specific functions may be outsourced over time to free internal resources due to shifting strategic priorities.

When deciding whether to use vendors or inhouse resources, consider the benefits and limitations of each approach.[179]

Outsourcing Benefits
- **Access to a larger talent pool.** Marketing agencies, consultancies, and technology vendors often attract talent focused on each organization's core area of expertise. For example, few hotels require enough graphic design work to make hiring a dedicated designer practical. A design agency, by contrast, may have many graphic designers on their staff to meet client demand.
- **Experience with a variety of projects.** Because most outsourced vendors work on projects for more than one client, they often have insights and experience beyond those a single hotel or hotel company can gather.
- **Rapid time-to-market.** Building inhouse capabilities usually takes time due to the need to attract, hire, and train staff. Outsourcing often allows hotel marketers to quickly supplement their teams with needed experience and expertise—and reduce commitments as priorities shift.

Outsourcing Downsides
- **Lack of independence.** When choosing a vendor to augment your team's abilities, you rely on the expertise and knowledge that vendor provides to accomplish your objectives. This creates a dependency that may cause issues for your business in the longer term if you shift directions or find that they cannot effectively meet your needs.
- **Limited control.** While you can reject work from vendors that fails to meet your brand or business standards—at least within the constraints of your contract—vendors have significant control of the processes and products they provide. Any disconnect between their processes and vision and your own may reduce your ability to achieve your goals.

Inhouse Benefits
- **Better understanding of your business.** No matter how closely a vendor works with you, it's likely that internal resources will have a deeper understanding of the details of your business. Many vendors focus exclusively on the hospitality industry to mitigate this limitation, but the very nature of most vendor relationships provides inhouse personnel an advantage here.
- **Total control of process and priorities.** When working with your own team, you have full control of your working processes—the ability to decide what, when, and how your resources will accomplish your goals. Vendors must split their priorities across multiple clients and may not provide you the level of control you may require for some aspects of your digital marketing and distribution activities.
- **Maintain your staff's knowledge and skills.** Vendors can help you get access to resources and skills quickly and easily. Unfortunately, those resources and skills remain with your vendor and introduce the risk of losing access if your vendor relationship changes.

Inhouse Downsides
- **Fewer available resources and tools.** Typically, an inhouse solution gives you access to fewer resources—human, procedural, and technological—than you can acquire from a vendor.
- **Staff retention issues.** While bringing components of your digital marketing inhouse gives you the ability to grow your institutional knowledge, frequently the loss of a single key individual from an internal team can hurt overall productivity.
- **May be more expensive.** When working with a vendor, your costs are typically borne across their clients, lowering your overall expenses. Any functions you bring entirely inhouse come with salaries, benefits, and training for your human resources, plus technology, additional implementations, and the need to keep up tools in line with industry standards on your own. These factors often—though not always—result in higher costs overall.

The key question when evaluating whether to manage a function inhouse or outsource it is, "Is this tool, technology, and/or role strategic to our organization?" Hotel marketers often use vendors so they can focus on the big picture, the strategy, and the operation of the hotel itself. Vendors play a complementary role, providing hotel staff the bandwidth to focus on those areas most important to the business overall.

No matter which direction you choose, your success depends on your ability to manage your vendor relationships and your overall strategy. As noted in the *Harvard Business Review*[180], "Outsource the work, not the leadership…when outsourcing, you can't manage through the contract, you have to manage through the people." Delegating to a vendor is no different, on a day-by-day basis, than delegating internally.

THE VENDOR MANAGEMENT LIFECYCLE

Once you have decided to engage a vendor, you can use a straightforward process for selecting the best possible one. This process (illustrated in Figure 1) allows you to determine the right vendor for your needs and ensure you get the greatest return on your spend.

1. Assess needs.
2. Identify qualified vendors.
3. Evaluate fit.
4. Negotiate contract.
5. Onboard and manage the vendor relationship.
6. Divest (if needed).

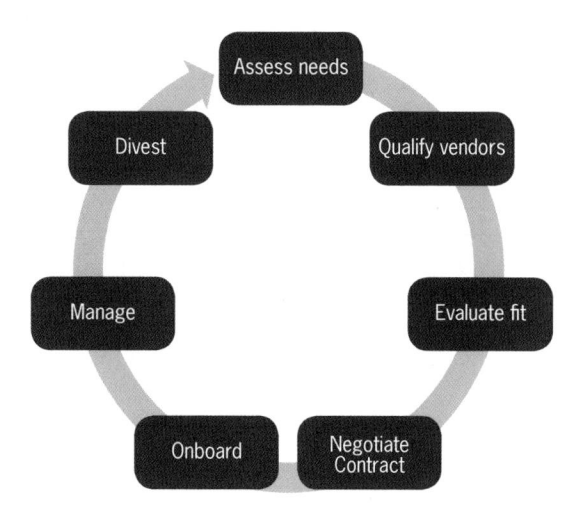

The Vendor Management Lifecycle

STEP 1: Assess Needs

As you begin your search for a new vendor, the first step is to discuss and document in detail the services and products you need for your hotel. While it is perfectly acceptable to have exploratory calls with vendors to "see what's out there"—sometimes you may not know what products and services exist to support your needs, let alone what your needs are—you should draft some basic requirements at your earliest opportunity in the process.

As RFP 365 notes, "What does their optimal size, location, and service portfolio include? Clarify which traits and features are necessities and which are on the 'wish list.' Be as specific as possible. The clearer the picture of your 'ideal' solution, the easier it will be to recognize…" the vendor who best meets your needs.[181]

Meet with all stakeholders from your team to ensure you've thought through all requirements you have of your vendor. We tend to operate in silos, so be sure that you have considered every department that may be impacted by a technology or vendor change.

Determine who within your organization will help you assess potential vendors. Make sure that you define your decision-making process with your team. Will only one person make the final decision based on input from other stakeholders? Will you choose based on consensus? Clarify roles for the evaluation process to streamline your final decision.

Additionally, develop a project plan and set expectations with your internal stakeholders around their time commitment to the process. Map out a timeline with deadlines so that all involved understand the timeframe within which you want to work to make the decision.

Finally, establish a target budget for your outsourced services. While you may not know what individual vendors or services cost, you will save yourself time later if you can at a minimum estimate what you can afford to spend to meet your needs. You may need to evaluate the cost of doing nothing—to help build a case for your owner to make the investment in an outside vendor.

Once you've defined your needs, begin formally contacting vendors to assess their capabilities and fit with your organization.

STEP 2: Identify Qualified Vendors

After defining your needs, create a target list of potential vendors. Scout them out in the exhibitor showcase at HSMAI conferences, review trade publications, conduct online searches and check their profiles and references on LinkedIn, and talk with others in your market and industry about which vendors they use:

- What do they like about their existing vendor?
- Who else did they consider?
- What would they like to see work better?

This will help you determine the appropriate vendors to meet with for your situation.

For simpler requirements, you may choose to simply contact the vendor directly and begin discussing your needs. For more complex engagements, you may want to draft a request for information (RFI) or request for proposal (RFP) instead.

An RFI is a preliminary document that asks vendors to detail their products, services, and capabilities. Hotel companies use this information to evaluate potential vendor candidates, who may then be invited to present their qualifications in person or participate in an RFP response.

RFI's and RFP's help you manage the expectations of the candidates but require a fair bit of work on your end. Ensure you are using a process that aligns with the size of the desired engagement.

STEP 3: Evaluate Fit

Once you have reached out to potential vendors, whether directly or via an RFI/RFP, begin to evaluate their ability to support your needs. As ContractWorks states, "focus on fit, not flare."[182]

You can easily be dazzled by robust presentations or sophisticated sales techniques. Focus always on your relationship with the vendor's team. As you're likely going to work closely with these individuals for a period of years, your ability to get along with them is as important to the success of the partnership as their technical or business skills.

Ensure each affected member of your team you identified during the requirements phase has the opportunity to meet with the potential vendors and have their questions answered. Gather feedback from internal stakeholders and work with potential vendors to identify and address any problem areas early to minimize or eliminate conflict later. No one likes surprises.

While contract negotiation typically follows the evaluation phase, it is often worthwhile to discuss potential terms during the evaluation itself to ensure alignment and fit. For larger vendor searches, many hotel marketers choose to use an evaluation scorecard (see the sample on page 250). This allows stakeholders an easy way to consistently assess each candidate vendor, while also providing a simple way to reduce conflicting opinions.

This scorecard also enables you to weigh your options. No vendor will likely have 100% of what you need, but by weighting what functions or features are most important to you, you will more easily be able to decide in the end. An added benefit to this is the discussion that can take place with your fellow stakeholders around which product features are most important to them and why. This can create clearer alignment.

Additionally, you may wish to speak with references. If others in your market or network use the vendor, speak with them too about their experience as it is rare that a potential vendor will connect you with a client who is dissatisfied with their service.

REQUIREMENT (Score 1-10)	WEIGHT	VENDOR A	VENDOR B	VENDOR C
Quality	3.0	8	8	7
Chemistry/Fit	3.0	7	8	9
Trust	3.0	6	7	7
Scalability of Resources	3.0	9	7	8
Relevant Experience	3.0	9	9	9
Development Methodologies	3.0	5	5	6
Technology Focus	3.0	8	8	8
Proximity	2.5	7	7	7
Size	2.0	8	5	6
Cost	2.0	8	6	7
Compliance	2.0	8	8	8
References	2.0	4	7	7
Warranties/Guarantees	1.5	8	8	9
Financial Position	1.0	8	7	7
Certifications	.5	8	8	8
TOTAL SCORE		253.5	248.5	260
RANKING		2	3	1

Sample vendor evaluation scorecard

Take the time to find the vendor who best suits your needs. When possible, establish a pilot program, working with one or more vendor candidates on a low-risk, small-scale implementation of their service to determine how well your teams work together in practice, and how well their solution meets your needs.

Once you've determined the best candidate, move on to negotiating a contract.

STEP 4: Negotiate Contract

Contract negotiations can range in complexity from a few simple discussions and rounds of review to weeks or months of back-and-forth to find mutually agreeable terms. As the legal implications of contracting fall outside the scope of this program, we will offer just a few tips for effective negotiation.

- SERVICE LEVELS: What is an acceptable service level from your vendor? How regularly will you interact? How rapidly do you expect them to respond to you? Do you expect faster response during particular periods? What remedies do you expect if they fail to meet agreed-upon service levels? What remedies are you prepared to offer if you fail to meet some portion of the agreement?

- PRICING: What pricing model does your vendor use? Are costs fixed or do they scale based on room count, property count, use, marketing spend, or other factors? How will their charges to you change as your company grows (or shrinks)? Can pricing change while the agreement is in effect or only during renewal periods? Remember that you're not always looking to achieve the lowest cost; you're looking to receive the greatest value.

- DATA OWNERSHIP: If any data collection is ta king place—your guest data, your usage data—who has ownership and accountability for the privacy of this data?

- TECHNOLOGY DEPENDENCIES: Does this vendor or technology rely on any other technology to function? How are updates handled? What about new advancements in technology?

- TERM AND RENEWALS: How long is the agreement in effect? Does the contract auto-renew at the end of its period or are you (or the vendor) required to explicitly agree to renew? Which party—you or the vendor—can terminate the agreement and for what reasons? What resources do you own at termination? Who owns the data collected? If your relationship doesn't work out, are you able to move to an alternative provider—or move services inhouse—without violating the agreement?

Obviously, there are many other elements to include in a contract that will help you meet your goals and protect you from risk. Consult with your attorney or qualified legal counsel before signing any agreement with a vendor. But remember, your lawyer can only do so much. It will often be your responsibility to represent the business and ensure the contract specifies what you expect of the vendor. Make sure you have negotiated and reviewed the contract carefully to get what you need.

STEP 5: Onboard and Manage the Vendor Relationship

At this stage, your primary concern is building a healthy relationship with the outsourced team. In fairness, you have likely been working on that relationship throughout the selection and contracting process. But now they're not just "some vendor." They're your partner, an extension of your team. Ensure effective onboarding and ongoing management.

- CLEAR ROLES AND RESPONSIBILITIES: Are you and your vendors clear on your respective roles and responsibilities? Ensure you've outlined expectations and have a clear understanding of who on the vendor's team will deliver on those. Similarly, make your team easy to work with too. Keep the lines of communication open so your vendors know who to contact when they need something.
- SHARED ACCOUNTABILITY: Have you consistently outlined what success looks like for your vendors? Do you hold each other accountable for reaching those objectives? Use regular checkpoints to review progress and hold one another accountable for delivery against your goals.
- REPORTING AND FEEDBACK: Do the measures exist that show you and your vendor the progress towards your goals? Who is responsible for validating those measures? If you're relying on your vendor to produce reports of their progress, do you fully understand those reports? While it is absolutely the vendor's responsibility to track its progress, you are ultimately accountable for the business results. Make sure you can effectively evaluate their activity and results—and that you are providing your vendor with actionable feedback of how their actions are working for your property.

The keys to a successful relationship are communication, trust, and integrity. Do you trust what your vendor tells you? Do they trust you? Can you rely on one another to do what you say you'll do? Can you have difficult conversations, focused on solving problems? In the words of Harvard Fellow William Ury, "Be soft on the person, hard on the problem."[183]

The stronger your professional relationship, the better your results will be.

STEP 6: Divest (If Needed)

Unfortunately, vendor relationships don't always work out. Whether your needs change or the vendor's services evolve, sometimes your vendor can no longer meet your needs. This will require transitioning to a new vendor, taking the service inhouse, or dropping the service altogether.

The following questions can help you prepare for that situation.

- What does it take to terminate the contract? Many contracts have some form of termination clause or the ability to buy out the rest of the contract period. If you're unhappy with your existing vendor be aware of any auto-renewals and prepare to terminate prior to those going into effect.
- When is it appropriate to alert your existing vendor? While you typically would rather not blindside an existing vendor, and would prefer to leave on good terms, you also must protect your business. Existing service level agreements in your contract should require your current vendor to continue support during any transition. At the same time, ensure you have everything in place as soon as possible to make the transition as smooth as you can.
- Do you have an alternative provider? Assuming you still will require the service your existing vendor provided, are you

prepared to move to a new vendor or are you ready to move the services inhouse? Have you identified who will do the work and when they are available to take over? Do you have a project plan for the transition?

- What support do you require from the existing vendor during transition? Often during transition, you may require your existing vendor to continue providing support. This may include day-to-day operational service and training for your team and/or new vendor. Talk through how this will work in practice with your existing vendor once you've informed them of your intent to cancel, then hold each party accountable to ensure a smooth transition.
- How long will transition take? Are you ready for the transition? Do you have a project plan to guide you through the transition? Are all stakeholders aware of the transition and what it requires of them?
- What costs will you have to account for during transition? Frequently during a transition, you may have to pay both the new vendor and the existing one at the same time. Ensure you have the budget to support the transition fully and minimize any unnecessary risks.
- What lessons have you learned that you can apply to the new situation? What can you take from the existing relationship to help you get better results from the new vendor or your internal team?

Handling your vendor relationships from needs assessment through to day-to-day management and, when necessary, divestiture takes effort. But done well, it also yields excellent results for your hotel(s). Work closely with your vendors throughout the lifecycle to ensure they have all the information they need. Then manage them effectively to ensure they will help you achieve all the goals you have.

CONCLUSION

Vendor management represents a critical component of your digital marketing skills. Due to resource constraints and other factors, few hotel marketers do everything by themselves. Instead, they use the right blend of inhouse and outsourced team members to reach their goals. Vendors ideally represent partners for your hotel, as dedicated to your success as any other member of your team. You should hold them accountable just as you would a member of your team. Ultimately, you're looking to work together to achieve results. Manage your vendors effectively and efficiently and you'll be able to do just that.

SAMPLE CHDM EXAM QUESTIONS

1. Which of the following would be considered an upside to outsourcing a project? (select all that apply)
   a. An outsourced vendor likely has more experience with a variety of projects
   b. An outsourced vendor likely has access to a larger talent pool than you
   c. Cost savings
   d. Faster time to market
   e. More control over the project

2. What is the benefit of using a weighted scorecard to evaluate vendors during the selection process? (select all that apply)
   a. Allows stakeholders an easy way to consistently assess each candidate vendor
   b. Provides a simple way to reduce conflicting opinions
   c. Ensures you get the best price
   d. Creates closer alignment between stakeholders
   e. All of the above

Answers
1 = a, b, & d
2 = a, b, & d

NOTES

Chapter 34: Regulations Marketers Need to Know

There are a few areas of law and regulation that impact marketing around the world. This chapter does not provide legal advice, but is intended to increase your awareness of these issues. Consult with your company's legal counsel if you have any questions.

PRIVACY: GDPR AND CCPA

If you have been in an IT or web meeting in the last few years, you have probably heard the initials GDPR, which stands General Data Protection Regulation. In 2018, the European Union implemented GDPR, requiring certain disclosures, data protections, and the "right to be forgotten."

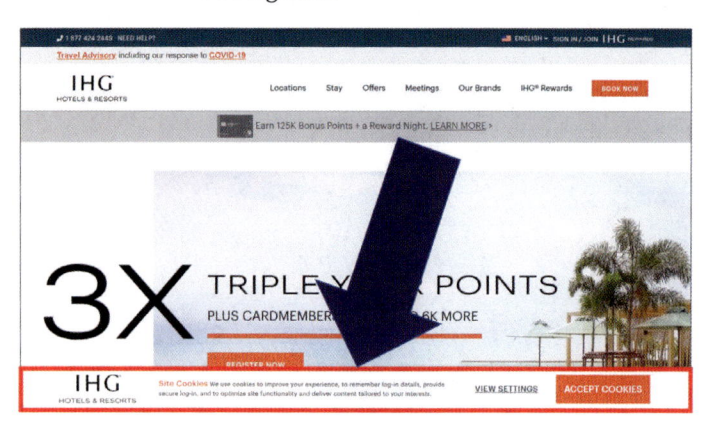

The ubiquitous "warnings" about site cookies were put in place as a result of privacy regulations.

While GDPR is European legislation, it impacted every company with customers or businesses in Europe. Regardless of presence or customers in Europe, most U.S.-based companies have tried to comply with this—not only do they want to comply with E.U. law, but they knew the U.S. would not be far behind in introducing similar regulations. California was among the first and introduced the CCPA, or California Consumer Protection Act, which took effect on January 1, 2020.

These regulations are intended to protect consumers and allow them to have control over their personal data. The most important aspect for marketers to know is that these laws allow people to request the data a company has about them, or request that their data be deleted. Therefore, it is important that you have a policy and guidelines in place to deal with privacy-related requests from your guests/prospective guests, and that the key points of customer contact understand these policies and guidelines.

GDPR versus CCPA

	GDPR	CCPA
Scope	EU residents' personal data processed	California residents' personal data collected
Application threshold	None	For-profit entity with annual revenue over $25M; or receives information about over 50,000 California residents, households, or devices annually, or derives at least half of its annual business revenue from selling personal information
Consent to collect process	Voluntary, freely given, specific, informed and unambiguous (absent other legitimate basis)	Not required
Right to access	Right to access all EU personal data processed	Right to access CA personal data collected in last 12 months, delineate between sold and transferred
Right to portability	Must export and import certain EU personal data in a user-friendly format	All access requests must be exported in user-friendly format no import requirement
Right to correction	Right to correct errors in EU personal data processed	Not included
Right to start processing	Right to withdraw consent or otherwise stop processing of EU personal data	Right to opt-out of selling CA personal data only; must include opt-out link on website
Right to stop automated decision making	Right to require a human to make decisions that have a legal affect	Not included
Right to stop third-party transfer	Right to withdrawal of consent for data transfers involving second purposes of special categories of data	Right to opt-out of selling personal data to third parties
Right to erasure	Right to erase EU personal data, under certain conditions	Right to erase CA personal data collected, under certain conditions
Right to equal services and prices	At most, implicitly required	Explicitly required
Private right of action damages	No floor or ceiling	Floor of $100 and ceiling of $750 per consumer per incident
Regular enforcement penalties	Ceiling at 4% of global annual revenues	No ceiling - $7500 per violation

COOKIES

We have reviewed various aspects of cookies in previous chapters. While it is not currently directly regulated, some companies are starting to self-regulate to either be good corporate citizens or to ward off legislation and lawsuits. As a result, we are seeing a change in the use of cookies. Many companies, including Apple, have phased out the use of third-party cookies, and Google announced that it will eliminate third-party cookies in 2023.

First-party cookies

First-party cookies are collected and stored in your browser directly by websites you visit. The website uses these cookies to recognize you when you come back to the site. This may mean you are automatically logged in, your language preference is recognized, you are sent to relevant pages, and other things that can make the user experience better.

Third-party cookies

Third-party cookies are cookies that are placed in your browser by someone other than the website you are on (they are placed by a third-party). This allows for cross-site tracking, retargeting, and ad-serving. Third-party cookies are often placed by ad networks.

Web cookies: Different flavors [184]

	FIRST-PARTY COOKIES	THIRD-PARTY COOKIES
WHO HOSTS	The domain you're visiting	Ad servers, social media sites, commenting aggregators, live-chat pop-ups, etc.
WHERE TRACKED	The domain you're visiting and, in rare instances, other sites	Users across many domains
MAIN PURPOSE	Smoother site access	Enabling adware
WHAT THEY DO	Remember logins, preferences, shopping cart items, etc.	Retarget prospective customers as they move from site to site

As covered in Chapter 20 (Display Media), a lot of the targeting we can do today is done by aggregating third-party cookies, meaning we can target based on broad search history. With the impending elimination of third-party cookies by Google, a lot of companies are scrambling to figure out how to approach this. There is other technology being developed to try to make up for the loss of third-party cookies, and this will evolve over time. In the meantime, the latest buzzword is "contextual advertising," utilizing publishers whose content is relevant to the advertisers. While certainly not a new term, it is taking on more prominence as people consider how to effectively target in a third-party cookie-less world.

AMERICAS WITH DISABILITIES ACT (ADA)

The Americans with Disabilities Act (ADA) went into effect on July 26th, 1990. The ADA is a civil rights law that made it illegal to discriminate against people based on disability in the areas of employment, **public accommodation**, public services, transportation, and telecommunications.

Title III of the Americans with Disabilities Act specifically prohibits discrimination on the basis of disabilities in places of public accommodations, commercial facilities, and some private entities. **Websites are considered a public accommodation** because the goods and services offered on the site are being offered to the general public.

- Websites must be ADA compliant or risk lawsuits
- There are no defined standards for ADA compliance
- Web Content Accessibility Guidelines 2.0 AA (WCAG 2.0 AA) are widely used as the current standard
- The general rule of thumb is: Can the person with a disability use your site and book rooms and ADA rooms with the same level of ease as non-disabled people?

There are both site content issues (things like information required regarding ADA accommodations) and technical issues (things like font size, colors, tags, etc.) that need to be addressed on your website. To test the technical aspects of your site, run your URL through this ADA test tool: https://wave.webaim.org/.

It is not uncommon for hotels to get complaint or demand letters from attorneys. Even if you are compliant, there is a good chance that you will receive a complaint or demand letter, as there are law firms that will blast out these demand letters in hopes of quick settlements.

The two main best practices are:

1. Ensure your site is ADA compliant (to the best of your ability).
2. Understand your company's guidelines for dealing with complaint letters. In most cases, they should be dealt with by your legal department.

CAN-SPAM

The CAN-SPAM Act is a 2003 U.S. law that sets the rules for commercial email, establishes requirements for commercial messages, and gives recipients the right to have you stop emailing them. While the law has a lot of detail, the U.S. Federal Trade Commission highlights seven key areas:

1. Don't use deceptive subject lines.
2. Identify the message as an ad.
3. Tell recipients where you're located.
4. Tell recipients how to opt-out of receiving future emails from you.
5. Honor opt-out requests promptly.
6. Monitor what others are doing on your behalf.

Non-compliance can be costly. Each separate email in violation of the CAN-SPAM Act is subject to penalties of up to $43,792.

> **FUN FACT**
>
> CAN-SPAM is an acronym for Controlling the Assault of Non-Solicited Pornography And Marketing. Though this is not where the term SPAM comes from, this was Congress trying to be clever. The term SPAM for junk email precedes this legislation and is in reference to the British Comedy Troop Monty Python skit from 1970.

INFLUENCERS

Over the past decade, social media influencers have become more prevalent in commercial marketing efforts, and as such, have come under scrutiny and regulation. The U.S. Federal Trade Commission (FTC) has developed specific guidelines for influencers, the key aspects of which are around disclosure:

- When to Disclose: The influencer should disclose when they "have any financial, employment, personal, or family relationship with a brand." If posting from abroad, U.S. law applies if it's reasonably foreseeable that the post will affect U.S. consumers. Foreign laws might also apply.
- How to Disclose: Should be clear and obvious.

SAMPLE CHDM EXAM QUESTIONS

1. If an influencer posts from abroad, U.S. law does not apply even if the post will affect U.S. consumers
   a. True
   b. False

2. Which type of cookies are placed in your browser by someone other than the website you are on?
   a. First-party
   b. Second-party
   c. Third-party

3. Which privacy regulation addresses EU residents' personal data?
   a. CCPA
   b. GDPR

Answers
1 = b
2 = c
3 = b

NOTES

GLOSSARY OF DIGITAL MARKETING TERMS[185]

As the silos in hotel organizations continue to erode, marketing professionals are increasingly expected to engage at a higher level with asset managers and owners (not to mention GMs, sales teams, and revenue management).

In those interactions, marketers must demonstrate their knowledge of their own discipline AND all the hotel's operations and functions that run parallel with it. This kind of business acumen validates your proficiency and shows those colleagues and stakeholders that they can trust you and rely on your performance.

One easy way to brush up on your business acumen is to sharpen your understanding of the acronyms, jargon, and terminology used in and around the business of hotels. It will strengthen your skills, build your reputation as a knowledgeable team member, and form the foundation for your future success.

For a thorough overview of revenue management terminology, see Evolving Dynamics: From Revenue Management to Revenue Strategy, the study guide for HSMAI's Certified Revenue Management Executive (CRME) certification. Learn more at www.hsmai.org/crme.

301 Redirect	A method of redirecting a visitor from one web page to another web page. This type of redirect is to be used for permanent redirects. For example, you own websiteA.com and websiteB.com but you only want one website. You can 301 redirect all the traffic from websiteB.com to websiteA.com so that all visitors end up on websiteA.com.
302 Redirect	A method of redirecting a visitor from one web page to another web page, used for temporary situations only. For permanent redirects, instead use a 301.
404 Error	The error message that appears when a visitor tries to go to a web page that does not exist.
Ad Extensions	Additional pieces of information that can be added to Google Adword ads, including reviews, address, pricing, callouts, app downloads, sitelinks, and click-to-call. Ad extensions help advertisers create richer, more informative ads that take up more on-page real estate, which generally lead to higher Click Through Rates.
Ad Manager Account	An advertising account on Facebook that allows you to run ads on the Facebook Ad Network.
Ad Network	A grouping of websites or digital properties (like apps) where ads can appear. For example, Google has two ad networks: the search network (text ads that appear in search results) and the display network (image ads that appear on millions of websites that have partnered with Google).
AdWords	Google AdWords. A Google owned program that is used by advertisers to place ads on Google search results pages, on YouTube, and on Google ad network sites. AdWords is the primary platform for PPC advertising.
Algorithm	A process or set of rules that computers follow to perform a task. In digital marketing, algorithm usually refers the sets of processes Google uses to order and rank websites in search results. The SEO industry gives various Google algorithms their own nicknames like Penguin (which analyzes the quality of links pointing to a website) and Panda (which assesses the quality of the content on a website). The main ranking algorithm in SEO is referred to as "the core algorithm."
Algorithm Update	A change made to a Google algorithm. Updates typically affect the rankings of websites. Google makes hundreds of adjustments to their algorithms throughout the year, as well as several major updates each year.
Alt Tag	See Tag, Alt
Anchor Text	The visible, clickable text in a hyperlink.
AVE	Advertising Value Equivalent. In public relations, AVE measures the cost of the media space, or time, devoted to your story based on advertising value.
Average Position	A metric in Google AdWords that helps advertisers understand where, on average, their ads are showing in Google search results pages. There are usually 4 available ad slots at the top of a search result page (where 1 is the first ad, 2 is the second ad, etc.), so for the best results advertisers typically want an average position between 1-4. Average position 5+ indicates that your ads are showing at the bottom of the search results page.
Backlink	Also known more plainly as a "link," this is when one website hyperlinks to another website using html href code. Backlinks are used by Google in their SEO ranking factors, with the basic idea being that if "website A" has incoming backlinks from other strong websites (websites B, C, and D), the links are votes of trust for website A, and website A gains some authority from B, C, and D through the links.

Banner Ad	A popular type of digital image ad that can be placed across various websites.
Bing	A search engine that provides search services for web, video, image, and map search products. Bing is owned and operated by Microsoft, and it powers Yahoo! Search.
Bing Ads	A platform that provides pay-per-click advertising on both the Bing and Yahoo! search engines. The service allows businesses to create ads, and subsequently serve the ads to consumers who search for keywords that the businesses bid on. This platform also offers targeting options such as location, demographic, and device targeting.
Black Hat	Slang for unethical tactics to influence website rankings, like article spinning, mass directory link building, or negative SEO.
Blog	Short for "web log." A web page or a website that is regularly updated with new written content. Blogs are an important section of a website in digital marketing, as they offer fresh new content on a regular basis which can help attract new visitors, engage existing visitors, and give authority signals to Google.
Bot	Sometimes referred to as a "crawler" or "spider." An automated program that visits websites for specific reasons. A spam bot visits websites for nefarious reasons, often showing in Google Analytics as junk traffic. However, Google uses a bot to crawl websites so that they can be ranked and added to Google search.
Bounce Rate	The percentage of visitors to a website that leave without clicking or interacting with any portion of the page. For example, if 100 people visit a website, and 50 of them immediately leave, the website has a bounce rate of 50%. Websites aim to have as low a bounce rate as possible, and averages tend to be between 40-60%.
Breadcrumbs	Breadcrumbs display the directory path of the current folder or webpage and provide one-click access to each of the parent directories. Like breadcrumbs in the story "Hansel and Gretel," they allow you to retrace your steps back to where you started.[186]
Campaign	A series of advertising messages that share a theme, and market a product or service. In the context of digital marketing, campaigns can be run through search and display network advertising platforms (e.g., Google, Bing), social media, email, and/or other online platforms.
Canonical Tag	See Tag, Canonical
Code	The languages used to build a website. The most commonly used languages in web design are HTML, CSS, JS, and PHP.
Content	Any form of media online that can be read, watched, or interacted with. Content commonly refers specifically to written material, but can also include images and videos.
Conversion Rate	The rate at which visitors to a website complete the predefined goal. It is calculated by dividing the number of goal achievements by the total number of visitors. For example, if 100 people visit a website and 10 of them complete the conversion goal (like filling out a contact form) then the conversion rate is 10%.
Cookie	A cookie is a small piece of text sent to and stored in your browser by a website you visit. Cookies help websites remember information about your visit.
CPA	Cost Per Acquisition. A metric in paid advertising platforms that measures how much money is spent to acquire a new lead or customer. It is calculated by dividing the total spend by the number of conversions, for a given period. For example, if in a month a PPC account spends $1000 dollars and gets 10 conversions (leads), then the cost per acquisition is $100.
CPC	Cost Per Click. The amount of money spent for a click on an ad in a Pay-Per-Click campaign. In the AdWords platform, each keyword will have an estimated click cost, but the prices change in real time as advertisers bid against each other for each keyword. Average CPCs can range from less than $1 for longtail or low-competition keywords, to upwards of $100 per click for competitive terms, primarily in legal, insurance, and water damage restoration industries.
CPM	Cost Per Thousand (M is the roman numeral for 1,000). The amount an advertiser pays for 1,000 impressions of their ad. For example, if a publisher charges $10 CPM, and your ad shows 2000 times, you will pay $20 for the campaign ($10 per 1000 impressions x 2). Measuring ad success with CPM is most common in awareness campaigns, where impressions are more important than conversions or clicks.
Crawler	An automated program that scans websites. The name reflects how the software "crawls" through the code, which is why they are sometimes also referred to as "spiders." See also "Bots."
CRO	Conversion Rate Optimization. A branch of digital marketing that aims to improve the conversion rate of web pages, thus making the pages more profitable. Conversion rate optimization combines psychology with marketing and web design to influence the behavior of the web page visitor. CRO uses a type of testing called "A/B split testing" to determine which version of a page (version A or version B) is more successful.
CTA	Call to Action. A type of online content that drives the user to click-through to engage with a brand. This can be an image, button, link, etc. that encourages someone to book, download, register, call, or act in any way.

CTR	Click Through Rate. The ratio of how many times an advertisement was clicked on, versus how many times it was shown. It is calculated by dividing the ad's clicks by the ad's impressions. For example, if an ad is shown to 100 people, and 10 of them click the ad, then it has a click through rate of 10% (10 clicks / 100 impressions = 10%).
CRM	Customer Relationship Management. The practices, strategies, and technologies that companies use to manage and analyze customer interactions and data throughout the customer lifecycle, with the goal of improving customer relations, retention, and sales growth.
Dashboard	A web page that contains and displays aggregate data about the performance of a website or digital marketing campaign. A dashboard pulls information from various data sources and displays the info in an easy-to-read format.
Description Tag	See Tag, Description
Digital Marketing	A catchall term for online work that includes specialized marketing practices like SEO, PPC, CRO, web design, blogging, content, and any other form of advertising on an internet-connected device with a screen. Traditionally, television was not considered digital marketing, however the shift from cable television to internet streaming means that digital advertising can now be served to online TV viewers.
Direct Traffic	Website visits with no referring website.
Directory	A website that categorically lists websites with similar themes. Some directories like chambers of commerce (a list of businesses in one geographic area) can be helpful for SEO; however widespread abuse of spam directories led Google to discount links from directories whose sole purpose was selling links.
Display Ads	Ads on a display network which include many different formats such as images, flash, video, and audio. Also, commonly known as banner ads, these are the advertisements that are seen around the web on news sites, blogs, and social media.
Display Network	A network of websites and apps that show display ads on their web pages. Google's display network spans over 2 million websites that reach over 90% of people on the internet. Businesses can target consumers on the display network based on keywords/topics, placement on specific webpages, and through remarketing.
Duplicate Content	Refers to instances where portions of text are found in 2 different places on the web. When the same content is found on multiple websites, it can cause ranking issues for one or all the websites, as Google does not want to show multiple websites in search results that have the exact same information. This type of duplicate content can occur because of plagiarism, automated content scrapers, or lazy web design. Duplicate content can also be a problem within one website—if multiple versions of a page exist, Google may not understand which version to show in search results, and the pages are competing against each other. This can occur when new versions of pages are added without deleting or forwarding the old version, or through poor URL structures.
Earned Media Value (EMV)	A means to assign a dollar value to various actions associated with different social media content types. EMV allows marketers to assign a numerical value to their efforts, helping them to understand the ROI of their campaigns more fully. It is a subjective measure as there is no one, standardized way to calculate EMV. One common calculation is: # of users reached (impressions, reach, etc.) or # of actions taken (likes, comments, shares, etc.) x CPM
EAT	An acronym often used when talking about SEO. It stands for Expertise, Authority, and Trust. The Google algorithm that determines page rank looks at these important areas.
Ecommerce (or E-Commerce)	Electronic Commerce. A classification for businesses that conduct business online. The most common form of ecommerce business is an online retailer that sells products direct to the consumer.
Email Automation	A marketing system that uses software to automatically send emails based on defined triggers. Multiple automated emails in a sequence are used create user funnels and segment users based on behavior. For example, an automation funnel could be set to send email 1 when a person provides their email address, then either email 2a or 2b would be sent based on whether the person clicked on the first email.
External Link	A link that points at an external domain.
Facebook Ads Manager	A tool for creating Facebook ads, managing when and where they'll run, and tracking how well campaigns are performing on Facebook, Instagram, or their Audience Network.
Facebook Business Page	A public webpage on Facebook created to represent a company. Using a business page gives users access to Facebook Ads Manager. It also allows businesses to engage with users (i.e. page likes, message responses, post content).
Featured Snippet	A summarized piece of information that Google pulls from a website and places directly into search results, to show quick answers to common and simple queries. Featured snippets appear in a block at the top of search results with a link to the source. Featured Snippets cannot be created by webmasters; Google programmatically pulls the most relevant information from an authoritative site. Most featured snippets are shown for queries like "what is ____" or "who invented ____."

Filter	Popular social media and personalized search sites can determine the content seen by users, often without their direct consent or cognizance, due to the algorithms used to curate that content.
Friendly URL	A web address that is easy to read and includes words that describe the content of the webpage. This type of URL can be "friendly" in two ways. 1) It can help visitors remember the Web address, and 2) it can help describe the page to search engines. This is one of the most basic search engine optimization techniques.
Google	Company behind the search engine giant Google.com. Founded in 1998, Google now controls approximately 80% of the search market. Google has also expanded to include many software services, both directly related to search, and targeted towards consumers outside of the search marketing industry like Google Chrome (a web browser), Google Fiber (internet service), Gmail (email client), and Google Drive (a file storing platform). Google is owned by parent company Alphabet.
Google AdWords	Google's online advertising service. This system allows advertisers to reach customers through their search and display networks. AdWords offers several cost models which vary by bidding strategy and company goals. Advertisers can bid on keywords which allows their ads to show in Google search results and on Google's network of partner websites.
Google Algorithm	A mathematical programmatic system that determines where websites will appear on Google search result pages for any given number of queries. Sometimes also called the "Core" algorithm, though this is a less specific term. Google's algorithm is constantly updated (approximately 500-600 times a year, or two times per day), which can have varying levels of impact on the rankings of websites across the world. Google's actual algorithm is kept deliberately secret to prevent webmasters from manipulating the system for rankings, though Google does publicly state their suggested "best practices" for appearing higher in search results.
Google Analytics	A Google platform that allows webmasters to collect statistics and data about website visitors. Sometimes abbreviated "GA," Google Analytics allows webmasters to see where web traffic comes from and how visitors behave once on the site.
Google Maps	The location and navigation service provided by Google. Using maps.google.com, users can search for stores, restaurants, businesses, and landmarks anywhere in the world. Typically, users will find routes to nearby establishments including local businesses using Maps.
Google My Business	A free tool for businesses and organizations to manage their online presence across Google, including Search and Maps. By verifying and editing business information, the owner can help customers find their business or any relevant information about it. Most brands own this listing, but hotels can manage/submit updates.
Google Partner Agency	An agency that is certified by Google for meeting certain requirements.
Google Reviews	Reviews left using the Google My Business platform. Reviews are on a 1-5-star scale, and include a brief message written by the reviewer. Reviews can show up in the knowledge graph in Google searches, and have been shown to positively correlate with SEO rankings. (See also Google My Business)
Google Search Console	Previously Google Webmaster Tools. A no-charge web service by Google for webmasters. It allows webmasters to check indexing status and optimize visibility of their websites.
Hashtag	A phrase beginning with the symbol "#" used in social media as a way for tagging content for users to find. Adding hashtags to a post allows users to find that post when searching for that topic. This can be used for finding users looking for broad topics on social media, as well as niche, detailed topics.
Header	Can refer to either the top portion of a webpage that typically contains the logo and menu, or the section of HTML in a website's code that contains important information about the site.
Header Tag	See Tag, Header
HTML	Hypertext Markup Language. A set of codes that are used to tell a web browser how to display a webpage. Each individual code is called an element, or a tag. HTML has a starting and ending element for most markups. Hyper means it is not linear, so it is possible to go to any place on the internet and there is no set order.
HTTP	Hypertext Transfer Protocol. The protocol used by the world wide web to define how data is formatted and transmitted, and what actions web browsers and web servers should take to respond to a command. When you enter a website into your web browser and press enter, this sends an HTTP command to a web server, which tells the server to fetch and send the data for that website to your browser.
HTTPS	Hypertext Transfer Protocol Secure. A secured version of HTTP, which is used to define how data is formatted and transmitted across the web. HTTPS has an advantage over HTTP in that the data sent when fetching a webpage is encrypted, adding a layer of security so that third parties can't gather data about the webpage when the data is sent from the server to the browser.
Hyperlink	An HTML code that creates a link from one webpage to another web page, characterized often by a highlighted word or image that takes you to the destined location when you click on that highlighted item.

Impression	Share Used in pay-per-click advertising, this metric refers to the percentage of times viewers have seen an advertiser's ad, in relation to the total possible amounts that ad could have been seen. If an ad campaign's impression share is 70%, then the ads showed 7 out of 10 possible times.
Inbound Marketing	The activities and strategies used for attracting potential users or customers to a website. "Inbound" is a more recent euphemism for what has traditionally been called "SEO." Inbound marketing is crucial to having a good web presence, as it's used as a way to attract prospective customers by educating and building trust about your services, product, and/or brand. See also "Organic."
Index	When used as a noun, index refers to all the web pages that Google has crawled and stored to be shown to Google searchers (e.g., "The Google index has billions of websites"). When used as a verb, it refers to the act of Google copying a web page into their system (e.g., "Google indexed my website today, so it will start appearing in their search results").
Keyword	A word or phrase that describes the contents of a web page. Keywords help search engines match a page with an appropriate search query.
Keyword Density	The percentage of how often a keyword appears on a webpage in relation to the total words on that webpage.
Keyword Phrase	A group of two or more words that are used to find information in a search engine. Sometimes, when searching for something, one single keyword does not provide the information you seek, where a keyword phrase allows you to string multiple words together to find better information.
Keyword Priority	An overall score that combines keyword metrics to create a single, sortable number you can use to effectively prioritize keywords.
Keyword Stuffing	When a web page uses a keyword too often or superfluously, with the intent of manipulating search engines. This type of behavior is frowned upon and can lead to either algorithmic devaluation in search, or a manual penalty from Google.
Knowledge Graph/Panel	A system that Google launched to understand facts about people, places, and things, and how these entities are all connected. A knowledge graph displays on the SERP and is intended to provide answers, not just links, to search queries so that users do not have to navigate to other sites to gather the information.
Landing Page	The destination webpage a user lands on after clicking on a link (either in an ad or anywhere else). Some landing pages are designed with the purpose of lead generation, and others with the purpose of directing the flow of traffic throughout a site.
Latent Semantic Indexing (LSI) Keywords	Keywords that are semantically related to your primary keyword. They are not limited to synonyms or words with similar meanings. Google rewards websites which include relevant LSI keywords with higher rankings and more traffic.
Link Profile	The cumulative grouping of all links pointing to a particular website. A link profile can be used to determine a website's power, trust, subject matter, and content. Link profiles are important for determining where a website ranks in Google search results. If a website has a high number of links from websites that are not trusted, adult in nature, spammy, or against guidelines, the link profile will have a negative effect on rankings. If a website has a high number of links from websites that are strong providers of content or reputable sources of information it will have a positive effect on rankings.
LinkedIn	A social networking website oriented around connecting professionals to jobs, businesses, and other professionals in their industry. LinkedIn is also a strong platform for marketing, job posting, and sharing professional content.
Local 3-Pack	The top three results Google determines most geographically relevant to a local search. These three results will show at the top of the SERP in a special list accompanied by a map. The map pack shows up for queries with local intent, a general business type, or a "near me" search.
Local Citation	Anywhere online that a business is mentioned by name. Business directories like Moz, Foursquare, or Yelp are made of local citations. Being listed correctly on these sites is an important ranking factor for local search. They provide search engines with credible information about your business so the search engine understands the business exists, is legitimate, and that what you say about your business is true and accurate.
Local Search	A search to find something within a specific geographic area, such as "downtown hotel DC." Local search results can appear in many different places on a SERP but are typically accompanied by map pins. These results show the address and phone number of the company with a link to directions, if appropriate. Sometimes these listings are grouped into a "local pack."
Long Tail Keyword	A keyword phrase that is longer in length and hyper-specifically matches a user search query. A long tail keyword gets fewer searches per month but has a higher search intent, and typically less competition by companies looking to serve up content to that search query. For example, a regular keyword might be "Austin web designer" but a long tail keyword would be "affordable Austin web designer that makes WordPress sites."
Lookalike Audience	A targeting option offered by Facebook's ad service. This audience is created from a source audience (e.g., fans of your Facebook page, an email list), and from this list Facebook will identify common characteristics between audience members. Facebook will then target users that exhibit similar interests or qualities.

Meta Description	One of the meta tags that gives a description of the page in 160 characters. The meta description is an important aspect of a webpage because it is what appears in Google searches and other search engine results.
Meta Keywords	A specific meta tag that displays the specific keywords addresses in a page. After meta keyword markup was abused on some websites, listed keywords no longer apply to how a page is categorized by Google and other search engines.
Meta Tag	See Tag, Meta
Metasearch Engine (or Aggregator)	A search tool that uses another search engine's data to produce its own results from the internet. A typical metasearch engine pulls off the results from several search engines, say Google and Bing, and then applies its own algorithms in most cases to re-order the results. A hotel metasearch compiles the room rates from numerous booking websites and OTAs onto a singular platform. This focuses the shoppers/users onto one site, reducing the need to browse multiple sites. Examples: Trivago and Kayak.
Moz	Local Software that creates and maintains business listings on the sites, mobile apps, and directories that factor into local search engine results. Moz Local makes it easy to push business listings to the major data aggregators, plus other important sites and apps. Like YEXT.
NLP	Natural Language Processing. Allows computers to "understand" the contents of documents, including the contextual nuances of the language within them. The technology can then accurately extract information and insights contained in the documents as well as categorize and organize the documents themselves.[187]
Open Graph Tag	See Tag, Open Graph
Organic	A source of traffic to a website that comes through clicking on a non-paid search engine result. Organic traffic is a main measurement of an SEO campaign and grows as a site ranks better for keywords, or ranks for more keywords in search engines.
OTA	Online Travel Agency. Allows users to book hotel rooms, flights, train tickets, etc. These sites may be focused on travel reviews, trip fares, or both. Examples include Expedia and Booking.com.
PDF	A digital document format that provides a digital image of text or graphics. PDF's are the preferred document type when uploading documents to the internet because of the ease of use and the ability to import or convert them easily. PDFs can be read and indexed by Google just as a normal web page can.
Personalized Search Results	Results a user sees in a search engine that aren't just based on the traditional ranking factors, but also on the information that the search engine has about the user at the given time, such as their location, search history, demographics, or interests.
Pixel	A pixel is a tag or a block of code placed within your site's code that allows you to collect data about user behavior and is stored in a server. For example, a Facebook pixel can be put on pages of your website, and when the "pixel fires," it tells Facebook to show ads of a product the person saw on your website.
Position	The placement in Google search results that a site is in for a specific query.
PPC	Pay-Per-Click. An online advertising model in which advertisers are charged for their ad once it is clicked. The PPC model is commonly associated with search engine and social media advertising like Google AdWords and Facebook Ads. Advertisers bid for ad placement in a search engine's sponsored links when a user searches a keyword related to the business offering.
Quality Score	Google AdWords' rating of the relevance and quality of keywords used in PPC campaigns. These scores are largely determined by relevance of ad copy, expected click through rate, and the landing page quality and relevance. Quality score is a component in determining ad auctions, so having a high score can lead to higher ad rankings at lower costs.
Query	The term given for what a user types and searches using search engines like Google, Bing, and Yahoo. Examples of queries include "Austin electrician," "how do I know if I have a raccoon in my attic," "distance to nearest coffee shop," and many more.
Rankings	A general term for where a website appears in search engine results. A site's "ranking" may increase or decrease over time for different search terms, or queries. Ranking is specific to each keyword, so a website may have keywords that rank on the first page, and others that don't. Google ranking is made up of 200+ components or ranking factors to determine where a website ranks.
Readability	Readability is the ease with which a reader can understand the written text.
Reciprocal Link	Two websites linking to each other, typically for the express purpose of increasing both search engine rankings. These types of links are sometimes deemed manipulative by search engines, which can incur a penalty or devaluation against both sites.

Redirect	A way by which a web browser takes a user from one page to another without the user clicking or making any input. There are various types of redirects (the most common of which is the 301 redirect), which serve different purposes. Typically, this helps improve user experience across a website.
Referral	A medium denoted in Google Analytics that represents a website visit that came from another website (as opposed to coming from a Google search, for example). When users click on a link to another, external webpage, they are said to have been "referred" there.
Remarketing	Also known as retargeting, a type of paid ad that allows advertisers to show ads to customers who have already visited their site. Once a user visits a site, a small piece of data called a "cookie" will be stored in the user's browser. When the user then visits other sites, this cookie can allow remarketing ads to be shown. Remarketing allows advertisers to "follow" users around in attempts to get the user back to the original site.
Responsive Web Design	A philosophy of creating a website that allows all the content to show correctly regardless of screen size or device. Your website will "respond" to the size of the screen each user has, shrinking and reorganizing on smaller screens, and expanding to fill appropriately on large ones.
Rich Snippets	Describes structured data markup that operators can add to existing HTML so that search engines can better understand the information that is contained on each web page. Major search engines use this markup to present richer search results, allowing users to more easily find the information they are looking for.
ROAS	Return On Ad Spend. A PPC marketing metric that demonstrates the profit made as compared to the amount of money spent on the ads. Like ROI.
ROI	Return On Investment. For a business to receive a positive ROI, they must earn more money using marketing channels than they are spending on the marketing itself.
RSS	Really Simple Syndication. A way for users to keep track of updates to multiple websites (news sites, blogs, and more) in one place, as opposed to having to manually check in on every single site individually. An RSS Feed is a place where all updates are tracked together, in an easily viewable format.
Schema	Markup Code that is added to the HTML of a website to give search engines more relevant information about a business, person, place, product, or thing. Also known as rich snippets or structured data.
Search Engine	A program that searches an index of information and returns results to the user based on corresponding keywords. The most well-known search engines are Google, YouTube, Bing, and Yahoo.
Search Network	A group of websites in which ads can appear. Google's Search Network, for example, is a group of Google & non-Google websites that partner with Google to show text ads.
SEM	Search Engine Marketing. A nebulous term that can apply to either 1) any digital marketing that involves the use of a search engine, or 2) only paid digital marketing that involves a search engine. There is not an industry standard as to which definition is correct, however the latter is most used.
SEO	Search Engine Optimization. The process of getting traffic from the free, organic, or natural search results on search engines. Primary search results are listed on the search engine results page based on what the search engine considers most relevant to users.
SEO, Off-Page	Includes components like social media, articles, and references on other sites that give you "authority" according to Google and other search engines.
SEO, On-Page	Includes things you can control on your site, like keywords and meta tags.
SERP	Search Engine Results Page. The page that search engines show in response to a query by a searcher. This page will look different depending on the search engine (Google, Yahoo, Bing, etc.), but the main component is the list of websites or blue links that provide answers to the query.
Sessions	A metric in Google Analytics that measures one user interacting with a website during a given period, which Google defaults to 30 minutes. A session is not dependent on how many pages are viewed, so if a person goes to a website and looks around at different pages for 20 minutes, it would count as 1 session.
Sitelink	An ad extension in Google AdWords that appears below the main ad copy which links to a specific page on the website (e.g., Contact Us, About Us, etc.). Ads can have from 2-6 sitelinks.
Sitemap	An XML file or page on a website that lists all the pages and posts for search engines to see. This document helps search engines quickly understand all the content that they should be aware of on a particular website.
Slug	A portion of URL that comes after .com (or .org, .edu, etc.).

Source	A term in Google Analytics that helps webmasters classify where traffic is coming from (i.e., the "source" of the web traffic). Source can be a search engine (for example, Google) or a domain (website-example.com)
Spam	A broad term that includes many different nefarious activities in digital marketing that are done either to help a website rank better or to harm a competitor website. Spam is often seen in the form of hundreds or thousands of low-quality backlinks that were built by a black hat SEO to manipulate rankings.
Spider	See Bot and Crawler.
Structured Data	A system of pairing a name with a value that helps search engines categorize and index your content.
Tag, Alt	Describes what is in an image on a website, and its function on the page. Screen readers for the blind and visually impaired read out this text to make an image accessible. Alt tags and title tags strengthen the message toward search engine spiders to improve the visibility of the site within search engines. The alt and title attributes of an images are commonly referred to as alt tag or alt text and title tag.
Tag, Canonical	A way of telling search engines that a specific URL represents the master copy of a page. Also known as rel canonical.
Tag, Description	A piece of HTML code that provides a short description of a web page and is included in the code, but is not visible on the page itself. If a web page has a description tag, Google shows it if there is semantic similarity between the description tag and the content of the web page, and there is similarity between the user's search query and the content of the description tag. If a page does not have a description tag, Google typically shows sentence fragments on the page that contain the search query.
Tag, Header	Used in HTML for categorizing text headings on a web page. They are the titles and major topics of a web page and help indicate to readers and search engines what the page is about. Header tags use a cascading format where a page should have only one H1 (main title) but beneath can be multiple H2s (subtitles) and every H2 can have H3s beneath (sub-sub titles) and so on.
Tag, Meta	HTML snippet added to a webpage's code that add contextual information for web crawlers and search engines. Search engines use meta data to help decide what information from a webpage to display in their results. Example meta tags include the date the page was published, the page title, author, and image descriptions.
Tag, Open Graph	Snippet of code that cause your selected picture and marketing text to appear when users share content from your site on Facebook, tweet links to your content, or post to Instagram.
Tag, Title	An HTML element that is used to describe the specific topic of a web page. Title tags are displayed in the tabbed top bar of a web browser. In SEO, it is best practice to have descriptive title tags featuring your main keywords, rather than something basic like "home." In addition to the SERP, they also appear in web browsers and social networks.
Thin Content	Any content that doesn't add value to your searchers.
Title Tag	See Tag, Title
Tracking Code	A script, often placed in the header, footer, or thank you page of a website that passes information along to software tools for data gathering purposes. Tools like Google Analytics and Google AdWords utilize tracking codes so that they can track information about users who view a site.
Twitter	A social media platform where users interact, or "tweet," by posting a message or replying to a message in 140 characters or less. Each keystroke on a keyboard is considered a character. Twitter is used to share information and links, and utilizes hashtags to categorize information. Tweets are typically public and can be seen by anyone. If you are followed by another user, that user will see your tweets in their feed. Similarly, you will the see the tweets of anyone you follow in your feed.
Twitter Advertising	Allows marketers to promote a tweet on users feeds without that user having to follow your brand for it to appear on their feed. These advertisements can be used to grow brand awareness, gain more followers, extend social media reach, and/or reach out to prospective customers about a product or service.
UNAP	URL, Name, Address, Phone Number. An important ranking factor for search engine optimization. Consistency in website address, name, address, and phone number citations is an important piece of a local SEO Campaign.
Unique Visitors	A metric used in web analytics to show how many different, unique people view a website over a period of time. Unique visitors are tracked by their IP addresses. If a visitor visits the same website multiple times, they will only be counted once in the unique visitor's metric.
URL	Uniform Resource Locator. The address of a web page. The URL refers to what specific web page a web browser is viewing.
URL (Link) Shortener	A website that will create a short URL or web page address from a long one so that the short version, which is easier to remember and enter, can be used instead.

UX	User Experience. A customer's experience when interacting with a product (e.g., a website). User experience design is the process of enhancing user satisfaction and loyalty by improving the ease of use and pleasure provided in the interaction between the customer and the product. The concept most commonly applies to digital fields today.
Visitors	A metric in Google Analytics that quantifies a user of a website over a particular period of time. Visitors are often broken down between "new visitors" who are browsing for the first time in the allotted time period, or "returning visitors" who have already browsed at least once in the given time frame.
Visits	An old term in Google Analytics which was recently changed to "sessions."
Voice Search	Search queries that are performed by a user speaking into a mobile device, digital assistant, or computer.
Web 2.0	The second major phase of development of the World Wide Web, marked by a shift from static web pages to dynamic content, as well as social media and user-generated content.
Website	A document or group of documents that are accessible on the World Wide Web.
Wireframe	A cursory layout drawing of a webpage that acts as the first step in the design process.
Yahoo! Advertising	Yahoo and Bing ads are both run through the Bing Ads platform. These search engines share advertising networks.
Yahoo! Search	The third largest search engine in the U.S., owned by Yahoo and powered by Bing.
Yelp	A social review platform and search engine that allows users to leave reviews for businesses. Yelp also offers an advertising program which gives advertisers the ability to show their marketing assets to qualified Yelp users based on keyword searches.
Yext	A software tool designed to manage a business's location-related information on multiple directory websites. It uses a process called Power Listings so multiple listings and sites can be managed in one spot. Similar to Moz.
YouTube	A video sharing website bought by Google in 2006. YouTube is part of Google's ad network. YouTube is currently the 2nd most used search engine in the world.
YouTube Advertising	YouTube offers advertising in 6 different formats. Display ads, overlay ads, skippable video, non-skippable video ads, bumper ads, and sponsored cards. These ads can all be created and run through the Google AdWords platform.

ABOUT THE AUTHORS

Dan Wacksman is the founder of Sassato LLC. Sassato helps hotel management companies, ownership groups, hotels/hotel groups, and related technology companies with strategic planning and improving their marketing, distribution, technology, and implementations.

Dan has over 20 years of experience in the hotel and travel industry. Before forming Sassato, he was Senior Vice President of Marketing and Distribution for Outrigger Hotels and Resorts. He oversaw marketing, digital, loyalty/CRM, contact center operations, OTA relationships, and overall distribution strategy. Prior to Outrigger, with GTA (one of the largest travel wholesalers) he was managing director for China and regional director for Asia with responsibility for offices throughout the region. Dan also served as general manager of Aoyou.com, an OTA based in Beijing, and director of strategic development for Travelport where he was involved in acquisitions, integrations, and strategic initiatives.

Dan is the co-creator and instructor of the popular Hotel Digital Marketing Essentials online course and also teaches a digital marketing class at the University of Hawaii. Dan recently completed a two-year appointment as chair of HSMAI's Marketing Advisory Board, and still serves on the board. Dan was recognized by HSMAI as one of the Top 25 Extraordinary Minds in Hospitality Sales, Marketing, and Revenue Optimization.

Holly Zoba is the founder of Scout Simply (https://scoutsimply.com), a training company that helps hotels find more revenue through a combination of sales and marketing technology.

Holly began her career with Hospitality Partners where she spent 10 years as the VP of sales and marketing. She spent several years as the SVP of Hospitality with Signature Worldwide Training where she learned to execute the principles of adult learning and developed training programs for Best Western, Hilton, IHG, Smith Travel Research and Caesar's Entertainment. Prior to launching her own company, Holly became a full stack web application developer (MERN).

She is a past chair of the HSMAI Marketing Advisory Board.

A frequent industry author and speaker, she is also a recipient of the Top 25 Most Extraordinary Minds in Sales and Marketing for her work on advocacy marketing.

ACKNOWLEDGEMENTS

This publication on digital marketing for hotels would not have been possible without the help, insight, and contribution of many in the travel industry who were called upon for their insights, best practices, case studies, and feedback along the way.

HSMAI thanks the following individuals for their contributions, their insights, and their willingness to share their expertise in order to make this publication a more valuable learning tool.

Anil Aggarwal
CEO
Milestone Internet Marketing

Stuart Butler, CHDM
Chief Marketing Officer
Myrtle Beach Convention & Visitors Bureau

Robert Cole
Founder-CEO
RockCheetah

Michael Goldrich, CHDM
Global Head of Digital Marketing
Club Quarters

John Jimenez
VP of E-commerce
Noble Investment Group

Juli Jones, CAE
Vice President
HSMAI

James Jack La Russo
Global Marketing Director
The Travel Corporation (ttc.com)

Kelly McGuire, Ph.D.
Principal
ZS

Delana Meyer, CHDM
Owner
DRM Consulting, LLC

Adele Gutman Milne
Host of the Hospitality Reputation Marketing podcast

Rosalyn Ransaw
Digital Marketing Manager
Red Roof

Dean Schmit
Founder
Base Camp Meta

Katarina Stanisic
Managing Director
BWH Hotel Group

Zack Regner, CHDM, CHBA
Maui Liaison
Hawaii Chapter of HSMAI

Kathleen Tindell
Director of Education & Certification
HSMAI

Russell Tindell
Assistant Editor
HSMAI

All members of HSMAI's Marketing Advisory Board 2020-2021

ENDNOTES

[1] "What Is Digital Marketing?" American Marketing Association, 16 Mar. 2021, www.ama.org/pages/what-is-digital-marketing/.

[2] Barone, Adam. "Digital Marketing." Investopedia, December 30, 2020, https://www.investopedia.com/terms/d/digital-marketing.asp.

[3] Blog, Interactive Schools. "50 Million Users: How Long Does It Take Tech to Reach This Milestone?" Interactive Schools, Interactive Schools, 21 Feb. 2018, blog.interactiveschools.com/blog/50-million-users-how-long-does-it-take-tech-to-reach-this-milestone.

[4] Blog, Interactive Schools. "50 Million Users: How Long Does It Take Tech to Reach This Milestone?" Interactive Schools, Interactive Schools, 21 Feb. 2018, blog.interactiveschools.com/blog/50-million-users-how-long-does-it-take-tech-to-reach-this-milestone.

[5] Garman, Erica. "Earned Media, Owned Media, Paid Media." Titan Growth, 11 May 2021, www.titangrowth.com/what-is-earned-owned-paid-media-the-difference-explained/.

[6] Merkle, Mary. "Digital Marketing Report: Q2 2020." Merkle, https://www.merkleinc.com/thought-leadership/white-papers/digital-marketing-report-q2-2020. June 8, 2021.

[7] "A short history of the Web." CERN, https://home.cern/science/computing/birth-web/short-history-web, June 8, 2021.

[8] "A short history of the Web." CERN, https://home.cern/science/computing/birth-web/short-history-web, June 8, 2021.

[9] "NCSA Mosaic for MS Windows." National Science Foundation, https://www.nsf.gov/od/lpa/news/03/images/mosaic.6beta.jpg, June 8, 2021.

[10] Heisler, Yoni. "In Pictures: A visual history of Netscape Navigator." IDG Communications, https://www.arnnet.com.au/slideshow/557401/pictures-visual-history-netscape-navigator/, June 8, 2021.

[11] Team Position². "'Jerry and David's Guide to the World Wide Web' Shuttered." Position², December 29, 2014, https://www.position2.com/blog/jerry-davids-guide-world-wide-web-shuttered.

[12] from the Internet Archive Wayback Machine, https://web.archive.org/web/19981202230410/http://www.google.com/, June 8, 2021.

[13] Nielsen, Jakob. "Nielsen's Law of Internet Bandwidth." Nielsen Norman Group, Apr. 4, 1998; Updated Sep. 27, 2019, https://www.nngroup.com/articles/law-of-bandwidth/.

[14] "Desktop vs Mobile vs Tablet Market Share Worldwide." StatCounter GlobalStats, https://gs.statcounter.com/platform-market-share/desktop-mobile-tablet/worldwide/#monthly-200901-202010, June 8, 2021.

[15] From Our World in Data, https://ourworldindata.org/grapher/daily-hours-spent-with-digital-media-per-adult-user, June 8, 2021.

[16] Sterling, Greg. "Survey: 118 million smart speakers in US, but expectation is low for future demand." MARTECH, January 8, 2019, https://martech.org/survey-reports-118-million-smart-speakers-in-u-s-but-the-expectation-of-future-demand-is-way-down/.

[17] Petrock, Victoria. "Voice Assistant and Smart Speaker Users 2020." Insider Intelligence, November 16, 2020, https://www.emarketer.com/content/voice-assistant-and-smart-speaker-users-2020.

[19] eMarketer, October 2020

[20] Fox, Linda. "Marriott and Expedia's battle over commissions could trigger industry-wide overhaul." Phocuswire, January 8, 2019, https://www.phocuswire.com/marriott-expedia-commission-negotiations, June 19, 2021.

[21] HOME2 SUITES BY HILTON Fact Sheet. 2020, https://newsroom.hilton.com/assets/HM2S/docs/Fact_Sheet/Home2_fact-sheet.pdf.

[22] For a comprehensive look at customer segmentation, see chapter 6 of HSMAI's publication Evolving Dynamics: From Revenue Management to Revenue Strategy | https://americas.hsmai.org/certification/publications-study-guides/#ED

[23] Vaghina, Veronika. "Marketing Funnel [All in One Guide For Beginners + Examples]." XCart, July 1, 2019, Updated July 8, 2019, https://www.x-cart.com/blog/marketing-funnels.html.

[24] Rennie, Alistair, Jonny Protheroe, Claire Charron, and Gerald Breatnach. "Decoding Decisions: Making sense of the messy middle." Think with Google, July 2020, https://www.thinkwithgoogle.com/consumer-insights/consumer-journey/navigating-purchase-behavior-and-decision-making/, June 8, 2021.

[25] "Travel Trends: 4 Mobile Moments Changing the Consumer Journey." Think with Google, November 2015, www.thinkwithgoogle.com/consumer-insights/travel-trends-4-mobile-moments-changing-consumer-journey/.

[26] Rennie, Alistair, Jonny Protheroe, Claire Charron, and Gerald Breatnach. "Decoding Decisions: Making sense of the messy middle." Think with Google, July 2020, https://www.thinkwithgoogle.com/consumer-insights/consumer-journey/navigating-purchase-behavior-and-decision-making/, June 8, 2021.

[27] Textor, C. "Number of outbound tourists departing from China from 2010 to 2019 (in millions)." Statista, June 2020, https://www.statista.com/statistics/1068495/china-number-of-outbound-tourist-number/.

[28] "Huānyíng to the new Chinese traveller." McKinsey & Company, November 2018, https://www.mckinsey.com/industries/travel-transport-and-logistics/our-insights/huanying-to-the-new-chinese-traveler

[29] "Ask the hotel experts: 'Attracting Chinese tourists is no longer one-size-fits-all'." SiteMinder, May 10, 2019, https://www.siteminder.com/r/marketing/hotel-digital-marketing/attract-chinese-tourists-hotel/.

[30] Whiddington, Richard. "Understand The 2020 Chinese OTA Landscape In 5 Graphs." Jing Culture & Commerce, March 5, 2021, https://jingculturecommerce.com/fastdata-ota-report-2020/. June 25, 2021.

[31] "What Travelers Want in 2021." Expedia Group, May18, 2021, https://advertising.expedia.com/blog/research/expedia-group-research-what-travelers-want-2021/. June 23, 2021.

[32] Patel, Neil. "How Loading Time Affects Your Bottom Line." NeilPatel.com, https://neilpatel.com/blog/loading-time/, June 8, 2021.

[33] This section was adapted with permission from Max Starkov from an original article by Max Starkov and Denis Strekalov titled "Hyper-Interactive Consumers," originally published in HOTELS magazine.

[34] DePalma, Donald A. and Paul Daniel O'Mara. "Can't Read, Won't Buy – B2C." CSA Research, June 30, 2020, https://insights.csa-research.com/reportaction/305013126/Marketing.

[35] Ramaswamy, Sridhar. "How Micro-Moments Are Changing the Rules." Think with Google, April 2015, https://www.thinkwithgoogle.com/marketing-strategies/app-and-mobile/how-micromoments-are-changing-rules/.

[36] "Digital Travel Sales, By Device." eMarketer, May 2021, https://forecasts-na1.emarketer.com/584b26021403070290f93a2b/5851918a0626310a2c1869dd, June 8, 2021.

[37] Clement, J. "Share of global mobile website traffic 2015-2021." Statista, April 28, 2021, https://www.statista.com/statistics/277125/share-of-website-traffic-coming-from-mobile-devices/.

[38] Chaffey, Dave. "Mobile marketing statistics compilation 2021." Smart Insights, March 3, 2021, https://www.smartinsights.com/mobile-marketing/mobile-marketing-analytics/mobile-marketing-statistics/.

[39] "2020 Global Smartphone Users." Newzoo 2020, Global Mobile Market Report, May 2020, https://www.smartinsights.com/mobile-marketing/mobile-marketing-analytics/mobile-marketing-statistics/. July 1, 2021.

[40] "Optimize your website for mobile." Google Ads Help, https://support.google.com/google-ads/answer/7323900?hl=en, June 14, 2021.

[41] "Google advice: Switch your m-dot domain to responsive before the mobile-first index rollout." Search Engine Land. June 20, 2017. https://searchengineland.com/google-advice-switch-m-dot-domain-responsive-mobile-first-index-rollout-277446. January 10, 2018.

[42] "M.dot vs. Responsive vs. Progressive: What's the Right Solution for Your Company?" Mobify. May 7, 2015. https://www.mobify.com/insights/m-dot-responsive-progressive-whats-the-right-solution/. January 10, 2018.

[43] "Choose a mobile configuration." Google Search Central, https://developers.google.com/search/mobile-sites/mobile-seo. July 1, 2021.

[44] "Techie Traveler." Lab42 Blog. March 23, 2012. http://blog.lab42.com/techie-traveler. November 18, 2013.

[45] Deloitte Digital, 55 The Data Company. "Milliseconds make Millions: A study on how improvements in mobile site speed positively affect a brand's bottom line" 2019.

[46] "Social Media, Mobile and Travel: Like, Tweet, and Share Your Across the Globe." WebFX Blog. http://www.webfx.com/blog/social-media-mobile-travel/. May 28, 2019.

[47] Petrov, Christo. "57 Mobile vs. Desktop Usage Statistics For 2021 [Mobile's Overtaking!]." TechJury, March 29, 2021, https://techjury.net/blog/mobile-vs-desktop-usage/#gref, June 17, 2021.

[48] Dolliver, Mark. "Deal-Seekers 2020 Economizing in Ways Old and New." eMarketer, April 15, 2020, https://content-na1.emarketer.com/deal-seekers-2020, November 15, 2020.

[49] Parrish, Melissa. "Mobile for Marketing: Is It a Channel or a Device?" Forrester Blogs. March 4, 2011.

[50] Atmosphere Research Group US Online Leisure Travel Benchmark Survey, October 2011.

[51] "Traveler's Road to Decision 2011." Think with Google, October 24, 2012, http://www.thinkwithgoogle.com/insights/library/studies/travelers-road-to-decision-2011/.

[52] "The 2014 Traveler's Road to Decision." Google, November 22, 2017, http://storage.googleapis.com/think/docs/2014-travelers-road-to-decision_research_studies.pdf; and McGuire, Caroline. "Google reveals the top 10 travel searches of 2016 in the US." The Daily Mail, November 22, 2017, http://www.dailymail.co.uk/travel/travel_news/article-4047968/Was-listening-geography-class-Google-reveals-10-travel-searches-2016-Grand-Canyon-them.html.

[53] "How Micro-Moments Are Reshaping the Travel Customer Journey." Think with Google. https://www.thinkwithgoogle.com/marketing-resources/micro-moments/micro-moments-travel-customer-journey/. November 19, 2017.

[54] Gevelber, Lisa and Oliver Heckmann. "Travel Trends: 4 Mobile Moments Changing the Consumer Journey." Think with Google. November 2015. https://www.thinkwithgoogle.com/consumer-insights/travel-trends-4-mobile-moments-changing-consumer-journey/. January 10, 2018.

[55] Gevelber, Lisa and Oliver Heckmann. "Travel trends: 4 mobile moments changing the consumer journey." Think with Google, November 2015, https://www.thinkwithgoogle.com/consumer-insights/consumer-trends/travel-trends-4-mobile-moments-changing-consumer-journey/.

[56] "How Quality Online Content Impacts Your Hotel's Performance: Webinar Highlights." trivago Hotel Manager Blog. April 27, 2017. http://hotelmanager-blog.trivago.com/en-us/trivago-online-content-webinar-recap-2017/. January 10, 2018.

[57] "How Mobile Influences Travel Decision Making in Can't-Wait-to-Explore Moments." Think with Google. July 2016. https://www.thinkwithgoogle.com/consumer-insights/mobile-influence-travel-decision-making-explore-moments/. January 10, 2018.

[58] Feldkamp, Jeanne. "Travel UGC: A Goldmine Hiding in Plain Sight." Stackla.com. https://stackla.com/blog/travel-ugca-goldmine-hiding-in-plain-sight/. January 10, 2018.

[59] Knapton, Sarah. "Facebook users have 155 friends - but would trust just four in a crisis." The Telegraph. January 20, 2016. http://www.telegraph.co.uk/news/science/science-news/12108412/Facebook-users-have-155-friends-butwould-trust-just-four-in-a-crisis.html. January 10, 2018.

[60] Anderson, Chris. "In the millennial, social-media-centric age, Instagrammable hotels stand out." Hotel Management. September 19, 2017. https://www.hotelmanagement.net/sales-marketing/millennial-age-instagrammable-hotels-stand-out. January 10, 2018.

[61] Adapted from "2017 Content Marketing Framework: 5 Building Blocks for Profitable, Scalable Operations." Content Marketing Institute. http://contentmarketinginstitute.com/2016/10/content-marketing-framework-profitable/. November 11, 2017.

[62] "How to Overcome Content Marketing Struggles." eMarketer. March 23, 2015. https://www.emarketer.com/Article/How-Overcome-Content-Marketing-Struggles/1012255. January 10, 2018.

[63] "You Are Your Content: State of Content 2017." Accenture Interactive. https://www.accenture.com/us-en/_acnmedia/PDF-44/Accenture-You-Are-Your-Content-Survey-Screen.pdf?la=en#zoom=50. January 10, 2018.

[64] "The 4C Content Production Framework." Tim Peter & Associates. January 31, 2017.

[65] Schaefer, Mark W. The Content Code (Louisville, TN: Mark W. Schaefer, 2015).

[66] Rose, Robert Rose. "The 2017 Content Marketing Framework." Content Marketing Institute. October 7, 2016. http://contentmarketinginstitute.com/2016/10/content-marketing-framework-profitable/. January 10, 2018.

67 Stemler, Sam. "28 Video Marketing Statistics You Need to Know in 2020." Boast, November 14, 2019, https://boast.io/28-video-marketing-statistics-you-need-to-know-in-2020/.

68 Chaffey, Dave. "Video marketing statistics to know for 2020." Smart Insights, February 11, 2020, https://www.smartinsights.com/digital-marketing-platforms/video-marketing/video-marketing-statistics-to-know/.

69 "The Top 16 Video Marketing Stats for 2016."Adelie Studio. http://www.adeliestudios.com/top-16-video-marketing-statistics-2016/. January 7, 2018.

70 A portion of this section was adapted with permission from Paolo Boni from an original article by Paolo Boni titled "Want to Attract More Online Travel Shoppers? Tell Your Hotel's Story with Video," originally published on HotelExecutive.com

71 "Infographic: Social and Mobile Make Summer Travel a Breeze." Column Five Media for Rasmussen College, October 24, 2012, http://www.rasmussen.edu/student-life/blogs/main/socialand-mobile-make-summer-travel-a-breeze/.

72 Reused with permission. "6 Creative Ways to Use Your Existing Hotel Media." Leonardo. October 24, 2012. http://blog.leonardo.com/6-creative-way-to-use-your-existing-hotel-media/

73 "Video Best Practices Guide for Marketers." Marketing Profs and Thomson Reuters Multimedia Solutions, January 15, 2012, http://thomsonreuters.com/content/news_ideas/white_papers/financial/video_best_practices_guide_for_marketers.

74 Used by permission from Leonardo.

75 Hardwick, Joshua. "How Do Search Engines Work and Why Should You Care?" ahrefsblog, April 27, 2021, https://ahrefs.com/blog/how-do-search-engines-work/.

76 "Search Engine Market Share Worldwide." StatCounter GlobalStats, https://gs.statcounter.com/search-engine-market-share, June 8, 2021.

77 For a history of all of Google's updates see https://moz.com/google-algorithm-change or https://www.searchenginejournal.com/google-algorithm-history/.

78 "Alt Text." Moz, https://moz.com/learn/seo/alt-text, June 9, 2021.

79 "Google search results: the evolution of the SERPs." Digital Guide, Ionos by 1&1, https://www.ionos.com/digitalguide/online-marketing/search-engine-marketing/the-evolution-of-google-search-results-1998-to/, June 9, 2021.

80 "Canonicalization." Moz, https://moz.com/learn/seo/canonicalization, June 9, 2021.

81 "Canonicalization." Moz, https://moz.com/learn/seo/canonicalization, June 9, 2021.

82 Singhal, Amit. "Introducing the Knowledge Graph: things, not strings." The Keyword, Google, May 16, 2012, https://blog.google/products/search/introducing-knowledge-graph-things-not/.

83 Shewan, Dan. "How Google Hummingbird Changed the Future of Search." The WordStream Blog, December 27, 2017, https://www.wordstream.com/blog/ws/2014/06/23/google-hummingbird.

84 "Google RankBrain." Moz, https://moz.com/learn/seo/google-rankbrain, June 9, 2021.

85 "Search Quality Rating Guidelines." Google, October 2020, https://static.googleusercontent.com/media/guidelines.raterhub.com/en//searchqualityevaluatorguidelines.pdf, June 9, 2021.

86 "Evaluating page experience for a better web." Google Search Central Blog, Google, May 28, 2020, https://developers.google.com/search/blog/2020/05/evaluating-page-experience.

87 Walton, Philip. "Web Vitals." web.dev, April 30, 2020, Updated July 21, 2020, https://web.dev/vitals/#core-web-vitals.

88 Fishkin, Rand. "In 2020, Two Thirds of Google Searches Ended Without a Click." SparkToro, March 22, 2021, https://sparktoro.com/blog/in-2020-two-thirds-of-google-searches-ended-without-a-click/.

89 Law, Thomas J. "Google SERPs: Features and How to Improve Your Ranking in 2021." Oberlo, November 22, 2020, https://www.oberlo.com/blog/serp-google-search-engine-results.

90 Soulo, Tim. "Ahrefs' Study Of 2 Million Featured Snippets: 10 Important Takeaways." ahrefsblog, May 29, 2017, https://ahrefs.com/blog/featured-snippets-study/, June 17, 2021.

91 Answer the Public, https://answerthepublic.com/.

92 Enge, Eric. "Mobile Voice Usage Trends in 2020." Perficient, June 30, 2020, https://www.perficient.com/insights/research-hub/voice-usage-trends.

93 Petrock, Victoria. "US Voice Assistant Users 2019." eMarketer, July 15, 2019, https://www.emarketer.com/content/us-voice-assistant-users-2019, June 14, 2021.

94 Petrock, Victoria. "Voice Assistant and Smart Speaker Users 2020." eMarketer, November 16, 2020, https://www.emarketer.com/content/voice-assistant-and-smart-speaker-users-2020.

95 Sterling, Greg. "Study: 48% of consumers use voice assistants for general web search." Search Engine Land, July 23, 2019, https://searchengineland.com/study-48-of-consumers-use-voice-assistants-for-general-web-search-319729.

96 "Introduction to Structured Data." Google Search. https://developers.google.com/search/docs/guides/intro-structured-data. January 25, 2018.

97 "Introduction to Structured Data." Google Search. https://developers.google.com/search/docs/guides/intro-structured-data. January 25, 2018.

98 Aufreiter, Nora, Julien Boudet, and Vivian Weng. "Why marketers should keep sending you e-mails." McKinsey & Company, January 1, 2014, https://www.mckinsey.com/business-functions/marketing-and-sales/our-insights/why-marketers-should-keep-sending-you-emails.

99 "Cendyn/ONE's CRM, Loyalty, and Data-Driven Marketing Platform Powers AMResorts' Guest Communications." Hotel Online, December 1, 2015, https://www.hotel-online.com/press_releases/release/cendyn-ones-crm-loyalty-and-data-driven-marketing-platform-powers-amresorts/.

100 "What Travelers Want in 2021." Expedia Group, May18, 2021, https://advertising.expedia.com/blog/research/expedia-group-research-what-travelers-want-2021/. June 23, 2021.

[101] Seavers, Dan. "What is Advertising Value Equivalency?" Talkwalker, November 7, 2018, https://www.talkwalker.com/blog/advertising-value-equivalency.

[102] Seavers, Dan. "Advertising value equivalency: Do AVEs ad value to your PR measuring?" Talkwalker, November 7, 2018, https://www.talkwalker.com/blog/advertising-value-equivalency.

[103] Bredava, Anna. "Share of Voice: What It Is, Why It Matters & How to Measure It." Search Engine Journal, April 20, 2020, https://www.searchenginejournal.com/share-of-voice/359752/#close.

[104] "TripBarometer 2017/18 Global Report." Tripadvisor, January 2019, https://mk0tainsightsjao4bom.kinstacdn.com/wp-content/uploads/2018/10/TripBarometer-2017-2018.pdf, June 11, 2021.

[105] "The Hotel Review Sites You Should Monitor." ReviewTrackers, Augst 19, 2020, https://www.reviewtrackers.com/blog/hotel-review-sites/.

[106] Proserpio, Davide and Giorgos Zervas. "Study: Replying to Customer Reviews Results in Better Ratings." Harvard Business Review, February 14, 2018, https://hbr.org/2018/02/study-replying-to-customer-reviews-results-in-better-ratings, June 19, 2021.

[107] von Adams, Karin. "Global Social Network Users 2020." Insider Intelligence, December 8, 2020, https://www.emarketer.com/content/global-social-network-users-2020, June 11, 2021.

[108] Kemp, Simon. "Digital 2021: Global Overview Report." We Are Social, and Hootsuite, https://wearesocial.com/digital-2021, June 11, 2021.

[109] Kemp, Simon. "Digital 2021: Global Overview Report." We Are Social, and Hootsuite, https://wearesocial.com/digital-2021, June 11, 2021.

[110] "Social Networks: Average Time Spent by US Adult Social Network Users, 2015-2022." eMarketer, May 2020, https://www.emarketer.com/chart/236260/social-networks-average-time-spent-by-us-adult-social-network-users-2015-2022-minutes-per-day-nov-2019-vs-april-2020, June 14, 2021.

[111] Kemp, Simon. "Digital 2021: Global Overview Report." We Are Social, and Hootsuite, https://wearesocial.com/digital-2021, slide 93, June 11, 2021.

[112] "Social listening: Your launchpad to success on social media." SproutSocial, https://sproutsocial.com/social-listening/, June 11, 2021.

[113] "A History of Social Media Algorithms." dcustom, 2019, http://dcustom.com/wp-content/uploads/2019/02/History-of-Social-Media-Algorithms_2019_v1.pdf, June 11, 2021.

[114] Koumchatzky, Nicolas and Anton Andryeyev. "Using Deep Learning at Scale in Twitter's Timelines." Twitter blog, May 9, 2017, https://blog.twitter.com/engineering/en_us/topics/insights/2017/using-deep-learning-at-scale-in-twitters-timelines, June 11, 2021.

[115] "A History of Social Media Algorithms." dcustom, 2019, http://dcustom.com/wp-content/uploads/2019/02/History-of-Social-Media-Algorithms_2019_v1.pdf, June 11, 2021.

[116] "A History of Social Media Algorithms." dcustom, 2019, http://dcustom.com/wp-content/uploads/2019/02/History-of-Social-Media-Algorithms_2019_v1.pdf, June 11, 2021.

[117] Iqbal, Mansoor. "Facebook Revenue and Usage Statistics (2021)." Business of Apps, May 24, 2021, https://www.businessofapps.com/data/facebook-statistics/, June 11, 2021.

[118] Smith, Keran. "25 Facebook Advertising Statistics That Will Blow Your Mind."Lyfe Marketing, August 7, 2019, https://www.lyfemarketing.com/blog/facebook-advertising-statistics/, June 11, 2021.

[119] YouTube, https://www.youtube.com/intl/en-GB/about/press/, June 14, 2021.

[120] YouTube, https://www.youtube.com/intl/en-GB/about/press/, June 14, 2021.

[121] Stout, Dustin W. "Social Media Statistics 2021: Top Networks By the Numbers." Dustin Stout, https://dustinstout.com/social-media-statistics, June 11, 2021.

[122] Stout, Dustin W. "Social Media Statistics 2021: Top Networks By the Numbers." Dustin Stout, https://dustinstout.com/social-media-statistics, June 11, 2021.

[123] LinkedIn, https://news.linkedin.com/about-us#Statistics, June 11, 2021.

[124] Stout, Dustin W. "Social Media Statistics 2021: Top Networks By the Numbers." Dustin Stout, https://dustinstout.com/social-media-statistics, June 11, 2021.

[125] "Hotel Snapchat Marketing – 13 Proven Tactics." Millionmetrics, August 21, 2017, https://www.millionmetrics.com/hotel-snapchat-marketing/, June 11, 2021.

[126] Stout, Dustin W. "Social Media Statistics 2021: Top Networks By the Numbers." Dustin Stout, https://dustinstout.com/social-media-statistics, June 11, 2021.

[127] Zenn, Jacqueline. "9 Ways to Measure Your Brand's Social Media Health." Mashable. June 11, 2012. http://mashable.com/2012/06/11/social-media-brand-data/#qL895kx0TqqJ. January 10, 2018.

[128] *Influencer Marketing Benchmark Report.* Influencer Marketing Hub and Upfluence, 29 Mar. 2021, influencermarketinghub.com/influencer_marketing_benchmark_report_2021.pdf.

[129] "Time Spent on Mobile Apps Surpasses Television Viewing." Bloomberg.com, Bloomberg, 11 Sept. 2015, www.bloomberg.com/news/videos/2015-09-11/time-spent-on-mobile-apps-surpasses-television-viewing.

[130] Guttmann, A. "U.S. Ad Blocking Cost 2020." Statista, 6 Feb. 2018, www.statista.com/statistics/454473/ad-blocking-cost-usa/.

[131] Ewing, Mike. "71% More Likely to Purchase Based on Social Media Referrals [Infographic]." HubSpot Blog, 29 Mar. 2021, blog.hubspot.com/blog/tabid/6307/bid/30239/71-More-Likely-to-Purchase-Based-on-Social-Media-Referrals-Infographic.aspx?__hstc=212364107.2c6053498c9622a05396af056ad0720c.1615646842502.1615646842502.1615646842502.1&__hssc=212364107.2.1615646842503&__hsfp=120531889.

[132] "Disclosures 101 for Social Media Influencers." Federal Trade Commission, Nov. 2019, www.ftc.gov/system/files/documents/plain-language/1001a-influencer-guide-508_1.pdf.

[133] "Disclosures 101 for Social Media Influencers." Federal Trade Commission, Nov. 2019, www.ftc.gov/system/files/documents/plain-language/1001a-influencer-guide-508_1.pdf.

134 "Influencer Marketing Benchmark Report." Influencer Marketing Hub and Upfluence, 29 Mar. 2021, influencermarketinghub.com/influencer_marketing_benchmark_report_2021.pdf.

135 "Influencer Marketing Benchmark Report." Influencer Marketing Hub and Upfluence, 29 Mar. 2021, influencermarketinghub.com/influencer_marketing_benchmark_report_2021.pdf.

136 "Influencer Marketing Benchmark Report." Influencer Marketing Hub and Upfluence, 29 Mar. 2021, influencermarketinghub.com/influencer_marketing_benchmark_report_2021.pdf.

137 Day, Charli. "Are You Absolutely Sure Your Social Media Marketing Budget Is Ready for This Year?" Agorapulse, 9 Jan. 2020, www.agorapulse.com/blog/social-media-marketing-budget-plans/.

138 "The Crane Resort Taps into the Power of Guest Storytelling to Boost Their Bottom Line with Flip.to." Flip.to, www.flip.to/news/the-crane-resort-taps-into-the-power-of-guest-storytelling-to-boost-their-bottom-line-with-flip-to.

139 "Premier Inn Pillows Go Viral." Premier Inn, www.premierinn.com/gb/en/news/2021/premier-inn-pillows-go-viral.html, June 14, 2021.

140 Agrawal, Swadhin. "51+ SEO Statistics For 2021: Facts, Trends & SEO By The Numbers." DigitalGYD, May 29, 2021, https://www.digitalgyd.com/seo-statistics/, June 217, 2021.

141 "Search Engine Market Share Worldwide." StatCounter GlobalStats, https://gs.statcounter.com/search-engine-market-share, June 8, 2021.

142 "Data Usage & Control Primer: best practices & definitions." Interactive Advertising Bureau, November 15, 2013, http://iab.net/data_primer.

143 Programmatic Advertising & Media Buying. Marketing Land, https://marketingland.com/library/display-advertising-news/display-advertising-programmatic-media-buying, January 18, 2018.

144 IAB contributors. "IAB Wiki - Glossary of Interactive Advertising Terms." Interactive Advertising Bureau, November 15, 2013.

145 Facebook Business Help Center, https://www.facebook.com/business/help/, June 10, 2021.

146 "The Best Facebook Ad Formats For Hotels." Fuel, March 20, 2017, https://www.fueltravel.com/blog/the-best-facebook-ad-formats-forhotels/.

147 "Best Practices for Promoting Hotel Inventory Using Travel Ads." Facebook Business, April 30, 2019, https://www.facebook.com/business/help/872000339596842.

148 Cohen, David. "LinkedIn Overhauled the Reporting Experience in Its Campaign Manager." AdWeek, July 26, 2018, https://www.adweek.com/performance-marketing/linkedin-overhauled-the-reporting-experience-in-its-campaign-manager/.

149 "Sponsored Content tips." LinkedIn Marketing Solutions, April 30, 2019, https://business.linkedin.com/marketing-solutions/success/best-practices/sponsored-content-tips.

150 Estis Green, Cindy, Mark V. Lomanno, and Matt Carrier. Demystifying the Digital Marketplace: Spotlight on the Hospitality Industry, Part 3. Kalibri Labs, 2018.

151 Schaal, Dennis. "The Definitive History of Online Travel." Skift.com. June 2016.

152 U.S. Consumer Travel Report, Eighth Edition, Phocuswright, July 2016, https://www.phocuswright.com/Travel-Research/Technology-Innovation/U-S-Consumer-Travel-Report-Eighth-Edition, June 14, 2021.

153 "The difference between margin and markup." AccountingTools, April 10, 2021, https://www.accountingtools.com/articles/what-is-the-difference-between-margin-and-markup.html.

154 Search, Shop, Buy: The New Digital Funnel. Phocuswright, June 2015, https://www.phocuswright.com/Travel-Research/Consumer-Trends/Search-Shop-Buy-The-New-Digital-Funnel, June 14, 2021.

155 Lerner, Steven. "Expedia Group, Booking Holdings spent more than $11B on marketing (mostly to Google) in 2019." PhocusWire, March 6, 2020, https://www.phocuswire.com/booking-holdings-expedia-group-marketing-spend-2019.

156 "A Closer Look At Expedia's Operating Expenses." Forbes, April 8, 2019, https://www.forbes.com/sites/greatspeculations/2019/04/08/a-closer-look-at-expedias-operating-expenses/?sh=71b6c5277ab6.

157 Portions of the Best Practices section are adapted from the HSMAI white paper "Best Practices for Your Online Distribution & Marketing Strategy" published December 2010.

158 www.merriam-webster.com

159 Wikipedia

160 "Global AI Survey: AI proves its worth, but few scale impact." McKinsey & Company, November 22, 2019, https://www.mckinsey.com/featured-insights/artificial-intelligence/global-ai-survey-ai-proves-its-worth-but-few-scale-impact.

161 Fletcher, Wilson. "Digital-first: the essential modern business mindset." Medium, October 23, 2018, https://medium.com/thehumanlayer/digital-first-the-essential-modern-business-mindset-9e116f61407e.

162 "How to Use Predictive Analytics in Data-Driven Marketing." Marketing Evolution, January 29, 2021, https://www.marketingevolution.com/knowledge-center/the-role-of-predictive-analytics-in-data-driven-marketing.

163 Kearns, Michael and Aaron Roth, "The Ethical Algorithm: The Science of Socially Aware Algorithm Design," Oxford University Press, November 1, 2019.

164 IBM Cloud Education. "Machine Learning." IBM Cloud Learn Hub, July 15, 2020, https://www.ibm.com/cloud/learn/machine-learning.

165 Green-Lerman, Hillary. "Ask a Data Scientist: What is Machine Learning?" CodeAcademy, February 16, 2018, Updated July 14, 2020, https://www.codecademy.com/resources/blog/what-is-machine-learning/.

166 Bergdahl, Jacob. "4 Business Strategies for Implementing Artificial Intelligence." Towards Data Science, January 20, 2021, https://towardsdatascience.com/4-business-strategies-for-implementing-artificial-intelligence-24deff39158c.

167 Bergdahl, Jacob. "4 Business Strategies for Implementing Artificial Intelligence." Towards Data Science, January 20, 2021, https://towardsdatascience.com/4-business-strategies-for-implementing-artificial-intelligence-24deff39158c.

168 Bergdahl, Jacob. "4 Business Strategies for Implementing Artificial Intelligence." Towards Data Science, January 20, 2021, https://towardsdatascience.com/4-business-strategies-for-implementing-artificial-intelligence-24deff39158c.

169 Stanway-Williams, Caitlin. "The 'integrators': Why fusing creativity and data drives marketing performance." Datasine, January 20, 2020, https://datasine.com/2020/01/20/the-integrators-why-fusing-creativity-and-data-drives-marketing-performance/, February 3, 2021.

170 Bergdahl, Jacob. "4 Business Strategies for Implementing Artificial Intelligence." Towards Data Science, January 20, 2021, https://towardsdatascience.com/4-business-strategies-for-implementing-artificial-intelligence-24deff39158c.

171 Bergdahl, Jacob. "4 Business Strategies for Implementing Artificial Intelligence." Towards Data Science, January 20, 2021, https://towardsdatascience.com/4-business-strategies-for-implementing-artificial-intelligence-24deff39158c.

172 Thompson, Stuart A. and Charlie Warzel. "Twelve Million Phones, One Dataset, Zero Privacy." The New York Times, December 19, 2019, https://www.nytimes.com/interactive/2019/12/19/opinion/location-tracking-cell-phone.html.

173 Singel, Ryan. "NetFlix Cancels Recommendation Contest After Privacy Lawsuit." Wired, March 12, 2010, https://www.wired.com/2010/03/netflix-cancels-contest/.

174 "Fitness app Strava lights up staff at military bases." BBC News, January 29, 2018, https://www.bbc.com/news/technology-42853072.

175 Dastin, Jeffrey. "Amazon scraps secret AI recruiting tool that showed bias against women." Reuters, October 10, 2018, https://www.reuters.com/article/us-amazon-com-jobs-automation-insight/amazon-scraps-secret-ai-recruiting-tool-that-showed-bias-against-women-idUSKCN1MK08G.

176 Knight, Will. "The Apple Card Didn't 'See' Gender—and That's the Problem." Wired, November 19, 2019, https://www.wired.com/story/the-apple-card-didnt-see-genderand-thats-the-problem/.

177 "Choice Hotels' intelligent process automation nets satisfied clients and cost savings." ZS, https://www.zs.com/about/our-impact/choice-hotels-automation-nets-satisfied-clients-and-cost-savings, June 10, 2021.

178 "Overview of Attribution modeling in MCF." Google Analytics Help, https://support.google.com/analytics/answer/1662518?hl=en. July 6, 2021.

179 Adapted from "CMO's Boost In-House Marketing Skills." The Wall Street Journal, May 2, 2017, http://deloitte.wsj.com/cmo/2017/05/02/cmos-boost-in-house-marketing-skills/; Robles, Patricio. "In-house agency versus on-site agency: Weighing the pros and cons." eConsultancy, June 9, 2017, https://econsultancy.com/blog/69148-in-house-agency-versus-on-site-agency-weighing-the-pros-and-cons; and, Smale, Thomas. "In-House or Outsourced? How Do You Decide?" Entrepreneur, March 1, 2017, https://www.entrepreneur.com/article/289844.

180 Cramm, Susan. "Outsource the Work, Not the Leadership." Harvard Business Review, July 19, 2010, https://hbr.org/2010/07/outsource-thework-not-the-lea.

181 Duin, Anna. "Strategic Sourcing & Other Vendor Management Best Practices." RFP 365, September 3, 2015, http://www.rfp365.com/blog/vendor-management-best-practices-strategic-purchasing.

182 Naughter, Tara. "4 Vendor Management Best Practices." ContractWorks, July 20, 2017, https://www.contractworks.com/blog/4-vendor-management-best-practices.

183 Fisher, Roger and William Ury. Getting to Yes: Negotiating Agreement Without Giving In (New York: Penguin Books, 2011), 11.

184 Lutkevich, Ben. Third-party cookie. TechTarget, https://whatis.techtarget.com/definition/third-party-cookie. July 6, 2021.

185 The following sources were used and sometimes quoted to compile this glossary.

- Weber, John Leo. (July 7, 2017). The Ultimate List of Digital Marketing Terms. https://www.geekpoweredstudios.com/digital-marketing-glossary/
- Cline, Mary. (March 28, 2017). Digital Marketing Glossary. https://www.mdsdecoded.com/blog/digital-marketing-glossary/
- Digital marketing in 2018: A glossary every marketer should have. (September 12, 2018). https://www.tworiversmarketing.com/blog/blog-entry/
- 2018/09/12/digital-marketing-in-2018-a-glossary-every-marketer-should-have/
- The Ultimate List of Digital Marketing Glossary of Terms to Know. (October 15th, 2018). https://www.punith.com/digital-marketing-glossary/

186 "Breadcrumbs." TechTerms, https://techterms.com/definition/breadcrumbs, June 10, 2021.

187 "Natural language processing." Wikipedia, https://en.wikipedia.

NOTES

NOTES